HARD PLASTIC DOLLS, II

Identification and Price Guide

by Polly and Pam Judd

Jill by Vogue Dolls, Inc: pop-up advertisement from *Playthings* magazine, March 1957 (see page 228).

Published by Hobby House Press

Grantsville, Maryland 21536

Acknowledgements

Many people from all over the United States have helped mold this book. Their inquiries and contributions have helped us add to the original *Hard Plastic Dolls* book. We wish to thank all of the people who spoke to us as we traveled, sent us letters, and offered ideas and encouragement. It is great fun to be associated with all the "doll" people.

Our special thanks and appreciation to Mr. Richard Sherin, Chief Museum Conservator of the Strong Museum in Rochester, New York, for his help with the conservation of hard plastic dolls.

Mr. H.B. Samuels, of the Reliable Toy Co., helped us with the Coronation Section.

Vivien Brady-Ashley, Sandra Crane, Marianne Gardner, Marge Meisinger and Nancy Roeder were very helpful with Alexander pictures and information.

Mary Elizabeth Poole really helped start this book with her wonderful suggestions and boxes of research.

Dorothy Hesner, one of the first collectors of hard plastic dolls, could remember the "Good Old Days."

The Cleveland Doll Club always encouraged us and gave us support when we needed it.

The following people contributed pictures, information and ideas: Barbara Andresen, Phyllis Appell, Patricia Arches, Mary Ann Bauman, Ester Borgis, Laura May Brown, Beatrice Campbell, Nancy Carlton, Ruth Casey, Nancy Catlin, Barbara Comienski, Athena Crowley, Mary Jane Cultrona, Kathryn Davis, Sherri Dempsey, Jean Dicus, Sharlene Doyle, Diane Hoffman, Kathy George, Sally Herbst, Dorothy Hesner, Virginia Ann Heyerdahl, Jill Kaar, Helen Keefe, Eunice Kier, Chree Kysar, Lois Janner, Arline Last, Diane Loney, Christine Lorman, Kim Lusk, Margaret Mandel, Glenn Mandeville, Elizabeth Martz, Ruth Moss, Shirley Niziolek, Roslyn Nigoff, Elsie Ogden, Pat Parton, Thelma Purvis, Louise Schnell, Lois Seketa, Betty Shriver, Carmen Smotherman, Sandra Strater, Elaine Timm, Pat Timmons, Mary Ann Watkins and Gigi Williams.

We also wish to thank our editor, Donna H. Felger, and the entire staff of Hobby House Press, Inc.

Hard Plastic Dolls, II is an independent study by the authors Polly & Pam Judd and published by Hobby House Press, Inc. The research and publicaton of this book were not sponsored in any way by the manufacturers of the dolls, the doll costumes and the doll accessories featured in this study. Photographs of the collectibles were from dolls, costumes or accessories belonging to Polly or Pam Judd at the time the picture was taken unless otherwise credited with the caption.

The information as to the ownership pertains to documentary materials contemporary with the doll or doll's accessories. Ownership of the registered trademark, the trademark or the copyright may have expired or been transferred to another owner.

The values given within this book are intended as value guides rather than arbitrarily set prices. The values quoted are as accurate as possible but in the case of errors, typographical, clerical or otherwise, the authors and publisher assume no liability nor responsibility for any loss incurred by users of this book.

Additional copies of this book may be purchased at $14.95 from
HOBBY HOUSE PRESS, INC.
1 Corporate Drive
Grantsville, Maryland 21536
1-800-554-1447
(please add $4.75 per copy for postage)
or from your favorite bookstore or dealer.

Printing in the United States of America

ISBN: 0-87588-421-0

Table of Contents

Preface

Our first book, *Hard Plastic Dolls*, was a beginning in the identification of hard plastic dolls. Since it was intended to be a small paperback handbook that could easily be carried and stored, it was necessarily limited in scope. In the second book we have added a number of companies and dolls which were not in book one.

The following dolls are included in this book:
1. All-hard plastic
2. Dolls with vinyl heads and hard plastic bodies
3. Baby dolls with hard plastic heads and cloth, latex and rubber bodies

Hard Plastic Dolls, I covered 84 companies. This was by far the majority of the companies which made hard plastic dolls. *Hard Plastic Dolls, II* will add other manufacturers and concentrate on companies which did not have as many pictures and information as in the first book.

Foreign hard plastic dolls are very interesting and collectible. They are now appearing more and more in the American market. Individual companies and countries have different and unusual hard plastic material. Some of it appears to be celluloid which is the original base of the hard plastic material developed during World War II. While different, these dolls are beautiful and very collectible.

Since the identification of clothes is very important to collectors of these dolls, there will be even more space given to company brochures, catalogs and advertisements of the fashions of that period than in the first book.

There is a section of suggestions for the conservation of doll clothing from the hard plastic era.

There are additions to the identification features found at the end of the first book. For the most part, the authors have not repeated these identification tips. For more complete details, please consult the section at the end of *Hard Plastic Dolls, I.*

One special addition to the Identification Section is research of the small *Ginny*-type and "Chubby-type" dolls which were so popular. Pictures of their bodies have been included for easy reference. This has been requested by many of our readers.

For ease of identification and understanding, this book will have the same general format as *Hard Plastic Dolls I* and have many cross references. The abbreviation "HP" means hard plastic and will be used throughout the book.

Finally, at the back of this book there will be a price update of the dolls in *Hard Plastic Dolls, I* which have seemed to have changed in value. Prices of the dolls in this book will continue to appear under the picture.

The Beginning of Hard Plastic Dolls

The very tiny doll in *Illustration 1* belongs to Dorothy Hesner of Cicero, Illinois. Her mother had a little gift and embroidery store in Chicago during World War II. About 1943 or 1944 she began selling these tiny hard plastic dolls. During the war toys were scarce, and Dorothy repainted hundreds of these for her mother who put them in pretty card boxes along with fabric, scissors, needles and thread and sold them for sewing kits. Dorothy dressed this doll in a Girl Scout uniform, and she still has it today.

Plastic was used in the various services during the war. Wally Judd, our husband and father, was a soldier in the U.S. Air Force in Alaska. He repaired airplanes using plastic, and he made a beautiful small hard plastic locket for Polly and sent it to her. Someway this substance found its way into civilian life during the war years and into the lives of the happy children who lived near the little gift shop in Chicago.

Kimport reported in their *Doll Talk* magazine in January-February of 1974 that the first real plastic doll was put out by Ideal Novelty Company in 1940 but was discontinued after about a year due to war restrictions on materials. The body and legs were in one piece. The arms were movable and all of it was a radically different texture that looked and felt like human flesh. It could be pinched, wrinkled and became warm to the touch. The heads were made of hard plastic and the bodies were kapoc stuffed. It was a great success but the fortunes of war prevented it from continuing on to become a very profitable commercial enterprise.

However, it was a beginning. Today, as the 20th century draws to a close, we look back on that early era and to the very first hard plastic dolls and remember how beautiful they were.

Illustration 1. Tiny HP doll costumed by Dorothy Hesner. *Dorothy Hesner Collection.*

In 1946 the Sears catalog showed many of the composition dolls which were quickly manufactured for children who had not had many dolls during World War II. While a few of their other baby dolls had hard plastic heads, Sears proudly presented a baby doll and toddler, "For the first time! Made entirely of Plastic." This doll, made by Ideal, still has original clothes and is in the collection of Mary Elizabeth Poole.

SEE: *Illustration 2. Mary Elizabeth Poole Collection.*

First All-Hard Plastic Doll Offered by Sears: 15in (38cm); toddler and 14in (36cm) baby; advertised as having lifelike hands and feet; separate fingers and toes; molded, tinted hair; sleep eyes with real lashes; dressed in sunsuits in assorted colors, styles, materials; 1946.
This doll was made by Ideal.

SEE: *Illustration 3. 1946 Sears Christmas catalog. Barbara Andresen Collection.*

1.   2.   3.

How To Use This Book

This book is set up in the same format as *Hard Plastic Dolls, I*. There are several ways to use this book depending upon the reader's knowledge of a doll. If the doll is marked and you know the company name, turn immediately to the company section and look up the company name which appears in alphabetical order. You will find a list of dolls and their characteristics, dates of production if possible and a current price range.

If the doll is marked but you do not know the company name (example "R & B"), turn to the Doll Marks Guide on page 233. You will find these letters indicate the Arranbee Company. Then turn to the Arranbee section for pictures and more references. Most marked hard plastic dolls have their numbers, letters and symbols listed in the Doll Marks Guide. This is one of the few parts of the Doll Identification Guide of *Hard Plastic Dolls, I* which is repeated in this book.

If the doll is unmarked or if the mark is not listed, turn to the Doll Identification Guide. There, at the beginning of the section you will find another Table of Contents listing the various doll characteristics which will help you. Examples are arm hooks, eyes and fasteners. There are many others. In this section the doll features will help you narrow the possibilities and refer you back to the doll company. Often there will be references to the page numbers of specific identification details in *Hard Plastic Dolls, I*. The authors have tried not to duplicate the information unless it is very important.

When you have exhausted these options and still have not identified your doll, there is an excellent section "Differences Among Hard Plastic, Composition and Vinyl Dolls" in *Hard Plastic Dolls, I*. This will help you determine if your doll is hard plastic.

The authors are very appreciative and thankful to the many, many people who took the time to write to us about their dolls and send us new information and wonderful pictures. This book is really the result of their efforts.

The abbreviation "HP" for hard plastic has been used throughout this book.

Pricing Hard Plastic Dolls

Prices unless otherwise noted would be for dolls from excellent to mint-in-box condition and include original clothes. Dealers were consulted in many parts of the United States, and they agreed that in today's selling market, collectors are looking for and willing to pay these prices for pristine dolls. Dolls not in this condition are selling for *considerably* less.

Local prices also will vary. It is true that what is eagerly sought in one section of the country will sell sluggishly in another location. In general hard plastic dolls are still excellent sellers.

Dolls that were presumed to be rare have a way of appearing after a book is published showing their pictures or citing high prices for them. When this happens, collectors and dealers will have to adjust to a downward scale.

Actually this is an excellent time for collectors who are looking for specific dolls, but do not want to pay high prices, and enjoy renovating and redressing dolls, to purchase them. If this is done, the original clothing should be kept and stored near the doll. However, it must always be kept in mind that these dolls will command lower prices if they are resold.

A Note About Plastics

by Richard W. Sherin

All plastics are polymers. Basically, they consist of many small units (called monomers) which have been linked together chemically. In addition, they can contain a number of other materials to give them color and other desirable physical properties. Research has shown that most types are susceptible to deterioration caused by oxygen and ultraviolet radiation. While we can't eliminate oxygen very readily, we can, as described above, minimize exposure to UV. Some plastics are created by the addition of water molecules; as they age, they can lose this water and therefore become a different material with very different properties. About this we can do little. Others, such as polyvinylchloride (PVC), turn yellow as they age and give off hydrochloric acid (HCl). This acid could be potentially harmful to susceptible materials nearby. Celluloid (cellulose nitrate) plastics — Kewpie dolls are an example — are especially sensitive to alkaline materials. Celluloid is also flammable and can self-destruct, giving off nitric acid HNO_3...again potentially destructive to nearby materials. Early forms of celluloid may smell of oils such as camphor, added initially as a plasticizer but which (eventually) made the celluloid harder, and somewhat less flammable.

Any odor associated with plastic has to be due either to some incomplete curing process or to some form of decomposition. Research into the deterioration mechanisms of plastics is still in its infancy. Only recently have conservators recognized the types of problems peculiar to plastics and begun to seek appropriate remedies (if any exist). An improperly chosen solvent or cleaning solution may activate an odor by partly dissolving the surface. The novice should seek expert advice before attempting any cleaning beyond water and should take the time to carefully record any observations for collective benefit.

While it appears that much plastic deterioration is inherent and inevitable, we can still slow it down somewhat by following some of the preceding suggestions.

Doll Conservation

by Richard W. Sherin

Authors' Note: Richard W. Sherin is Chief Museum Conservator at the Strong Museum in Rochester, New York. The Strong Museum's collection of some 20,000 dolls is the most comprehensive in any museum. Before assuming his present position, Mr. Sherin was Assistant Conservator of Decorative Arts and Furniture at the Indianapolis Museum of Art. He holds a Master of Arts degree in the Conservation of Historic and Artistic Works from Cooperstown (NY) Graduate Program.

If at all possible, store your doll collection in a cool, dry and clean environment. Higher temperatures accelerate unwanted chemical reactions and lead to the more rapid deterioration of both a doll and its accessories. Relative humidity control is also very necessary and often critical. Maintain the relative humidity as close as you can to 50 percent year round. Avoid attics and cellars.

As a general rule, it is better to store a doll and its original box separately. These boxes usually are of poor quality; they are often highly acidic and can be very damaging when direct contact is permitted between the doll and the box. The best solution is to store the doll by itself in an archival box of appropriate dimension. Padding it with neutral tissue paper will help secure the doll's position. Store clothing and other accessories in a second box, taking care to wrap each piece with the same inert tissue. If the doll must remain in its original box, use tissue or two-ply acid-free matt board to isolate it (from the material[s] of the box) the best way you can. Do not use any tapes or glues for this; simply wrap or cut-and-fit dry.

Dolls in storage should be regularly inspected to guarantee their well-being. Reorient and repack the dolls where appropriate in order to minimize creasing of clothing fabrics and to maintain the proper form.

The nature of the lighting under which dolls are displayed is also very critical for optimum preservation. Generally, two types of (light) sources are commonly employed — incandescent (regular light bulbs) and fluorescent (tubes). Both can be used, but be aware that the latter emits considerable ultraviolet (UV) radiation. Very high in energy, UV causes severe damage to organic materials (textiles, wood, paper, etc.) in the form of embrittlement, fading, shrinkage, and discoloration. If fluorescent tubes are used, make sure to also install UV-filtering plastic sleeves over each one. These can be purchased from a reliable lighting firm and their use will eliminate over 95 percent of this very harmful energy. Whatever your light source, the level of visible light at the doll should not exceed five (5) footcandles. A dimmer switch is the easiest solution here. Even then the exposure should be limited as much as possible.

A & H Doll Mfg. Corp.

The registered trademarks, the trademarks and the copyrights appearing in italics within this chapter belong to A & H Doll Mfg. Corp.

A & H Doll Mfg. Corp. had one of the most innovative and comprehensive doll lines in the hard plastic era. The dolls were popularly priced and designed to appeal to many different types of customers. The dolls themselves were rarely marked but were usually well tagged.

Today they are not the most expensive of collectible dolls but if the dolls are found mint-in-box and tagged, they are pretty and appealing. They also document the entire period of hard plastic dolls.

Dolls of Destiny: Advertisement from *McCall's Needlework*, Fall-Winter 1953-1954. These dolls were one of the first hard plastic dolls to be authentically dressed in historical costumes. An innovation at the time, they were expensive ($8.95) and came in a beautiful blue brocade box. The costumes were lovely and well made. Each doll carried her own storybook written by a well-known children's author and historian. The dolls are (a) *Mary Todd Lincoln*, (b) *Marie Antoinette*, (c) *Elizabeth Woodville Grey*, (d) *Martha Washington*, (e) *Queen Isabella*, (f) *Betsy Ross*, (g) *Queen Elizabeth I*, (h) *Empress Josephine*, (i) *Empress Eugenie*, (j) *Molly Pitcher*, (k) *Priscilla Alden* and (l) *Queen Victoria*. (For general characteristics, see *Illustration 5*.)

In 1953 hard plastic dolls were new and the cost was high. Today these same "Dolls of Destiny" are considered to be one of the less expensive collectible dolls. However, the costumes are unusual and made with attention to detail.

MARKS: "Pat's Pending" (back); "Doll of Destiny and name of doll" (dress tag)
SEE: *Illustration 4. McCall's Needlework*, Fall-Winter 1953-1954.
PRICE: $35-45

4. a   j   k   l

5.

6.

Dolls of Destiny *Molly Pitcher* (right) HP: 12in (31cm); head turning walker; jointed at neck, arms and legs; molded shoes with bow (see Identification Guide, *Hard Plastic I*, page 283A); closed mouth; 2nd and 3rd fingers on each hand molded together; two dimples on each knee; sleep eyes; molded lashes; black, white and yellow colonial style dress with green striped underskirt; white hat, collar, apron; carries a copper pitcher which was made in Italy; 1953-1954.

> **MARKS:** "A Doll of Destiny//Molly Pitcher//1754-1832" (dress tag) "Pat's Pending" (back)
> **SEE:** *Illustration 5.*
> **PRICE:** $35-45

Dolls of Destiny *Priscilla* (left): HP; 12in (31cm); gray rayon dress and cape; white apron and bonnet; 1953-1954.

> **MARKS:** "Doll of Destiny//Priscilla//1604-1680" (dress tag) "Pat's Pending" (back)
> **SEE:** *Illustration 5.*
> **PRICE:** $35-45

Dolls of Destiny *Betsy Ross* (right): HP; 12in (31cm); (see *Illustration 5* for general characteristics); 1953-1954.

There were at least two different materials used for the dresses of *Betsy Ross*. Both were green to follow the famous painting which was used in many schoolbooks. The picture was painted by Charles Weisgerber and exhibited at the Columbian Exposition in Chicago in 1893. The *Betsy* on the right has the book which was included with each doll. She has a pair of toy scissors hanging at her waist.

> **MARKS:** "Doll of Destiny//Betsy Ross 1752-1836" (dress tag of both dolls); "Pat's Pending" (back)
> **SEE:** *Illustration 6.*
> **PRICE:** $35-45

7.

George Washington: HP; 8in (20cm); green velvet coat; maroon pants with gold braid; white lace jabot; tricorn hat; white wig; circa early 1950s.

    MARKS: None (doll); "A Marcie Doll" (box)

    SEE: *Illustration 7.*

    PRICE: $10-12

8.

Gigi Identification: (see also Identification Guide, page 237).

    This doll came in at least three forms:

1. An early all-HP hip pin straight leg walker
2. A later all-HP with regular walking mechanism and bent knees
3. Vinyl head doll with HP body and regular walking mechanism with bent knees and rooted hair

The skin color is a light, clear flesh tone with a lovely natural type coloring; the eyebrows are delicately painted; the sleep eyes have molded lashes; deep red coloring on tiny lips; standard arm hooks (see *Hard Plastic Dolls, I,* page 264I); molded ear stands away from body toward the back of the head; head turning walker; no dimples above fingers; dimples above toes; two lines above ankles on bent knee model; good detail on fingernails and toenails; large navel.

Gigi: HP; 8in (20cm); dressed in outfit seen in brochure on page 3, No. 8; red print jumper with rickrack and lace trim; matching bonnet; "Rau Sklikits" on inside of snap.

    MARKS: None (doll)

    SEE: *Illustration 8.*

    PRICE: $25-35

Gigi: HP; 7½in (19cm) head-turning walking doll; standard arm hook (see Identification Guide, *Hard Plastic Dolls, I,* page 265K); 2nd and 3rd fingers molded together; straight legs; two lines under knees; two dimples behind knees; finely sculptured toes with two dimples over them; no dimples on hands; black and white striped skirt with pink felt top and two embroidered black crosses; lace on sleeves; No. 709; (for picture of body, see Identification Guide, page 237); mid 1950s.

    MARKS: None (doll)

    SEE: *Illustration 9. Pat Parton Collection.*

    PRICE: $25-35

9.

***Gigi* Brochure:** HP; 8in (20cm); (for general characteristics, see page 11); head turning walker; hair may be set; circa 1955.

No. 7240—DRESSED DOLL
No. 724—OUTFIT ONLY
Lipstick Red and White Furry Trimmed skating costume with White Boots and Ice Skates.

★ A *Gigi* DOLL ★

GIGI DOLL OUTFITS
may be purchased Separately
*No. 729—Leatherette Sport Jacket outfit only.
*No. 730—Rain Outfit Only
*No. 7300—Dressed Doll in Rain Outfit
*Not illustrated

No. 725—OUTFIT ONLY
A real fur coat fully lined, with a matching hat and muff.

★ A *Gigi* DOLL ★

No. 7260—DRESSED DOLL
No. 726—OUTFIT ONLY
An exquisite formal gown of taffeta threaded with gold with a darling net stole to match.

8 Inch Dress-up Dolls

Gigi ©
DOLLS & OUTFITS

DRESSED DOLL $**1**⁹⁸

OUTFIT ONLY $**1**⁰⁰

"*Gigi*" and her Custom Made Outfits are sold at leading department and toy stores everywhere. Fine dressmaker detail with handy snaps for easy changes. Choose from the widest selection of dainty clothes suitable for every occasion.

Each and every outfit is a rare delight . . . expertly made to the last detail. You'll love making Gigi your best dressed doll.

MANUFACTURED BY
A & H DOLL MFG. CORP.
WOODSIDE 77, N. Y.

MY NAME IS

Gigi ©

White and gold Majorette Costume with Boots and Baton to lead the parade.

No. 7200
Dressed Doll
No. 720
Outfit Only

I WALK - I SIT - I SLEEP
I TURN MY HEAD
YOU CAN SET MY HAIR
AND CHANGE MY CLOTHES

10.

No. 7010—DRESSED DOLL
No. 701—OUTFIT ONLY
A dainty pastelle organdy skirt with felt top, natural straw up-turned hat to complete outfit.

★ A *Gigi* DOLL ★

No. 7020—DRESSED DOLL
No. 702—OUTFIT ONLY
Luscious pink or aqua organdy dress with matching bonnet and purse.

No. 7030—DRESSED DOLL
No. 703—OUTFIT ONLY
Little people cotton print with contrasting color chintz apron and adorable straw bonnet.

★ A *Gigi* DOLL ★

No. 7040—DRESSED DOLL
No. 704—OUTFIT ONLY
Cherry red dress, lace trimmed, with darling little apron and black straw hat.

No. 7270—DRESSED DOLL
No. 727—OUTFIT ONLY
Blue denim jeans with a red and white checked blazer, up-turned hat and glasses.

★ A *Gigi* DOLL ★

No. 7280—DRESSED DOLL
No. 728—OUTFIT ONLY
Davy Crockett Outfit, suede fringed jacket and shirt. Leatherette brown belt, rifle and shoulder sling with real fur-tailed cap.

No. 7050—DRESSED DOLL
No. 705—OUTFIT ONLY
Rose print dress trimmed with pink with adorable pink bonnet to match.

★ A *Gigi* DOLL ★

No. 7060—DRESSED DOLL
No. 706—OUTFIT ONLY
Black and white striped taffeta skirt and lace trimmed felt top, black straw hat.

11.

12

No. 7070—DRESSED DOLL
No. 707—OUTFIT ONLY
Black and white gibson dress with belt and sailor straw hat.

★ A *Gigi* DOLL ★

No. 7080—DRESSED DOLL
No. 708—OUTFIT ONLY
Pink checked sun dress with white pique jacket, with darling natural straw hat.

No. 7090—DRESSED DOLL
No. 709—OUTFIT ONLY
Adorable guimpe dress, striped skirt and net sleeves and black straw hat.

★ A *Gigi* DOLL ★

No. 7100—DRESSED DOLL
No. 710—OUTFIT ONLY
Orange dress with smart forest green jacket and matching hat.

No. 7110—DRESSED DOLL
No. 711—OUTFIT ONLY
Tiny print yellow dress with charming yellow apron and fashionable black straw hat.

★ A *Gigi* DOLL ★

No. 7120—DRESSED DOLL
No. 712—OUTFIT ONLY
Gold matelasse lounging set, smart contrasting trousers with gold slippers.

No. 7130—DRESSED DOLL
No. 713—OUTFIT ONLY
Smart Navy Blue hat and coat trimmed with white collar and cuffs and white matching purse.

★ A *Gigi* DOLL ★

No. 7140—DRESSED DOLL
No. 714—OUTFIT ONLY
A delightful rickrack trimmed cotton print dotted with lace and matching hat.

2.

No. 7150—DRESSED DOLL
No. 715—OUTFIT ONLY
Tiny red print on white cotton, sweet little apron with beautiful blue ribbon bow for hair.

★ A *Gigi* DOLL ★

No. 7160—DRESSED DOLL
No. 716—OUTFIT ONLY
Highly styled tiny polka dot cotton with flower trimmed felt cloche.

No. 7170—DRESSED DOLL
No. 717—OUTFIT ONLY
Charming cotton print trimmed with velvet and lace and natural straw hat.

★ A *Gigi* DOLL ★

No. 7180—DRESSED DOLL
No. 718—OUTFIT ONLY
Delightful school dress trimmed with velvet with perky straw hat.

No. 7190—DRESSED DOLL
No. 719—OUTFIT ONLY
Complete Nurse's costume with cute little cape and Nurse's cap.

★ A *Gigi* DOLL ★

No. 7210—DRESSED DOLL
No. 721—OUTFIT ONLY
Beach Costume with fashionable knit top and Hat to Match.

No. 7220—DRESSED DOLL
No. 722—OUTFIT ONLY
Yellow and Red Cowgirl Costume complete with Vest, Hat and Boots.

★ A *Gigi* DOLL ★

No. 7230—DRESSED DOLL
No. 723—OUTFIT ONLY
Gold and White Fluffy Ballet Costume and adorable little Crown on head.

13.

14.

Gigi and Revolving Carousel Wardrobe: HP with vinyl head; 8in (20cm); (for other general characteristics, see page 11); plastic carousel is transparent; holds new couturier wardrobe for 1957.

Lil' Sister with Carousel Wardrobe: all-vinyl baby doll; winks, coos, sleeps, wets, drinks; 1957.

SEE: *Illustration 14. Playthings,* March 1957.

PRICE: $25-35 (*Gigi*)
$10-15 (*Lil' Sister*)

15.

Hits for '58: advertisement in *Playthings,* February 1958.

As late as 1958 A & H was advertising some hard plastic dolls complete with doll wardrobes.

SEE: *Illustration 15.*

Prize Packages: A & H was one of the early companies to make hard plastic dolls for the mass market. Like similar companies, they were still making the popular inexpensive "fashion" dolls into the 1960s. They featured *Belles in Bells, Teens in Bells, Gigi in Bells, Lil' Sister in Bells, Belles of Nations* and other famous dolls.

MARKS: None (doll); "A & H Dolls" (engraved on bottom of bell)
SEE: *Illustration 16. Playthings,* March 1962.
PRICE: $20-25 (in bell)

16.

Dutch Girl in Bell: HP; 8in (20cm); sleep eyes; blonde wig; high-heeled shoes with hole in the bottom of the shoes; jointed at neck, shoulders, hips; dressed in Dutch costume with purple skirt; white dotted swiss top; felt Dutch cap; one of *Belles of Nations*; 1962.

This doll has high-heeled shoes like the doll in the "Unknown" section of *Hard Plastic Dolls, I* (see *Illustrations 519* and *520*, page 234).

    MARKS: None (doll); "A & H Dolls" (engraved on bottom of bell)

    SEE: *Illustration 17.*

    PRICE: $20-25

17.

Birthstone Dolls: This is an advertisement for 9in (22cm) dolls called *Birthstone Belles:*

1. January	Garnet	7. July	Ruby
2. February	Amethyst	8. August	Sardonyx
3. March	Aquamarine	9. September	Sapphire
4. April	Diamond	10. October	Opal
5. May	Emerald	11. November	Topaz
6. June	Pearl	12. December	Turquoise

    SEE: *Illustration 18. Playthings*, March 1962.

    PRICE: $10-12 each

18.

Costume Styled for *Julie* Walking Doll: boxed "Czech" outfit made for *Julie* and all 8in (20cm) walking dolls; beautiful red print skirt with black felt vest; white organdy blouse trimmed with lace; traditional Czech lace headpiece with multi-colored ribbon streamers; gripper snap says "RAU SKLIKITS" on inner part of snap; circa 1955-1957.

MARKS: "Styled for Julie//Czech//A & H Mfg. Corp."
SEE: *Illustration 19. Pat Parton Collection.*
PRICE: $5-7

19.

Active Doll Corporation

The registered trademarks, the trademarks and the copyrights appearing in italics within this chapter belong to Active Doll Corporation.

Scotch Lassie: HP; 7in (18cm); sleep eyes with lashes painted above eyes; painted-on shoes (see Identification Guide, *Hard Plastic Dolls, I,* page 285H); blonde hair; Scotch plaid skirt with red and gold ribbon top. Other dolls in the series included *American Bride, French Miss, Greek Miss, Swedish Lass, Brazil Miss, Dutch Miss, Irish Lass, German Miss, Spanish Senorita, Italian Miss, British Princess;* circa 1955.

MARKS: None (doll); "Active Doll Corporation//'I am one of the beautiful Dolls of Many Lands' " (box)
SEE: *Illustration 20.*
PRICE: $6-10

20.

Admiration Doll Company

This company made an inexpensive line of dolls which they advertised in *Playthings* in the early 1960s. Their hard plastic was a light hollow material that was used in these later dolls. They also made vinyl high-heeled dolls. There was a minimum of sewing in their costuming.

21.

Girl: inexpensive HP; 7½in (19cm); *Ginger* characteristics unless otherwise noted (see Identification Guide, *Illustration 238*); pink wig; large sleep eyes (see Identification Guide, *Illustration 246*); heavy eyebrows; unusual curves in arms; non-walker; original clothes still stapled on doll; green polka dot top; pink, green and black skirt; white paint over exposed toes to imitate shoes; *Ginger* arm hook (see *Hard Plastic Dolls, I*, page 266N); circa 1962-1965. This doll is similar to the Midwestern *Mary Jean* (page 150) but it does not have the *Mary Jean* arm hooks.

MARKS: "Admiration//Toy Co.//A1 75//Made in Hong Kong" (back)
SEE: *Illustration 21. Barbara Comienski Collection.*
PRICE: $6-10

Alden's

The Alden mail order catalog was used extensively during the hard plastic era. They advertised many dolls from known companies. They also had a line of dolls made exclusively for them.

Lil Megotoo: HP with vinyl head; 8in (20cm); walker; doll cost 88 cents; each outfit also cost 88 cents; outfits included bride dress; travel suit; majorette costume with baton; fall coat; roller skate outfit with skates; Red Cross nurse outfit; chemise dress; tea party dress; 1958. Information came from advertisement from Davison's Store of Atlanta, Georgia, November 9, 1958.
This doll was also sold through the Alden's catalog.

22.

SEE: *Illustration 22.*
PRICE: $10-15

Alexander Doll Company, Inc.

The registered trademarks, the trademarks and the copyrights appearing in italics within this chapter belong to the Alexander Doll Company, Inc., unless otherwise noted.

In 1946 the Alexander Doll Company resumed production of their composition dolls, but very quickly turned to the new hard plastic material. By 1948 they were using hard plastic for many dolls including *Babs Ice Skater* (see *Hard Plastic Dolls, I*, page 115), *Alice in Wonderland* (see *Hard Plastic Dolls, I*, page 22), *McGuffey Ana* (see *Hard Plastic Dolls, I*, page 20), *Margaret O'Brien, Little Women* and others. They continued to use the *Margaret* face and introduced a new charmer named *Maggie*. Most of these dolls were not marked. However, their clothes were usually labeled.

The early hard plastic dolls had a deep flesh color painted on their bodies. This can be seen at the arm and leg joints. Their costumes were made of cottons, organdies, net and other materials of the period. Even today, many of these dolls still retain the transitional "quiet glow." Collectors today eagerly seek these early dolls.

Using the new innovations in plastic and cloth, by 1951 Madame Alexander's dolls had become the pace-setter of the 1950s, and she became a leader in both the doll and fashion industries.

23.

24.

Bride: HP; 14in (36cm); fully jointed; lovely red hair with soft curls; white organza over taffeta dress; long tulle veil edged with lace; tiny stiff cap with flowers at each side; green foil wrist tag with "Madame Alexander" on it; circa 1948 or 1949. Many of these early hard plastic Alexander dolls were not marked with the company name. Usually the dress was tagged.
    MARKS: "Madame Alexander" (dress tag)
    SEE: *Illustration 23. Sandra Crane Collection.*
    PRICE: $325-400 (more for larger doll)

Ringbearer: HP; 12in (31cm); toddler; fully-jointed; blonde wig over molded hair; sleep eyes; wearing white satin suit; pillow carries wedding ring; early gold cloverleaf tag; circa 1948-1950. This unusual doll is sometimes called *Precious* or *Lovey Dovey*. He was also sold with just his molded hair and no wig.
    MARKS: "Alexander" (head)
    SEE: *Illustration 24. Nancy Roeder Collection.*
    PRICE: $500-600

Knuckle-head Nellie: HP; 14in (36cm); red caracul wig; original white organdy over a satin dress; trimmed with bows; 1950. Madame Alexander often advertised on the back cover of *Playthings* and this picture was on the back cover of the May 1950 issue. The advertisement says, "...Inspired by Mary Martin's great performance in 'SOUTH PACIFIC'." In the lower right hand corner is a picture of Madame Alexander in a locket. Many of the advertisements from this period showed this locket.

    SEE: *Illustration 25. Playthings,* May 1950.

    PRICE: $600-700

"KNUCKLE-HEAD NELLIE"
... Inspired by Mary Martin's great
performance in "SOUTH PACIFIC"

25.

Cinderella: painted HP; 15in (38cm); jointed at neck, shoulders, hips; *Margaret* face; dressed in long blue satin gown with side panniers; trimmed in silver braid; silver necklace and bracelet; clothes all original; blonde formal wig with chignon held with net and jeweled gold headpiece; glass slippers; 1950. The skin color of this doll has not faded. The satin dress has retained its blue color. This is very unusual because the blue often turns to a pink or lavender shade. It has been preserved well.

    MARKS: None (doll); "Madame Alexander//New York//All Rights Reserved" (tag)

    SEE: *Illustration 26.* (Color Section, page 40).

    PRICE: $600-700 in this condition; less if fading has taken place

Pink Bride: early HP with beautiful skin tone; 14in (36cm); blonde mohair wig in original set; sleep eyes; pink satin dress with scoop neck and lace ruffle; high-necked net inset with net sleeves attached; pink net veil over a flower headpiece; pink slip and panties; nylon stockings; pink leather slippers with tiny bow; bouquet of pink flowers with matching floorline drop ribbons; all original; circa 1950. Around 1950 fashion-conscious brides could choose pink as a bridal color. While it was fashionable, it never became very popular. Madame Alexander, always a fashion leader, followed the trend and made this unusual pink bride doll.

    MARKS: None; very few of these early *Margaret*-faced dolls were marked. "Madame//Alexander//New York, N.Y. U.S.A." (tag on dress)

    SEE: *Illustration 27.* (Color Section, page 95).

    PRICE: $500-600 + (rare doll — very few sample prices)

Early Hard Plastic Portrait Dolls

At the beginning of the 1950s Madame Alexander designed a set of wonderful Pre-Portrait dolls which carried the Fashion Award label. These were done in the manner of some of the composition 21in (53cm) dolls with theatrical makeup and costumes. Six have so far been identified.

1. A bride which has come to be known as the *Victorian Bride*. So far these dolls have not been found in an Alexander box with a name on the label.
2. A lovely girl known as the so-called *Kathryn Grayson* doll. She, too, has not been found in a labeled box.
3. The *Champs-Elysees* is known as the "Lady with the Rhinestone Teardrop," and is dressed in a wonderful black lace dress over pink satin. She has been found in a labeled box.
4. A theatrical ballerina has been found in a box, and she has the name *Deborah*.
5. A beautiful doll, dressed in the manner of a Godey Lady, has been found in a box with the name *Judy* on it.
6. *Pink Champagne* is the name given to a wonderful red-headed doll according to the label on her box.

In the past few years these dolls have emerged in the same gowns in several areas of the United States. All of the dolls have clothes with fancy costume jewels and spangles handsewn in the theatrical way. Some have tags in the dresses. Others do not. Madame Alexander's design is elegant and the sewing is done in true couturier fashion.

Champs-Elysees (also known as the Lady with the Rhinestone Beauty Mark): HP; 21in (53cm); added eyelashes; blonde wig with bangs; tight strapless pink satin underdress; black lace over black tulle overdress; jeweled bracelets on both arms; black lace headpiece; round gold Fashion Academy Award tag; 1951. 1951 was the first year that Madame Alexander received the Fashion Award Gold Medal. She also received the medal in 1952, 1953 and 1954.

SEE: *Illustration 28* (Color section, page 33). *Vivian Brady-Ashley Collection.*

PRICE: (rare doll — very few samples prices)

28.

Victorian Bride: HP; 21in (53cm); *Margaret* face; normal eyelashes; dress in 3 sections; lacy net blouse that ties at waist; lined white satin bodice; draped satin skirt; five-section bustle; deep lace ruffle at bottom of skirt; lace veil formed like mantilla over stiffened bandeau; white flowers at each side of head; bouquet of white flowers in lace circle with narrow satin streamers; bodice has square snaps; skirt has round snaps; circa 1951.

MARKS: "Madame Alexander" embroidered cursive-type writing (tag)
SEE: *Illustration 29* (Color section, page 34). *Sandra Crane Collection.*
PRICE: (rare doll - very few sample prices)

Champs Elysees: HP; 21in (53cm); blonde off-the-face wig; Godey period costume; white lace three-quarter top; very wide pink taffeta ruffles which sweep around the front and are caught up at the waist in back; ribbon and flower-trimmed straw hat; 1951.

SEE: *Illustration 30* (Color section, page 35). *Diane Hoffman Collection.*
PRICE: (rare doll - very few sample prices).

Pink Champagne: HP; 21in (53cm); red wig with beautiful hair set; purple silk organza dress with underskirt; taffeta slip-pantie; decorated with beautiful multi-colored flowers and rhinestones down the right front of her dress; flowers are also on her left shoulder; pearl necklace and earrings; her loosed chignon is held by a hairnet studded with "diamonds;" circa 1951. The lovely doll was found in a box labeled "Pink Champagne."

SEE: *Illustration 31* (Color section, page 36). *Vivien Brady-Ashley Collection.*
PRICE: (rare doll - very few sample prices).

Deborah Ballerina: HP; 21in (53cm); *Margaret* face; set of false eyelashes over their normal lashes (when lost it is possible to see a heavily painted line on lid); brows painted with short strokes; full lips; elaborate chignon; painted fingernails; original clothes in two pieces; white satin bodice with neckline of tulle; lace skirt over tulle underskirt which is embroidered with rhinestones and pearls; satin panties with ruffled tulle; rhinestone and pearl choker necklace; round snaps; circa 1951.

SEE: *Illustration 32* (Color section, page 37). *Sandra Crane Collection.*
PRICE: (rare doll - very few sample prices).

Kathryn Grayson (so called): HP; 21in (53cm); *Margaret* face; dark makeup; full lips; heavy eyelashes; dress with tulle skirt and lace bodice with rhinestones; teardrop earrings; ornate necklace; flowers on each side of head; 1951.

SEE: *Illustration 33* (Color section, page 38). *Sandra Crane Collection.*
PRICE: (rare doll - very few sample prices).

34.

Kathy: HP; 15in (38cm); red pigtail wig; *Maggie* face; fully jointed; red and black pedal pushers; red corduroy weskit; white organdy blouse; black velvet cap with red feather; watch fob; roller skates; brown tie shoes; box for curlers; circa, 1951. *Kathy* was also made in 18in (46cm) and 23in (58cm) sizes. Another roller skating costume is a blue cotton knit one-piece body suit and a full circle skirt of pink gabardine. F.A.O. Schwarz pictured a blue two-toned dress with rickrack trim in their 1951 catalog.

> MARKS: Fashion Academy Award tag; brochure with "Kathy" on cover
>
> SEE: *Illustration 34. Nancy Roeder Collection.*
>
> PRICE: $400-425

35.

Maggie: HP; 14in (36cm); see *Hard Plastic Dolls, I* for general characteristics; unusual black pigtail wig; not a walker; Fashion Award sticker on bottom of the box; red dress with white organdy pinafore; circa 1951-1952.

> SEE: *Illustration 35. Marianne Gardner Collection.*
>
> PRICE: $375-425

Wendy Bride (doll on left): HP; 15in (38cm); walker; white taffeta long dress with white tulle overskirt; long tulle veil topped by lace bonnet; white bridal bouquet; long nylon stockings; satin shoes; *Maggie* face; 1953.

> SEE: *Illustration 36* (doll on left). *Marianne Gardner Collection.*
>
> PRICE: $340-370

36.

Rosamund (doll on right): HP; 15in (41cm); long yellow taffeta bridesmaid dress with yellow tulle overskirt; originally she carried a hat box with curlers; doll was inspired by the book *Rosamund* by Maria Edgeworth; *Maggie* face: 1953. The doll also came in an 18in (46cm) size. The dress came in other pastel colors also.

SEE: *Illustration 36* (doll on right).
Marianne Gardner Collection.
PRICE: $340-370 15in (41cm)
$425-475 18in (46cm)

•

Annabelle: HP; 15in (38cm); *Maggie* face; shown in 1952 F.A.O. Schwarz catalog; inspired by Kate Smith's stories of Annabelle; 1952.

SEE: *Illustration 37. Playthings,* August 1952.
PRICE: $400-425

37.

Tommy Bangs: HP; 15in (38cm); all original light pants with dark blue coat with double set of buttons; pink shirt; from Louisa M. Alcott's book *Little Men;* 1952 only.
Other dolls in the series in 1952 include *Stuffy* and *Nat.*

See: *Illustration 38. Marianne Gardner Collection.*
PRICE: $700-750 +

38.

Stuffy: HP; 14in (33cm); *Maggie* face; blue, white and black checked pants; blue jacket and cap; from Louisa M. Alcott's book *Little Men;* all original except tie is missing; 1952 only.

MARKS: "Stuffy//Madame Alexander//New York U.S.A." (dress tag)
SEE: *Illustration 39. Patricia Arches Collection.*
PRICE: $700-750 +

39.

Glamour Girls: HP; 18in (46cm); used both *Maggie* and *Margaret* faces; seven different dolls; walking mechanism; each doll has a hat box and curlers; all the dresses are from the 1860s with full skirts and hoops; made for one year only, 1953.

1. Below *Blue Danube*: blue cotton print with pink and white flowers; black trim and ribbons; lace trim around neck and on puffed sleeves; stiff white lace bonnet.
SEE: *Illustration 40. Nancy Roeder Collection.*
2. Not pictured *Edwardian*: blonde wig; black taffeta and lace hat with pink ostrich feather; pink embossed cotton gown; black lace gloves.
3. Not pictured *Victorian*: formal pink taffeta gown; black velvet bodice; full skirt has a garland of pink roses; black and pink velvet ribbons trim outfit; black straw lace bonnet with pink rosebuds; tulle bow.
4. Not pictured *Godey Lady*: red taffeta gown and bonnet; gray fur cloth stole; red hatbox.
5. Not pictured *Civil War*: white taffeta dress; wide red sash; tiny red rosebuds and green leaves sewn on front of gown; white horse hair braid picture hat.
6. Not pictured *Queen Elizabeth II*: court gown of white brocade and blue Sash of Garter; jeweled coronet, earrings and bracelet; long white gloves.
7. *Picnic Day*: (See *Illustration 41*.)
PRICE: $600-800 each

40.

Glamour Girl: HP; 18in (46cm); walking mechanism; hat box and curlers; dressed in *Picnic Day*; strawberry pink dress with green leaves; wide green sash; trimmed with black val lace; large straw hat with pink rosebuds; 1953.

    SEE: *Illustration 41. Vivian Brady Ashley Collection.*
PRICE: $600-800

41.

24

Elaine of the Me and My Shadow Series: HP; 18in (46cm); portrait dolls; matching 7½in (19cm) miniature portrait dolls; garden party blue organdy dress trimmed with many rows of tiny val lace ruffles and stitching. The underdress is pink taffeta. There is a white taffeta hoop skirt and matching panties. The dress has puff sleeves, a round neck outlined with pearls and a big blue satin sash. There is a picture hat of white straw lace and pink satin slippers. 1954.
    SEE: *Illustration 42. Sandra Crane Collection.*
    PRICE: $600-800

The other dolls in the "Me and My Shadow Series" include:
1. *Mary Louise:* (See *Hard Plastic Dolls I,* page 26.)
2. *Blue Danube Waltz:* soft blue taffeta dance dress with side drapery of blue and gold striped taffeta; elaborate hairdo with a tiny gold coronet; gold necklace and jeweled bracelets (not pictured).
3. *Queen Elizabeth:* ornate white court gown with blue sash of the Order of the Garter; star and white orlon ermine cape; jeweled tiara, earrings and bracelet; long white gloves (not pictured).
4. *Cherie:* bouffant opera gown of heavy white satin gracefully draped with white roses; Goya pink taffeta opera coat is lined and fastened at the neck with a big bow; satin bag and the hairdress are rose trimmed (not pictured).
5. *Agatha:* iridescent taffeta Edwardian gown trimmed with delicate braid, flowers and pleated tulle; tight basque ends in a drapery which falls in a short train in back; ornate necklace; trimmed hat; white kid gloves; parasol (not pictured).

Victoria of Me and My Shadow Series: HP; 18in (46cm); 1850s costume; slate blue taffeta with side panniers and bustle drapery; narrow white silk braid; small hat of starched white lace with topknot of roses and forget-me-nots; fuchsia ribbons; fuchsia velvet reticule; 1954.
    SEE: *Illustration 43. Vivien Brady-Ashley Collection.*
    PRICE: $600-800

42.
    43.

Binnie Walker: HP; 15in (38cm); clothes in suitcase include gabardine coat, matching pillbox hat, white gloves, muff of pretend leopard, tartan school dress, nightgown, playsuit, blouse, pedal pushers, bonnet, shoes, socks, curlers for her Saran wig; head turning walker; sleep eyes; 1954.

    SEE: *Illustration 44.* Marshall Field & Co. 1954 Christmas catalog. *Barbara Andresen Collection.*

    PRICE: $500-600+

Binnie doll in a suitcase is all set for the Grand Tour. There's an impressive list of things to take packed in her cardboard suitcase. She's dressed for travel in her organdy dress with panties and net trimmed half slip, short socks and black slippers. She's stowed away a rayon gabardine coat, matching pillbox hat, little white gloves and muff of pretend-leopard, a tartan school dress, nightgown, playsuit, blouse, pedal pushers, bonnet, extra shoes, socks, and curlers to primp her Saran wig. Binnie walks, too, turns her head and closes her eyes. She's made of hard plastic, measures 15 inches tall. Cardboard suitcase with plastic handle is 17⅛x12x5 inches. For ages 6 to 12.
151 T7-8 . . . . $19.95

44.

Winsome Binnie Walker (*Cissy* face): HP; 25in (64cm) head turning walker; red curly hair; original tagged clothes; pink organdy dress; white lace hat; black shoes; white ankle socks; 1954-1955.

    MARKS: "Alexander" (head)

    SEE: *Illustration 45* (Color Section, page 40).

    PRICE: $225-275 15in (38cm)
              $250-300 18in (46cm)
              $325-400 25in (64cm)

Mary Ellen: HP with vinyl arms jointed at elbow; 31in (79cm); jointed at neck, shoulders, elbows, hips, knees; glued-on Saran wig; dressed in red taffeta redingote over dotted white taffeta (used on *Binnie Walker* the same year); white straw hat; exclusive outfit made for Marshall Field & Co.; 1955.

    MARKS: "MME ALEXANDER" (head); "#3122 Mary Ellen" (box)

    SEE: *Illustration 46. Marge Meisinger Collection.*

    PRICE: $425-500

46.

Mary Ellen: additional outfits in the Alexander catalogs.

1954

1. Long party dress of nylon net and lace over taffeta. She has pink satin slippers to match her pink satin sash. There is a circlet of flowers in her hair. She wears white kid gloves.
2. Heavy pile fleece red coat with brass buttons over a taffeta dress. A muff and hat are of leopard plush. She wears suede slippers and carries a hatbox with curlers and comb.
3. Nautical outfit consisting of a tailored dress with a pleated red taffeta skirt, a blue wool middy jacket with brass buttons and white collar and a white French beret with a red pompon. She wears white gloves and suede slippers.

1955

1. Period gown of aqua blue taffeta with tight bodice and bouffant skirt. There is a bonnet and wrist muff made of matching tulle and trimmed with rosebuds. The slippers are pink satin.
2. Bridemaid's gown of shimmering yellow taffeta which is trimmed with gold braid, appliqued flowers and rhinestones. The hat is a band with tiny flowers and gold mesh veil at each ear. The slippers are pink satin.

PRICE: $50-80 (mint-in-box outfit)

Lissy: HP; 12in (31cm); for general characteristics, see *Hard Plastic Dolls, I,* page 30. *Lissy* is very popular with collectors and is not as easy to find as some of the other Alexander dolls. She came as a bride, bridesmaid or ballerina. A wide selection of separate clothes and accessories were available. There was also a set of *Little Women* dolls (see *Hard Plastic Dolls, I,* page 32). In 1962 *Katie* and *Tommy* were made with a *Lissy* face for the 100th anniversary of F.A.O. Schwarz; in 1962 and 1963 a trousseau set with a doll called *Pamela* was made (see *Glamour Dolls of the 1950s & 1960s,* page 43).

MARKS: None (doll); most clothing marked with Alexander label

47.

48.

SEE: *Illustration 47. Nancy Roeder Collection.*

PRICE: $350-400

Kelly: HP; 12in (31cm); *Lissy* face; unjointed arms and legs; flat feet; (see *Hard Plastic Dolls, I* for comparison of *Lissy* and *Kelly*); pink nylon party dress with ruffles; 1959.

Lissy and *Kelly* were offered in a basic box with underwear or dressed in marked dresses. The 1958 Alexander catalog states that there was a large selection of clothes available. This dress was shown on a hanger with other clothes.

MARKS: None (doll)

SEE: *Illustration 48. Nancy Roeder Collection.*

PRICE: $400-500

Cissy:

Most of the doll manufacturers stopped making all-hard plastic dolls after 1957-1958. The Alexander Doll Company was one of the few that continued making some of them on into the 1960s. Like other companies, they did make some transitional dolls with vinyl heads.

Madame Alexander was a leader in the movement toward a more mature type of doll for children and her hard plastic *Cissy* was one of the first to have a high heel. A detailed explanation of the impact of *Cissy* on the doll world can be found in the *Glamour Dolls of the 1950s & 1960s*. *Elise*, a few years later, was also an all-hard plastic doll except for her arms. Because the hard plastic era spanned the decade from 1947 to 1957, *Cissy* was included in *Hard Plastic Dolls, I*, and some more pictures are included in this book. However, *Elise* fits the time frame of the book, *Glamour Dolls of the 1950s & 1960s* and her clothes for the most part reflect the fashions of that period. For more detailed information about *Elise* and her clothes, see *Glamour Dolls of the 1950s & 1960s*, pages 33 to 37. An *Elise Renoir* is pictured in *Illustration 51* (Color Section, page 95).

Cissy: HP head, body and legs; vinyl jointed arms; 20in (51cm) to 21in (53cm); high-heel feet; mature body; beautiful red taffeta formal with sweeping skirt; frothy sheer dotted swiss tulle stole that falls to the hem; ring; pearl necklace; circa 1957-1958.
MARKS: "Alexander" (head)
SEE: Front cover.
PRICE: $800 up

Cissy: #2283; silk ball gown with printed camellias; long cape stole of velvet lined to match gown; rhinestone pin at neckline; rhinestone necklace and matching solitaire earrings and ring; gold veil with matching flowers in hair; nylon panties; silk stockings; red high-heeled sandals; full hoop skirt; 1958.
MARKS: "Alexander" (head)
SEE: *Illustration 49. Glenn Mandeville Collection.*
PRICE: $700-800 up

Renoir Cissy: HP; 20in (51cm); long yellow satin dress with matching jacket; black sequin trim and handbag; net petticoat; black sandals; hat made of roses, violets and field flowers with black veil; "diamond" ring; 1961.
SEE: *Illustration 50. Marianne Gardner Collection.*
PRICE: $700-800 up

49.

50.

28

Elise Renoir: HP head and body with vinyl arms; 16½in (42cm); sleep eyes; high-heeled feet; mauve taffeta dress trimmed with lace; silk braid with reticule to match; cameo brooch; solitaire engagement ring; earrings; white straw hat trimmed with field flowers and pink veil; patented wig that can be washed and curled; 1963.

MARKS: "MME//Alexander" (back); "Alexander" (head)
SEE: *Illustration 51* (Color Section, page 95).
PRICE: $550-600

Cissette:

By 1957 most of the doll companies had almost totally ceased using the "injection mold" process for making hard plastic dolls. Most of the children and their mothers preferred the softer vinyl dolls with rooted hair and since the hard plastic doll was more expensive, the era of hard plastic dolls was almost over.

The Alexander Doll Company was an exception. They continued to make the *Cissette* and Alexander-Kin dolls of hard plastic. In 1957 they introduced *Cissette* which is still one of their most popular dolls. She had a slim, mature figure with lovely arms and legs and high-heeled feet. She competed with the small fashion dolls that led to the *Barbie®* fashion era.

Madame Alexander was an acknowledged expert in the entire fashion industry and *Cissette* wore the wonderful clothes of the glamorous years from 1957 to 1963. Her wardrobe was spectacular!

Cissette's wardrobe included street wear, sports outfits, formal gowns and historical period costumes. In 1961 an elegant doll with a special hairdo named *Margo* was part of the line. In 1962 *Cissette* was dressed as Jacqueline Kennedy. She had an unusual dark wig with a side part, a forehead curl and a row of soft curls at the collar line. From 1968 to 1973 a series of Portrette dolls with dazzling costumes was made. The Alexander Doll Company still uses hard plastic for the dolls for their new *Cissette* series.

Today this wonderful doll has been revived to the delight of collectors, and she is as beautiful and glamorous as ever.

Barbie® is a registered trademark of Mattel, Inc.

Cissette: HP; 10½in (27cm); adult body; high heeled; jointed at knees; dressed in light blue toreador pants; fancy nylon blouse; large pink nylon sash; pink rose at neckline; "diamond" earrings; pearl necklace.

MARKS: "MME Alexander" (back)
SEE: *Illustration 52* (Color Section, page 39).
PRICE: $275-300

53.

Cissette Portrette: 10½in (27cm); adult body; high heeled; jointed at knees.
Gold Rush (left): orange taffeta dress with black lace; black picture hat; 1963.
Gibson Girl (right): dark purple skirt; white and lavender striped blouse; purple hat with lavender feathers; 1963.
 MARKS: "Mme Alexander" (back)
 SEE: *Illustration 53. Louise Schnell Collection.*
 PRICE: $1400 (*Gold Rush*) $1200 (*Gibson Girl*)

Cissette Portrette: HP; 10½in (27cm); high heeled; jointed at knees.
Renoir (left): long dark blue dress trimmed with lace; red picture hat; 1968.
Scarlett (middle): dark green taffeta dress with black trim; green picture hat with white feather; 1968.
Agatha (right): red dress with lace trim; hat missing; 1968.
 MARKS: "Mme Alexander" (back)
 SEE: *Illustration 54. Louise Schnell Collection.*
 PRICE: $500-600 (*Renoir*) $500-550 (*Scarlett*) $575-595 (*Agatha*)

54.

Cissette Portrette: HP; 10½in (27cm); adult body; high heeled; jointed at knees.
Godey (left): pink taffeta dress with two ruffles at hemline; pink picture hat; 1968.
Southern Belle (middle): white dress with pleated ruffle at bottom of skirt; trimmed with lace with green ribbon running through it; large net picture hat trimmed with red roses; 1968.
Melinda (right): blue taffeta dress with ruffle at hemline; white lace collar; bonnet-type hat with blue net trim with ties at neck; 1968.
 MARKS: "Mme Alexander" (back)
 SEE: *Illustration 55* (Color Section, page 39). *Louise Schnell Collection.*
 PRICE: $500-575 (*Godey*) $500-575 (*Southern Belle*) $475-550 (*Melinda*)

56.

Jenny Lind: HP; 11in (28cm); high-heeled feet; jointed at knees; Portrette 1969; pink satin dress with pink satin over skirt; trimmed in lace; light and dark pink rosebud bouquet; blonde hair has center part and pulled to each side and fastened with rosebuds.
 SEE: *Illustration 56. Vivien Brady-Ashley Collection.*
 PRICE: $700-750+

Alexander-kins

The small 7½in (19cm) to 8in (20cm) dolls were first sold in 1953 and are still being sold today. Mothers and grandmothers started collections for their children because they were inexpensive and beautiful. The international dolls have helped children learn the countries of the world for the last 35 years. Many adult collectors consider that these dolls are the base of their collections. The newest tiny Alexanders are eagerly anticipated each year at the American International Toy Fair. Orders are quickly placed in local stores and new dolls join the beloved older ones.

Along with the international dolls, other small *Wendy Ann/Wendy/Wendi-kins/ Alexander-kins*, as they have been called, were in the Alexander catalogs each year. Over the years there has been an interest in these dolls by a group of collectors who have become specialists. The entire world of the regular *Wendy-kins, Alexander-kins* is different from the other world of Alexander doll collecting. Unexpectedly, these dolls have appreciated in price to a greater degree than most of the other Alexander dolls; a few sometimes command prices of over $1000. The list of dolls below is printed with the hope that collectors will be able to identify those rare dolls that seem to be selling at the highest prices.

1953
1. Agatha
2. Blue Danube
3. Civil War
4. Edwardian
5. Goya
6. Guardian Angel
7. Little Godey
8. Madeline
9. Little Southern Girl
10. Little Victoria
11. Peter Pan
12. Quiz-kin
13. Quiz-kin Bride
14. Quiz-kin Ballerina
15. Victoria

1954
1. Bible Characters
2. Agatha
3. Apple Annie
4. Blue Danube
5. Civil War
6. Elaine
7. Guardian Angel
8. Little Godey
9. Little Victoria
10. Mary Louise
11. Queen
12. Southern Belle
13. Victoria
14. Wendy Angel

1955
1. Garden Party
   (long gown; both straight leg
   non-walker and walker)
2. Baby Angel
3. Baby Clown
4. The Best Man
5. Bridesmaid
6. Curly-Locks
7. Davy Crockett Boy and Girl
8. Drum Majorette
9. Dude Ranch
10. Highland Fling
11. Juliet
12. Majorette
13. Melanie
14. Lady in Waiting
15. Little Minister
16. Mambo
17. Red Riding Hood
18. Rodeo
19. Romeo
20. Southern Belle
21. Waltzing

1956
1. Ballerina
2. Bridesmaid
3. Cousin Karen
4. Flower girl
5. Little Melanie
6. Melanie
7. Nurse
8. Parlour Maid
9. Pierrot Clown
10. Southern Belle
11. Story Princess

PRICES: Since there is a limited number of people willing to pay high prices for these dolls, local prices may be considerably less than national prices. To get the top prices, the seller may have to advertise nationally or even internationally.

1957
1. *Aunt Agatha*
2. *Aunt Pitty Pat*
3. *Bride*
4. *Bridesmaid*
5. *Cousin Grace*
6. *First Communion*
7. *Groom*
8. *Governess Nana*
9. *Graduation Party*
10. *Little Minister*
11. *Prince Charles*
12. *Princess Ann*

1958
1. *Bridesmaid*
2. *Edith the Lonely Doll*

1960
1. *Little Lady with Box of Cosmetics*

1961
1. *Amanda of Americana Group*
2. *Charity of Americana Group*
3. *Faith of Americana Group*
4. *Lucy of Americana Group*
5. *Maggie Mixup*
6. *Maggie Mixup Angel*
7. *Maggie Mixup with Watering Can*
8. *Maggie Mixup in Skating Costume*
9. *Maggie Mixup in Riding Habit*

1963
1. *Southern Belle*

1965
1. *1965-1972 Sewing Kit and Doll*

1968
1. *Easter Doll*

Davy Crockett Boy and Girl: HP; 8in (20cm); straight leg walker; boy has red caracul wig; girl has red "flip style" wig; both have mock suede clothes with fringe; belts have metal buckles; plush "coonskin" caps; 1955.

 SEE: *Illustration 57. Margaret Mandel Collection.*
 PRICE: $800-1000+ each.

57.

Continued on page 41.

32

Lady with the Rhinestone Beauty Mark (see page 20). Vivien Brady-Ashley Collection.

Alexander *Victorian Bride* (see page 21). *Sandra Crane Collection.*

Champs-Elysees (see page 21 and back cover). *Diane Huffman Collection.*

Alexander *Pink Champagne* (see page 21). *Vivien Brady-Ashley Collection.*

36

Alexander *Deborah* (see page 21). *Sandra Crane Collection.*

Alexander *Kathryn Grayson* (see page 21). *Sandra Crane Collection.*

Alexander *Cissette Portrettes* (left to right): *Godey Lady, Southern Belle, Melinda* (see page 30). *Louise Schnell Collection.*

Alexander *Cissette* in toreador pants (see page 29).

Alexander *Binnie Walker* (see page 26).

Alexander *Cinderella* (see page 19).

40

Continued from page 32.

Infant of Prague: HP; 8in (20cm); bent knee walker; unusual construction of hand; right hand molded so palm is in down position with 3rd finger curled under; left palm of hand faces upward; ornate jeweled crown and clothes; circa 1956.
    SEE: *Illustration 58. Vivien Brady-Ashley Collection.*
    PRICE: Not enough sample prices.

Angel: HP; 8in (20cm); *Maggie Mixup* face; bent knee walker; pink robe with gold trim; wings covered with gold design; circa 1960-1961.
    MARKS: "Alex" (back)
    SEE: *Illustration 59. Nancy Roeder Collection.*
    PRICE: $1200-1500 up

58.

59.

Bride and Groom: HP; 8in (20cm); bent knee walker; circa 1957.
    MARKS: "Alex" (back)
    SEE: *Illustration 60. Nancy Roeder Collection.*
    PRICE: $900-1000 pair

60.

61.

Little Women: HP; 8in (20cm); bent knee walker.

Madame Alexander loved to design dolls from fiction and the characters from *Little Women* were among her favorites. Most of the hard plastic dolls in various sizes were used for these famous dolls. The small dolls known as Alexander-kins have been used for these character dolls for many years and are still favorites with children and collectors.

> SEE: *Illustration 61. Toys and Novelties,* March 1964.
> PRICE: $650-725 set

62.

Little Genius: HP head and "Magic Skin" arms and legs; cloth body; 19in (46cm); eye shadow above eyes; hair in original set; all original yellow nylon dress with matching hat; matching yellow taffeta panties; dress trimmed with flowers; also came in 16in (41cm) and 23in (58cm); circa 1949.

> MARKS: "Little Genius//Alexander N.Y. U.S.A.//All Rights Reserved" (dress) "Alexander" (head)
> SEE: *Illustration 62. Mary Ann Bauman Collection.*
> PRICE: $275-325

Quiz-kin: HP; 7½in (19cm); straight leg non-walker; named after the television "Quiz Kids;" two buttons in back to make head move; all original pink organdy dress; 1953.

> SEE: *Illustration 63. Dorothy Hesner Collection.*
> PRICE: $400-550

63.

American Character Doll Co.

American Character Doll Co. was a leader in the manufacturing of dolls in the hard plastic era. In 1952 they published a catalog of the dolls made that year. On the first page they said, "For 33 years the American Character Doll Co. has manufactured dolls of the finest quality and craftsmanship, catering to children of all age groups.

"Our dolls have always appealed to parents because of their durability, and to children because of their beauty and play value.

"Some of our famous dolls that have become American 'Buy-words' are *TOODLES*, the first rubber doll; *SWEET SUE*, the first dolls with Saran wigs that could be washed, combed and curled; *TINY TEARS*, the only doll ever made that cries with real, wet tears."

SEE: *Illustrations 64* through *77*; These are the hard plastic dolls from this catalog.

Tiny Tears Characteristics: there are several different *Tiny Tears* dolls.
1. HP head; 18½in (47cm); rubber body which squeaks when pressed; very heavy doll (over four pounds); mouth with hole in it for bottle; sleep eyes with lashes; hole in nostrils close to eyes for tears; dimples above toes on feet and below fingers on hands; molded hair; circa 1950.
2. HP head; 15in (38cm); vinyl body; plastic has waxy look; mouth with hole for bottle; sleep eyes with lashes; holes in nostrils close to eyes for tears; dimples above toes on feet and below fingers on hands; individual fingers; rooted hair inset in skull cap; clothes not original; circa 1952 to 1955.
3. HP head; 12in (31cm); all-rubber body; mouth with hole for bottle; sleep eyes with lashes; holes in nostrils close to eyes for tears; individual fingers with dimples below fingers on hands and dimples above toes on feet; rubber body squeaks when pressed; head measures 11in (28cm) in circumference; molded hair; circa 1950.
4. HP head; 11in (28cm); vinyl arms, legs and body; plastic has waxy look; mouth with hole for bottle; sleep eyes with lashes; hole in nostrils close to eyes for tears; dimples above toes on feet and below fingers on hands; body squeaks when pressed; head 10in (25cm) in circumference; individual fingers; molded hair; circa 1952-1955.

Each of these types of dolls may come in different sizes. For pictures of these dolls see *Hard Plastic Dolls, I,* pages 48 to 50.

Sweet Sue Characteristics:
1. Rather light skin color but there is some blush in the checks.
2. The hair is coarse, rough and difficult to curl but it is pretty and washable.
3. The walkers have a spring in the arm joint which is distinctive to these dolls.
4. Many dresses are full-skirted with an attempt to imitate the hoop skirt, espe-cially in formal wear. The sleeves are often puffed below the elbow.
5. Shoes often have a snap closing.
6. Most wigs are blonde or reddish blonde.
7. Mouth is slightly off center.
8. Closed mouth.
9. Sleep eyes with lashes.

Sweet Sue Marks:
1. "A.C."
2. "Amer. Char."
3. Many of the dolls were unmarked.
   PRICE: $135-150   14in (36cm)
            $170-200   18in (46cm) - 20in (51cm)
            $235-250   24in (61cm)
            $275-350   30in (76cm)

Sweet Sue School Girl: HP; 14½in (37cm); dainty print dress of white embossed cotton with matching panties; neckline and circular skirt edged with pleated scalloped trim; two roses nestled at neckline; Saran hair gathered with two bows; doll on right is pictured in 1952 company catalog; doll on left wears the same dress.
   MARKS: None
   SEE: *Illustration 64. Sharlene Doyle Collection* (doll on left).
   PRICE: $135-150

Sweet Sue Birthday Party (left): light blue taffeta party dress with matching panties; French piping on neckline, waist and flounce; Saran hair with a rose and pink velvet bow.

Sweet Alice (right): blue satin-finished broadcloth dress; sheer white cross-bar lace-trimmed organdy pinafore; matching blue panties; long blonde Saran hair with black velvet bow; black patent leather pumps.
   SEE: *Illustration 65.*

64.   65.

Sweet Alice: HP; 16½in (38cm); turning head walker; arm hooked to heavy springs; closed mouth; sleep eyes; long blonde Saran wig; mouth off center; lashes painted under eyes; sheer white cross-bar organdy pinafore, lace trimmed; black velvet bow; blue satin-finish broadcloth dress with matching panties; black patent leather pumps; long white "Alice" stockings; in 1952 catalog. (For general American *Sweet Sue* characteristics, see page 43.)
   MARKS: "Made in U.S.A." (back)
   SEE: *Illustration 66* (Color Section, page 162).
   PRICE: $150-160

Sweet Sue Bride (left): heavy white satin gown with deep ruffle around skirt; Queen Elizabeth neckline with lace and satin ribbons; nylon tulle veil with lace and lillies of the valley trim; wired hoop slip and matching panties.

Mardi Gras (right): satin formal gown; circular skirt; deep cowl off-the-shoulder neckline; large pouf sash of contrasting color; ruffled hoop slip; matching panties; long Saran glamour bob pinned back with a rose; silver slippers.

SEE: *Illustration 67*. American Character 1952 catalog.

PRICE: $135-160   15in (38cm)
         $170-200   18in (46cm)
         $225-250   23in (58cm)

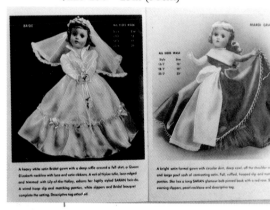

67.

Sweet Sue Co-Ed (left): red and green tartan taffeta with full skirt; important braid trim; "Gibson Girl" organdy sleeves; deep neckline with revers trimmed with lace; long wavy Saran hair.

Sunday Best (right): red taffeta brocade button-down dress; matching panties; deep white collar and cuffs trimmed with Val lace; straw hat over curled Saran hair; white parasol.

SEE: *Illustration 68*. American Character 1952 catalog.

68.

45

Sweet Sue Cotillion: a dream dress of satin lace; full skirt over taffeta slip; front is shirred nylon tulle ruffles; pink and blue rosebuds scattered over the tulle; form-fitting satin bodice; lace-edged flaired shoulder ruffles; ruffled hooped slip; matching panties; pearl necklace; satin slippers; hair is a Saran ponytail; matching chignon in carrying case.

SEE: *Illustration 69.* American Character 1952 catalog.

PRICE: $225-300

Tiny Tears: catalog says, "The only doll that cries real tears. Feed her she wets; place a pacifier in her mouth, squeeze her gently, and she weeps big, wet tears. You can hear her cry lustily. *Tiny Tears* drinks her bottle, wets her diaper, blows big soap bubbles, sleeps and can be bathed. She is made of molded rubber — fully jointed — and has a plastic head, sleeping eyes and lashes."

MARKS: "American Character" (head); some dolls have "Pat. No. 2.675.644" (head)

SEE: *Illustration 69.* American Character 1952 catalog.

PRICE: $50-55   11in (28cm)
$50-55   12in (31cm)
$50-55   15in (38cm)
$80-85   18½in (47cm)

69.

American Character Doll Company advertised widely on television. In connection with the "The Pinky Lee Show," they published a small cartoon and advertising doll book which cost 15 cents. Along with cartoon adventures of *Tiny Tears, Sweet Sue* and *Toodles,* pictures of the actual dolls in the 1955 line were shown in beautiful color. The cover is shown in *Illustration 70. Illustration 71* shows two adventures of *Sweet Sue.* 1. *Sweet Sue* stars on Pinky's T.V. show. 2. Life size *Sweet Sue* fools Pinky Lee.

SEE: *Illustration 70.*
      Illustration 71. 70.

71.

Life Size *Sweet Sue*: HP body and legs; vinyl arms; jointed at neck, shoulders, elbows, hips, knees; as big as a three-year-old-child; walks, sits, stands, kneels; rooted hair in vinyl head.

SEE: *Illustration 72* pictured in *Adventures of Pinky Lee, TIny Tears,* and *Sweet Sue* published by American Character Doll Company, 1955.

PRICE: $275-300

72.

Sweet Sue wardrobe from 1955 catalog "Adventures of *Pinky Lee, Tiny Tears,* and *Sweet Sue*"; published by American Character Doll Company. From left to right top row: *Springtime, Sweet Sue Coat, Sunday Best, Junior Prom.* From left to right middle row: *Birthday Party, Co-ed, Cotillion, Bride.* From left to right bottom row: *Schoolgirl, Teatime, Life Size Sweet Sue.*

SEE: *Illustration 73.* (Color Section, page 96).

Tiny Tears: HP head; jointed rubber body; 13in (33cm); both doll and layette were featured on the television program "Ding Dong School;" doll cries real tears if she is fed water from her bottle. The pacifier is placed in her mouth and then she is gently squeezed; doll also wets, blows bubbles, sleeps; doll is washable; layette includes embossed cotton dress, panties, bonnet, knit booties, sleeping garment, extra diaper, package of Kleenex tissues, bottle, sponge, soap, bubble pipe, washcloth, pacifier, instruction booklet; 1954.

MARKS: "American Character" (head); some dolls have "Pat. No. 2.675.644" (head)

SEE: *Illustration 74.* Marshall Field & Co. 1954 Christmas catalog. *Barbara Andresen Collection.* ·

PRICE: $55-60

Tiny Tears and her layette featured on Ding Dong School. Just feed her water from her bottle, place pacifier in her mouth, squeeze her gently, she cries real tears. She wets, blows bubbles, sleeps, can be bathed. Has movable, jointed rubber body and hard plastic head. Layette includes: embossed cotton dress, panties, bonnet, knit bootees, sleeping garment, extra diaper, package of Kleenex tissues, bottle, sponge, soap, bubble pipe, washcloth, pacifier and instruction booklet. 13 inches tall. For girls ages 4 to 10.
151 T2-64 . . . . **$7.95**

74.

Toodles "Potty Baby": HP head and molded rubber body; 13in (33cm) and 16in (41cm); advertisement first appeared in *Life Magazine*; the advertisement said "'Toodles the Potty Baby' makes a game out of teaching little girls the rules of baby care." The doll came with a layette. Other dolls advertised in 1949 included *Baby Sue, Sweet Sue* and *Little Sis* (a rubber doll).

    SEE: *Illustration 75. Playthings*, October 1949.
    PRICE: $50-70

75.

Annie Oakley: HP; 18in (46cm); fully jointed; unusual face; red and white cowgirl outfit; blonde hair; sleep eyes with unusual feathered eyebrows; eyelashes below the eyes and five lines to the side of the eye; arm hook (see Identification Guide, *Hard Plastic Dolls, I,* page 266P); 1955.

    MARKS: Small "P" (arm hook).
    SEE: *Illustration 76* (doll). *Diane Loney Collection.*
        Illustration 77. American Character Doll Co. catalog, 1955.
    PRICE: $170-200 (complete)

76.

77.

Betsy McCall: HP; 8in (20cm); beautiful bisque-like finish; rooted brown hair in a plastic skull cap covering or wig; blue sleep eyes with molded lashes; closed mouth; knee joints; 2nd and 3rd fingers molded together. *Betsy* has clothes which could be purchased, and *McCalls* magazine featured *Betsy* and her wardrobe each month in paper doll form; white and red gingham dress with white bias trim at neckline; white apron; all original; circa 1958. *Betsy McCall's* hair was either a wig or a plastic skull cap with inset hair.

   MARKS: "McCall Corporation" (on back in circle)
   SEE: *Illustration 78.*
   PRICE: $100-120

78.

Betsy McCall® is a registered trademark of the McCall Corp.

Arranbee Doll Company, Inc.

The Arranbee Company was a maker of fine dolls in the early 1950s, and the following pictures show the lovely dolls and their clothes.

It is interesting that in 1951 they were ahead of their time and were experimenting with vinyl dolls and parts. The *Nancy* doll was advertised as having a vinyl head, arms and legs. It was one of the few dolls with a vinyl head that had a wig. It was also one of the few hard plastic dolls made in the United States with a "Mama" voice box. (See *Illustration 79.*) A baby made that year also had a vinyl head. Most of the other dolls in their line were all-hard plastic.

The company was interested in clothes and fashion. The little girl dolls were dressed in the type of dresses fashionable for the little girls who owned them. They also made formal designer-type doll clothes for the older girls.

The 11in (28cm) *Littlest Angel* dolls were among their best sellers. They were *Ginny*®-type dolls that were larger and easier to manipulate than the small 8in (20cm) walking dolls. Today they are beloved by many collectors because of their cute "chubby" bodies and beautiful clothes.

In 1957, just before Arranbee was sold, they advertised an all-vinyl doll with 12 outfits. The book *Glamour Dolls of the 1950s & 1960s*, shows pictures of some of the vinyl dolls and company catalogs made when Arranbee became a division of Vogue.

Nanette: HP; 15in (38cm), 18in (46cm) and 23in (58cm); non-walking; sleep eyes; Dynel or Saran wig; came with comb, curlers and two-color instruction sheet; 1950.

1. (Upper right) *Party Formal:* full length sheer over ruffled satin hooped slip; picture hat.
2. (Center) *Roller Skater:* wide belted plaid jumper; peasant blouse; matching hair ribbon; roller skates.
3. (Lower left) *Tea Party;* short taffeta print party dress with ribbons and bows; carrying a little handbag.

   SEE: *Illustration 79. Playthings,* October 1950.

   PRICE: $140-165   15in (36cm)
   depending on outfit
   $180-220   18in (46cm)
   depending on outfit
   $225-300   23in (58cm)
   depending on outfit

79.

Nanette Cowgirl: HP; 14in (36cm); red felt skirt; black and white plaid top; black felt dress with silver trim; yellow tie; red felt cowboy hat; red felt boots with white trim; circa 1950-1956.
> MARKS: "R&B" (head)
> SEE: *Illustration 80. Marianne Gardner Collection.*
> PRICE: $150-180 (complete)

Nanette with Tiara: HP; 18in (46cm); head-turning walker; jointed at neck, arms and hips; beautiful plastic with excellent skin tone; red wig; sleep eyes with lashes under eyes; 2nd and 3rd fingers molded together; pink embroidered net formal dress over pink taffeta slip; white slip with hoop; pearl straps; pink flowers at waist; silver tiara on head; early 1950s.
> MARKS: "R&B" (head)
> SEE: *Illustration 81.*
> PRICE: $160-180

Nancy Lee: HP; 14in (36cm); deep rose velvet ball gown trimmed with feathers; pair of white half gloves; white cotton purse trimmed with gold braid; white anklets; gold shoes; tosca wig; all original; circa early 1950s.
> MARKS: "R&B" (head)
> SEE: *Illustration 82* (Color Section, page 96). *Lois Janner Collection.*
> PRICE: $150-180

80.

81.

Nancy Lee Skater: HP; 20in (51cm) without skates; blonde mohair wig; sleep eyes; all original red and white skating outfit; white skates; circa early 1950s.
  MARKS: "R&B" (head); "Nancy Lee 14106//R & B Quality Doll" (box)
  SEE: *Illustration 83. Vivian Brady-Ashley Collection.*
  PRICE: $250-300

83.

Nancy: HP; 14in (36cm); lovely skin tone with red on cheeks, hands and knees; pink skating outfit with various colors on trim around the skirt; all original including ice skates; circa early 1950s.
  MARKS: "Nancy" (tag)
  SEE: *Illustration 84. Sandy Strater Collection.*
  PRICE: $150-180

Nancy: HP body with vinyl arms, legs and head; 24in (61cm); walker; washable Dynel hair; says "Mama;" clothes patterned after children's clothes. This is a very unusual early Arranbee doll. During this period manufacturers were experimenting with the various types of plastic and vinyl. It is unusual to find a vinyl-headed doll with a wig. Other dolls advertised were *Angel Face* which also had a vinyl head, arms and legs; all-HP *Nannette; Dream Baby* with a soft vinyl head.
  SEE: *Illustration 85. Playthings,* July 1951.

84.

85.

52

Life Size *Nanette:* plastic body with soft vinyl head; 30in (76cm) head turning walker; sleep eyes; washable rooted Saran hair that can be combed and curled; came with four costumes; 1955.

  SEE: *Illustration 86.* 1955 Arranbee catalog. *Kathryn Davis Collection.*
  PRICE: $275-350

86.

***Nanette* Brochure:** HP with vinyl head; 15in (38cm), 18in (46cm) and 25in (64cm); head turning walker; jointed at neck, shoulders, hips and knees; sleep eyes; closed mouth; rooted Saran hair; individual fingers; guaranteed not to crack, peel or chip; 1955.

  MARKS: "17VW" (head)
  SEE: *Illustration 87.* 1955 Arranbee catalog. *Kathryn Davis Collection.*
      Illustration 88. 1955 Arranbee catalog. *Kathryn Davis Collection.*

87.

88.

53

Nanette Ballerina: HP with vinyl head; 18in (46cm); head turning walker; real lashes; sleep eyes; painted lashes under eyes; closed mouth; auburn rooted hair; individual fingers; jointed at neck, shoulders, hips and knees; peach satin bodice; beige net tutu with printed stars and circles; pink flowers at neckline; flat feet with pink ballet slippers; 1955. These dolls also came in a 15in (38cm) size. On her tag Arranbee advertised *Littlest Angel, Sweet Pea, Angel Face, Angel Skin* and *Dream Baby.*

    MARKS: "17VW" (back of head); "R&B Nanette//kneels//walks//sits//stands//turns her head//My Saran Hair is Rooted just like real Growing hair" (tag)

    SEE: *Illustration 89.*

    PRICE: $100-125

Nanette Beauty Shop Doll: HP; 15in (38cm); 18in (46cm) and 23in (58cm); head turning walker; complete with curlers and easy instructions for doing hair. The Arranbee doll at the bottom of the page in the middle is an all-vinyl *Nancy Lee* doll with 12 outfits.

    SEE: *Illustration 90. Playthings,* August 1957.

89. 90.

Littlest Angel All-HP Characteristics: 10½in (27cm) - 11in (28cm); open-closed mouth with slightly molded tongue; sleep eyes with molded eyelashes; painted eyelashes below the eye; hip pin walker (see Identification Guide, *Hard Plastic Dolls, I,* page 291D); 1954 dolls have straight legs; later dolls have jointed knees; individual fingers with 3rd and 4th fingers curving slightly inward; dimples above fingers and toes; arm hooks (see Identification Guide, pages 236). It is possible for these dolls to have no mark. However, the best clue to identification is the hip pin walker.

    MARKS: Most have "R&B" (head); the "R&B" is not always distinct and can wear off.

91.

Littlest Angel: HP; 11in (28cm); jointed at neck, shoulders, hips and knees; head turning walker; basic doll came with panties, shoes, socks, tag and box which showed some of the outfits; 1955. Boxed outfits were usually purchased separately, **SEE:** *Illustration 91. Sally Herbst Collection.*
PRICE: $55-75

Littlest Angel Brochure 1954: "The Busiest Girl We Know"

1. *Two Piece Sleeper:* yellow and blue knitted sleeper; little lamb embroidered on top.
2. *Sunsuit and Hat:* red and white sunsuit which can be used as a swimsuit. (See *Illustration 100.*)
3. *Sunsuit and Straw Hat:* blue sunsuit trimmed with lace; large straw hat.
4. *Three-Piece Pajama Set:* Two-piece pajamas with elegant matching robe and slippers.
5. *Afternoon Dress:* red and white peppermint dress; lace trimming; matching panties.
6. *Tennis Ensemble:* white shorts; blue and white halter and shirt; tennis cap; tennis racket.
7. *Organdy Birthday Dress:* dress with pink rosebuds; ruffles.
8. *School Dress:* lace-trimmed polka dot swiss organdy dress; magic slate and pencil.
9. *Overalls and Hat:* red and white checkered overalls and matching bonnet.
10. *Garden Party Dress:* pink dress with embroidery; rosebuds at waist; natural color straw bonnet.
11. *Beach Apparel:* bathing suit; salmon-colored robe and hood; special beach bag; slippers.
12. *Skating Costume:* black felt with silver trim; black hat; silver skates.
13. *Nurse's Uniform:* traditional nylon nurse's uniform; blue cape with red lining.
14. *Picnic Outfit:* pedal pushers; frilly peasant blouse; gold slippers; glasses.
15. *Bridal Gown:* gown embroidered with tiny flowers; illusion net veil; bridal bouquet.
16. *Formal Gown:* ruffled long dress; gold slippers.
17. *Roller Skating Set:* dungarees with red polka dot cuffs; matching handkerchief; halter; bonnet.
18. *Coat, Hat, Dress:* stylish hat and coat; lace trim; Christmas dress under coat.
19. *Fisherman's Outfit:* denim pants; shirt with fish on it; green straw hat; black boots; two fish and other fishing equipment in bag.
20. *Drum Majorette Costume:* fancy skirt; satin top with shiny buttons; high-stepping boots; peaked hat with plume.
21. *Ballerina Costume:* pink tulle; pink satin ballet slippers; rosebuds in hair. (See *Illustration 104.*)
22. *Two-Gun Tess:* brown leatherette riding skirt; two-pint hat; riding boots; twin pistols. (See *Illustration 103.*)
23. *Ski Outfit:* blue and white outfit with white ribbing; tassel cap; skis and poles. (See *Illustration 98.*)
24. *TV Lounging Clothes:* blue and silver oriental jacket; lounging slippers; glasses.

***Littlest Angel* Brochure 1955:** all dolls have jointed knees.
   SEE: *Illustration 92. Brochure from Kathryn Davis Collection.*

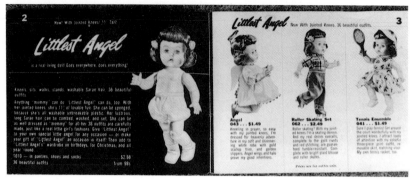

92.

***Littlest Angel* Brochure 1955:**
   SEE: *Illustration 93. Brochure from Kathryn Davis Collection.*

93.

***Littlest Angel* Brochure 1955:**
   SEE: *Illustration 94. Brochure from Kathryn Davis Collection.*

94.

Littlest Angel Brochure 1955:
SEE: *Illustration 95. Brochure from Kathryn Davis Collection.*

95.

Littlest Angel Brochure 1955:
SEE: *Illustration 96. Brochure from Kathryn Davis Collection.*

96.

Littlest Angel Brochure 1955:
SEE: *Illustration 97. Brochure from Kathryn Davis Collection.*

97.

Littlest Angel Brochure 1955: Not Photographed.
1. *Garment Bag:* plaid garment bag with hanger; #102.
2. *Travel Set:* plaid car bag with zipper: matching tote bag: #103.
3. *Travel Trunk:* metal trunk with drawer; #104.
4. *Gretel Metal Trunk:* trunk with three outfits and doll; sunglasses; extra shoes, socks, hangers; #151.
5. *Riding Habit Metal Trunk:* weekend package with three costumes and doll; hangers; glasses; extra shoes and socks; doll dressed in jodhpurs; #152.

Littlest Angel Brochure 1957 all dolls have jointed knees; buyer had choice of vinyl head with rooted hair (V1010) or hard head with foundation wig (H1010). This catalog had fewer descriptions than the previous two catalogs.

1. *Standard Doll in Box:* dressed only in panties, shoes, socks; #V1010 and #H1010. The doll with the hard head cost $2.59 and the doll with the vinyl head cost $2.98.
2. *R & B Surprise Doll All Packed to Go Bye Bye in Her 4 Color Gift Box:* Surprise Doll Book.
   A. *English Outfit:* #SD-1.
   B. *Chinese Outfit:* #SD-2; (see *Illustration* 106).
   C. *French Outfit:* #SD-3.
   D. *Russian Outfit:* #SD-4.
   E. *Italian Outfit:* #SD-5.
   F. *Dutch Outfit:* #SD-6.
   G. *Dressed Doll and Wonder Book:* #SD-10.
3. *Denim Smock:* #503.
4. *Checked Overalls:* #504.
5. *Ice Skater:* red velvet skating outfit with white trim and pompon; silver skates; matching hat with pompon; #509; (see *Illustration* 98).
6. *Artist's Outfit:* #512.
7. *Gretel Outfit:* #514.
8. *Red Riding Hood:* #516.
9. *Alice in Wonderland:* #517.
10. *Golf Outfit:* #519.
11. *Embroidered Nylon Dress:* #618.
12. *Square Dancer:* #620.
13. *Leather Jacket Set:* #623.
14. *Ballerina Outfit:* #613.
15. *Dress and Reversible Coat:* #612.
16. *Appliqued Nylon Dress:* #61.
17. *Formal Outfit:* #603.
18. *Formal Outfit:* #604.
19. *TV Outfit:* #609.
20. *Nylon Dress and Hat Outfit:* #611.
21. *Ski Outfit:* #616; (see *Illustration* 98).
22. *Cowgirl Outfit:* #607; (see *Illustration* 103).
23. *Riding Habit:* #617; (see Color Section, page 168).
24. *Formal Dress and Hat:* #707.
25. *Bridal Outfit:* #706; (see *Illustration* 105).
26. *Velvet Coat & Formal Dress:* #804.
27. *Borgana Fur Coat:* #709.
28. *Formal Dress with Fur Stole:* #803.
29. *Coat, Hat & Dress Set:* #705.
30. *Aqua Organdy Dress:* #312.
31. *Two-Piece Sleeper:* #301.
32. *Polka Dot Dress:* #310.
33. *Sunsuit and Parasol:* #308; dark suit with fancy trim.
34. *Lantern Print Dress:* #309.
35. *Red Plaid Dress:* #417.
36. *Three-Piece Pajama Set:* #412.
37. *Rain Outfit:* #413.
38. *Organdy Dress and Hat Set:* #414.
39. *Brown Strip Dress:* #416.
40. *Afternoon Dress:* #402; candy stripe and white dress.
41. *Tennis Outfit:* #404.
42. *Party Dress:* #406.
43. *Bermuda Shorts:* #407.
44. *Tic Tac Toe Print Dress:* #528.
45. *Cardigan and Hat:* #523.
46. *School Dress and Hat Set:* striped with print pinafore; #526.
47. *Taffeta Party Dress:* #529.
48. *Nurse's Outfit:* #510.
49. *Pleated Skirt and Blouse:* #527.

Littlest Angel Skier: HP; 11in (28cm); blue gabardine ski outfit with white knit and red braid trim; blue ski hat with white knit trim and pompon; wooden skis attached to black shoes; wood ski poles; outfit listed in 1954. It was listed as #065 in 1955 and #616 in 1957. This particular outfit was purchased mint-in-box which was the way most of the clothes were purchased at the time.

    MARKS: "R&B" (head and body)
    SEE: *Illustration 98.*
    PRICE: $55-75

Littlest Angel Skater: HP with vinyl head; 11in (28cm); red velvet skating costume with white trim; silver ice skates; all original; listed #509 in 1957 catalog. Other skating costumes include a black felt one with silver trim and black hat in 1954 and #054 a white knitted skating suit in 1955.

    MARKS: "R&B Doll Company" (body only)
    SEE: *Illustration 98.*
    PRICE: $45-65

98.

Littlest Angel in Jodhpurs (left): HP; 11in (28cm); white jodhpurs and blouse; red vest, jockey cap, boots; circa 1955-1957.

    MARKS: "R&B" (head)
    SEE: *Illustration 99* (Color Section, page 168).
    PRICE: $75-90

Littlest Angel: HP; 11in (28cm); red and white cotton print sunsuit in 1954 catalog; 1955 doll jointed at neck, shoulders, hips and knees; outfit could double for swimsuit.

    MARKS: "R&B" (head)
    SEE: *Illustration 100. Nancy Carlton Collection.*
    PRICE: $55-75

100.

Littlest Angel: HP; 10in (25cm); walking doll; sleep eyes; Saran wig can be combed and curled; wardrobe includes broadcloth dress, panty, party dress, lacy slip, corduroy coat, hat, organdy dress, overalls, blouse, robe, pajamas, sunsuit, slippers, shoes, socks; 1954.

    SEE: *Illustration 101.* 1954 Marshall Field & Co. Christmas catalog. *Barbara Andresen Collection.*

    PRICE: $80-100

Littlest Angel: HP; 10in (25cm); head turning walker; accessories include a mahogany reproduction of early American Tester bed; two-drawer wardrobe with mahogany finish; 1954.

    SEE: *Illustration 102.* 1954 Marshall Field & Co. catalog. *Barbara Andresen Collection.*

    PRICE: $55-75 (doll)

Littlest Angel has a heavenly wardrobe. She wears dress and panty, and the foot high wood trunk holds: broadcloth dress, panty, party dress, lacy slip, corduroy coat, hat, organdy dress, overalls, blouse, robe and pajama set, sun suit, slippers, shoes and socks. She's 10 inches tall, plastic, walks, sits and stands alone, closes her eyes. Saran wig can be combed and curled for your littlest Christmas angels, ages 4 to 10.
151 T2-87 .... **$15.95**

101.

give her a Doll to play with and love

[F] **Colonial bed** sure to bring sweet sugar plum dreams to any doll. Reproduction of early American Tester bed in fine mahogany finish. Dotted-Swiss canopy and spread, tufted mattress and bolster. 13¾x8½x 13 inches, big enough for 8-inch doll. Ages 4 to 10. **151 T2-89**.. **$7.95**
[G] **Littlest Angel. 151 T2-88**—10-inch doll in red pajamas........ **$4**
[H] **Two drawer wardrobe** with lots of room for pretend-mothers to store their children's clothes. Fine mahogany finish. Deep sliding drawers. 13½x9x5 inches, will hold wardrobe for dolls up to 11 inches tall. For girls age 4 to 10. **151 T2-90** **$7.95**

11

102.

103.

Littlest Angel Cowgirl: HP; 10½in (27cm); braided blonde wig with flowers in hair; blue eyes; all original cowgirl dress with brown leather-type skirt, collar and cuffs; white and blue checked blouse; felt hat; outfit #064 in the 1955 catalog.

  MARKS: "R&B" (head)
  SEE: *Illustration 103. Sally Herbst Collection.*
  PRICE: $55-75

Littlest Angel Ballerina: HP; 11in (28cm); pink ballerina costume #063; flowers and clip on each side of brunette wig; in 1955 brochure.

  MARKS: "R&B" (head)
  SEE: *Illustration 104. Sally Herbst Collection.*
  PRICE: $55-75

Littlest Angel Bride: HP; 11in (28cm); white bridal gown embroidered all over with tiny flowers; veil of illusion net; carrying a bouquet of white blossoms; #030 in 1955 brochure.

  MARKS: "R&B" (head)
  SEE: *Illustration 105. Sally Herbst Collection.*
  PRICE: $55-75

104.

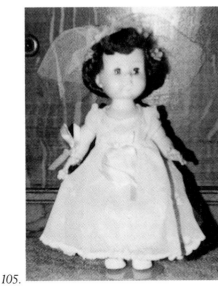

105.

106.

Littlest Angel with **Vinyl Head Characteristics:** HP with vinyl head; 11in (28cm); open/closed mouth with detailed molded tongue; molded eyelashes; jointed knees; pin-jointed walker (leg joints with pin hidden under body); sleep eyes with tiny eyelashes painted under the eyes; dimples on back of hands; rooted hair; arm hook (see Identification Guide, page 244). The 1957 brochure listed the vinyl head rooted hair doll for $2.98 and the hard head with foundation wig for $2.59. Both mothers and children preferred the rooted hair dolls.

> MARKS: Marks seen on these dolls: "R&B" (head); "R&B Doll Company" (body); "11"; "15"; "16"; "19"; "65"; "⊥."

Littlest Angel in Chinese Costume: HP with vinyl head; 11in (28cm); purple, gold and black print Chinese-style top with braid; rose pants; small paper umbrella; brunette rooted hair; blue eyes; listed in 1957 brochure as the "R & B Surprise Doll - all packed to go Bye-Bye in her 4 color Gift Box! Dressed 11in *Littlest Angel* Doll. 'Surprise Doll' Book;" 1957. Other Surprise Dolls included English, French, Russian, Italian and Dutch.

> MARKS: Inverted "T" (body); "Littlest Angel BOB #1010" (box)
>
> SEE: *Illustration 106.*
>
> PRICE: $75-95 The *Surprise Dolls* are hard to find.

Artisan Doll
(Artisan Novelty Co.)

The registered trademarks, the trademarks and the copyrights appearing in italics within this chapter belong to Artisan.

In 1950 the Artisan Doll Company introduced their new walking doll with a wardrobe of "California Originals" by Michele. Many of the costumes were labeled. The dolls had unusually widespread legs with a heavy walking mechanism. They were very beautiful. The advertisement said, "The dolls could walk, skate, stand alone, and do the splits. Her Ravon wig could be shampooed, combed, and waved." A less expensive doll was the same without the walking mechanism.

MARKS: None (doll); clothes sometimes had a tag
SEE: *Illustration 107. Playthings,* June 1950.
PRICE: $80-110

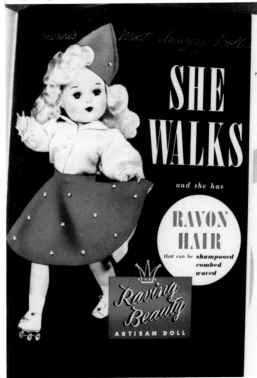

107.

General Characteristics for *Raving Beauty* and *Miss Gadabout:* HP; 20in (51cm); felt tongue with four teeth; wig that could be washed and curled; sleep eyes with real eyelashes; 2nd and 3rd fingers slightly curled; could sit, stand and walk with unusual hip action; Y on seat; 1950. The company made both walkers and non-walkers. (For more information and pictures, see *Hard Plastic Dolls, I,* page 56.)

MARKS: None (doll); clothes sometimes labeled

Raving Beauty: HP; 20in (51cm); (see page 63 for general characteristics). The first wardrobe of "California Originals" by Michele consisted of a square dance costume with brown or blue skirt; cowgirl costume with brown or light blue skirt; skating costume with blue or red gabardine skirt; pastel yellow or blue nightgown with black negligee; black net negligee with black bra and panties; print organdy matinee dress and hat; taffeta wedding gown; all costumes came with accessories; 1950.

    MARKS: None (doll); labels on some of the clothes
    SEE: *Illustration 108. Playthings,* June 1950.
    PRICE: $80-110

Raving Beauty: HP; 100 Series; (see page 63 for general characteristics); doll packed in silver and black tubular container; costumes include #102 sunsuit, #103 playtime costume in white or pastel green, #104 afternoon costume; #101 party costume of light blue taffeta; each costume had panties and shoes; 1950. This doll was not a walking doll. (For further information about Artisan dolls, see *Hard Plastic Dolls, I,* page 56.)

    MARKS: None (doll)
    SEE: *Illustration 109. Playthings,* June 1950.
    PRICE: $100-150

108.

109.

Raving Beauty Walking Doll: HP; 20in (51cm); (see page 63 for general characteristics); early 1950s.

  MARKS: None (most dolls)
  SEE: *Illustration 110* (doll on left).
        Playthings, April 1951.
        Illustration 111 (doll on right).
        Playthings, August 1951.
  PRICE: $100-150

Harry Waters, sales manager for Artisan Dolls, looking mighty pleased with the Raving Beauty Walking Doll, and with the opening of a permanent show room by Artisan at 200 Fifth Ave., New York.

110.

111.

Raving Beauty: HP; 20in (51cm); walking doll; (see page 63 for general characteristics); long yellow formal dress with matching underpants; pinkish satin slippers; tortoise and silver comb in hair; extra outfit of nylon black negligee; early 1950s.

    MARKS: None (doll); "Original Michele//California" (tag on dress); "Raving Beauty//Trademark//Walking Doll//No. 300//Artisan Novelty Company" (box)

    SEE: *Illustration 112. Sharlene Doyle Collection.*

    PRICE: $100-150

112.

Ava Milano Art Doll

The registered trademarks, the trademarks and the copyrights appearing in italics within this chapter belong to Ava Milano Art Doll Company.

Pamela: Italian; HP; 18in (46cm); flirty eyes; human hair wig; individual fingers; painted fingernails; closed mouth; crier box grill; beautiful green organdy dress trimmed with green felt and hand-painted rosebuds; petticoat and separate hooped skirt; pantaloons; leather shoes; matching umbrella; large straw hat; large beautifully printed box. This is an unusually beautiful doll. Both Lenci and Furga were also dressing similar hard plastic dolls in this manner.

    MARKS: "Pamela" (handwritten on head); "AVA//Milano//Art Doll//#35//Extra//Pamela" (box). The signed Pamela on the box and on the head is the same.

    SEE: *Illustration 113. Sandra Strater Collection.*

113.   **PRICE:** $125-150

Baby Barry Toys

The registered trademarks, the trademarks and the copyrights appearing in italics within this chapter belong to Baby Barry Toys.

Baby Barry: HP; 16in (41cm); open mouth with four teeth; felt tongue; braided blonde hair; blue sleep eyes; beige skirt with white blouse; white with blue trimmed suspenders; white shoes, socks and underwear; Y on seat; Wave-A-Doll Hair Kit came with the doll.

MARKS: "Made in USA//170" (back); "Universal Doll Corp.//New York//N.Y." (top of tag); "Style No. 17W//Description//All Hard Plastic//Saran Hair-Wave Kit//Manufactured by//Baby Barry Toys//New York, N.Y." (box); "Wave-A-Doll//Hair//Kit" (box)

SEE: *Illustration 114. Sharlene Doyle Collection.*

PRICE: $50-55

114.

Beddy-Bye and Bye-Bye Doll

The registered trademarks, the trademarks and the copyrights appearing in italics within this chapter belong to Duchess Doll Corp.

Travel Doll: HP; 7¼in (19cm); jointed at neck only; blonde wig; sleep eyes with brown painted lashes above eyes; four fingers molded together; molded painted shoes; included in kit are a gold dress with lace trim; blue flowered print nightgown; pink satin bathrobe; pants; curlers; green felt coat, hat; purse; circa mid 1950s. This company used a *Duchess* doll in their suitcase kit which was made to entertain children while traveling.

MARKS: "DUCHESS DOLL CORP// DESIGN COPYRIGHT //1949" (back of doll)

SEE: *Illustration 115. Marge Meisinger Collection.*

PRICE: $25-30

115.

Belle Doll & Toy Corp.

The registered trademarks, the trademarks and the copyrights appearing in italics within this chapter belong to Belle Doll & Toy Corp. unless otherwise noted.

116.

Saucy Walker® is a registered trademark of the Ideal Toy Corp.

Heddi Stroller: HP; 20in (51cm); head turning walker; Saran pigtail wig; *Saucy Walker*-type; 1952.

    SEE: *Illustration 116. Playthings*, July 1952.

    PRICE: $40-50

Bible Doll Co. of America

The registered trademarks, the trademarks and the copyrights appearing in italics within this chapter belong to Bible Doll Co. of America.

David: Very shiny HP; approximately 10in (25cm); raised eyebrows; caracul hair and suit; red belt and boots; came with brochure, "This is David, Your Little Friend From the Bible;" other dolls include Bible characters *Queen Ester, Miriam, Rebekah, Ruth* and *Joseph*; also came with an envelope marked, "Holy Land Earth from the Mount of Olives;" circa mid 1950s.

    SEE: *Illustration 117* (Color Section, page 224). *Eunice Kier Collection.*

    PRICE: Not enough sample prices.

Block Doll Corp.

The registered trademarks, the trademarks and the copyrights appearing in italics within this chapter belong to Block Doll Corp.

The Block Doll Corp. made many dolls for the mass market. Most of them were smaller, inexpensive dolls. They advertised regularly in *Playthings* and not only sold dolls to the public under their name, but they sold to other doll sales companies. Their *Answer Doll* was advertised as early as 1951 and was still advertised in 1957.

For a comparison of some of the collectible "chubby" dolls, see the Identification Guide, page 244.

Answer Doll: HP; 12in (33cm); fully jointed; sleep eyes; nods head "Yes" and shakes head "No." The company advertised that they had other hard plastic miniature dolls with movable parts and sleep eyes that were 5½in (14cm), 6½in (17cm) and 7½in (19cm).

SEE: *Illustration 118. Playthings,* March 1951.

PRICE: $45-55 (*Answer Dolls*)   118.

Baby Walker: HP; 10½in (27cm); straight leg walker; sleep eyes with molded eyelashes; eyelashes painted under eyes; closed mouth; jointed at neck, shoulders and hips; excellent skin tone; red cheeks and knees; dimples at back of elbows; line above and below knee; double line at front ankle; arm hook (see Identification Guide, page 244); dimples above fingers but not above toes; original clothes; white piqué print with red print roses; snap on dress reads, "Dot Snappers;" unusually nice quality doll; quality of clothing inferior; circa 1955.

MARKS: None (doll); "Baby Walker// Block Doll Corp." (box)

SEE: *Illustration 119.*

PRICE: $45-55

119.

120.

Answer Doll: HP; 12in (31cm); fully jointed; sleep eyes; press back and doll nods "yes;" press tummy and doll nods "no."

> SEE: *Illustration 120. Playthings, March 1957.*
> PRICE: $45-55

Chubby-Type: HP; vinyl head; 10½in (27cm); more highly arched eyebrows than Vogue and Arranbee chubby-type dolls; closed mouth; real eyelashes; painted eyelashes under eyes; deep flesh tone; head turning walker; sleep eyes; jointed knees; dimples on elbows; rooted hair; walker; circa 1957.

> MARKS: "Block Doll Product" (head)
> SEE: *Illustration 121. Mary Jane Cultrona Collection.*
> PRICE: $30-40

The Central Toy Manufacturing Corporation advertised 3 Block Doll Creations in 1949. These dolls were jointed only at the arms and were among the early inexpensive hard plastic dolls which became so popular. These were advertised "for jobbers and chain stores" and are today good examples of dolls who were made to be sold to other companies. This is one of the reasons so many dolls are hard to research. Unless the purchasing company put on a tag or labeled the box and it stayed with the doll over the years, it is almost impossible to identify. This is true of more expensive dolls also.

SEE: *Illustration 122. Playthings,* March 1949.
PRICE: $5-6 (as is)

121.

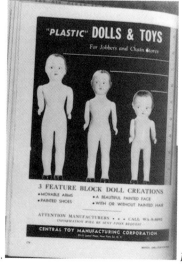

122.

Bonomi Company (Italy)

Annie: HP; sleep eyes with eyelids separate from the eyeballs; lids come down without the eyeballs rolling under; eyes move from side to side; jointed at neck, shoulders and hips; unusual walking mechanism which has instructions, "This doll can walk. Take it by its shoulders or by its waist and push it slowly forward leaning it alternately on one foot and on the other one. In case a leg should unlock from its mechanism, it is enough to make the doll sit down in order that it may be quite ready to walk again. Patented." Instructions were written in Italian, English and German; circa early 1960s.

123.

> MARKS: "Bonomi's original doll made in Italy,//Annie" (tag)
> SEE: *Illustration 123. Mary Elizabeth Poole Collection.*
> PRICE: $85-100

Chiquita Trinkets

These are inexpensive dress-me dolls sold to Chiquita Trinkets of Miami, Florida. They are unusual because they are tropical regional dolls. Dolls pictured include *Tropicana*, *Hansel* and *Gretel*, *Rumbera*, *Miss Muffet* and *Ballerina*. HP; 7½in (19cm); jointed at neck and shoulders; elegantly dressed in lovely organdies, quilted satins, chintzes; trimmed with sea shells and natural foliage; 1951.

> MARKS: "An Original//Chiquita Doll//Chiquita Trinkets, Inc. Miami Fla." (bottom of foot)
> SEE: *Illustration 124. Playthings*, March 1951.
> PRICE: $5-10

124.

Rumbero Doll: HP; 11in (28cm); jointed at neck and shoulders; mohair wig; sleep eyes with light lashes painted above eyes; molded-on shoes (see *Hard Plastic Dolls, I,* page 283A); all original multi-colored costume as shown in advertisement, upper left doll; 1951.

MARKS: None (doll); "An Original// Chiquita Doll" (tag shaped like a sombrero)
SEE: *Illustration 125.*
PRICE: $5-10

125.

Commonwealth Plastics Corp.

The registered trademarks, the trademarks and the copyrights appearing in italics within this chapter belong to Commonwealth Plastics Corp.

Dress-Me Dolls: Commonwealth advertised many different types of undressed dolls throughout the years of 1957 to 1965. Although they were still making hard plastic dolls in various sizes, they advertised in *Playthings* in November of 1959, that they had dolls from 6in (15cm) up. They had, "teen age dolls, adult dolls, baby dolls, boy dolls, colored dolls, vinyl dolls with rooted hair, plastic dolls with dynel, Saran and mohair wigs." They had absorbed the Lingerie Lou Company. (Note the logo in the corner of advertisement.)

SEE: *Illustration 126. Playthings,* March 1960.

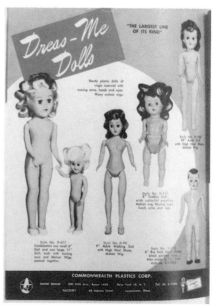

126.

Coronation Hard Plastic Dolls

The coronation of Elizabeth II of England took place in 1953 during the hard plastic doll era. A few of the English souvenir dolls were made of this material by Rosebud and Pedigree.

In the United States souvenir dolls of the coronation were very popular and some hard plastic coronation dolls were produced including the very popular Vogue *Ginny Coronation Doll*® and the lesser known *Beaux Arts Creations*® by Madame Alexander.

The Alexander Doll Company, Inc., catalog of 1953 showed a group of six dolls gracing a miniature spiral staircase. *Queen Elizabeth II* is in the center of the picture and *Princess Margaret Rose* is at the bottom of the stairs. The other four dolls were dressed in wonderful ball gowns with dazzling jewelry and headpieces. The catalog stated, "To own a truly beautiful and elegant doll is certainly the fondest wish of collectors young in heart. Madame Alexander's Beaux Arts Creations are without question the finest dolls ever made. All dolls in this group walk."

Other manufacturers in the United States made less expensive souvenirs, but all of the coronation dolls are colorful, beautiful and very collectible.

Alexander Doll Company

Beaux Arts Creations Queen Elizabeth: HP; 18in (46cm); elaborate white brocade court gown and blue Sash of the Garter; lavishly jeweled tiara, earrings, bracelet; long velvet robe has a cape and border of white fur cloth and silver braid; long white gloves; *Margaret* face; 1953.

   MARKS: "Alexander" (doll); "Madame Alexander//All Rights Reserved" New York U.S.A."
   SEE: *Illustration 127* (Color Section, page 89).
   PRICE: $900-1000 + (very few samples prices available)

Alexander Doll Company

Beaux Arts Creations Princess Margaret Rose: HP; 18in (46cm); blush pink faille taffeta court gown decorated with iridescent sequins; jeweled tiara and bracelet; earrings and necklace are of pearls; long white gloves (not shown); *Margaret* face; 1953.

   MARKS: "Alexander" (doll); "Madame Alexander//All Rights Reserved//New York U.S.A."
   SEE: *Illustration 128* (Color Section, page 90).
   PRICE: $900-1000 + (very few sample prices available)

Alexander Doll Company

Beaux Arts Creations Lady: HP; 18in (46cm); gown of petal soft pink satin; long brocaded satin coat of dove blue trimmed with rhinestone and lined in pink satin; rhinestone tiara (missing) and bracelet; rhinestone earrings; *Margaret* face; 1953. The dove blue satin coat has faded to almost the same color as the pink gown and coat lining. The thread has retained its dove blue color and can be seen upon careful examination. This type of fading often hampers identification for collectors.

    MARKS: "Alexander" (doll); "Madame Alexander//All Rights Reserved//New York U.S.A."

    SEE: *Illustration 129* (Color Section, page 91).

    PRICE: $900-1000+ (very few sample prices available)

Alexander Doll Company

Beaux Arts Creations Lady: HP; 18in (46cm); chartreuse taffeta gown trimmed with rosebuds; big sash of forest green taffeta; gold tiara set with green brilliants; *Margaret* face; 1953. The forest green taffeta has changed to a lovely brown but the green thread can be seen if inspected closely.

    MARKS: "Alexander" (doll); "Madame Alexander//All Rights Reserved//New York U.S.A."

    SEE: *Illustration 130* (Color Section, page 92).

    PRICE: $900-1000+ (very few sample prices available)

Alexander Doll Company

Beaux Arts Creations Lady: HP; 18in (46cm); white satin ball gown; rich red taffeta evening cape; tiny green, faded-to-brown, muff covered with red roses; hair simply arranged with single band of pearls; *Maggie* face; 1953.

    MARKS: "Alexander" (doll); "Madame Alexander//All Rights Reserves//New York U.S.A."

    SEE: *Illustration 131* (Color Section, page 93).

    PRICE: $900-1000+ (very few sample prices available)

Alexander Doll Company

DOLL NOT PHOTOGRAPHED

Beaux Arts Creations Lady: HP; 18in (46cm); youthful gown of aqua taffeta draped with flowing stole of nylon net embroidered with flowers and jewels; jeweled tiara and bracelet; pearl necklace; 1953. (Face unknown.)

Rosebud

Peeress Coronation Doll by L. Reese & Co.: HP; 15in (38cm); non-walker; beautiful brownish-red mohair wig; sleep eyes with real extra long eyelashes; arched eyebrows; eyelashes painted under eyes; molded open mouth and tongue with two tiny painted teeth; very red cheeks like HP English dolls; individual fingers; rather buxom breasts for a child doll; cryer in back with dots in the form of a six-pointed star; well-molded knees; all original heavy cream-colored satin formal dress with slip with crinoline; royal purple robe and royal hat with simulated ermine trim; Cinderella button shoes; 1953.

    MARKS: "Rosebud//Made in England//Pat. No. 667906" (back); "Rosebud" (head)

    SEE: *Illustration 132* (Color Section, page 94).

    PRICE: Not enough samples; very rare doll; seldom seen even in English doll books.

Peeress Coronation Doll™ is a registered trademark of L. Reese & Co.

Awin Trading Co. (England)

Coronation Walking Guardsman: HP; 24in (61cm); scarlet tunic; black trousers; belt; bearskin.

Awin was a marketing company which also advertised nylon shirts and boys melton knickers in the same issue of the newspaper.

    SEE: *Illustration 133. Daily Mirror,* May 30, 1953 (England).

Coronation Walking Guardsman™ is a registered trademark of the Awin Trading Co.

133.

Pedigree Company Soft Toys, Ltd. (Peter Darling Ltd.)

Coronation Doll: HP; 27in (69cm); hair may be combed; sleep eyes; exquisite flowing robe with sash and golden crown; 1952.

Advertised, "She walks, sits, laughs, recites, sings, and says her prayers in a real human voice." She laughs and says, "He, he, he. I love my mummy. My mummy taught me a rhyme." Says, "Little Bo Peep." Sings, "Oh dear what can the matter be!" Says a prayer.

    Pedigree is known to have sold *Playmate Dolls*. They also used the name Darling for some of their dolls. The advertisement says, "More than a doll — She's a 'Darling' Playmate."

    SEE: *Illustration 134. Daily Mirror,* May 30, 1953 (England).

    PRICE: Not enough sample prices.

Coronation Doll™ is a registered trademark of the Peter Darling Ltd.

134.

Vogue Dolls, Inc.

135.

Coronation Doll: HP; 8in (20cm); advertisement in *Playthings;* "Queen Elizabeth's Coronation//inspires a//Masterpiece in Miniature; *Ginny,* the Vogue Doll dressed as the Queen of Doll Land..truly Ruler of all the Young in Heart is gowned in a sumptuous white brocaded satin, trimmed with gold and lace. She is wearing the 'Order of the Garter' with a handmade medallion. Her robe is a majestic sweep of purple velvet trimmed with white fur. Climaxed by a pearl-and-golden Crown with scepter is the ultimate in beauty and artistry. A Limited Quantity."
SEE: *Illustration 135. Playthings,* March 1953.
PRICE: $1000 up

Ginny is a registered trademark of Vogue Dolls, Inc.

Duchess Doll Corp.

Coronation Doll: HP; 7½in (19cm) and 12½in (32cm); fully jointed; sleep eyes; white-on-white satin dress with lace and gold trim; gold crown; red velveteen cape; advertisement said, "Exquisite likeness of Queen of England." (See *Hard Plastic Dolls, I,* page 86 for picture of the doll.)
MARKS: "Duchess Doll Corp.//Design Copyright//1948" (back of doll)
SEE: *Illustration 136. Playthings,* March 1953.
PRICE: $35-40

Coronation Doll is a registered trademark of Duchess Doll Corp.

A and H Doll Mfg. Corp.

Donna Dolls Queen Elizabeth: HP; 12in (31cm); 18 other characters dressed in authentic costume; 1952.
Some doll companies were quick to capitalize on the prospect of the coronation of Princess Elizabeth of England. Long before the actual event, this doll was advertised in *Playthings,* July 1952.
SEE: *Illustration 137. Playthings,* March 1952.
PRICE: $45-50

Queen Elizabeth Doll is a registered trademark of the A and H Doll Mfg. Corp.

136.

137.

Doll Bodies (Dolls Of Far-A-Way-Lands, Inc.)

Coronation Doll: HP; 7½in (19cm); also 12in (31cm); jeweled tiara, necklace, bracelet, royal orders; sparkling formal dress of non-tarnishable silver metallic material covered with chantilly lace; royal blue sash; 1953.

  SEE: *Illustration 138. Playthings*, March 1953.

  PRICE: $35-40

Coronation Doll® is a registered trademark of Doll Bodies, Inc.

Reliable Toy Co. Ltd/Ltee.

Coronation Dolls:

A Little Queen for Coronation Festivities: HP; 8in (20cm); moving eyes; jointed at neck and shoulders only; mohair wig with tiara; colorful coronation robe; beautiful white satin dress with gold trim; painted shoes; ribbon across chest.

A Real Queen in her royal Raiment: HP; 11in (28cm); moving eyes; jointed at neck and shoulders only; dressed in beautiful white satin dress with ribbon and gold trimming; mohair wig with tiara; colorful coronation cape; satin panties; shoes and socks.

Coronation Walking Doll: HP; 12in (31cm); lead her by the hand and she could walk along with you; Saran hair that can be combed, brushed, curled and waved; beautifully dressed in her royal cape and tiara; panties; soft vinyl shoes and socks.

Queen of the Coronation Dolls: HP; 16in (41cm); moving eyes; Saran hair that can be combed, brushed, curled and waved; she could be lead along by the hand and walk; beautifully dressed in white satin with gold trim; royal robe with cape, panties, tiara, socks and soft vinyl shoes.

The above information is from page 15 of the 1953 Reliable catalog.

  SEE: *Illustration 139.*

Coronation Doll® is a registered trademark of the Reliable Toy Co. Ltd./Ltee.

138.

139.

Cosmopolitan Doll and Toy Corporation Types of Gingers

Today the Cosmopolitan *Ginger* dolls are widely collected. The collectors in their middle and late thirties remember these wonderful dolls who were very affordable. Like many of the small walking dolls, they had an extensive wardrobe and a wide variety of accessories. The sizes of the dolls ranged from 7½in (19cm) to 8½in (22cm). During the days of their manufacture, there were changes in their body styles to keep up with the latest innovations in doll technology.

An extensive study of *Ginger* characteristics and *Ginger* body styles can be found in the Identification Guide, page 238-239. Other information can be found in *Hard Plastic Dolls, I*, page 81.

Variations in the *Ginger*-type all-HP dolls include:

1. Early painted eyelash, straight leg non-walkers and walkers (see page 238).
2. Large sleep eye, straight leg walkers (see page 238).
3. Medium sleep eye, straight leg walkers (see page 238).
4. Small sleep eye, straight leg walkers (see page 238).
5. Bent knee walkers (see page 238, 239).
6. Bent knee and bent elbow walkers (see page 238).
7. Dolls with black flesh tone.

Ginger dolls with HP bodies and vinyl heads include:

1. Rooted hair, straight leg walkers (see page 238).
2. Rooted hair, straight leg walkers with Cha Cha heels (see page 238).

For pictures of the various body types see, Identification Guide page 238-239.

Most of the *Ginger* dolls had blue eyes but some dolls had green, brown and lavender eyes. These last dolls also had lavender hair.

The following marketing companies used one of the basic *Gingers:*

1. Terri Lee dressed them in Scout and Brownie Uniforms. (See *Hard Plastic Dolls, I*, page 82, *Illustration 186*).
2. Active *Mindy*
3. Midwestern *Mary Jean* (See page 150.)
4. Marcelle Boissier *Jeanette*
5. Admiration Girl (See page 17.) These are late dolls made in Hong Kong and have unusual arms and lightweight hard plastic.
6. Companies who made regional souvenirs.
7. Advertising dolls of various kinds including a perfume and cosmetic company who sold a Spanish doll.

Often the dolls sold to other companies had the large eyes and an inferior hard plastic. These were sold under different names.

Ginger not only had a large wardrobe, her accessories, furniture and books included:

1. Trunks and luggage
2. Hats
3. Stands and hangers
4. Wigs
5. Ice skates, roller skates and extra shoes
6. House, patio and lawn furniture
7. Wardrobes for clothing
8. Gift sets (See *Hard Plastic Dolls, I*, page 82, *Illustrations 183* and *184*.)
9. Cardboard doll house
10. *Little Golden Book* about *Ginger*
11. Packaged *Ginger* clothes that came to members of the *Ginger* "Doll of the Month Club"

Cosmopolitan also had permission to use costumes related to Disney characters and Disneyland. (See *Illustrations 146-148*.)

Other types of *Ginger* dolls made by Cosmopolitan include:

1. *Ginger Baby*.
2. *Miss Ginger* (See *Glamour Dolls of the 1950s & 1960s*, pages 81-84.)
3. *Little Miss Ginger* (See *Glamour Dolls of the 1950s & 1960s*, page 84.)

Painted Eye Ginger Nurse: HP; 8in (20cm); early doll with painted eyelashes above eyes; straight leg walker; medium eyes (see Identification Guide, *Illustration 421*); dressed as nurse in marked *Ginger* costume; circa 1954. Later painted eye *Gingers* came as jointed knee walkers.

> **MARKS:** None (doll); "Fashions for 'Ginger'//Cosmopolitan Doll & Toy Corp.// Jackson Heights, N.Y." (tag sewn into uniform)
> **SEE:** *Illustration 140. Pat Parton Collection.*
> **PRICE:** $45-50

Ginger: HP; 8in (20cm); walker; sleep eyes; advertisement said, "The only eight inch walking doll with a fully lined and stitched Saran wig." The extra outfits were boxed with shoes and socks; 1955 wardrobe.

> **SEE:** *Illustration 141. Playthings*, August 1955.

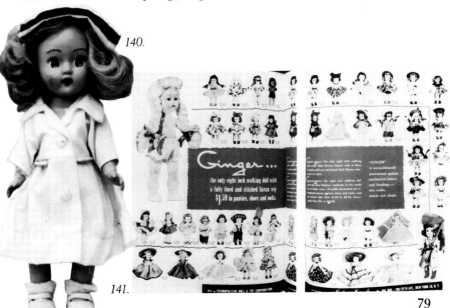

140.

141.

Ginger in Mexican Outfit: as shown in advertisement in *Playthings*, March 1955; cotton jumpsuit; white cotton blouse; matching straw hat with pompon trim; cowboy boots.

> **MARKS:** None (doll)
> **SEE:** *Illustration 142. Marge Meisinger Collection.*
> **PRICE:** $55-75+

Mousketeers: HP; advertised as "The only doll in the Mickey Mouse Club;" from left to right: *Ginger* in her Mickey Mouse Sweater Costume; *Ginger* in her Mousekarade Costume; *Ginger* in her official *Talent Roundup Costume;* vinyl *Mickey Mouse* mask included with each outfit; 1955.

> **SEE:** *Illustration 143.* *Playthings,* September 1955.
> **PRICE:** $75-100+ (very few sample prices available)

Ginger in Mouseketeer Mousekarade Costume: red jersey suit with Mickey Mouse patch; black belt, boots and cap with Mickey Mouse ears; 1955.

> **MARKS:** None (doll)
> **SEE:** *Illustration 144* (Color Section, page 167). *Marge Meisinger Collection.*
> **PRICE:** $75-100+ (very few sample prices available)

142.

143.

Ginger in Mouseketeer Official Talent Roundup Costume: blue felt skirt with white felt trim; blue top; white cowboy hat; cowboy boots; 1955.
   MARKS: None (doll)
   SEE: *Illustration 145. Marge Meisinger Collection.*
   PRICE: $75-100+ (very few sample prices available)

145.

Ginger visits Adventureland in Disneyland:
1. Cha-Cha-Cha Seniorita
2. Safari Girl
3. Oriental Princess
   SEE: *Illustration 146.* Ginger brochure, 1956.

Trousseau Series:
1. Bride
2. Bridesmaid
3. Bridesmaid
   SEE: *Illustration 146.* Ginger brochure, 1956.

146.

Ginger Visits Frontierland in Disneyland:
1. *Indian Princess*
2. *Frontier Girl*
3. *Pioneer Girl*

Ginger Visits Fantasyland in Disneyland:
1. *Blue Fairy*
2. *Cinderella*
3. *Dream Princess*
   SEE: *Illustration 147.* Ginger brochure, 1956.

147.

148.

Ginger Visits Tomorrowland in Disneyland:
1. *Rocket Pilot*
2. *Sun Princess*
3. *Space Girl*

Ginger Visits the Mickey Mouse Club:
1. *Mousekarade Costume*
2. *Official Treatment Roundup Costume*
3. *Official Mickey Mouse Club Costume*
   SEE: *Illustration 148.* Ginger brochure, 1956.

Ginger Gay Nineties Series:
1. Long dress with fur stole; doll has upswept hair.
2. Long dress with three ruffles on the skirt; embroidery trim on bottom of each ruffle; wide dark hat; dark hair.
3. Long dress with three net ruffles on skirt; light wide hat with feather trim; blonde hair.
   SEE: *Illustration 149.* Ginger brochure, 1956.

Ginger Activity Series: left to right

Upper row
1. Ice skating costume
2. Roller skating costume
3. Ballerina tutu

Lower Row
1. Beach clothes
2. Drum majorette uniform
3. Fireman uniform

   SEE: *Illustration 149.* Ginger brochure, 1956.

149.

Ginger Ballerina: HP; 7½in (19cm); *Ginger* characteristics (see Identification Guide, page 238); slightly different arm hook (see Identification Guide, page 238) and jointed elbows; yellow ballerina outfit; circa 1956-1957. The same doll was pictured in *Hard Plastic Dolls, I,* Unknown Section, page 234.

  MARKS: None (doll); "Fashions for Ginger Cosmopolitan Doll and Toy Company" (tag on dress)
  SEE: *Illustration 150.*
  PRICE: $35-40

150.

83

Cha Cha Heel Ginger: HP; vinyl head; 8in (20cm); *Ginger* characteristics (see Identification Guide, page 238) except for legs; head turning walker but legs have been restyled with medium heels; head has unusually nice vinyl with lovely color; sleep eyes operate smoothly; 1957.

This doll is rare because Cosmopolitan also introduced the high-heeled *Little Miss Ginger* on the right in the illustration. She was much more popular with the children.

    MARKS: "Ginger" (bottom of feet and shoes)

    SEE: *Illustration 151.*

        Illustration 152. Playthings, March 1957.

    PRICE: $35-50+ (very few sample prices available)

151.

152.

Ginger and Miss Ginger: advertisement in *Playthings*, March 1957; *Ginger* is HP; *Miss Ginger* is approximately 10in (25cm); vinyl; matching outfits for *Ginger* and her Slim Teen Age Sister; *Miss Ginger's* dresses came with silk stockings, high-heeled shoes and jewelry.

> **SEE:** *Illustration 153. Playthings,* March 1957.
> **PRICE:** $40-55 (*Ginger*)
> $40-55 (*Miss Ginger*)

Ginger Doll-Mate: promotion used in 1957 to sell more *Ginger* dolls and clothes. *Ginger* Doll-ers were given with the purchases. The customer could send five *Ginger* Doll-ers plus one real dollar ($1) plus a child's picture and she would receive a *Ginger DOLL-MATE* which could be dressed in any of *Ginger's* beautiful outfits. This was a masonite cut out doll in real lifelike color with the child's picture pasted on it.

> **SEE:** *Illustration 154. Playthings,* March 1957.

153.

154.

D & D Mfg. Co.

The registered trademarks, the trademarks and the copyrights appearing in italics within this chapter belong to D & D Mfg. Co.

Nun: HP; 12in (31cm); non-walking; Plastic Molded Arts characteristics (see *Hard Plastic Dolls, I* page 207); molded-on shoes painted white (see Identification Guide, *Hard Plastic Dolls, I,* page 283, *Illustration 612*); black taffeta nun's habit with rosary beads and cross at the waist. Printing on box says, "Attend Church regularly...//for the Family that Prays Together...Stays Together!" 1954.

  MARKS: None (doll); "No. 1400 Nun Doll//1954 D & D MFG. Co." (box)
  SEE: *Illustration 155.*
  PRICE: $25-30

155.

A. H. Delfausse Company

The registered trademarks, the trademarks and the copyrights appearing in italics within this chapter belong to A. H. Delfausse Company.

156.

Mademoiselle: HP; walking doll; no height given in advertisement; toddler doll; has wardrobe; 1953.
  SEE: *Illustration 156. Playthings,* March 1953.
  PRICE: $25-30

De Soto
Manufacturing Company

The registered trademarks, the trademarks and the copyrights appearing in italics within this chapter belong to De Soto Manufacturing Company.

157.

Randy Goes to the Circus: HP head; no other information available.

> SEE: *Illustration 157. Playthings,* March 1950.
> PRICE: $25-40

Diamont (Germany)

The registered trademarks, the trademarks and the copyrights appearing in italics within this chapter belong to Diamont.

Boy in Lederhosen: HP; 14in (36cm); molded hair under human hair wig; sleep eyes with real eyelashes; unusual closed mouth with deep indentation under chin; dimples on knees and elbows; jointed at neck, shoulders and hips; chubby body; black Bavarian hat; blue pants and red print shirt; cobbled leather shoes; circa mid 1950s. This doll has a wonderful character face which lends itself to the typical type of German hard plastic used in that country.

> MARKS: "Diamont" in oval (head)
> SEE: *Illustration 158. Shirley Niziolek Collection.*
> PRICE: $85-110

158.

159.

G. A. Doherty Co.

The registered trademarks, the trademarks and the copyrights appearing in italics within this chapter belong to G. A. Doherty Co.

***Susan's* Crochet Doll Kit:** HP; 7in (18cm); Duchess doll is used in the kit made by G. A. Doherty Co.; Duchess characteristics (see page 99); kit has materials to make a crocheted bride dress with satin, flowers, ribbon and D.M.C. crochet thread which were included in the kit; circa 1948-1950.

    MARKS: "Duchess Doll Corp.//Design Copyright//1948" (back)
    SEE: *Illustration 159.*
    PRICE: $12-15

Doll Bodies, Inc.
(Originally Lingerie Lou)

The registered trademarks, the trademarks and the copyrights appearing in italics within this chapter belong to Doll Bodies, Inc., unless otherwise noted.

Mary-Lu Walker: HP; 18in (46cm); walking doll; sleep eyes; painted eyelashes under eyes; ponytail or pigtail Dynel hair that is washable, brushable and combable; an assortment of 16 different dresses could be purchased for her or another 18in (46cm); 1955.

    SEE: *Illustration 160. Playthings,*
        March 1955 (top).
    PRICE: $40-45

160.

Mary-Lu: HP; 7¼in (19cm); Dynel hair that can be washed, combed and set; came with panties in a heat-sealed package; clothes could be purchased separately; walking doll with same characteristics as the Roberta doll; molded and painted shoes with bows in front (see Identification Guide, *Hard Plastic Dolls, I,* page 286K); fatter legs than most of the *Ginny®*-type dolls; 1955.

    MARKS: None
    SEE: *Illustration 160. Playthings,* March 1955 (bottom).
    PRICE: $6-12

Ginny® is a registered trademark of Vogue Dolls, Inc.

Continued on page 97.

Alexander 1953 Beaux Arts Creations, No. 2025, *Queen Elizabeth II* (see page 73).

Alexander 1953 Beaux Arts Creations, No. 2020B, *Princess Margaret Rose* (see page 73).

Alexander 1953 Beaux Arts Creations, No. 2020C, Lady (see page 74).

Alexander 1953 Beaux Arts Creations, No. 2020E, Lady (see page 74).

Alexander 1953 Beaux Arts Creations, No. 2020F, Lady (see page 74).

Rosebud (England) *Peeress Coronation* (see page 75).

Alexander pink *Bride* (see page 19).

Alexander *Elise Renoir* (see page 29).

American Character, page from company catalog, *Sweet Sue* (see page 47).

Arranbee *Nancy Lee* (see page 51). *Lois Janner Collection.*

Continued from page 88.

161.

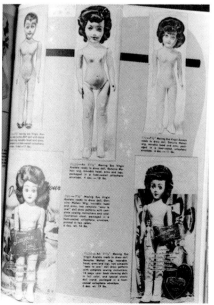

162.

Mary-Lu Walker: HP; 16in (41cm); open mouth with four teeth; sleep eyes with real lashes; lashes also painted under the eyes; excellent flesh tone; shiny hard plastic; all original; turquoise dress with white organdy collar; circa 1955.

> **MARKS:** "A Product of Doll Bodies Inc. New York 12, N.Y." (box); None (doll).
> **SEE:** *Illustration 161. Ruth M. Casey Collection.*
> **PRICE:** $50-60 (in box)

Dress-Me Dolls: HP; various sizes from 7½in (19cm) to 11½in (29cm); sleep eyes; some fully jointed; others jointed only at neck and shoulders; mohair wigs; packaged in heat-treated cellophane envelopes; 1955. These dolls were sold well into the 1960s, and they were packaged in many ways. Often they came with as many as 16 sewing patterns complete with sewing instructions. Some came with a 16-page-book of colored pictures of costumes of all nations. Stands were also available.

> **MARKS:** Usually none
> **SEE:** *Illustration 162. Playthings,* March 1955.
> **PRICE:** $5-15

97

Dress-me Doll: HP; 7½in (19cm); doll in plastic bra and pants; sewing kit with two dolls, two stands and two patterns, *Lingerie Lou's Doll Collection Book*.

    MARKS: None (doll)

    SEE: *Illustration 163. Playthings*, August 1952.

    PRICE: $12-15

Dolls of Faraway Lands: HP; authentically costumed dolls in satins, braids and taffetas; sleep eyes; jointed head and arms only; 1953. These dolls were advertised for collectors. They were packaged in gift window boxes and sold by Dolls of Far-A-Way Lands, Inc., a subsidiary of Doll Bodies, Inc.

    MARKS: "Dolls of Faraway Lands" (boxes)

    SEE: *Illustration 164. Playthings*, March 1953.

    PRICE: $5-10

163.

164.

Duchess Doll Corp.

Duchess was a very active company during the hard plastic era. They not only sold dolls under their name, but they sold dolls to other companies which were used in unusual and attractive kits to keep children busy and happy. (See G. A. Doherty Co., page 88 and Beddy-Bye and Bye-Bye Doll Company, page 67.)

Duchess Small Doll Characteristics: HP; 7in (18cm) to 8in (20cm); side-glancing or sleep eyes; painted, molded Virga-type shoes (see Identification Guide, *Hard Plastic Dolls, I,* page 284D); inexpensive clothing which was usually stapled on; 1st, 2nd, 3rd and 4th fingers molded together; arm hook (see Identification Guide, *Hard Plastic Dolls, I,* page 268V). The company was famous for their boxed "International Series" which was often given as a bonus at the local grocery store. They made other boxed dolls. They are very collectible today.

Dale Evans: HP; 8in (29cm); jointed at arms only; white cowgirl suit made of plastic; red plastic cuffs; red felt gun holster; gold buckle; white felt hat; white boots; clothes stapled onto doll; Virga-type shoes (see Identification Guide, *Hard Plastic Dolls, I,* page 285H); circa 1948.
  MARKS: "Duchess Doll Corp.// Design Copyright//1948" (back)
  SEE: *Illustration 165.*
  PRICE: $15-20

165.

166.

Miss Valentine of 1951: HP; 7-1/2in (19cm); dress is a white and red printed rayon gown trimmed with ribbon and decorated with gold braid; packaged in an acetate window box.

> MARKS: "Duchess Doll Corp.//
> Design Copyright//1948"
> (back)
> SEE: *Illustration 166. Playthings*, December 1951.
> PRICE: $15-20

Peter Pan and Tinker Bell: HP; 7in (18cm); Walt Disney characters 1st, 2nd, 3rd and 4th fingers molded together. This was made and advertised to take advantage of the movie *Peter Pan* which was released that year; 1953.

> MARKS: "Duchess Doll Corp//
> Design Copyright//1948"
> (back)
> SEE: *Illustration 167. Playthings*, May 1953.
> PRICE: $15-20 each

167.

Alice in Wonderland: HP; 12-1/2in (32cm) and 7-1/2in (19cm); sleep eyes; jointed at neck, shoulders and hips; issued in a "Dolls of all Nations" box; 1951. Walt Disney's production of *Alice in Wonderland* was released in August 1951. Other Disney characters by Duchess include *Cinderella* in 12-1/2in (32cm) and 7-1/2in (19cm) sizes and *Snow White* in the 7-1/2in (19cm) size only.

    MARKS: None (doll)
    SEE: *Illustration 168. Playthings*, August 1951.
    PRICE: $20-30

Italian Dream Girl: HP; 13in (33cm); blue sleep eyes with lashes; brunette wig; jointed at neck, legs and arms; arm hook (see Identification Guide, *Hard Plastic Dolls, I*, page 267S); painted, molded shoes (see Identification Guide, *Hard Plastic Dolls, I*, page 285I); 1st, 2nd and 3rd fingers molded together; red satin skirt; white organdy apron, blouse, scarf; carrying a small basket with a chick inside; excellent quality hard plastic; circa 1952. The doll in *Hard Plastic Dolls, I* on page 103, *Illustration 240, Violetta*, is also a Duchess doll.

    MARKS: None (doll); "A Duchess Dream Girl Doll - Italian" (box)
    SEE: *Illustration 169.*
    PRICE: $25

168.

169.

170.

Duchess advertised in 1953 that they had a new picture frame box. "This new Duchess DeLuxe Series brings to you the same incomparable Duchess Doll packaged in a real Picture Frame Box. The Picture Frame enables you to hang the Duchess Doll on the wall and also to stand it on a display counter by means of a built-in easel..."

SEE: *Illustration 170. Playthings,* March 1953.

PRICE: $15-20

Eegee
(Goldberger Doll Mfg.
Co., Inc.)

The registered trademarks, the trademarks and the copyrights appearing in italics within this chapter belong to Goldberger Doll Mfg. Co., Inc.

Gigi Perreau: HP body and vinyl head; 20in (51cm); Dynel rooted washable hair; fully-jointed body; open mouth with teeth; Ninon dress; 1952. Gigi Perreau was a Universal-International starlet. Eegee promised dealers a promotional package which included personal appearances with Gigi Perreau, theater tie-ins from coast-to-coast, free photo prints with the doll and free newspaper mats.

SEE: *Illustration 171. Playthings,* September 1952.

PRICE: $65-100

171.

Susan Stroller: HP; 23in (58cm); head turning walker; Saran hair with curlers; sleep eyes; crying mama voice; sleep eyes; 1953.

> MARKS: "Eegee" (head); "EE-GEE" (body); or none
>
> SEE: *Illustration 172. Playthings*, February 1953.
>
> PRICE: $50-55

172.

Effanbee Doll Corp.

The registered trademarks, the trademarks and the copyrights appearing in italics within this chapter belong to Effanbee Doll Corp.

Howdy Doody: Composition heads and hands; stuffed cloth body; 23in (58cm); 19in (48cm); sleep eyes; molded hair; dressed in cowboy costume with scarf with "Howdy Doody" on it; 1947-1949.

> MARKS: "Effanbee" (head)
>
> SEE: *Illustration 173. Playthings*, March 1949.
>
> PRICE: $150-200 19in (48cm)
> $200-250 23in (58cm)

173.

174.

Electronic Doll: 28in (71cm); jointed at neck, shoulders and hips; sings, laughs, talks and says her prayers in a human voice when you press the button; sings, "London Bridge's Falling Down" and "Mary Had a Little Lamb;" says, "Now I Lay Me Down to Sleep;" pink dress with black and white checked trim; 1950.

    SEE: *Illustration 174.* Advertisement for Effanbee Dolls...a Division of Noma Electric Corp.

    PRICE: $125-175 + (very few sample prices available)

By the early 1950s doll wardrobes became very important. Dress designers in France and the United States also designed beautiful doll clothes for many different types of dolls. Madame Schiaparelli designed doll clothes for her daughter, Gogo, and Effanbee persuaded her to design a collection of clothes for their *Honey* doll. These dolls were limited to America's finest stores on a franchise basis. Only one franchise was allowed in a city. At that time Effanbee was a division of Noma Electric Corp.

    SEE: *Illustration 175. Playthings,* July 1951.

175.

Schiaparelli Doll: HP; 18in (46cm); close-fitting blonde wig; sleep eyes; jointed at neck, shoulders and hips; walker; beautiful flesh color; pink embossed organdy with darker pink roses; black shoes; white socks; *Honey Walker* mold; 1951. (Costume may not be original.)

MARKS: "Effanbee" (back)

SEE: *Illustration 176. Ester Borgis Collection.*

PRICE: $250-325 + depending on costume (rare doll — very few sample prices)

Tintair Honey: HP; 16in (41cm); sleep eyes; red coloring on knees and back of hand; jointed at neck, arms and legs; blonde hair (almost white); turquoise glazed waffle dress with white organdy sleeves and yoke trimmed in eyelet organdy; pink shoes; pink bows in hair; all original; boxed set includes "Glossy Chestnut" and "Carrot Top" non-poisonous hair color; applicator; curlers; 1951.

MARKS: "Effanbee" (neck); "I am the Tintair Doll (4 curlers) An Effanbee Durable Doll" (tag front); "A New Effanbee Playmate//May You and your Tintair Dolly have many happy times together// Trademark Reg//Made in U.S." (tag back)

SEE: *Illustration 177* (doll in box, Color Section, page 163).

Illustration 178 (advertisement). *Playthings*, August 1951.

PRICE: $225-300 + (as pictured in box)

176.

Every little girl's

EFFANBEE DOLL CO.

178.

105

Honey Bride: HP; 14in (36cm); head turning walker; sleep eyes with real eyelashes; jointed at neck, shoulders and hips; red headed wig; all original satin bride dress with full skirt ending in a graceful train; looped fringe trim around a flattering shawl; bib collar; taffeta petticoat over crinoline; taffeta panties; white satin slippers; 1952.

> **MARKS:** "Effanbee" (head); "Effanbee" (back)
> **SEE:** *Illustration 179* (Color Section, page 166).
> **PRICE:** $170-200 14in (36cm)
> $180-225 16in (41cm) depending on costume
> $195-240 18in (46cm) depending on costume
> $275-325 24in (61cm) depending on costume

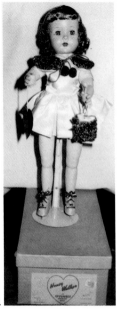

Honey Walker Ice Skater: HP; 18in (46cm); sleep eyes; jointed at neck, shoulders and hips; beautiful skin color; all original white skating costume; fur capelet and muff; 1951-1953.

> **MARKS:** Effanbee (back); "Honey Walker" (box and tag)
> **SEE:** *Illustration 180. Gigi Williams Collection.*
> **PRICE:** $195-240

180.

Elite Creations

Vicki: HP; 8in (20cm); facial characteristics and tubular arm hooks of the *Pam*₌ doll (see *Hard Plastic Dolls, I*, Identification Guide, page 2660); does not have the molded slippers of *Pam*₌; the toes have excellent detail with dimples above toes; jointed at neck, shoulders, hips and knees; red, black and yellow plaid shirt; blue jeans; red shoes; brown pigtails; (see body construction, Identification Guide, page 239); mid 1950s.

> **MARKS:** None (doll); "Elite Creations" (brochure)
> **SEE:** *Illustration 181. Ester Borgis Collection.*
> **PRICE:** $30-40

Pam® is a registered trademark of Fortune Toys, Inc.   *181.*

Brochure with Doll: from left to right:
1. Roller skating outfit with dark print skirt and white top; roller skates.
2. Tennis outfit; shorts and top; tennis racket.
3. Jeans and shirt shown on doll in picture.
4. Nurse's uniform.
Poem on Right Side of Doll
"To make your Vicki doll look smart
Select her wardrobe from this chart
Run over to your local store
Don't leave before you see some more."
   SEE: *Illustration 181. Ester Borgis Collection.*

***Vicki* Brochure:**
   SEE: *Illustration 182. Ester Borgis Collection.*
   PRICE: $5-10 (individual outfit in box)

182.

183.

***Vicki* Brochure:**
   SEE: *Illustration 183. Ester Borgis Collection.*
   PRICE: $5-10 (individual outfit in box)

107

| No. 402 BRIDESMAID | No. 401 BRIDE | No. 407 PINAFORE | No. 403 HAT AND COAT | No. 412 BALLERINA | No. 405 PARTY DRESS |

184.

Vicki **Brochure:** right hand picture only:
1. Bride in white rayon dress with net veil.
2. Bridesmaid in pink rayon dress with flower in hair.
   SEE: *Illustration 184. Ester Borgis Collection.*
   PRICE: $5-10 (individual outfit in box)

Eugenia Doll Company, Inc.

The registered trademarks, the trademarks and the copyrights appearing in italics within this chapter belong to Eugenia Doll Company, Inc., unless otherwise noted.

Pam, the Perm-O-Wave Doll: HP; 14in (36cm); human hair wig which could be set in any style with the popular Perm-O-Wave curlers; the curlers could also be used to give home permanents to the mother and daughter; included also a plastic makeup cape, comb, barrette and carrying case; 1949. This was one of the earliest home permanent dolls.

    SEE: *Illustration 185. Playthings,* April 1949.

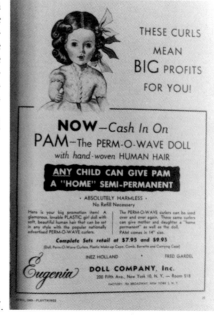

185.

Doll in Child's Dress: HP; 18in (46cm); (for general characteristics, see *Illustration 187*); organdy dress with lace trim; 1947-1949.

> **MARKS:** None (doll); "A Personality// Play-Mate" (box)
> **SEE:** *Illustration 186. Betty Shriver* Collection.
> **PRICE:** $150-175

Doll in Pink Dress in Box: HP; 18in (46cm); beautiful wig; feathered eyebrows; sleep eyes with five lines painted at each side of eye; nail polish; 2nd and 3rd fingers molded together and slightly curved; body similar to *Nancy Ann Style Show* doll; red on knees and hands; wide Y on seat; pink organdy dress with circular fluted hat; 1947-1949.

> **MARKS:** None (doll); "A Personality// Play-Mate" (box)
> **SEE:** *Illustration 187. Sherry Dempsey* Collection.
> **PRICE:** $150-175

Nancy Ann Style Show® is a registered trademark of Nancy Ann Storybook Dolls, Inc.

187.

186.

109

Juliette Bridal Doll: HP; 21in (53cm); human hair wig; jointed at neck, shoulders and hips; closed mouth; 1947.

SEE: *Illustration 188. Playthings,* March 1947.

PRICE: $175-200

188.

J.K. Farnell & Co. Ltd. (England)

The registered trademarks, the trademarks and the copyrights appearing in italics within this chapter belong to J.K. Farnell & Co. Ltd.

Plastic Dolls: HP; various sizes; dolls were made through the 1960s and possibly into the 1970s. Small girl and boy dolls were sold to sales companies who costumed a line of souvenir dolls such as soldiers, Scottish dolls, Welsh dolls, and so forth.
The Farnell company made a line of Alpha Toys. In the 1930s they made cloth dolls which were similar to Chad Valley or Norah Wellings dolls. They used the trademark names of *Joy Day* and *Alpha Cherub Dolls.*

MARKS: "Alpha" (back) on some of the hard plastic dolls; none on other dolls

Fleischaker Novelty Company

The registered trademarks, the trademarks and the copyrights appearing in italics within this chapter belong to Fleischaker Novelty Company.

Little Girl of Today: HP body; head, arms and legs made of soft plastic which feels like real flesh; molded hair doll is 22in (56cm); rooted hair doll is 22in (56cm) and 28in (71cm); rooted human hair; glassine eyes; talks and walks when guided; dressed in organdy dress with matching one available for little girls; pictures of hair styles for the doll and hairdressing tips were available in an accompanying brochure; 1951.

This was a very early rooted hair doll.

SEE: *Illustration 189. Playthings,* June 1951.
Illustration 190. Playthings, June 1951.

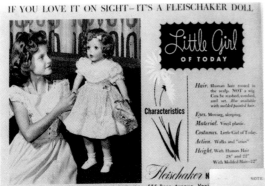

189.

190.

Fortune Toys Incorporated

The registered trademarks, the trademarks and the copyrights appearing in italics within this chapter belong to Fortune Toys Incorporated, unless otherwise noted.

One of the most popular dolls sold by Fortune Toys Incorporated was a small walking doll which competed with *Ginny®*. Although the dolls had the same characteristics, they were sold as *Pam, Ninette* and *Starlet, the Lustercreme Doll*. There may have been others also sold under the Fortune name. Fortune was connected with Beehler Arts and Ontario Plastics.

Virga was also another company connected with Beehler Arts and Ontario Plastics. They sold dolls with the same characteristics called *Lucy®, Schiaparelli GoGo®, Lolly Pop®, Play-Mates®, Play-Pals®* and others.

Kim, another company, used the same address as Beehler Arts on their dolls' boxes. These dolls were called *Kim*.

Other dolls with the same characteristics were sold by Doll Bodies, Grant Plastics, Niresk Industries, Plastic Molded Arts, Roberta Dolls and Norma Dolls.

There is a difference in the quality of both the hard plastic and the costuming of these dolls. For more information and pictures of these dolls, see the Identification Guide, page 242. It is difficult to know which company sold a doll originally unless it has a tag or is in a marked box.

The following characteristics are common to all these dolls:
1. 7½in (19cm) to 8in (20cm) in height. However, a few are as tall as 9in (23cm). (See *Illustration 366* in the Virga section.)
2. Tube-like arm hook (see Identification Guide, *Hard Plastic Dolls, I*, page 266O).
3. Molded-on T-strap shoes (seen Identification Guide of this book, page 252I).
4. Sleep eyes.
5. Crease in center of kneecap.
6. Seamline cut through the back part of ear.
7. Many with molded hair under wig.
8. Deep indentation under lower lip (no dimple).
9. 2nd and 3rd fingers molded together.

The Fortune company made other types of dolls which are shown in *Hard Plastic Dolls, I*, pages 241-244.

Ninette: HP; 8in (20cm) head turning small walking doll; 24 outfits available; 1955. This doll competed with *Ginny®*.
Clothes shown in advertisement include:

1. *Morning dress*
2. *Spring dress*
3. *Bridal dress*
4. *Cowgirl outfit*
5. *School dress*
6. *Lounging ensemble*
7. *Garden outfit*
8. *Ski outfit*
9. *Clown outfit*
10. *Majorette outfit*
11. *Halloween outfit*
12. *Little Miss Muffet*
13. *Formal dance gown*
14. *Red ensemble*
15. *Party dress*

191.

MARKS: None (body)
SEE: *Illustration 191. Playthings*, April 1955.
PRICE: $25-30

Ginny® is a registered trademark of Vogue Dolls, Inc. *Lucy®, Schiaparelli GoGo®, Lolly Pop®, Play-Mates®* and *Play-Pals®* are registered trademarks of Virga. *Kim®* is a registered trademark of the Kim company.

See *Illustration 192* on page 139.

Pam: The box for the *Pam* doll advertised "Michele Cartier//presents//Pam//and// her fabulous wardrobe." For pictures of *Pam* dolls, see pages 101 and 102, *Hard Plastic Dolls, I.* The individual clothing boxes which could be purchased separately were inscribed with the same words.

MARKS: None (doll)
SEE: *Illustration 193. Marge Meisinger Collection.*
PRICE: $30-35 (doll)

193.

G.H. & E. Freydberg, Inc.

The registered trademarks, the trademarks and the copyrights appearing in italics within this chapter belong to G.H. & E. Freydberg, Inc, unless otherwise noted.

Mary Jane: HP; 17in (43cm); made in imitation of *Terri Lee®*; closed mouth that is wider than *Terri Lee®*; flirty eyes; eyebrows more arched than *Terri Lee®*; painted eyelashes on side of eye; redder flesh color and more glossy than *Terri Lee®*; head turns as it walks; 2nd and 3rd fingers molded together; more slender body than *Terri Lee®*; sleep eyes; doll dressed in bright pink dress with lace trim; green pajamas; green, brown and white checked robe; checked shirt and jeans; 1953.

MARKS: None (doll); "Mary Jane" (tag sewn into clothes)
SEE: *Illustration 194.*
PRICE: $150-175

194.

Terri Lee® is a registered trademark of the Terri Lee Dolls, Inc.

Mary Jane: two pages of advertising the doll and her clothing; 1953.
SEE: *Illustration 195. Playthings,* June 1953.

195.

Furga (Italy)

The registered trademarks, the trademarks and the copyrights appearing in italics within this chapter belong to Furga.

Girl in Blue Dress: Italian HP; 14in (36cm); dark skin tone; blonde wig; sleep eyes with long Italian (very long) lashes; feathered eyebrows; two-toned pink lips; jointed at neck, shoulders and hips; all original; blue rayon long dress and matching hat with pink trim; cotton teddy; circa mid 1950s.

> **MARKS:** "Furga" (head); "Made in Itali" (stamped on chest); "Made in Italy" (tag sewn into clothes)
> **SEE:** *Illustration 196. Jill Kaar Collection.*
> **PRICE:** $125-150

196.

Grant Plastics, Inc.

A few of the doll companies of the 1950s specialized in the "Dress-Me" type dolls. A handful actually did the manufacturing. Others acted as national wholesalers and sold to companies who dressed the dolls. They also sold to regional wholesalers who in turn sold in smaller lots to doll shops, doll hospitals and to local people who wanted to dress a few to sell for profit or sell at a bazaar. Even today similar dolls made of vinyl can be found in the local craft shops.

Grant Plastics, Inc., advertised in *Playthings* magazine and their line was extensive.

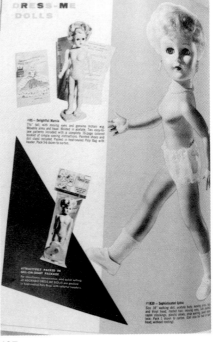

197.

Marcia: HP; 7½in (19cm); sleep eyes; jointed at neck and shoulders; two easy-to-sew patterns included with a complete 16-page colored booklet of simple sewing instructions; painted shoes; doll stand included; packed in heat-sealed poly bag; one of the *Adorable Dress-Me Dolls*; circa 1959-1963.
MARKS: None (doll)
SEE: *Illustration 197* (doll on left).
   Playthings, March 1961.
PRICE: $5-10

Sylvia: HP with vinyl head; 18in (47cm); walking doll; rooted hair; jointed at neck, shoulders and hips; sleep eyes; silk panties; rayon socks; drop earrings; pearl necklace; could also be ordered with hard plastic head and mohair wig; 1961.
One of the *Adorable Dress-Me Dolls*.
MARKS: None (doll)
SEE: *Illustration 197* (doll on right).
   Playthings, March 1961
PRICE: $5-10

Suzie: HP; 8in (20cm); toddler doll; mohair wig; jointed at neck, shoulders and arms; white shoes painted on over toes; (see *Illustration 428E*); sleep eyes; came with panties; one of the *Adorable Dress-Me Dolls*; circa 1959-1963; Dorothy Hesner of Chicago has such a doll and states, "Included was lots of printing which told how to dress the doll. Cottons and silks were the best. Use a curling iron to press the clothes. For fur trim use angora."

      MARKS: None (doll); "Adorable Dress Me Dolls//Sizes 7½ inch//to 20in (51cm) with moving eyes and moving parts//New Style Coiffeurs//Grant Plastics, Inc. Made in U.S.A." (cardboard attached to top of plastic bag)

      SEE: *Illustration 198. Playthings*, March 1961.

      PRICE: $5-10

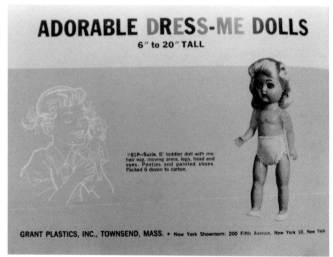

ADORABLE DRESS-ME DOLLS
6" to 20" TALL

#81P—Suzie. 8" toddler doll with mohair wig, moving arms, legs, head and eyes. Panties and painted shoes. Packed 6 dozen to carton.

GRANT PLASTICS, INC., TOWNSEND, MASS. • New York Showroom: 200 Fifth Avenue, New York 10, New York

198.

Kathleen: HP; 11in (28cm); flat feet; sleep eyes; mohair wig; jointed at neck, shoulders and hips; individually packed in heat-sealed poly bag; doll stand included; one of the *Adorable Dress-Me Dolls*; circa 1959-1963.

      MARKS: None (doll)

      SEE: *Illustration 199* (doll on left). *Playthings*, March 1961.

      PRICE: $5-10

Priscilla: HP; 12in (31cm); high-heeled feet; mohair wig; jointed at neck, shoulders and hips; packed in heat-sealed poly bag; leotard and high-heeled shoes included; one of the *Adorable Dress-Me Dolls*; circa 1959-1963.

      MARKS: None (doll)

      SEE: *Illustration 199* (second from left). *Playthings*, March 1961.

      PRICE: $5-10

Linda: HP; 12in (31cm); teenage high-heeled feet; jointed at neck, shoulders and hips; mohair wig; high-heeled plastic shoes included; packed in heat-sealed poly bag; one of the *Adorable Dress-Me Dolls*; circa 1959-1963.

      MARKS: None (doll)

      SEE: *Illustration 199* (third from left). *Playthings*, March 1961.

      PRICE: $5-10

Gretchen: HP; 7½in (19cm); chubby baby doll-type; jointed at neck, shoulders and hips; sleep eyes; dynel wig; molded painted shoes (see *Illustration 198*); packed in heat sealed poly bag; circa 1959-1963.
    MARKS: None (doll)
    SEE: *Illustration 199* (fourth from left). *Playthings*, March 1961.
    PRICE: $5-10

Donna: HP; 7½in (19cm); sleep eyes; jointed at head and shoulders; mohair wig; stand included; painted shoes (see *Hard Plastic Dolls, I*, page 284D); one of the *Adorable Dress-Me Dolls*; circa 1959-1963.
    MARKS: None (doll)
    SEE: *Illustration 199* (fifth from left). *Playthings*, March 1961.
    PRICE: $5-10

Pamela: HP; 8in (20cm); sleep eyes; mohair wig; jointed at head and shoulders; high heeled; stand included; packed in heat resistant poly bag; one of the *Adorable Dress-Me Dolls*; circa 1959-1963.
    MARKS: None (doll)
    SEE: *Illustration 199* (sixth from left). *Playthings*, March 1961.
    PRICE: $5-10

Karen: HP; 7½in (19cm); sleep eyes; mohair wig; colorful removable plastic bra and panty set; painted shoes; packed in heat-sealed poly bag; stand included; one of the *Adorable Dress-Me Dolls*; circa 1959-1963.
    MARKS: None (doll)
    SEE: *Illustration 199* (seventh from left). *Playthings*, March 1961.
    PRICE: $5-10

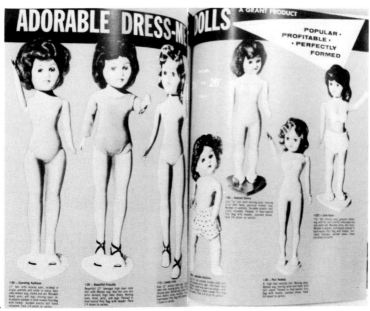

199.

Eileen: HP body with vinyl head; 20in (51cm); jointed at neck, shoulders, hips and knees; mohair wig; high-heeled feet; packed with earrings, necklace and bracelet; pearl tiara; 1960.

In 1959 they changed the finish on the faces of their dolls and advertised them as having "A New Sun-Tone." The dolls could be purchased dressed or undressed. *Eileen* was poly-packed in a box. It is one of the *Adorable Dress-Me Dolls.*

    MARKS: None (doll)
    SEE: *Illustration 200. Playthings,* March 1960.
    PRICE: $10-12

200.

    A reader, Elizabeth Woodward, of Leavenworth, Kansas, has reported that she has a doll like the "unknown" one on page 234, *Illustrations 519* and *520* in *Hard Plastic Dolls, I.* She said it was a "Dress-Me" doll. Grant made such a doll and sold it in a poly bag with a cardboard label. We are grateful to everyone who wrote to us through Hobby House Press, Inc., and many of the ideas and pictures in this book have come from these people. We enjoy each and every letter.

J. Halpern Company (Halco)

The registered trademarks, the trademarks and the copyrights appearing in italics within this chapter belong to J. Halpern Company.

In the early 1950s the J. Halpern Company advertised rather large "Pretty as a Picture" dolls. They advertised in *Playthings* in 1951 but no further advertisements for the company could be found. Upper left: doll in checked long dress with umbrella and purse. Middle right: *Baby Fluffee*. Lower left: doll in formal dress with white stole. In 1951 their 12-page catalog featured these and many other dolls.

SEE: *Illustration 201. Playthings*, April 1951.

Baby Fluffee: HP head with magic skin body; 24in (61cm); flirty blue sleep eyes; blonde mohair wig; off-white dress with pink ribbons; the same embroidery design is on bonnet and skirt of dress; rubber panties which have a tendency to melt onto magic skin body; circa 1951.

MARKS: None (doll); navy blue tag with gold writing, "Superb//Halco//Brand//Made in U.S.A.//Baby Fluffee//featherweight"
SEE: *Illustration 202. Sandy Strater Collection.*
PRICE: $50-65

201.

202.

119

Bride doll: HP; 29in (74cm); gown of lustrous white rayon satin; illusion veil; white slippers; 1951.

Bridesmaid: HP; 29in (74cm); flowered dress with ruffle around bottom of skirt; 1951.

SEE: *Illustration 203. Playthings*, June 1951.

PRICE: $85-110

203.

Hardy Different Toys

The registered trademarks, the trademarks and the copyrights appearing in italics within this chapter belong to Hardy Different Toys.

Girl in White Dress: HP; 14in (36cm); light brown mohair wig; blue sleep eyes; white satin and net trimmed with gold rickrack costume; 1949. The owner was given this doll for a Christmas present in 1949. It had been purchased at Schrafft's in New York City.

MARKS: "Made in USA" (back); "Hardy Different Toys// Trade Mark//New York, N.Y. 23 E. 49th St." (on diamond shaped tag)

SEE: *Illustration 204. Mary Elizabeth Poole Collection.*

PRICE: $75-100

204.

P. J. Hill Co.

The registered trademarks, the trademarks and the copyrights appearing in italics within this chapter belong to P. J. Hill, Co., unless otherwise noted.

Based in Newark, New Jersey, this is another marketing company which sold by mail order. They purchased dolls from known companies and advertised them heavily in the hobby and "pulp" magazines of the 1950s. Today we would say that they "discounted" them. The dolls sold widely and well, and today they are very collectible. Most of them are unmarked.

Cindy Walker: HP; 14in (36cm), 20in (51cm) and 23in (58cm); braided hair; sleep eyes; head-turning walker; jointed at neck, shoulders and hips; mama voice; *Saucy Walker* look-alike; extra wardrobe could be ordered including hat and coat ensemble, bridal ensemble, plaid vinyl rain cape, ballerina outfit, hostess coat and sheer nightgown; 1955.

SEE: *Illustration 205. Workbasket*, November 1955.

PRICE: $25-35

205.

Saucy Walker® is a registered trademark of the Ideal Toy Corporation.

121

Hollywood Doll Manufacturing Co.

Queen for a Day: HP; 6in (15cm); painted eyes looking upward; molded hair under wig; swivel head; protruding lower stomach; 1st, 2nd, 3rd and 4th fingers molded together; red velvet robe with mock fur trim; white satin and lace dress; gold crown; 1947. The doll was made for the popular program "Queen for a Day." It was advertised in *Playthings*, March 1947.

    MARKS: Star "Hollywood Dolls" (back)
    SEE: *Illustration 206.*
    PRICE: $28-30

Western Series Cowboy: HP; 5in (13cm); sleep eyes; no eyelashes; molded hair; all fingers molded together; original clothes; black cowboy hat; red checked shirt; imitation brown leather pants; black painted-on shoes; circa 1947.

    MARKS: "Hollywood Dolls" in circle (back); wrist tag says "Cowboy;" box labeled
        "A Hollywood Doll//Western Series//Cowboy."
    SEE: *Illustration 207.*
    PRICE: $20-30

206.

207.

Advertisement in *Playthings*, September 1952: list of dolls and other items available in 1951.

Princess Series
Lucky Star Series
Nursery Rhymes
Little Friends
Playmates
Toyland Series
Sweetheart Series
Lullaby Baby Series
Western Series

Everyday Series
Cradle Series
Baby Buggy Series
The Lucky Star Doll
Queen for a Day
The Wishing Doll
Old Mother Witch
The Nun
Peter Rabbit

Bunny Rabbit
Bridegroom
Ballerina
Undressed
Bedtime Dolly
Little Snow Baby
Doll Stands
Cradle
Carriage

SEE: *Illustration 208.*

208.

Non-walking doll: HP; 8in (20cm); unusual shiny brown wig; non-walking doll; unusual brown sleep eyes; molded eyelashes; no painted lashes; jointed at neck, shoulders and hips; straighter legs than most of the small *Ginny*®-type dolls; individual fingers; arms have unusual indentations at the elbows; arms and legs are not strung like similar dolls but move well; feet have dimples above toes; only slight indentation for navel; mid 1950s; (see Identification Section, *Illustration 415.*)

> **MARKS:** Large Star with "A Hollywood Doll" around outer edge (back)
> **SEE:** *Illustration 209. Marge Meisinger Collection.*
> **PRICE:** $25-35

209.

Ginny® is a registered trademark of the Vogue Dolls, Inc.

123

Rock-a-Bye Baby: HP; 5in (13cm); jointed neck and arms; all original in box; white taffeta with lace and ribbon trim; circa 1949-1951.

   MARKS: "Hollywood Doll" in circle (back); "Hollywood Doll" (arm tag); "Rock-a-by-Baby" (box)

   SEE: *Illustration 210. Pat Parton Collection.*

   PRICE: $16-20

210.

Horsman Dolls, Inc.

The registered trademarks, the trademarks and the copyrights appearing in italics within this chapter belong to Horsman Dolls, Inc.

Pitter Patty: HP head; soft body; vinyl arms and legs; 19in (48cm); sleep eyes; crier; heart beat mechanism without winding; plastic curlers for curling her hair.

   SEE: *Illustration 211. Playthings,* November 1951.

   PRICE: $50-65

211.

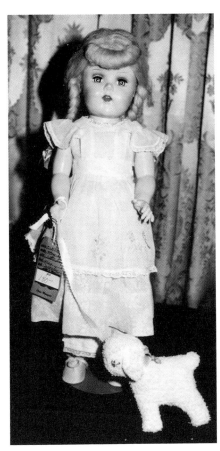

212.

Mary Had a Little Lamb: HP; 18in (46cm); excellent color; blonde mohair wig; black eye shadow; orange feathered eyelashes; Y on backside; all original (possibly dressed by Mollye Goldman); pink embossed organdy dress; white organdy apron; white pantaloons; circa 1953-1955.

MARKS: "Horsman" (head)
SEE: *Illustration 212. Ester Borgis Collection.*
PRICE: $85-110

Little Girl: HP; 16in (41cm); excellent color; sleep eyes; open mouth with four teeth; felt tongue; individual fingers; original clothes; pink taffeta dress with plaid taffeta trim; early 1950s.

MARKS: "Horsman" (head); "This Horsman doll has Saran hair, sleep eyes; real lashes." (tag)
SEE: *Illustration 213. Gigi Williams Collection.*
PRICE: $70-90

213.

125

Bright Star: HP; 15in (38cm); sleep eyes; open mouth with teeth; original clothes; head turning walker; pretty ponytail; blue piqué dress with white collar and cuffs; red and white braid only on one collar and down the front; Saran hair; blue plastic shoes; early 1950s.

MARKS: None (doll); "Bright Star// Horsman//All Plastic// Lightweight and Non-Breakable//Lifelike and Washable//Arms, Legs, Head Moves" (tag)

SEE: *Illustration 214. Chree Kysar Collection.*

PRICE: $70-90

214.

Mary Hoyer Doll Mfg. Co.

The registered trademarks, the trademarks and the copyrights appearing in italics within this chapter belong to Mary Hoyer Doll Mfg. Co.

Bride: HP; 14in (36cm); glass-like sleep eyes; closed mouth; 2nd and 3rd fingers slightly curled; pointed chin; tiny face in comparison with other hard plastic dolls; beautiful porcelain-like skin color; standard arms (see Identification Guide, *Hard Plastic Dolls, I*, page 262A); real lashes and lashes painted under eyes; eye shadow; jointed in neck, arms and legs; no molded hair under wig; gray eyebrows; original satin dress with net overskirt; bodice with net ruffle; matching veil; late 1940s to mid 1950s.

MARKS: "Original//Mary Hoyer//Doll" in circle (back); "Mary//Hoyer//Dolls" (box)

SEE: *Illustration 215* (Color Section, page 168). *Pat Parton Collection.*

PRICE: $350-400+ depending on costume; prices vary in different sections of the country.

Mary Hoyer Dollies: (for general characteristics, see *Illustration 215*). From left to right: girl in handknit beige dress; Mary Hoyer labeled nurse's outfit with blue cape and hat with a red cross of felt; gray skirt and Mary Hoyer labeled burgundy sweater set; dark green short coat and hat set; beige and white tennis outfit with tennis racket; late 1940s to mid 1950s.

MARKS: "Original//Mary//Hoyer//Doll" in circle (back)
SEE: *Illustration 216. Sharlene Doyle Collection.*
PRICE: $350-400+ depending on costume; prices vary in different sections of the country

216.

217.

Doll in Three-Piece Knitted Bathing Outfit: HP; 14in (36cm); (for general characteristics, see *Illustration 215*). Mary Hoyer sold dolls and doll patterns through a mail order business in Reading, Pennsylvania. This doll wears a deep pink three-piece bathing suit knitted from an original pattern.

MARKS: "Original//Mary Hoyer// Doll" in circle (back).
SEE: *Illustration 217.*
PRICE: $350-400+ depending on costume; prices vary in different sections of the country

Molded Hair *Mary Hoyer:* HP; 14in (36cm); (for general characteristics, see *Illustration 215*). It is not unusual for a Mary Hoyer doll to have slightly molded hair under the original wig. This doll has a dark brown wig over the molded hair.

    MARKS: "Original//Mary Hoyer// Doll" in circle (back)

    SEE: *Illustration 218. Helen Keefe Collection.*

Walking Doll in *Polly Prim* Outfit: HP; 14in (36cm); (for general characteristics see, *Illustration 215*); for $.75 plus the regular price of $4.95, a walking doll could be ordered; doll came with Dupont nylon washable wig; the same doll with a hand-curled wig was $3.50; other items which could be ordered included a sewing kit to make a *Polly Prim* outfit; a ready-to-wear *Polly Prim* outfit; yarn kits and accessories; Dolly Wave set; wardrobe trunks; *Sun Bonnet Sue* Child's Sewing Kit; and *Sun Bonnet Sue* outfit ready to wear.

    SEE: *Illustration 219. McCall's Needlework,* Fall-Winter 1953-1954.

219.

218.

Twins: HP; 14in (36cm); boy (see *Hard Plastic Dolls, I,* page 112) and girl; (for general characteristics, see *Illustration 215*); 1953. The advertisement said, "You and your little girl will find real enjoyment in these famous twin dolls." The girl has a Dupont nylon washable wig that can be combed or waved. The boy's hair is of curly lamb's wool dyed brown or black. Both came undressed but with shoes and stockings.

> MARKS: "Original//Mary Hoyer//Doll" in circle (back)
>
> SEE: *Illustration 220. McCall's Needlework,* Spring-Summer 1953.

Mary Hoyer: HP; 14in (36cm); advertisement for yarn kits and accessories; kit to make Western Costume was $1.00; western boots were $.35; kits included all necessary materials, buttons, simple instructions; sports accessories available included roller skates, ice skates, skis and tennis rackets.

> SEE: *Illustration 221. McCall's Needlework,* Winter 1949-50.

220.

221.

Gigi: HP; 18in (46cm); sleep eyes; only about 2000 of these dolls were made by the Frisch Doll Company; pink long satin dress; pink straw hat; early 1950s.

MARKS: "Original//Mary Hoyer//Doll" in circle (back)

SEE: *Illustration 222. Kathy George Collection.*

PRICE: $400-500 + (very few sample prices available)

222.

Ideal Toy Corporation

The registered trademarks, the trademarks and the copyrights appearing in italics within this chapter belong to Ideal Toy Corporation, unless otherwise noted.

The Ideal Toy and Novelty Company was one of the doll industry's leaders during the hard plastic era. Today's collectors have realized that their *Toni®*, *Saucy Walker* and *Miss Curity* dolls are very beautiful and very collectible. Prices have risen accordingly.

The authors were happy to have presented the company catalogs in *Hard Plastic Dolls, I* and in this book they have attempted to show the unusual and rarer dolls in the Ideal line.

Many readers have asked us for more information about the wonderful Ideal babies. We have featured some of them in this volume. Perhaps the doll we have been asked to identify most often is the all-hard plastic *Plassie Toddler* which is one of the most beautiful of all the hard plastic babies. (See *Illustrations 224-226*).

Just before the company went out of business we asked the Ideal Public Relations Department to try to find out if there were unmarked Ideal dolls. They contacted foremen on the line who had been there in the 1950s, and they said that some of the regular lines were unmarked and purchased for special orders. They particularly made the *Toni*®-type dolls in formal dresses for special orders.

Because many of their customers wanted the new vinyl heads with rooted hair, they substituted these vinyl heads for hard plastic heads or hard plastic heads for vinyl heads as they had requests. They sold regular dolls to the leading mail order houses and also made special dolls for them, both marked and unmarked.

For detailed information about Ideal dolls, see *Hard Plastic Dolls, I*, pages 122-163.

Plassie: HP head with pliable synthetic rubber body; 16in (41cm), 19in (48cm) and 22in (60cm); cries when leg is squeezed; sleep eyes with real lashes; separate fingers; fingers so flexible that doll can clasp her hands; cotton-stuffed body; dress of embroidered sheer pastel cotton; matching bonnet; cotton slip; panties; rayon socks; imitation leather shoes; 1946. This is a very early doll with a hard plastic head and a magic skin body.

SEE: *Illustration 223*. Sears catalog, Christmas 1946. *Barbara Andresen Collection*.

PRICE: $50-100 (depending on size and costume)

223.

Plassie Toddler: both dolls are all-HP; 14in (36cm).

Most of the Ideal babies and toddlers during this period had a hard plastic head and a "Magic Skin" or cloth body, but the *Plassie Toddler* was listed in the 1949-1950 catalog as having "a new all plastic body, sleeping eyes, fully jointed, mohair wig." (See *Hard Plastic Dolls, I,* page 131.) Ideal did offer changes in doll specifications and parts in this catalog. Probably some doll buyers wanted to offer their customers the molded hair dolls which mothers often preferred instead of wigs which could be pulled off easily by children.

Both dolls are similar but they have different characteristics. Doll on left: blue sleep eyes; painted lashes under the eyes; closed mouth; painted brown hair.

MARKS: "Made in U.S.A.//Pat. No. 2252077" (head); "Ideal Doll//14" (back)

Doll on right: hazel sleep eyes; eyebrows; lashes painted under eyes; painted brown hair; molded curls on back of head; open mouth; pink blush on cheeks, elbows and chest; original shoes and socks.

MARKS: "14//Ideal Doll//Made in U.S.A." (head); "Ideal Doll//14" (back); "An Ultra Fine Product//An//Ideal Doll//Made in USA//Ideal Novelty & Toy Co.//Long Island City//New York" (tag)

SEE: *Illustration 224* (front). *Elaine Timm Collection.*
Illustration 225 (back). *Elaine Timm Collection.*

PRICE: $75-100

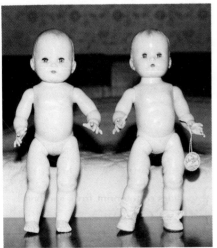

224.

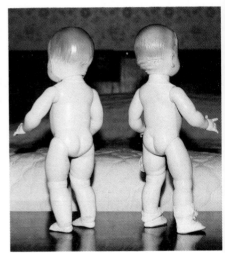

225.

Plassie Toddler: HP; 14in (36cm); sleep eyes; jointed at neck and shoulders; dark wig with curls; dressed in yellow organdy dress and bonnet with the unique Ideal trim around the bottom of the dress; circa 1949-1950. This doll was in the 1949-1950 catalog (see *Hard Plastic Dolls, I,* page 131, *Illustration 310*).

MARKS: "14//Ideal Doll//Made in U.S.A." (head); "Ideal Doll//14" (body)

SEE: *Illustration 226. Ruth Moss Collection.*

PRICE: $75-100

226.

227.

228.

Betsy Wetsy: HP head; synthetic rubber body; 12in (31cm) and 16in (41cm); sleeping eyes with real lashes; six-piece layette and nursing bottle; dressed in knitted shirt, flannel diapers, knitted bootees; layette includes cotton print frock and bonnet, rayon socks, imitation leather shoes; 1946.

SEE: *Illustration 227.* Sears catalog, Christmas 1946. *Barbara Andresen Collection.*

PRICE: $80-100

Which Doll is the *Toni*: advertisement for the *Toni*® doll which was a "take-off" on the famous commerical of the time, "Which twin has the Toni Home Permanent?"

SEE: *Illustration 228. Family Circle,* December 1950.

Toni® is a registered trademark of The Gillette Co.   **133**

Toni® **Family Common Characteristics:** HP; closed mouth; sleep eyes with lashes; painted lashes below eyes; individual fingers with four dimples on back of hand; two dimples behind the knee; standard arm (see Identification Guide, *Hard Plastic Dolls, I,* page 262A); line around wrist; usually well marked; pretty flesh tone; Y on seat; washable and curlable hair.

MARKS: "Ideal Doll"
"P 90" 14in (36cm)
"P 91" 16in (41cm)
"P 92" 19in (48cm)
"P 93" 21in (53cm)
"P 94" 22½in (57cm)

PRICE: P 90 $150-180
P 91 $160-190
P 92 $190-250
P 93 $275-330
P 94 $350-400+ (very few sample prices available)

Toni, Ideal's Nylon Haired, Nylon-Dressed Beauty: HP; introduction of Bur-Mil nylon permanent pleated dress for *Toni®* doll; 1953.
SEE: *Illustration 229. Playthings,* March 1953.

Toni® **in Pleated Dress:** HP; 21in (53cm); (for general characteristics, see above); medium blue nylon accordian-pleated dress; pink leather shoes; rose ribbon sash; rose wrist ties on arms; blue satin ribbon in hair; petticoat not attached to dress; lace on dress, petticoat and panties is the same.
MARKS: "P-93" (neck and back)
SEE: *Illustration 230. Jean Dicus Collection.*
PRICE: $400 up (rare doll; very few sample prices)

229.

230.

Toni® is a registered trademark of The Gillette Co.

Toni: HP; 16in (41cm); blonde wig; all original tagged dress; pink top and blue and gold skirt; excellent skin coloring; came with *Toni Wave Kit; circa 1952*.

MARKS: "Ideal Doll P 91" (head)
SEE: *Illustration 231* (Color Section, page 166).
PRICE: $160-180

***Toni* Patterns:** HP; (for general characteristics, see page 134). Many patterns were available "at your favorite pattern counter." The advertising stated the patterns could also be worn by "famous Ideal's other 'Dolls with a Purpose:' Harriet Hubbard Ayer, Betsy McCall and Miss Curity."
SEE: *Illustration 232. McCall's Needlework*, Fall-Winter 1953-1954.

232.

233.

Harriet Hubbard Ayer: HP body and vinyl head; came in 14in (36cm), 16in (41cm), 19in (48cm) and 21in (53cm); introduced at New York Toy Fair in February 1953; came with eight-piece harmless *Harriet Hubbard Ayer* cosmetic kit, beauty table and booklet of instructions; 1953.

> **MARKS:** "MK 14 Ideal Doll" (head); "Ideal Doll" (back)
>
> **SEE:** *Illustration 233. Playthings,* March 1953.
>
> **PRICE:** $140-180 14in (36cm)
> $175-200 16in (41cm)

Miss Curity: HP; 14in (36cm); (for general characteristics, see page 134); unusual picture of dark-haired *Miss Curity;* made only in 14in (36cm) size; included with the doll was a complete Bauer & Black first aid kit; box included a booklet of first aid play instructions; 1953.

> **MARKS:** "P 90//Ideal Doll//Made in USA" (head); "Ideal Doll//P 90" (back)
>
> **SEE:** *Illustration 234. Playthings,* March 1953.
>
> **PRICE:** $200-225

234.

Mary Hartline (Toni® P-94): HP; 22½in (57cm); closed mouth; sleep eyes with lashes; painted lashes below eyes; individual fingers with four dimples on back of hand; two dimples behind the knee; line around wrist; usually well marked; pretty flesh tone; Y on seat; washable and curlable hair; grill in stomach; 1952.

> **MARKS:** "Ideal" (head); "P 94" (body); "P 93" (arms)
> **SEE:** *Illustration 235. Patricia Arches Collection.*
> **PRICE:** $300-350 up (rare doll)

Toni®: HP; 22½in (57cm); unusually large *Toni®* doll; all original; red dress with rickrack trim around neckline; gold belt and shoes; excellent skin coloring; black wig; sleep eyes; (for general *Toni®* P 94 characteristics, see *Illustration 325*).

> **MARKS:** "P 94" (back of head)
> **SEE:** *Illustration 236. Chree Kysar Collection.*
> **PRICE:** $300-350 up (rare doll)

Betsy McCall® (Toni® family): vinyl head with wig; HP body; 14in (36cm); closed mouth; sleep eyes and lashes; wears real *Betsy McCall®* clothes just like the dresses little girls shopped for at department stores; fully-jointed; an easy-to-sew pattern came with every *Betsy McCall®*; there were also paper dolls of *Betsy* each month in *McCall's®* magazine; all original outfit; rose skirt with straps and white blouse; 1953.

> **MARKS:** "McCall Corp." (head); "P 90//Ideal Doll" (back)
> **SEE:** *Illustration 237* (Color Section, page 169).
> **PRICE:** $150-170

235.

Betsy McCall® is a registered trademark of McCall Corp.

Toni® is a registered trademark of The Gillette Co.   236.

137

Saucy Walker: HP; 22in (56cm); jointed head turning walker; flirty rolling eyes; Saran wig which could be brushed and waved; grill in stomach (see Identification Guide, *Hard Plastic Dolls, I,* page 276D); open mouth with two teeth; individual fingers; painted eyelashes under eyes; pin-jointed walker with unpainted Ideal screw type pin (see Identification Guide, *Hard Plastic Dolls, I,* page 290B); straight legs; red dot in corner of eye; double crease behind knee; circa 1952.

MARKS: "Ideal" (head)
SEE: *Illustration 238. Sharlene Doyle Collection.*
PRICE: $125-150 22in (56cm)
        $70-100 16in (41cm)

Lolly: HP; 9in (23cm); walker with turning head; pin-jointed walker; pin covered with paint; two dimples on knees; painted-molded hair with curls covering ear; individual fingers; closed mouth; molded lashes; not original clothes; circa early 1950s. This is the doll listed as *Tiny Girl* on page 143 of *Hard Plastic Dolls, I.* Elizabeth Woodward of Leavenworth, Kansas, wrote to tell us her name. Kathryn Davis of Toledo, Ohio, supplied the Ideal brochure. We thank them both.

SEE: *Illustration 239. Ideal Brochure.*
PRICE: $25-30

238.

239.

138

Inez Holland House

The registered trademarks, the trademarks and the copyrights appearing in italics within this chapter belong to Inez Holland House.

Starlet: HP; 7½in (19cm); wardrobe consists of school dresses, "Sunday best," sportswear, bridal party and special costumes; costumes were stain resistant and wiped clean with a damp cloth; circa 1957.
Inez Holland House was a company which sold many types of dolls made by other manufacturers.
    MARKS: None (doll)
    SEE: *Illustration 192.* Luster-Creme Shampoo Starlet Brochure.
    PRICE: $30-35

192.

Jolly Toys

The registered trademarks, the trademarks and the copyrights appearing in italics within this chapter belong to Jolly Toys.

Girl in Pink Dress: HP; 16in (41cm); sleep eyes; beautiful blonde wig; open mouth with two teeth; jointed at neck, shoulders and hips; all original; pink taffeta dress with lace trim; rose at waistline; snap slippers; circa 1954-55.
    MARKS: None (doll); "Jolly Toys" (tag)
    SEE: *Illustration 240. Ester Borgis Collection.*
    PRICE: $60-75

240.

Joy Toys, Inc.

Talking Doll: Speaks in English, Spanish, French or Portuguese; company advertised that they made rubber dolls, composition dolls, talking dolls and plastic dolls; 1951. **SEE:** *Illustration 241. Playthings*, May 1951.

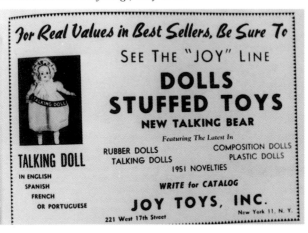

241.

Kim Dolls

Fairy: HP; 8½in (22cm); (for general characteristics, see Virga *Hi Heel 'Teen, Illustrations 368, 369*). This is an example of several satellite marketing companies operating from one main company. Both boxes had the same address (47 West St., New York City). Both dolls had wardrobes designed for the individual doll. However, the costumes fit both dolls. Circa 1956-1957.

> **MARKS:** None (doll); "Kim//Ready to Dress" (box)
> **SEE:** *Illustration 242. Marge Meisinger Collection.*
> **PRICE:** $20-25

242.

Kim in Jodhpur Outfit: HP with vinyl head; 7½in (19cm); (for general characteristics, see Fortune-Virga dolls, page 112); original costume; circa 1956-1957. This doll wears the same costume as the Virga doll in *Illustration 364*. Both dolls were made by the Beehler Arts Company and distributed under different names.

MARKS: None (doll); "Kim//Riding Outfit" (box)

SEE: *Illustration 243. Patricia Arches Collection.*

PRICE: $20-25

243.

Käthe Kruse

The registered trademarks, the trademarks and the copyrights appearing in italics within this chapter belong to Käthe Kruse.

Because cloth dolls had become very expensive for Käthe Kruse to manufacture in the 1950s, she turned to the German Schildkröte celluloid firm for help in making a new doll made entirely of a mixture of celluloid and plastic. This has now come to be called hard plastic. However, it is not quite the same material as the hard plastic made in the United States during this period.

A few years later production on these dolls ceased and a new doll was designed and produced which had a type of hard plastic head and a cloth body.

Model Hanne Kruse: European HP head; 9¾in (25cm); cloth body; German-style dress with white apron; all original; circa 1957.

MARKS: "Original//Käthe Kruse// Model//Hanne Kruse" (tag); "G.M.6.H. 885" (label in dress)

SEE: *Illustration 244. Beatrice Campbell Collection.*

PRICE: $250-275 up

244.

141

Badebaby: HP; approximately 12in (31cm); head was that of "Rumpumpel" doll; body made by Rheinische Gummi und Celluloid Fabrik Co. (turtle symbol); entirely washable; 1963-1974.

    MARKS: None (doll)
    SEE: *Illustration 245. Mary Elizabeth Poole Collection.*
    PRICE: $300-350 up (very few sample prices available)

245.

#5934/10 Gretchen (left) and #5964/1 Hansel (right): all-HP; 16in (41cm); unusual sleep eyes (the lid comes down and the whole ball of the eye does not roll); wigs; *Gretchen* is dressed in the traditional German jumper; *Hansel* is dressed in Bavarian-type short pants with suspenders of braid; circa mid 1950s.

    MARKS: Turtle in Diamond//"Modell//Käthe Kruse//T46"
    SEE: *Illustration 246. Mary Elizabeth Poole Collection.*
    PRICE: $375-400 up each

#5934/11 Susi (left) and **#5954/6 Jane** (right): all-HP; 16in (41cm); unusual sleep eyes (the lid comes down and the whole ball of eye does not roll); wigs; dressed in traditional jumpers of the young German schoolgirl; mid 1950s.

    MARKS: Turtle in Diamond//"Modell//Käthe Kruse//T46" (head)
    SEE: *Illustration 247. Mary Elizabeth Poole Collection.*
    PRICE: $375-400 each

246.
      247.

Mimerle: German HP head; cloth body; approximately 12in (31cm); polka dot dress with white apron; human hair pigtail wig; painted eyes; purchased in 1972. The quality of the hard plastic head on this doll is not quite the same as that on the earlier all-HP dolls.

MARKS: "Original//Käthe Kruse// Stoffpuppe" (tag)

SEE *Illustration 248. Mary Elizabeth Poole Collection.*

PRICE: $300-400 up

248.

Mrs. Lavalle

The registered trademarks, the trademarks and the copyrights appearing in italics within this chapter belong to Mrs. Lavalle.

249.

Cuddlee Bride Walking Doll: HP; 8in (20cm); jointed at neck, shoulders and hips; sleep eyes; came complete with seven outfits; price complete in 1956, $2.98. This is another of the popular small walking dolls which was marketed by a special company. In this case it was a mail order company. It is impossible from the advertisement to identify the doll.

SEE: *Illustration 249. House Beautiful,* October 1956. *Margaret Mandel Collection.*

PRICE: $25-30

Lenci (Italy)

The Lenci company is known for their cloth dolls of the 1920s and 1930s. However, the well-known Italian company has been making many different kinds of dolls and novelties throughout their existence.

After World War II they used the new hard plastic for several different lines of dolls. They had been making the cloth *Miniatures* and *Mascotte* dolls dressed in provincial costumes, and they continued to make provincial dolls in the new plastic material. These dolls are dressed in the usual quality costumes of the House of Lenci.

From left to right:

Girl from Sardinia: HP; 6in (15cm); beautiful hand-painted face with the Lenci two-tone lips; side glancing eyes; tiny hand-painted eyelashes; fingers molded together; light brown wig; red felt skirt and bolero with metallic trim; black apron with embroidered waistband; white cotton print scarf under her brown felt headdress; 1950s.

   MARKS: "Lenci//Torino//Made in Italy//Samughed//Sardegna" (tag)

   SEE: *Illustration 250* (Color Section, page 223).

   PRICE: $40-50

Girl from Valsarentino: HP with vinyl arms; 6in (15cm); lovely flesh tone to the hard plastic; well-painted face with the usual Lenci two-tone lips; side-glancing eyes with tiny painted eyelashes; blue eye shadow above eyes; red felt skirt and top; blue and red plaid scarf; white print apron; gold necklace with "Torino" engraved on it; black felt provincial hat with blue and white ribbons; 1950s.

   MARKS: "Lenci//Torino" (tag sewn into seam of dress)

   SEE: *Illustration 250* (Color Section, page 223).

   PRICE: $40-50

Lovely Doll

251.

U.S. Marine, U.S. Army, U.S. Air Corps: HP; 7in (18cm); fluttery eyes; high arched eyebrows; lashes painted above eyes; one-piece body; arm and neck joints, 2nd and 3rd fingers molded together; painted-on shoes with bows (see *Hard Plastic Dolls, I*, Identification Guide, page 286J); standard arm hook; two marks on palms of hands; molded painted hair; dressed in traditional uniforms; circa 1954.

   MARKS: None (doll); "A Lovely Doll//Movable eyes, Movable arms, Movable head" (box)

   SEE: *Illustration 251.*

   PRICE: $15-18 each

McCall's Patterns and Kits

The registered trademarks, the trademarks and the copyrights appearing in italics within this chapter belong to McCall's, unless otherwise noted.

Pattern for Dy-Dee® Doll: patterns for a lacy party dress: embroidered Sunday coat; sunsuit; bunting; came in sizes for 11in (28cm), 13in (33cm), 15in (38cm) and 20in (51cm) dolls.

SEE: *Illustration 252. McCall's Needlework,* Winter 1949-1950.

XMAS FOR DOLLY

Dress a Dy-Dee Doll in the Xmas spirit. She'll wear a lacy party dress under her embroidered Sunday coat. Cute sunsuit outfit. A bunting for sleepy-time. For dolls 11, 13, 15, 20 ins. No. 632, blue transfer, 25c.

252.

Dy-Dee® is a registered trademark of the Effanbee Doll Corp.

145

No. 1720. Bicycling outfit for a Sweet Sue doll—pedal pushers, jersey blouse and kerchief. Also, three other outfits. For dolls 15, 18, 21 inches tall. Pattern, electric blue transfer, 35c.

1720

No. 1706. Sunsuit for a Toni doll—back, front and sleeves cut in one piece; zippered closing. Also, three other outfits. EASILY MADE. For dolls 14, 16, 19, 21 inches tall. Pattern, 35c.

1706

No. 1809. Appliquéd felt skirt for Maggie and Alice dolls. Petti-blouse, knitted sweater and cap, party dress. Also, other clothes. For 15, 18 in. dolls. Pattern, McCall's Blue* transfer, 35c.

1809

1809

* "McCall's Blue" transfer stamps on light or dark material.

Patterns for Dolls: HP dolls; various sizes depending on dolls; patterns for pedal pushers with jersey blouse and kerchief for *Sweet Sue*® dolls; sunsuit for *Toni*® dolls; appliqued felt skirt for *Maggie*® and *Alice*® dolls; party dress for *Maggie*® and *Alice*® dolls; 1953-1954.

SEE: *Illustration 253. McCall's Needlework*, Fall-Winter 1953-1954.

253.

Betsy McCall: HP; 14in (36cm); pictures of costumes from some of the McCall patterns available at local stores; advertised as "easily made, close with zippers."
SEE: *Illustration 254. McCalls Needlework,* Fall-Winter 1953-1954.

254.

Doll Kits for Majorette Cowgirl and Skater: HP walking dolls; complete kit included doll, wool yarn, accessories and instructions.
SEE: *Illustration 255. McCall's Needlework,* Fall-Winter 1953-1954.
Illustration 256. McCall's Needlework, Fall-Winter 1953-1954.

255. MᶜCALL'S   256.

Fad of the Month Club Doll: offer to readers of *McCall's Needlework;* you could select a sewing kit to dress the club doll as a *Bride, Angel* or *Sweet Genevive;* each month there was another offering; dolls were all-HP.

SEE: *Illustration 257. McCall's Needlework,* Fall-Winter 1953-1954.

257.

McCall's Needlework Magazine (D.M.C. Corp.)

Famous Women in History Crochet Costume Instructions Book: for HP "Dress Me" type dolls. Costumes include:
1. Top left - *Marie Antoinette*
2. Top right - *Queen Elizabeth*
3. Center left - *Joan of Arc*
4. Center right - *Cleopatra*
5. Bottom left to right - *Queen Ester, Queen Isabella, Betsy Ross, Empress Josephine* and *Mary, Queen of Scots.*
   SEE: *Illustration 258. McCall's Needlework,* Fall-Winter 1953-54.

Marie Antoinette®, Queen Elizabeth®, Joan of Arc®, Cleopatra®, Queen Ester®, Queen Isabella®, Betsy Ross®, Empress Josephine® and *Mary, Queen of Scots®* are registered trademarks of D.M.C. Corp.

148

258.

259.

Romeo and Juliet: HP; 32in (81cm); mannequins which were used by the sewing classes of Bedford High School (suburban Cleveland, Ohio) for a project in costume design: *Juliet* is dressed in pink velvet and lace with a chiffon scarf; *Romeo* wears a dark blue tunic with a medium blue cape; circa 1950s.

> **MARKS:** "McCall" (base of doll)
> **SEE:** *Illustration 259. Thelma Purvis Collection.*
> **PRICE:** No price samples available.

Midwestern Mfg. Co.

The registered trademarks, the trademarks and the copyrights appearing in italics within this chapter belong to Midwestern Mfg. Co, unless otherwise noted.

260.

Mary Jean: HP; 8in (20cm); blonde hair; large eyes; jointed at neck, shoulders and hips; arm hook (see Identification Guide, page 236E); dress has blue top with blue, black and yellow print skirt; gold ribbon sash; walking mechanism, head does not turn; separate fingers; white shoes painted over bare feet so toes show through; (see Identification Guide, page 251E); all original clothes; excellent skin color; doll has most *Ginger*® characteristics but the hard plastic is inferior; arm hooks (see Identification Guide, page 238); circa 1954-1956.

> **MARKS:** None (body); "I'm Mary Jean//A Product of Midwestern Manufacturing Co." (box)
> **SEE:** *Illustration 260.*
> **PRICE:** $23-26

Ginger® is a registered trademark of Cosmopolitan Toy and Doll Corporation.

261.

Suzy Stroller: HP; 16in (41cm) and 19in (48cm); walker; 1953.

Midwestern Mfg. Co. made a line of inexpensive dolls for the mass market. In the same magazine they advertised "America's Famous Character Dolls", 6½in (17cm), 7½in (19cm) and 11in (28cm).

MARKS: Most bodies of Midwestern dolls are unmarked but the boxes usually have the Midwestern name on them.

SEE: *Illustration 261. Playthings,* March 1953.

PRICE: $50-75

Nancy Ann Storybook Dolls, Inc.

The registered trademarks, the trademarks and the copyrights appearing in italics within this chapter belong to Nancy Ann Storybook Dolls, Inc., unless otherwise noted.

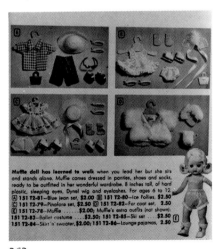

Muffie doll has learned to walk when you lead her but she sits and stands alone. Muffie comes dressed on panties, shoes and socks, ready to be outfitted in her wonderful wardrobe. 8 inches tall, of hard plastic, sleeping eyes, Dynel wig and eyelashes. For ages 6 to 12.
Ⓐ 151 T2-81—Blue jean set, $2.00 Ⓑ 151 T2-80—Ice Follies, $2.50
Ⓒ 151 T2-79—Pinafore set, $2.50 Ⓓ 151 T2-82—Fur coat set, 2.50
Ⓔ 151 T2-78—Muffie . . . . . . $2.00; Muffie's extra outfits (not shown):
151 T2-83—Ballet costume . . . $2.50; 151 T2-85—Ski set . . . $2.50
151 T2-84—Skirt 'n' sweater, $2.00; 151 T2-86—Lounge pajamas, 2.50

262.

Muffie Identification: *Muffie* was introduced in 1953 to compete with the small dolls such as *Ginny*∗. They were introduced as "Playtime Dolls." They came both dressed and undressed in a basic box. Nancy Ann produced an extensive wardrobe for these tiny 8in (20cm) dolls, constantly changing the line to compete with the many other small dolls which flooded the market.

Nine basic types of dolls are shown in the Identification Section, pages 240, 241. All are similar except #9 which was made after the original company was sold.

Muffie: HP; 8in (20cm); jointed on head, arms and legs only; Dynel wigs and eyelashes; sleep eyes; pictured is a blue jean set, pinafore set, Ice Follies costume, fur coat set; 1954. According to the advertisement, this was the year that *Muffie* learned to walk.

SEE: *Illustration 262.* Marshall Field & Co. 1954 Christmas catalog. *Barbara Andresen Collection.*

PRICE: $85-100+ (according to costume)

151

263.

Nancy Ann *Muffie* Brochure: (top to bottom)
Left to right: Row 1
    501 White dress with red trim and hair ribbon.
    502 Pink dress with blue trim and hair ribbon.
    503 Dress with red skirt and red and white polka dot top.
    504 Dress with rose top; white print skirt; rose hair ribbon.
    505 Dress with blue top with rickrack trim; yellow skirt with blue print.
    506 Dress with blue top trimmed with lace; pink print skirt.
    507 Blue and white striped dress trimmed in red; red hair ribbon.
    508 Pink dress trimmed with blue; large blue hair ribbon.

Left to right: Row 2
  601 Lavender and white striped dress; white tam.
  602 Yellow dress with deeper yellow trim; straw hat with one daisy.
  603 Blue print dress with pattern of white stripes with blue polka dots; red cloche.
  604 Dress with brown top; white skirt; white and brown tam.
  605 Multi-colored polka dots on white dress; blue neck inset; straw hat with red ribbon.
  606 Blue jumper with red checked top; red straw hat.
  607 Red and white striped sailor dress; white and red tam.
  608 Blue organdy party dress with light lavender trim; blue straw hat trimmed with matching flowers.
Left to right: Row 3
  701 Summer dress with red top; print skirt with matching sleeves; navy blue straw hat trimmed with flowers.

264.

702 Scotch plaid in red and blue; matching plaid tam.
703 Yellow and blue print dress with large blue collar; natural straw hat trimmed with flowers.
704 High-waisted dress with red and white striped skirt and solid red top; red straw hat trimmed with ribbon.
705 Combination dress with yellow print skirt and blue top; yellow straw hat trimmed with matching flowers.
706 Dress with blue and pink plaid skirt and white top; white and navy blue tam.
707 Pink dress trimmed with white print braid; pink straw hat.
708 Lavender print dress trimmed with lace; matching straw hat trimmed with flowers.
Left to right: Row 4
801 Blue and white print sunsuit; glasses; matching blue hair ribbon.
802 Playsuit with blue jeans and red and white checkered shirt; red straw hat; glasses.
803 Traditional Scotch Lassie costume; green and red plaid skirt; black suit coat and Scotch hat with feather; large red purse.
804 Bedtime costume with pink, blue and green robe.
805 Lounging outfit with blue pants; yellow metallic wrap-around top; gold shoes; blue hair ribbon.
806 Pink ballerina costume; pink ballerina shoes; pink hair ribbon.
807 Light blue ice skating costume trimmed with a ruffle; pink puff hair piece.
808 Red and white ski outfit with matching hat; ski boots.
Left to right: Row 5
809 Red and white polka dot dress; matching plain red hat.
810 White coat and hat trimmed with black.
811 Yellow raincoat with hood; red ribbons for braided hair.
812 Blue coat with blue and white checked trim on collar and hat.
901 Bridal gown with long veil; bouquet.
902 Blue party dress; white fur stole and hat.
903 Rose dress with lace trim; white fur coat and tam.
Left to right: Row 6
907 Gift box with assorted clothes and accessories.
908 Red wardrobe trunk with doll included in red and white striped dress trimmed in blue; clothes, accessories and extra shoes included.
Left to right: Row 7
915, 916, 917, 918, 919, 920 Accessories in plastic and boxed containers.
921 Undressed *Muffie* with some of her wardrobes.
SEE: *Illustration 263*. Nancy Ann brochure.
       Illustration 264. Nancy Ann brochure.
PRICE: $115-125 up for doll and mint outfit
       $25-55 for unopened boxed outfit

The Nancy Ann company was sold to Albert Bourla and stockholders and they made an "International Series" which was introduced at the American Toy Fair in New York in 1967. Hong Kong was rapidly becoming the center of doll manufacturing and the clothes for this series were made there.

This doll was not in production very long because children wanted the teenage dolls. Although it is different from the other *Muffie* dolls, it has a charm of its own and is rare. (See Identification Guide, page 241.)

MARKS: None (doll)

154

Spanish Muffie: HP; 8in (20cm); head-turning walker with plastic mechanism; beautiful skin tone but different from earlier Nancy Ann dolls; mouth painted inside lines to make it appear smaller; eyelashes painted under eyes; legs wider and heavier than other Nancy Ann dolls; one line on seat; dressed in red taffeta with black lace and gold braid trim; lace mantilla with crown-like pseudo comb in front holding it up; gold earrings; black underclothes; stockings and shoes; all original, (see Identification Guide, page 241); 1967.

MARKS: None (doll)
SEE: *Illustration 265* (Color Section, page 165).
PRICE: $80-100 (The price of this doll has been rising because it is difficult to find.)

Around the World Muffie: HP; 8in (20cm); (for general characteristics, see *Illustration 265*); packed in see-through package; 1967.

MARKS: None (doll)
SEE: *Illustration 266. Chree M. Kysar Collection.*
PRICE: $80-100

266.

Debbie was made in both all-HP and HP with a vinyl head. Nancy Ann, following the general trend, introduced vinyl heads in the *Muffie, Debbie* and "Style Show" lines in the mid and later 1950s. This book shows the HP *Debbie. Debbie* with the vinyl head was shown in *Head Plastic Dolls, I*, page 191.

The HP *Debbie's* arm hooks are shown in this book in the Identification Guide, page 235. The arm hooks of *Debbie* with the vinyl head are shown in *Hard Plastic Dolls, I*, page 268U.

MARKS: "Nancy Ann" (head)

155

267.

Debbie: HP; 10½in (27cm); molded hair under lovely long blonde wig; jointed at neck, shoulders and hips; knees are not jointed; head turning walker; closed mouth; sleep eyes with molded lashes; heavy dark painted lashes under eyes; individual fingers; blue checked cotton dress; organdy apron with pink rickrack trim; yellow straw hat; pink plastic purse with "Debbie//By//Nancy Ann" printed on it; white slip attached to dress; 1955.

      MARKS: "Nancy Ann" in raised letters on back of head; these letters wear off easily; dress tag says, "Styled By Nancy Ann//Nancy Ann Storybook Dolls Inc.// San Francisco, California"

      SEE: *Illustration 267. Marge Meisinger Collection.*

      PRICE: $65-85

Debbie: clothes

      Left: pink coat; blue taffeta dress; blue shoes and socks; white fur piece and muff; white cotton panties; clothes in small Nancy Ann pink box with large polka dots; dress and coat not tagged.

      Right: satin bride dress with lace trim; net veil; bouquet of flowers; white satin slippers; white cotton panties; dress has Nancy Ann tag; large blue polka dot Nancy Ann box.

      MARKS: "Storybook Dolls by Nancy Ann//Debbie's Special Occasion Styles" (boxes)

      SEE: *Illustration 267. Marge Meisinger Collection.*

      PRICE: $25-50 (boxed outfit)

Debbie: HP; 10½in (27cm); according to the advertisement, the dolls were "Big and Little Sister dolls with look-alike costumes;" outfits could be purchased separately. There were over 60 different "look-alike" costumes; 1955.

      SEE: *Illustration 268. Playthings,* August 1955.

268.

Roy Rogers and **Dale Evans:** HP; 8in (29cm); excellent quality dolls; medium dark skin tone; standard arm hooks (see Identification Guide, *Hard Plastic Dolls, I,* page 265K); feet like small Nancy Ann Storybook Dolls but no shoes painted on; dressed in Rodeo costumes; Nancy Ann gripper snaps (see Identification Guide, page 247); *Roy* has tan chaps; jeans; red, white, green and yellow plaid shirt; ears that stand away from head; lariat around wrist; *Dale* has same shirt; suede skirt; brown suede boots with yellow painted trim; Nancy Ann panties; both dolls have white cowboy hats; 1955.

It's Roy and Dale!

270.

MARKS: None (dolls)
"Nancy Ann Storybook Dolls Inc. of California 3R Roy Rogers" (box)
"Nancy Ann Storybook Dolls Inc. of California 3D Dale Evans" (box)
SEE: *Illustration 269* (Color Section, page 221). *Nancy Catlin Collection.*
PRICE: $100-125 each; (rare dolls — very few sample prices)

Roy Rogers and **Dale Evans:** HP; 8in (20cm); advertisement says, "Every detail of clothing is authentic 'Roy Rogers' right down to the boots, belts and Roy and Dale's famous white felt hats. Three different surefire 'western' outfits: *Rodeo, Roundup* and *Parade;*" walkers; real eyelashes; dolls pictured are wearing rodeo outfits.
SEE: *Illustration 270. Playthings,* July 1955.
PRICE: $100-125 each

Nancy Ann Style Show Series **Brochure:** all-HP.

MARKS: None (body and head); silver tag on wrist which listed the name of the doll and told of other available *Style Show* Dolls.

SEE: *Illustration 271.* Nancy Ann brochure.
Illustration 272. Nancy Ann brochure.

PRICE: $400-475

271.

272.

The beautiful Nancy Ann *Style Show* doll is very popular with collectors. The clothing is beautifully designed and made. The *Style Show* doll is usually all-HP and it is rarely seen with a vinyl head mint-in-box. Since it is not marked, it is difficult to identify. This late 1950s' doll still has lovely material and costume design. The gripper snap matches the material (see Identification Guide, page 247).

MARKS: "18V" (head); none (body); "2403" (bottom of box and also inside box)

Nancy Ann Style Show Doll: HP with vinyl head; 18in (46cm); sleep eyes; closed mouth; same general body characteristics as all-HP doll; color on knees and wrists; 2nd and 3rd fingers molded together and curved forward; head-turning walker; excellent details on hands, wrists and ears; beautiful rooted hair; blue dress taffeta with lace trim on skirt and sleeves; rose sash and skirt trim; hat trimmed with flowers and wide rose ribbon; same underwear as used on the all-HP doll; stockings; gripper snaps (see *Illustration 424*, left).

MARKS: "18V" (head); none (body); "2403" (bottom of box, also inside box)
SEE: *Illustration 273* (Color Section, page 164). *Nancy Arches Collection.*
PRICE: $300-400 (very few sample prices available)

159

The world of *Nancy Ann Storybook Dolls* is a wonderful place for collectors. Not only were there different types of bodies and series, but the actual material was changed as Nancy Ann coped with changes and shortages. The different body styles were shown in *Hard Plastic Dolls, I*. This book shows a few of the intricate variations of dolls in a single series. A collector can pursue these dolls for years and continue to find beautiful new models. They also can store these dolls in a very small space. No wonder they are popular!

274.

Sisters Go to Sunday School: HP; *Little Sisters* all 3½in (9cm); black pupil sleep eyes; *Big Sister* is 5in (13cm); black pupil sleep eyes; all have high white boots. *Big* and *Little Sisters* always had matching dresses. However, the material among different sets of dolls varied, even within a one-year-period.

> SEE: *Illustration 274. Marianne Gardner Collection.*
>
> PRICE: $35-55 each

275.

Little Sisters Go to School: HP; 3½in (9cm); black pupil sleep eyes. This shows the progress and change in the plastic of one type of doll. The doll on the left has a very clear hard plastic. The second and third dolls each are more waxy. The doll on the right has a very yellow waxy hard plastic. The two dolls on the left are wearing the same dress. One is red and white; the other is green and white. The second doll from the right has a pale blue dress and the dress of the doll on the right is red and white.

> SEE: *Illustration 275. Marianne Gardner Collection.*
>
> PRICE: $35-55 each

continued on page 169

Ideal *Betsy McCall.*
(see page 137).

American Character
Sweet Alice (see page 44).

Effanbee *Honey Tintair* (see page 105). *Pat Parton Collection.*

Nancy Ann *Style Show* doll with vinyl head (see page 159). *Pat Arches Collection.*

164

Nancy Ann International *Muffie* (see page 155).

Effanbee *Honey Bride* (see page 106).

Ideal *Toni* (see page 135).

Cosmopolitan *Ginger Mouseketeer* (see page 80). *Marge Meisinger Collection.*

Rosebud *Miss Rosebud* (see page 199). *Virginia Heyerdahl Collection.*

Arranbee *Littlest Angel* in jodhpurs (see page 59).

Mary Hoyer *Bride* (see page 126). *Pat Parton
Collection.*

continued from page 160

Easter Dolls: HP; 5in (13cm); the doll on left is a painted-eye pinch face, circa 1948-1950 doll; the other two dolls are painted-eye dolls, circa 1951; all are dressed in cream-colored taffeta with tiny flowered print; large garden-type straw hats with a rose on top. Nancy Ann occasionally made special boxes for holiday dolls as can be seen in this illustration.

SEE: *Illustration 276. Marianne Gardner Collection.*

PRICE: $35-55 each

276.

Over the Rainbow #409: HP; 6in (15cm); painted eye; from "All-Time Hit Parade Series;" dressed in pink with black lace.

Maytime: HP; 6in (15cm); painted eye; #302 from "Operetta Series." The 300 and 400 series were quite elaborately dressed. Most of them had large hats.

SEE: *Illustration 277. Marianne Gardner Collection.*

PRICE: $35-55 each

277.

Beauty: HP; 5in (13cm); painted-eye pinch face; #156 orange organza dress with lace and orange metallic stripe around skirt; from *Beauty and the Beast.* (doll on left)

See Saw Marjory Daw: HP; 5in (13cm); painted-eye pinch face; #177 white taffeta dress with gold metallic stripes. (doll on right) There were many metallic fabrics used in this series.

SEE: *Illustration 278. Marianne Gardner Collection.*

PRICE: $35-55 each

278.

Niresk Industries, Inc.

The registered trademarks, the trademarks and the copyrights appearing in italics within this chapter belong to Niresk Industries, Inc., unless otherwise noted.

This Chicago marketing company was one of the largest sellers of dolls in the United States. They advertised in hobby and so-called "pulp" magazines in the 1950s. They purchased dolls from the original doll manufacturers and sold them at low cost. They imitated the more expensive dolls. Usually the dolls were not marked. Look-alike dolls included the Vogue *Ginny*®, Alexander ballerinas, Ideal *Saucy Walker*® and many, many others. Their advertisements continued into the advent of the high-heeled vinyl dolls.

Nina Ballerina: HP body with vinyl head; 20in (51cm); rooted Saran hair; sleep eyes; jointed at neck, shoulders and hips; thigh-length hose; frothy net skirt; gleaming lamé bodice spangled with sequins; Capezio ballet slippers; does splits and high kicks; see *Hard Plastic Dolls, I,* page 72, 1955.

SEE: *Illustration 279. Workbasket,* November 1955.
PRICE: $50-75

279.

Ginny® is a registered trademark of Vogue Dolls, Inc.
Saucy Walker® is a registered trademark of Ideal Toy Corp.

Hollywood Bride with Seven-Outfit Trousseau: HP body with vinyl head; 18in (46cm); rooted hair; sleep eyes; walking doll; jointed at neck, shoulders and hips; outfits include coat and beret, hostess gown, ballerina, plastic raincoat, sheer nightgown and afternoon dress; 1955.

SEE: *Illustration 280. Workbasket,* November 1955.

PRICE: $50-75

280.

Janie Pigtails: HP; 8in (20cm); Saran wig, head-turning walker; sleep eyes with real lashes; fully jointed; wardrobe and accessories available; hair can be styled to suit her costume; *Ginny®* look-alike; 1953. This advertisement should be compared with the Plastic Molded Arts *Joannie Pigtails®* advertisement in *Playthings,* March 1953; (see *Illustration 293*).

MARKS: None (doll)

SEE: *Illustration 281. Movieland,* October 1953

PRICE: $25-35

281.

Ginny® is a registered trademark of Vogue Dolls, Inc.
Joannie Pigtails® is a registered trademark of P.M.A., Inc.

171

Norma Originals, Inc.

The registered trademarks, the trademarks and the copyrights appearing in italics within this chapter belong to Norma Originals, Inc.

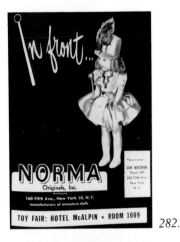

282.

Majorette: HP; 7½in (19cm); jointed at arms and neck; mitten hands; dressed as majorette with baton and plumed hat; 1951.

> **MARKS:** None (doll)
> **SEE:** *Illustration 282. Playthings,* March 1951.
> **PRICE:** $12-15

Norma Bride: HP; 8in (20cm); beautiful wig of long curly red hair; sleep eyes with molded lashes; no lashes painted on doll; standard arm hook; jointed at neck, shoulders and hips; molded-on slipper shoe with white only around bottom of shoe and not on straps (unusual) (see Identification Guide, page 252); lovely satin bride dress trimmed with lace; net veil with ornate lace; flowers at wrist; characteristics of Fortune and Virga dolls (see page 112); exceptional quality doll; mid 1950s.

> **MARKS:** None (doll); "A Norma Original" (wrist tag)
> **SEE:** *Illustration 283. Marge Meisinger Collection.*
> **PRICE:** $35-40

283.

Martha Washington: HP; 7½in (19cm); jointed at arms and neck; PMA characteristics (page 177) except that it has mitten hands; rose colonial dress; blonde wig; educational story came with doll; circa early 1950s. Brochure in box says that there was a "Fact and Fiction Series," "International Series," "Bridal Series," "American Series," "Sport Series" and a "Petite Series" which were only 5½in (14cm) tall.

> **MARKS:** None (doll)
> **SEE:** *Illustration 284.*
> **PRICE:** $15

284.

Groom: HP; 7½in (19cm); (see Fortune characteristics, page 112); painted-on black shoes (see Identification Guide, *Hard Plastic Dolls, I*, page 285H); black felt suit with white felt vest; rayon tie; black top hat; all original; circa early 1950s. The Norma company made very unusual and attractive boxes.

> **MARKS:** None (doll); "Norma Originals//Made to be loved//104 The Groom" (box)

SEE: *Illustration 285.*
PRICE: $20

285.

Old Cottage Toys

The registered trademarks, the trademarks and the copyrights appearing in italics within this chapter belong to Old Cottage Toys.

During World War II it was difficult to get dolls for children. Mrs. M. E. Fleischmann started to make dolls for her daughter and by the end of the war, she was making dolls commercially. At first she used whatever materials were available. By 1948 Mrs. Fleischmann registered the trademark "Old Cottage Toys."

Her daughter joined the company as co-owner when she grew up, and they employed talented craftsmen who used much handwork in the construction of both the dolls and the clothes. The clothes were well made with beautiful detail and a child could dress and undress the dolls. Soon the company developed a line of wonderful character dolls. Their 1970 catalog listed 56 different dolls. They were sold in Harrods and the Liberty department store in London and other leading stores in both England and the United States. The mail order firm of Mark Farmer in California also carried them.

Their output never kept up with the demand and because of the handwork, the dolls were never inexpensive. As time passes, the dolls become more and more collectible. **GENERAL CHARACTERISTICS:** In the late 1940s Mrs. Fleischmann developed a compound with hard plastic characteristics which she used for the movable head of the doll. The faces were beautifully sculptured and the colors bright and lifelike. There was excellent detail in the hand-painted faces.

The body was made of tightly stuffed, flesh-colored felt which was jointed with a special wire armature which allowed the head, arms and legs to move freely.

An unusual characteristic of these dolls was the large flat feet which are so carefully balanced that the doll can stand with no other support.

173

The dolls originally came in 8in (20cm) to 9in (23cm) and 11in (28cm) to 12in (31cm) sizes when dressed, but later the larger dolls were dropped from the line. These larger dolls are now quite rare and valuable.

TYPES OF DOLLS: historical figures; fairy tale figures; nationality dolls; English characters including the *London Policeman, Guardsman, Pearly King* and *Queen.* Another favorite doll was the one-piece felt baby with blonde curls.

Probably the most popular were the Victorian children. Pam purchased one in Harrods on her first trip overseas when she was 16. Years later when she returned to England and Harrods, she was disappointed when the saleswoman told her that they were so scarce and expensive that they only sold them during the Christmas season.

DESIGN CENTRE OF LONDON: The Council of Industrial Design selects the finest crafts in production for exhibition at the Design Centre in London. These products are allowed to be tagged with the Design Centre label. Some of the Old Cottage Dolls carry this tag along with the tag printed with the registered trademark of the company.

Mrs. Fleischmann was commissioned by Metro-Goldwyn Mayer to make a Japanese doll representing the film *Teahouse of the August Moon* which appeared on the film's showcard. She also made a doll to promote the film *Gigi.* The British Broadcasting Company asked her to make characters for a television broadcast, and she made *Tweedledee* and *Tweedledum*, characters from *Alice Through the Looking Glass.*

PRESERVATION WARNING: Care should be taken with the storage of these dolls. The hard plastic-type material of the Old Cottage Dolls has been known to "collapse." The dolls should be placed away from direct sunlight, heat, cold, and so forth. However, so far this does not seem to be a common occurrence.

286.

Scotland Boy: HP-type head with felt body; 9in (23cm); unusually large feet and shoes; painted face; nicely sculptured head; three lashes on side of eye; Stuart plaid kilt, scarf, hatband and cuffs of shoes; black velvet jacket; lace jabot and cuffs.

    MARKS: None (doll); picture of cottage with "Registered//Trade Mark" (tag); "Old// Cottage//Doll//Made in// England" (reverse side of tag)

SEE: *Illustration 286.*
PRICE: $70-95

Winter Girl in Kate Greenaway Style: (see page 173 for general characteristics); 9in (23cm); black flannel dress; blue brocade apron; white collar and cap trimmed in lace.
  MARKS: See *Illustration 174*.
  SEE: *Illustration 286*.
  PRICE: $70-95

Amy: for general characteristics see page 173; 10in (25cm); dressed in blue dotted dress; white organdy apron; blonde pigtail wig; white shoes and socks; 1969. This doll was advertised in the 1971 Mark Farmer catalog.
  MARKS: See *Illustration 286*; other tag says "as selected for the Design//Center//London"
  SEE: *Illustration 287. Mary Elizabeth Poole Collection.*
  PRICE: $85-110

Baby: entire doll one-piece felt; 4-3/4in (12cm); blonde curly wig; pink baby dress and matching bonnet; 1969.
  MARKS: None
  SEE: *Illustration 287. Mary Elizabeth Poole Collection.*
  PRICE: $40-45

Goose Girl: for general characteristics, see page 173; red felt dress and shoes; print apron and matching kerchief; plastic goose.
  SEE: *Illustration 288. Mary Elizabeth Poole Collection.*
  PRICE: $85-95 (small doll)
    $100-130+ (larger size)

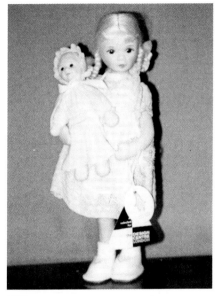

287.

288.

Tweedledum and Tweedledee: 10in (25cm); for general characteristics, see page 173; unusually large head; English schoolboy uniform; royal blue felt shirt; beige felt pants; blue and beige felt cap; 1968. These dolls were made for the English British Broadcasting Company for a television broadcast. They were schoolboy characters from *Through the Looking-Glass* by Lewis Carroll.

> **MARKS:** "Old Cottage Dolls" on tag; "Dee" and "Dum" written on the left shirt collar of each doll.
>
> **SEE:** *Illustration 289. Christine Lorman Collection.*
>
> **PRICE:** $600 + (very few sample prices available)

289.

Ontario Plastic Inc.

The registered trademarks, the trademarks and the copyrights appearing in italics within this chapter belong to Ontario Plastic, Inc., unless otherwise noted.

Paula Sue: HP; 8in (20cm); non-walking; sleep eyes with plastic eyelashes; deep clefts under nose; no painted eyelashes; arm hook similar to Vogue *Ginny*® with squared-off plastic piece holding a metal ring (see Identification Guide, page 235); original clothes; white dress with multi-colored ribbon trim; unusual gripper snap closing (see Identification Guide, page 247); for body comparison with other 8in (20cm) (see Identification Guide, page 241); mid 1950s.

> **MARKS:** "Ontario Plastic Inc.// Rochester N. Y." (back)
>
> **SEE:** *Illustration 290. Marge Meisinger Collection.*
>
> **PRICE:** $20-25

290.

Ginny® is a registered trademark of Vogue Dolls, Inc.

P & M Doll Company

The registered trademarks, the trademarks and the copyrights appearing in italics within this chapter belong to P & M Doll Company, unless otherwise noted.

THE DOLL THAT DOES EVERYTHING!

- SITS!
- KNEELS!
- BENDS!
- WALKS!

P & M's
Paula Mae
MAGIC
KNEE ACTION DOLL

WHITE & COLORED DOLLS

Our Brand New

ALL VINYL CREATIONS

are consistent in every way with the fine quality our customers have come to expect from P&M. And, of course, all beautifully costumed in the P&M manner, in keeping with the prevailing trend in infants' attire. Here, indeed, quality predominates though the retail prices are designed to produce volume sales.

We are featuring All Vinyl Dolls and also our Paula Mae Walking Doll

291.

Paula Mae Magic Knee Action Doll: HP body with vinyl head; rooted hair; *Saucy Walker®* look-alike; sits, kneels, bends and walks; 1955.

SEE: *Illustration 291. Playthings,* March 1955.

PRICE: $50-60 (white doll)
$65-80 (black doll)

Saucy Walker® is a registered trademark of the Ideal Toy Corp.

P.M.A. Dolls, Inc. (Plastic Molded Arts)

The registered trademarks, the trademarks and the copyrights appearing in italics within this chapter belong to Plastic Molded Arts, unless otherwise noted.

Plastic Molded Arts was a company which marketed many inexpensive dolls during the 1950s. Many of these dolls were featured in *Hard Plastic Dolls, I,* pages 207-211. This book shows illustrations of the *Ginny®*-type dolls by PMA which were not pictured in the earlier book.

Although there are none of these inexpensive small "fashion and character" type dolls in this book, as a convenience to the reader, the characteristics of these dolls are repeated below.

PMA Characteristics:
1. Double triangle mouth.
2. Molded eyelashes.
3. Heavy eyelashes beneath eyes.
4. Ear mold runs through ear.
5. 2nd and 3rd fingers molded together.
6. Two lines on palm of hand.
7. The tiny early dolls often have eyelashes above eye and no molded or imitation eyelashes.
8. The great majority have sleep eyes.
9. Most of the dolls have the standard arm hook (see Identification Guide, *Hard Plastic Dolls, I,* page 264H).
10. Molded and painted shoes with bow detail. There are several different types (see *Hard Plastic Dolls, I,* page 283A, B and C for details on shoes).

Ginny® is a registered trademark of Vogue Dolls, Inc.

PMA Characteristics of Ginny®-type dolls:
1. Head-turning walkers.
2. Sleep eyes.
3. The early dolls have real eyelashes. The later dolls have molded eyelashes.
4. Washable Saran wigs on HP dolls; rooted, washable hair on vinyl-headed dolls.
5. Heavy painted eyelashes (usually around entire eye).
6. Molded-on slippers which are painted, unpainted or just the bottom part is painted toes.
7. Standard arm hook (see *Hard Plastic Dolls, I*, Identification Guide, page 264I).

Joanie Pigtails: HP; 8in (20cm); Saran wig; head turning walker; sleep eyes with real lashes; heavily painted eyelashes around entire eye; molded-on slipper shoes which are sometimes painted and sometimes left in natural color (see Identification Guide, *Illustration 431*); standard arm hook (see *Hard Plastic Dolls, I*, Identification Guide, page 264I); 1953.
Niresk Industries marketed a *Janie Pigtail®* during the same year using the same basic doll (see Illustration 281).
MARKS: None (doll)
SEE: *Illustration 292. Playthings*, March 1953.
PRICE: $20-40 (depending on outfit)

Joanie Pigtails Wardrobe and Travel Case: HP; 8in (20cm); (for general characteristics, see *Illustration 292*); case include dress, panties, curlers, two-piece pajamas, shoes, mirror, comb and brush; not a walker; 1953.
MARKS: None (doll)
SEE: *Illustration 293. Playthings*, April 1953.
PRICE: $35-40+

Ginny® is a registered trademark of Vogue Dolls, Inc.

Janie Pigtails® is a registered trademark of Niresk Industries.

292.

293.

Joanie Walker: HP; 8in (20cm); (for general characteristics see page 178); molded slipper feet (see Identification Guide, page 252); pointed arched eyebrows; circa 1953.

> MARKS: None (doll); "Joanie Walker//P.M.A. Dolls, Inc" (box)
> SEE: *Illustration 294.*
> PRICE: $25-35

Joanie-the Wedding Belle: HP; 8in (20cm); (for general characteristics, see page 178); white satin wedding gown with matching panties; Saran wig; party dress and matching panties; pocketbook; comb; mirror; curlers; advertisement said, "Something old-bridal veil//something new-wedding slippers//something borrowed-wedding ring//something blue-wedding garter;" not a walker; 1953. *Joanie* came with a travel case with metal locks and a plastic handle.

> SEE: *Illustration 295. Playthings,* June 1953.
> PRICE: $35-40

Stepping Steppers: HP; 11in (28cm); head turning walker; washable Saran wig; sleep eyes; wardrobe available; plain plastic shoes with plastic bow; 1953.

> SEE: *Illustration 296. Playthings,* March 1953.
> PRICE: $10-15

294.

295.

296.

Chubby Type Girl: HP; 10½in (27cm); head turning walker; hidden pin walker (see *Hard Plastic Dolls, I*, page 291D); 2nd and 3rd fingers molded together; dimples on back of hands; toes all molded together; clothes not original; arm hook (see Identification Guide, page 236); circa mid 1950s.

> **MARKS:** "Plastic Molded Arts Co.// L.I.C. New York" (back)
> **SEE:** *Illustration 297. Helen M. Keefe Collection.*
> **PRICE:** $20-30

297.

298.

Miss Joan: HP; 12in (31cm); sleep eyes with eyelashes painted under eyes; jointed at neck, arms, hips and above knees; unusually nice doll; brunette hair; excellent skin color; arm hook (see Identification Guide, page 236); 2nd and 3rd fingers molded together and curving inward; all original; dressed in lace underwear with stockings and high-heeled shoes; circa 1957.

There are very few all-HP high-heeled dolls.

> **MARKS:** "Pat's Pend." (doll); "Miss Joan 1200//P.M.A. Dolls Inc." (box)
> **SEE:** *Illustration 298.*
> **PRICE:** $25-35

299.

Little Miss Joan: HP; 9in (23cm); Saran wig; walking doll; jointed at neck, shoulders, hips and knees; high heeled; came with outfits to purchase separately including a mink stole; 1957.

This is an unusual size for a high-heeled doll, especially one with bent knees.

> **SEE:** *Illustration 299. Toys and Novelties*, February 1957.
> **PRICE:** $25-35

Paris Doll Company

The registered trademarks, the trademarks and the copyrights appearing in italics within this chapter belong to Paris Doll Company, unless otherwise noted.

Rita Majorette: HP; 29in (74cm); walker; open mouth with teeth and felt tongue; lines above and below knees; dimples on knees; very "bulky" doll; *Mary Hartline®* look-alike; white majorette outfit trimmed with gold; circa early 1950s.

> **MARKS:** None
> **SEE:** *Illustration 300. Nancy Carlton Collection.*
> **PRICE:** $125-150

Mary Hartline® is a registered trademark of the Ideal Toy Corp.

300.

Rita: HP; 29in (74cm); walking doll; (see *Illustration 300* for general characteristics); large "bulky" doll that can wear little girl dresses. The 1951 doll was all-hard plastic. Later the doll was made with a vinyl head and increased 2in (5.1cm) in size. (See *Illustration 302.*)

    MARKS: None (doll)
    SEE: *Illustration 301. Playthings*, March 1951.
    PRICE: $125-150

Rita: HP body with vinyl head; 31in (79cm); (see *Illustration 300* for general characteristics); rooted hair; dressed in red and white checked rayon taffeta dress with braid trimmed collar; short puffed sleeves; red plastic belt; red shoes.

    MARKS: None (body)
    SEE: *Illustration 302.* Marshall Field & Co. 1954 Christmas catalog. *Barbara Andresen Collection.*
    PRICE: $125-150

301.

302.

Pedigree Company Soft Toys Limited

The name "Pedigree" was first used in 1942 for dolls and toys made at the Triang Works at Merton, London, England. The company registered the name "Pedigree" as a trademark that year. They have issued a large line of dolls for a long time. During the 1950s many of their dolls were modeled after those made in the United States. Most of them have the Pedigree signature on the head.

The company was proud of their high standards of workmanship and made the entire dolls in their factory. Their clothing and accessories were also of high quality and lasted well through many hours of children's play.

During the 1950s they had several factories in England as well as one in Belfast, Northern Ireland. There were ten factories in Canada, South Africa and New Zealand. They not only made many dolls, but they had a line of toys, prams, tricycles, toy trains and many other things.

In addition to the dolls shown in this book, their line during these years included:

1. *Magic Skin* dolls
2. Hard plastic dolls with vinyl heads
3. A popular 10in (25cm) *Fairy* with a mohair wig and wand
4. A 19in (48cm) *Elizabeth* teenage-type doll which was produced for *Woman's Illustrated* magazine. The doll's clothes were designed by the magazine's fashion expert, Veronica Scott. Patterns could be purchased from the magazine.
5. A 20in (51cm) head-turning walking boy doll with flirty eyes and molded curly hair painted brown.
6. Black versions of their popular dolls
7. Well into the 1960s they made hard plastic *Tartan* dolls in 12in (31cm), 14in (36cm), 15in (38cm) and 17in (43cm) sizes. Some of the dolls had musical movements within their body.
8. In the 1960s they made hard plastic character dolls in such natural costumes as *Swiss Miss, Dutch Girl* and *Welsh Girl*. Other character dolls included *Red Riding Hood, Madame Butterfly, Chloe* (black doll), *Kathleen of Ireland, Tommy Atkins, Manuel the Matador* and *Abdul the Turk*.
9. Other character dolls included *Robin Hood, Mary Had a Little Lamb* and *Ride a Cock Horse*.

Little Princess: One of the most desirable Pedigree hard plastic dolls is the lovely *Little Princess* modeled after Princess Anne. She was featured in an article in the magazine *Woman's Illustrated.* She says, "My name is 'Little Princess.' I am a special doll because I'm the first doll in the land. Norman Hartnell, the Queen's Dressmaker has designed the pretty lace trimmed frock I am wearing. All the other dolls will be envious because Normal Hartnell has designed so many pretty clothes for me...Pierre Balmain has planned a Paris wardrobe of clothes for me, too."

SEE: *Illustration 303. Mary Elizabeth Poole Collection.*
Illustration 304. Mary Elizabeth Poole Collection.
PRICE: No sample prices available.

Little Princess: HP; 14in (36cm); jointed at neck, shoulders and legs; blonde mohair wig; lovely color with red cheeks; sleep eyes; white and red dotted dress with red rickrack trim; all original; purchased by owner in 1953.

SEE: *Illustration 305. Mary Elizabeth Poole Collection.*

304.

303.

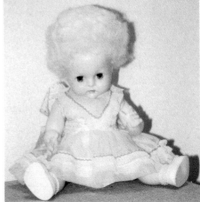

305.

AN IRISH SKIRT AND SHAWL TO MAKE
Designed by Sybil Connolly of Dublin

YOU can make this pretty Irish skirt and shawl for "Little Princess" very easily.

All you need is a piece of bright red, thin felt, 18 inches square. Now cut it into a circle (like the diagram below) which measures 18 inches across. Find the centre of the circle and cut out a round hole measuring 3¼ inches across.

Cut a little slit down from the edge of this circle so that dolly can get into her skirt easily, and fasten opening with a hook and eye.

The shawl is made from a triangle of black woollen material (as in diagram 2), and you can trim it very prettily with wool fringing, that Mummy can make or buy for you.

TWO PIECES . . .
NO SEAMS . . .

306.

307.

308.

Little Princess Pattern: An Irish Skirt and Shawl to Make; Designed by Sybil Connolly of Dublin; 1953.

> SEE: *Illustration 306. Woman's Illustrated*, Special Design. *Mary Elizabeth Poole Collection.*

Doll in Knit Outfit: HP; 22in (56cm); head-turning walker; flirty eyes; washable wig; grill in stomach; open mouth with teeth; pin-jointed walker with unpainted Ideal screw-type pin (see Identification Guide, *Hard Plastic Dolls, I*, page 290B); individual fingers; painted eyelashes under eyes; *Saucy Walker®*-type; circa 1953.

The English people wear their "woolies" for most of the year. Knitting is still popular and mothers and grandmothers make many doll clothes for the children. Because of this, it is sometimes difficult to find original clothes on English dolls. This wonderful doll has a complete knitted outfit including outer wrap, dress, full slip, separate undershirt, panties and shoes. She was purchased in Warwick, England.

> MARKS: "Pedigree//England" (head)
> SEE: *Illustration 307.*
> PRICE: $80-90

Pin-Up Doll: HP; 14in (36cm); "Magic Nylon" blonde hair; face slightly different from the Ideal *Toni®* doll but the body is almost the same; skin tone darker and brighter; bright red cheeks which are traditional with English dolls; Y on backside; came with "Pin-Up Play Perm Wave Kit," creme shampoo; 1952. There were six dolls in different "teenage" dresses.

> MARKS: "Pedigree//Made in England" (head)
> SEE: *Illustration 308. Pat Parton Collection.*
> PRICE: $65-85 (in original clothes)

Saucy Walker® is a registered trademark of the Ideal Toy Corp.
Toni® is a registered trademark of The Gillette Co.

185

309.

Costume Dolls: European HP; 6½in (15cm); sleep eyes with hand-painted lashes above eyes; no molded lashes; pretty faces; non-walkers; doll on left has shoes and socks painted over the mold; doll on right has no paint on feet. These dolls were sold to companies in European countries as well as in Great Britain who dressed them in provincial outfits and sold them as "tourist" dolls in their own country. These dolls are of excellent quality.

    MARKS: "Made in England" (body)
    SEE: *Illustration 309. Marge Meisinger Collection.*
    PRICE: $30-35

310.

Delite Doll: HP; 7in (18cm); jointed at neck and arms only; blue sleep eyes with no lashes; molded non-painted hair; mitten hands with deep dimples above each finger; "Precision moulding for true to life definition of limbs; modelled by a sculptor — a specialist in doll design" (printed on side of box); 1950s.

    MARKS: "Pedigree (in triangle//Made in//England" (back); "Pedigree Delite Dolls" (box)
    SEE: *Illustration 310.*
    PRICE: $6-7 (in box)

Toddler: HP; (22cm); wind-up walking doll; circa 1953.

    SEE: *Illustration 311. Woman's Illustrated. Mary Elizabeth Poole Collection.*

311.

Pressman Toy Corp.

Fever Doll with Hospital Bed: HP; 7in (18cm); part of doctor-nurse set; painted eyes; open mouth for thermometer; mechanism to make face red on inside of jaw; jointed arms and legs only; bed is 8½in (22cm); bed fully HP; windup crank operates a hospital bed, came in doctor-nurse sets; circa 1955.

Advertisement says, "This super-realistic Doctor-Nurse-Small Fry Hospital set featuring the Fever Doll — a 'patient' that actually runs a temperature and gets red in the face when lowered on the adjustable hospital bed."

MARKS: "Pressman Toy Corporation//Made in U.S.A.//Pat. Pend." (doll)
SEE: *Illustration 312.* (left)
      Illustration 313. Playthings, March 1955. (right)
PRICE: $25 (for working set)

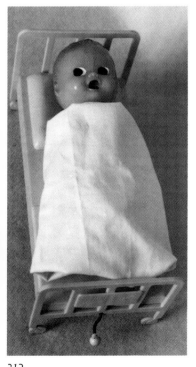

312.

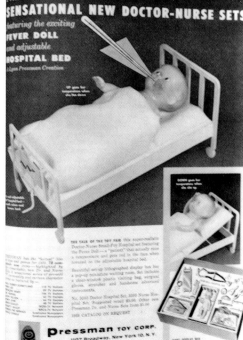

313.

Reina Doll Corp.

The registered trademarks, the trademarks and the copyrights appearing in italics within this chapter belong to Reina Doll Corp.

Best Dressed Doll in America: HP; 13in (33cm); fully jointed; mohair wigs; hand-painted faces; packed individually in gift window box; 1950.

SEE: *Illustration 314. Playthings,* March 1950.

PRICE: $15-25

314.

Reliable Toy Co. Ltd./Ltee (Canada)

The registered trademarks, the trademarks and the copyrights appearing in italics within this chapter belong to Reliable Toy Co. Ltd/Ltee.

Established in 1920 in Toronto, Canada, the Reliable Toy Co. has a long tradition of making fine dolls. Originally they manufactured stuffed animals but in 1933 they started to make dolls. In that year they made a *Shirley Temple* doll.

Through World War II the company made composition dolls. Two of their most popular were *Maggie Muggins* and Olympic champion ice skater *Barbara Ann Scott.*

According to Mr. L. S. Samuels, the hard plastic or injection mold process dolls were excellent dolls but expensive to make. Reliable made the doll bodies themselves, and they have been one of the few doll makers on this continent to continue this rather than relying on foreign makers.

Probably their most famous doll during the hard plastic era was the *Queen Elizabeth II* doll made for the coronation. (See page 94.)

Plassikins: HP; 15in (38cm); head-turning hip-pin walker with painted outside pins (see Identification Guide, *Hard Plastic Dolls, I,* page 290A); sleep eyes with molded lashes; open/closed mouth with two painted teeth; excellent color with rosy cheeks; diamond seat pattern (see Identification Guide, *Hard Plastic Dolls, I,* page 282A); all original pink glazed cotton dress and hat; brown shoes; circa 1954.

MARKS: "Reliable" in script (back)

SEE: *Illustration 315* (Color Section, page 224).

PRICE: $55-80

Dress-Me Doll: HP; 12in (31cm); sleep eyes; very pointed eyebrows; jointed at neck and shoulders only; wig; four fingers molded together; sold in sealed plastic bags; circa 1956-1962.

MARKS: "Reliable" (back)
"Reliable//all plastic//Dress Me Doll//Sleeping Eyes// Movable head and arms; Reliable Toy Co. Limited// Toronto.Montreal.Vancouver." (cardboard at top of plastic bag)
SEE: *Illustration 316. Elsie Ogden Collection.*
PRICE: $10-15

Indian: dark HP; 11in (28cm); gold flannel Indian outfit; multi-colored braid trim and headband; sleep brown eyes; molded lashes; small tuft of mohair attached to front of painted molded hair; circa mid 1950s.

MARKS: "Reliable//Made in Canada" (body)
SEE: *Illustration 317. Pat Parton Collection.*
PRICE: $25-30

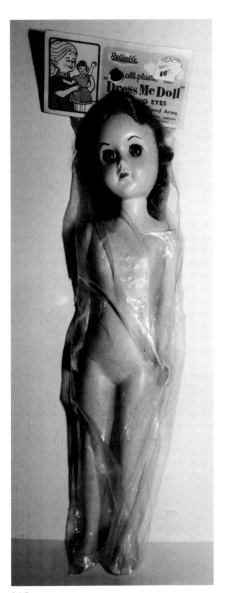

316.

317.

189

Richwood Toys, Inc.

The registered trademarks, the trademarks and the copyrights appearing in italics within this chapter belong to Richwood Toys, Inc., unless otherwise noted.

The Richwood Enterprises Company was located in Annapolis, Maryland, and made a *Ginny*-type doll before *Ginny* was named. *Sandra Sue* dates from the late 1940s to the late 1950s. Her beautiful wardrobe followed the style changes of the period.

Sandra Sue was made first with a flat foot to accommodate little girl and sports clothes. Later she was made with a high-heeled foot when the mature fashions were popular. (See Identification Guide, page 239.) Like the Alexander *Elise* doll with the jointed foot and the Cosmopolitan *Ginger* with the Cha Cha Heel, the *Sandra Sue* doll offered a choice to mothers who were concerned about the new mature dolls.

The following features were advertised:
1. Slender figure designed for stylish clothes.
2. Ball jointed and can sit, stand, move her head and arms.
3. Walking doll with a smooth all-metal mechanism.
4. A beautiful face created by a famous sculptor (possibly Agop Agopoff).
5. Moving eyes with tiny eyelashes.
6. Hand-decorated face with a different expression on each doll.
7. Saran wig which is stitchblocked, durable, washable and combable.
8. Porcelain-like finish specially processed on all parts.
9. A hospitalization policy which gave an exclusive lifetime guarantee of unbreakability.
10. A playworld of clothes, furniture, accessories and play equipment scaled just for her.

Sandra Sue Skater: HP; 8in (20cm); walker head does not turn; sleep eyes; highly arched, thin, dark orange eyebrows and eyelashes below the eyes; closed mouth; thin legs; flat feet; 1st, 2nd and 3rd fingers molded together; Y on seat; loop arm hook (see Identification Guide, *Hard Plastic Dolls, I*, page 263F); all original clothes; red flannel skating skirt and pants; blue knit sweater with white over sweater trimmed with braid; white mittens; red stockinette cap; white skates; red knee socks; blonde hair; mid 1950s.
  MARKS: "2" (inside of right arm); "0" (inside of left arm)
  SEE: *Illustration 318* (Color Section, page 220).
  PRICE: $65-80

Louisa May Alcott Dolls, Beth, Amy, Marmee, Meg and *Jo:* the company brochure says "The charm and wholesomeness of the real life story of Louisa May Alcott's 'Little Women' make it a favorite of girls today just as it was one of mine. It gives me great pleasure to present my interpretaion of the unforgettable characters of Marmee, Meg, Beth, Amy, and Jo in the wonderful book for today's little women."
  SEE: *Illustration 319*. Company brochure from *Kathryn Davis Collection*.
  PRICE: $65-75 each (without box)
    $80-100 each (with box)

Ginny® is a registered trademark of Vogue Dolls, Inc.
Elise® is a registered trademark of The Alexander Doll Co., Inc.
Ginger® is a registered trademark of Cosmopolitan Toy & Doll Corporation.

319.

Sandra Sue Brochure:
"Sandra Sue's trim little figure with its tiny waistline makes it possible for her to have clothes styled in fashions suitable for both the pre-teenage girl and the glamorous young lady. All of her coats have the fitted waist and flared skirts so popular this season.

"Sandra can look so grownup in her beautiful evening gowns and bridal outfits. She can look like a real little girl in her pretty short dresses or her winter sports clothes."
SEE: *Illustration 320.* Richwood Company brochure from *Kathryn Davis Collection.*
PRICE: $25-50 (outfits mint-in-zippered plastic bag)

320.

Sandra Sue Brochure:

Variety is the spice of life, and *Sandra Sue* had an outfit for every occasion. All of the designs in *Sandra Sue's* wardrobe were styles which America's best-dressed little girls were wearing in the 1950s.

SEE: *Illustration 321.* Company brochure from *Kathryn Davis Collection.*

321.

Sandra Sue Brochure:

SEE: *Illustration 322.* Company brochure from *Kathryn Davis Collection.*

322.

Sandra Sue: (for general characteristics, see page 190). This doll was advertised in *Hobbies* magazine. It suggested that this early high-heeled doll was not only a play doll, but it was also an excellent collector's item.

SEE: *Illustration 323. Hobbies,* March and April 1958. *Marge Meisinger Collection.*

SANDRA SUE

First high heel doll to be manufactured in an excellent collector's item, and a little 8" charmer for playtime, too. Available in 4 hair colors as pictured for only $1.98. "Little Women" outfits are $2.98 additional. Folder describing other outfits and Colonial Furniture sent on request. Postage extra.

THE DOLL HOUSE
229 Grand St.,
Morgantown, W. Va.

323.

Sandra Sue: This lovely doll had a beautiful extensive wardrobe. Today these tiny clothes are hard to identify. The following clothes were sold on a hanger in a plastic zippered bag. Accessories were sold in a round plastic container.

1. Accessories: white hat and shoes with various colored jewelry.
   SEE: *Illustration 324. Elsie Ogden Collection.*
   PRICE: $15-20
2. Formal dress: green taffeta long dress trimmed with lavender flowers.
   SEE: *Illustration 325. Elsie Ogden Collection.*
   PRICE: $15-20
3. Playsuit: white top with red shorts.
   SEE: *Illustration 326. Elsie Ogden Collection.*
   PRICE: $15-20

324.　　　　　325.　　　　　326.

Sandra Sue Furniture: "Sandra Sue is proud to be the only doll for whom a complete authentic set of furniture has been designed. The early Colonial homes of historic Annapolis have been the inspiration for this beautiful furniture."
1. Top: genuine mahogany Duncan Phyfe extension table with matching chairs. The table seats four dolls without leaf and six with leaf. The chairs are covered in a provincial print.
2. Left: the mahogany-finish tester bed is almost 12in (31cm) long and comes complete with canopy, bedspread, pillow, pillowcase and mattress. The canopy, bedspread and pillow are of crisp white material. All materials are washable.
3. Right: the 12in (31cm) solid mahogany wardrobe contains a shelf for hats and a hanging bar with tiny hangers for ensembles of clothes.

The *Sandra Sue* dolls were made in Annapolis, Maryland.

SEE: *Illustration 327.* Company brochure from *Kathryn Davis Collection.*

327.

Sandra Sue Furniture Not Pictured:
1. Mahogany chest-on-chest with brass-handled drawers that open.
2. Mahogany vanity and stool with white dimity skirts; mirror.
3. Mahogany bureau with mirror; brass handles; drawers that open.
4. Bright red sliding board with ladder and silver sliding surface.

Additional Clothes Not Pictured: stylish clothes for high-heeled doll (circa 1956-1957).
1. Afternoon dress of powder puff muslin print with wide sash; straw hat.
2. Two-piece nylon polka dot short bridesmaid dress; nylon petticoat; bouquet.
3. Two-piece gold print afternoon party dress with jewel trim; straw hat.
4. Sophisticated evening gown with very full white nylon skirt and strapless red and silver bodice. (See *Hard Plastic Dolls, I,* page 216, *Illustration 473.*)
5. Jewel-trimmed black taffeta tea dance dress; matching hat. (See *Hard Plastic Dolls, I,* page 216, *Illustration 473a.*)
6. Nylon embroidered organdy party dress; matching straw lace hat.
7. Two-piece dress with sheer white nylon top and velvet skirt.
8. Checked taffeta suit with ruffled petticoat; separate jacket; straw hat.
9. Blue jeans with plaid cuffs; matching plaid shirt; white sailor hat.
10. Scotch suit with authentic details; wool jacket; plaid tartan and garters.
11. Bathing suit of jersey with satin panel; beach hat; terry cloth beach jacket.
12. Two-tone organdy party dress with lace trim; contrasting sash and flowers.
13. Velvet and gold tea dance dress; white taffeta petticoat; gold Juliet cap.

Tina Sue: NOT PHOTOGRAPHED (circa 1956-57): *Tina Sue* is an 8in (20cm) jointed soft vinyl baby doll; sparkling sleep eyes with tiny lashes; came with diapers and booties. A spool cradle could be purchased separately.

Cindy Lou: painted HP; 14in (36cm); head-turning walker; pin-jointed knees; auburn wig; beautiful flesh tones; sleep eyes with lashes; arm hooks (see Identification Guide, page 236); painted fingernails; medium blue felt lined skirt, jacket, pants; pink top and gloves; skates are attached to shoes; advertised in December 1951 *House and Garden* magazine; original price was $11.20. Although the brochure says the doll is 14in (36cm), it actually measures almost 15in (38cm).

    MARKS: "Made In U.S.A." in circle (back); box shows a picture of a clock with "Cindy Lou" written across it. Around the clock is "Round the Clock Doll Fashions//Highland, Maryland"

    SEE: *Illustration 328. Marge Meisinger Collection.*

    PRICE: $85-115 (in original clothes)

Cindy Lou "Round the Clock Fashions":

1. Blue taffeta dress with blue velvet trim; gold shoes.
2. Red calico skirt; white top with red rickrack trim; white cotton petticoat.

Clothes came in see-through plastic top box with the clock logo in the lower right corner.

    MARKS: "Round the Clock Fashions" (on box)

    SEE: *Illustration 329. Marge Meisinger Collection.*

    PRICE: $20-30 (boxed outfit)

328.

329.

Cindy Lou Round the Clock Fashion Brochure:
SEE: *Illustration 330. Marge Meisinger Collection.*

330.

SEE: *Illustration 331. Marge Meisinger Collection.*

331.

332.

Roberta Doll Co., Inc.

The registered trademarks, the trademarks and the copyrights appearing in italics within this chapter belong to Roberta Doll Co., Inc.

The Roberta Doll Company was one of the early companies in the hard plastic field. In 1950 they were offering all plastic character dolls, girl dolls, bride dolls and baby dolls (featuring plastic heads with latex and vinyl arms and legs). That year they introduced *Baby Babette*.

SEE: *Illustration 333. Playthings, March 1950.*

333.

197

Rosebud (England)

The Rosebud Company began after World War II. They started with composition dolls but by 1950 they were making baby dolls of hard plastic which were sent around the world until the mid 1960s. *Woman's Weekly* magazine featured *Rosebud* twin dolls and knitted outfits that were designed for them. Readers could send to the magazine to purchase the doll.

Many sizes of dolls were made by injection molding (hard plastic method) from 6in (15cm) to 21in (53cm). However, many of the dolls were small. The famous beautiful Rosebud doll box was popular with English children everywhere.

Rosebud and Mattel of the United States began to work together in 1964 as each started with the pull string talking mechanism. Mattel took over Rosebud in 1967.

Chiltern was a company which marketed Rosebud dolls. Their coronation *Peeress* was issued in 1953 dressed in velvet and wearing a tiara. This was in honor of the Queen's coronation that year. (See Coronation Section, page 75 and Color Section, page 94.)

Baby: HP; 5½in (14cm); sleep eyes; molded hair; very rosy cheeks; Ÿ on backside; two dimples in each knee; unusual right hand construction; 2nd, 3rd and 4th fingers folded under which allows the baby to suck its thumb; left hand has individual fingers; doll was sent to owner from South Africa; 1950s to the mid 1960s. This was a very popular doll which was sold around the world. Stores in Sweden, in particular, sold many of these dolls.
MARKS: "Rosebud//Made//In//England" (back)
SEE: *Illustration 334. Virginia Ann Heyerdahl Collection.*
PRICE: $15-25

Fairy Dolls: HP; 6½in (16cm); jointed at arms only; net dress with gold sparkle trim; Ÿ backside; sleep eyes; individual fingers; usually boxed in lovely Rosebud box; sent to the owner from South Africa; mid 1950s.
MARKS: "Rosebud//Made in England//Patent Pending" (body)
SEE: *Illustration 335. Virginia Ann Heyerdahl Collection.*
PRICE: $25-35

334.
335.

Baby Rosebud Toddler: HP; 6½in (17cm); came in beautiful box; sold as a "Dress-Me" type of doll; mothers and grandmothers often crocheted or knitted "woolies" for this doll; mid 1950s.

MARKS: "Rosebud//Made in England//Patent Pending" (body)

SEE: *Illustration 336. Virginia Ann Heyerdahl Collection.*

PRICE: $25-35

336.

Miss Rosebud: HP; 7½in (19cm); painted eyelashes above sleep eyes; 3rd and 4th fingers joined together; non-walker; all original pink net dress with pink embroidery and blue net trim; pink underdress; parasol of same material and color; unusual medieval style dress; circa mid 1950s.

MARKS: "Miss Rosebud" (body); "Rosebud" (head)

SEE: *Illustration 337* (Color Section, page 167). *Virginia Ann Heyerdahl Collection.*

PRICE: $35-40

Miss Rosebud: HP; 7in (18cm); sleep eyes; no eyelashes; excellent quality doll; red dress; red striped apron; sold as a tourist doll in Copenhagen; mid 1950s.

MARKS: "Miss Rosebud" (back); "Gudrun//Formby//Danish Design// Copenhagaen Denmark (tag)

SEE: *Illustration 338. Marge Meisinger Collection.*

PRICE: $30-35

338.

Miss Rosebud (doll on right): HP; 7in (18cm); (for general characteristics, see *Illustration 337*); painted lashes above eyes; mohair wig; non-walker; had two different types of feet; dolls were often dressed in national costumes; mid 1950s.

Sarold Girl (doll on left): 7in (18cm); jointed at neck, shoulders and hips; unusual molded, painted raised eyebrows; metal arm hook (see Identification Guide, page 235); non-walker; mid 1950s.
> MARKS: "Miss Rosebud" (back);
> "Sarold" (back)
> SEE: *Illustration 339. Marge Meisinger Collection.*
> PRICE: $30-35 each

Miss Rosebud: HP; 7½in (19cm); straight-leg walker; painted eyelashes above eyes; dressed in kilt and black velvet jacket; *Ginny*-type doll; mid 1950s.
> MARKS: "Rosebud" signed in script (head)
> SEE: *Illustration 340. Barbara Comienski Collection.*
> PRICE:$30-35

339.

340.

Société Français Fabrication Bébé et Jouets

The registered trademarks, the trademarks and the copyrights appearing in italics within this chapter belong to the Société Français Fabrication Bébé et Jouets.

Like most other doll manufacturers throughout the world, S.F.B.J. began experimenting with doll molds after World War II. By 1947 they had begun to produce dolls using modern plastic material. During the early 1950s they made dolls in both rigid and flexible plastics. Their hair styles and clothes followed the latest fashions for French children. In keeping with modern clothes, these dolls often wore sportswear including slacks and bathing suits.

Girl: composition-plastic body; lighter plastic head; 15in (38cm); jointed at neck, shoulders and hips; inset eyes; lovely flesh tone on face; closed mouth; early 1950s.
MARKS: "Jumeau" (head)
SEE: *Illustration 341. Roslyn Nigoff Collection.*
PRICE: $85-125 + (in original clothes)

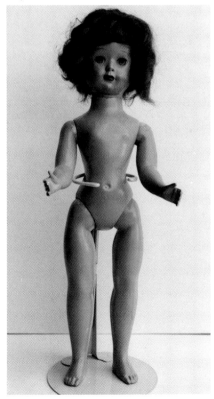

341.

Sarold (England)

The registered trademarks, the trademarks and the copyrights appearing in italics within this chapter belong to Sarold.

342.

Girl: HP; 8in (20cm); jointed at neck, shoulders and hips; no defined toes; molded raised eyebrows; metal arm hook (see Identification Guide, page 235); dolls have different faces but otherwise have same characteristics; non-walking doll; early 1950s. Sarold registered a trademark number 689831 on June 14, 1950. They made inexpensive dolls and are believed to have sold quantities of hard plastic dolls to Woolworths. (See World Wide Dolls, page 230 and Rosebud Dolls, page 198).

MARKS: "Sarold" (body)
SEE: *Illustration 342. Marge Meisinger Collection.*
PRICE: $20-30 (in original clothes)
IDENTIFICATION FEATURE: Raised eyebrows

Sayco Doll Corporation

The registered trademarks, the trademarks and the copyrights appearing in italics within this chapter belong to Sayco Doll Corporation.

The *Miss America Pageant Doll* was made about 1959 which was later than most of the other "chubby" hard plastic type dolls. There is only one picture of her in this book but there is a large section in *Glamour Dolls of the 1950s and 1960s*, pages 203-206. There are pictures of her entire wardrobe of 50 costumes. Her wardrobe reflects the fashion changes at the end of the 1950s: (see Identification Guide, page 247 for gripper snap fastener).
MARKS: "s" (head); or "Sayco" (head); or some dolls are unmarked.

343.

Miss America Pageant Doll-Wave: HP with vinyl head; 10¾in (27cm); brochure says 11in (28cm); rooted hair; excellent flesh color with rosy cheeks; unusually long eyebrows; sleep eyes with molded lashes; no painted eyelashes; flat, but beautiful face; small gap between neck and head; jointed at shoulders, neck, hips and knees; arm hooks (see Identification Guide, *Hard Plastic Dolls, I*, page 268U); individual fingers; dimples above fingers but not toes; "chubby" type; original Wave uniform; metal stars on collar; red chevron on sleeve; pocketbook with USA on it; doll came with 50 outfits which could be purchased; circa 1959.

    MARKS: Small "s" (head)

    SEE: *Illustration 343.*

    PRICE: $50-70 (including box and brochure)
              $25-50 (outfits)

Dream Girl Costume: Sayco made a line of outfits called *Dream Girl* which fit all 8in (20cm) walking dolls. One of these included a pretty pink felt skirt and pink sweater set; white shoes; the inner part of the gripper snap on the skirt says, "Dot Snapper;" circa 1955-1957.

    MARKS: "Dream Girl//by Sayco// Sayco Doll Corp." (box)

    SEE: *Illustration 344. Pat Parton Collection.*

    PRICE: $10-12

344.

Standard Doll Co.

The registered trademarks, the trademarks and the copyrights appearing in italics within this chapter belong to Standard Doll Co.

Ar-Doll Debuteens: HP; 15in (38cm); character dolls; sleep eyes; Saran hair that can be shampooed, combed, washed and curled; series includes a *Bride, Bridesmaid, Glamour Girl, Cinderella, Carmen* and *Alice in Wonderland*; unusual talking dolls with human voices; 1951.

Miniature Character Dolls: HP; 8in (20cm) sleep eyes with lashes; series includes *Brides, Bridesmaids, Dolls of all Nations* and *Famous Characters of Fact and Fiction*; 1951.

    SEE: *Illustration 345. Playthings,* March 1951.

    PRICE: $20-25 15in (38cm)
              $10-12 8in (20cm)

345.

Stephanie Playthings, Inc.

The registered trademarks, the trademarks and the copyrights appearing in italics within this chapter belong to Stephanie Playthings, Inc.

346.

Stephanie and *Stephan:* HP; 30in (76cm); walking dolls; 1950.
> SEE: *Illustration 346. Playthings,* June 1950.
> PRICE: $80-90 each

Tanzpuppe-Sweetheart (Western Germany)

The registered trademarks, the trademarks and the copyrights appearing in italics within this chapter belong to Tanzpuppe-Sweetheart.

347.

Vatican Guard: European HP; 7in (18cm) key wind dancer; molded hair; red, yellow and purple felt uniform; black tam; circa 1960s.
> MARKS: "Western Germany" (leg); "Tanzuppe DBGM1669844" (box)
> SEE: *Illustration 347.*
> PRICE: $18-25

Terri Lee, Inc.

The registered trademarks, the trademarks and the copyrights appearing in italics within this chapter belong to Terri Lee, Inc., unless otherwise noted.

Terri Lee and Jerri Welcome a New Baby Sister: HP; 16in (41cm); glued-on wig of various colors; distinctive features and eyes which are painted; very heavy doll; many clothes available that were all well made; red dots painted in nose like old china dolls; thicker lips than the *Mary Jane®* which is a *Terri Lee* look-alike; four fingers molded together with separate thumb; single line on seat. *Linda Lee* is an all-vinyl doll; 1951.

> MARKS: Early doll "Terri Lee, Pat. Pending;" later doll marked "Terri Lee"
> SEE: *Illustration 348. Playthings,* March 1951.
> PRICE: $200-250 (dolls with special outfits may be much higher)

Gene Autry: HP; 16in (41cm); (see general characteristics for *Terri Lee* dolls, *Illustration 348*); face painted differently; original red checked shirt; blue jeans; brown belt; 1947.

> MARKS: "Terri Lee, Pat. Pending" (body)
> SEE: *Illustration 349. Kathy George Collection.*
> PRICE: $500-600 (very few sample prices available)

Benjie: HP; 16in (41cm); (see general characteristics for *Terri Lee* dolls, Illustration 348); lamb's wool wig; white sweater top with red trim; red short pants; red and white socks; white hat; 1952.

> MARKS: "Terri Lee" (back)
> SEE: *Illustration 350. Kathy George Collection.*
> PRICE: $350-450 (very few sample prices available)

Mary Jane® is a registered trademark of G., H. and E. Freydberg, Inc.

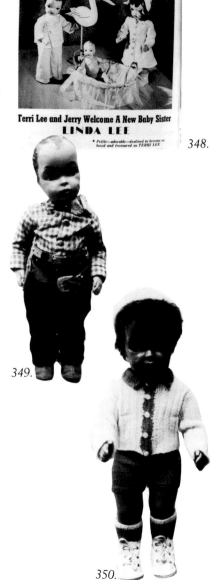

Terri Lee and Jerry Welcome A New Baby Sister **LINDA LEE**
• Petite—adorable—destined to become so loved and treasured as TERRI LEE
348.

349.

350.

Southern Belle: HP; 16in (41cm); (for general characteristics, see page   ); catalog description of outfit says, "Here I am, a true Southern Belle in taffeta dress, trimmed in narrow black velvet ribbon. I wear a rosebud chintz apron and large bow in my curls. My full petticoat and long pantaloons are eyelet trimmed. Whenever I wear this costume, Jerri pretends he's a gallant gentleman from the deep South."

   MARKS: "Terri Lee, Pat. Pending" (back)
   SEE: *Illustration 351* (Color Section, page 217).
   PRICE: $275-300

A Day in the Life of Terri Lee: HP; (for general characteristics see, *Illustration 348*); E. toe dancing costume of silver lamé and nylon tulle; silver kid toe slippers; F. official Brownie uniform; G. gay squaw skirt and white blouse in cotton; H. percale playdress in assorted colors; J. silver lamé evening coat with taffeta lining, formal gown of nylon tulle, satin and taffeta in pastels, silver slippers; K. lounging pajamas, housecoat, felt Elly Elf slippers; L. nylon can-can slip and panties; 1951.
D. *Baby Linda* is all vinyl. A layette, playpen and wardrobe trunk could be purchased separately.

   SEE: *Illustration 352.* May Company, Cleveland, Ohio, Christmas catalog, 1951.

352.

Tiny Terri and Tiny Jerri: HP; 10in (25cm); glued-on wigs; *Jerry* has a fur wig; sleep eyes; head-turning walker; painted features that are identified with *Terri Lee*; 1st, 2nd and 3rd, fingers molded together; red and blue checked matching shirts and blue jeans; circa 1956.

   MARKS: "C" (back in circle)
   SEE: *Illustration 353* (Color Section, page 218).
   PRICE: $135-150 (*Tiny Terri Lee*)
                      $170-185 (*Tiny Jerri Lee*)

206

Terri Lee Get in the Swim: HP; (for general characteristics see, page 205); beach bag and swim kit complete with beach sandals, beach towel, sunglasses, sunsuit, bandana, beach coat, swimsuit, and life saver; 1953.

 SEE: *Illustration 354. Playthings,* June 1953.

Jerri Lee, Tiny Jerri, Connie Lynn, Tiny Terri, Terri Lee; Baby Linda: matching outfits; cotton clothes with striped trim in various colors; 1957.

 SEE: *Illustration 355. Toys and Novelties,* February 1957.

354.   355.

Togs and Dolls Corp.

Mary Jane: HP body and vinyl head; unusual large sleep eyes with lashes; golden brown hair; jointed at neck, arms and legs; head-turning walker; 2nd and 3rd fingers molded together; dimples below fingers and on knees; all original; pink checked dress with white lace and black ribbon and rickrack trim; black leather shoes; circa 1955-1957.

 MARKS: None (doll); "My name is Mary Jane//I am made of Celanese acetate plastic//I have 36 pretty outfits//Do you have them all?" (tag)

SEE: *Illustration 356.*
PRICE: $75-100

356.

Uneeda Doll Company, Inc.

The registered trademarks, the trademarks and the copyrights appearing in italics within this chapter belong to Uneeda Doll Company, Inc.

Needa Toddles: HP head; vinyl arms and legs which are wired on; composition body; 22in (56cm); open mouth with two teeth; dimples on knees; walking apparatus advertised as "Magic Muscle;" Saran wig with curly hair; 1951.
A 1952 advertisement gives the height as 23in (58cm). The doll pictured has long braids.
    MARKS: Some dolls have a "20" on head
    SEE: *Illustration 357. Playthings*, September 1951.
    PRICE: $65-85

Magic Fairy Princess Doll: HP body with vinyl head; 18in (46cm); pink rooted hair; jointed at neck, shoulders, hips and knees; sleep eyes; original fairy costume; white satin top; white net tutu with glitter; plastic wings; silver slippers; circa 1957.
    MARKS: "Uneeda" (head); "210" (body); "The//Magic//Fairy//Princess Doll//
            Walks, Sits, Bends//Her Knees//Rooted//Washable Hair//by Uneeda" (tag)
    SEE: *Illustration 358. Roslyn Nigoff Collection.*
    PRICE: $50-70

357.

358.

Unica (Belgium)

The registered trademarks, the trademarks and the copyrights appearing in italics within this chapter belong to Unica.

    The Unica Company was founded in 1921 and made many beautiful and innovative dolls. By 1940 it had become one of the most important manufacturers in Europe, employing up to 400 people and using the most advanced techniques.

    Its premises were destroyed during World War II but by 1950 it again had become a prominent manufacturer. In the early 1960s its activities slacked down because it had failed to understand the growing demand for cheaper items. It did not cope with the ever-growing competition of cheap labor from the Orient.

    In 1971 a fire completely destroyed the manufacturing facilities, archives, and so forth. The owners decided not to reconstruct the plant and converted their activities to wholesaling of general toys.

    Since then they have become one of the leading toy importers and distributors in Belgium. The dolls made by Unica, especially in the periods 1930-1939 and 1947-1965, are much in demand by collectors but very few seem to be left.

    The above information came from J. Libeer, Managing Director of the present Unica Company.

Many of the dolls have a deep tan skin tone and they are very beautiful and cleverly designed. They are usually well marked, often with a crown of some type. Like many of the hard plastic dolls made outside of the United States, the hard plastic doll in *Illustration 359* has a cryer placed inside.

Blonde Rooted Hair Doll: European HP; 14in (36cm); head covered with unusual rubber cap holding rooted blonde hair which is glued to head; cap can be seen in photograph; brilliant blue sleep eyes with lashes; 2nd and 3rd fingers molded together; cryer inside body; clothes not original; circa 1955-1958.

> **MARKS:** "UNICA//(Picture of Crown)//Belgium" (back)
> **SEE:** *Illustration 359. Private Collection.*
> **PRICE:** $35-50

359.

Valentine Dolls, Inc.

The registered trademarks, the trademarks and the copyrights appearing in italics within this chapter belong to Valentine Dolls, Inc.

Mona Lisa: HP; 12in (31cm); painted lashes under sleep eyes; jointed at neck, arms and hips; molded P.M.A. shoes under regular shoes (see *Hard Plastic Dolls, I*, Identification Guide, page 283A); unusually flat arms; doll came with wardrobe in trunk; original dress with yellow piqué skirt and sleeves, white top and trim; other clothes include a blue striped taffeta dress and pants with lace trim; red cotton print bathing suit with white and navy print towel; blue plastic bathing hat; extra shoes and socks; two curlers on card; circa mid 1950s.

> **MARKS:** "Your new Mona Lisa Doll has Saran hair that can be washed-combed-waved-curled"; (tag); none (doll)
> **SEE:** *Illustration 360* (Color Section, page 223). *Pat Parton Collection.*
> **PRICE:** $60-80

Ballerina Dolls: HP with vinyl head; height unknown; initial offering by company of a ballerina doll that was jointed at the knee and ankle; shoes by Capezio.

Dressmaker Doll: HP; sewing form came with doll; no patterns needed; trimmings and basic materials and sleeve board included; brochure explained the few simple steps to follow.

> **MARKS:** Not given in advertisement but these dolls often had "VW" and a number on their heads
> **SEE:** *Illustration 361. Playthings,* April 1955.
> **PRICE:** $45-65 each

361.

Virga Doll Company

The registered trademarks, the trademarks and the copyrights appearing in italics within this chapter belong to Virga Doll Company, unless otherwise noted.

The Beehler Arts Company had several divisions of their company which sold many different lines of dolls. As early as August 1949 they advertised their 5in (13cm) Virga Doll series in *Playthings*.

In the mid 1950s their various divisions made *Ginny*® look-alikes that were called *Lucy, GoGo, Lolly Pop, Play-mates, Play-Pals, Kim*®, *Pam*®, *Ninette*® and *Starlet Lustercreme Shampoo Doll*®, and others. The quality of their dolls was uneven and they offered dolls in most price ranges. Each year they presented a new line of dolls, clothes and accessories which were colorful and appealed to children.

For the most part, the *Ginny*®-type dolls had the same body characteristics but like most of the doll companies of the 1950s, they purchased from the manufacturers of doll parts and often took what was available. The list of doll characteristics given on page 112 of the Fortune chapter applies to the majority of the Beehler Arts dolls.

Virga Doll Series: HP; 5in (13cm); 12 in series; dolls wear pastel dresses which illustrate nursery rhymes; five have colorful party dresses; the bridal party consists of a bride, maid-of-honor and bridesmaid; jointed at neck, shoulders and hips; facial coloring and shoes have special lacquer paint; 1949.
Beehler Arts was one of the first companies to sell hard plastic dolls. Their extensive Virga line was popular for many years.
Illustrated are 1. a nursery rhyme doll; 2. a party doll with a feather on her hat; 3. bride.
    MARKS: None (doll)
    SEE: *Illustration 362. Playthings*, August 1949.

The party doll, the bride and the nursery-rhyme doll are representative of the Five-Inch Virga Doll series in which each doll is patterned after the same mold.

362.

Lolly-Pop Walking Doll: HP; 8in (20cm); head-turning walker; Fortune *Pam*® characteristics except for arm hook; standard arm hook (see Identification Guide, *Hard Plastic Dolls, I*, page 265K); molded-on slippers (see Identification Guide, *Illustration 431*); purple rayon embossed dress with white nylon trim; purple wig, all original clothes; mid 1950s.

Poem on box: A Virga Doll for little girls.
Has hair that washes, also curls.
A Virga doll to dress and play,
The perfect doll to share your day.

MARKS: None on doll; "Virga//play//mates//LOLLY-POP//WALKING DOLL" (box)

SEE: *Illustration 363* (Color Section, page 219).

PRICE: $50-80+ (in box)

Playmate in Jodhpurs: HP; 8in (20cm); head-turning walker; for general characteristics, see Fortune section, page 112; all original; red jodhpurs; red flannel jacket and hat; black boots; mid 1950s.

The *Kim*® doll on page 141 has the same riding outfit as the Virga doll. Both dolls were made by the same company and marketed under a different name.

MARKS: None (body); "Virga//play//mates//WALKING DOLL//Riding Habit 198" (box)

SEE: *Illustration 364.*

PRICE: $50-80+

364.

Schiaparelli GoGo Skater: HP; 8in (20cm); (see page 112 for general characteristics); of Fortune-Virga and other Beehler Arts dolls.

Madame Schiaparelli, the French clothes designer of the 1950s, designed a line of beautiful clothes for the Virga Company (see *Hard Plastic Dolls, I*, page 241 and *Glamour Dolls of the 1950s and 1960s*, page 220 for more information).

MARKS: None (doll); "Schiaparelli" (tag sewn into dress)

SEE: *Illustration 365. Nancy Carlton Collection.*

PRICE: $85-100 (more for exceptional costumes)

Kim® is a registered trademark of Kim Doll Co.
Pam® is a registered trademark of Fortune Toys, Inc.   365.

Lucy: HP; 9in (23cm); blonde wig; sleep eyes with molded lashes; high arched eyebrow; head-turning walker; standard arm hooks; jointed at neck, shoulders and hips; individual fingers; dimples above each finger; two dimples on each knee; excellent toe detail; no dimples above toes; boxed clothes include a white piqué dress with red polka dot top and cape; blue polka dot plastic rain cape; green felt jacket, shoes, stockings, and so forth; circa 1955.

    MARKS: None (doll); "My Name Is Lucy 'I walk'//by Virga" (printed on inside of box)

    SEE: *Illustration 366. Marge Meisinger Collection.*

    PRICE: $50-80 (in box)

366.

Play-Pals Walking Doll: HP; 9in (23cm); pin-jointed head-turning walker; sleep eyes; molded lashes; blonde mohair wig; pointed painted eyebrows; individual fingers; dots over fingers; no dots over toes; deep impression under nose; beautiful flesh tone with rosy cheeks; two dimples on each knee; wardrobe includes white and pink dress trimmed with lace; pink robe with blue bias trim; yellow pajamas with pink bias trim; inside part of gripper snap says "RAU SKLIKITS;" circa mid 1950s.

    MARKS: None (doll); "Virga Play-Pals//Walking Doll//Manufactured by Beehler Arts Ltd." (box)

    SEE: *Illustration 367. Pat Parton Collection.*

    PRICE: $50-80 (in box)

367.

Hi Heel 'Teen:

This doll was an inexpensive doll which competed with the "glamour" high-heeled dolls which were popular about 1957-1965. The Beehler Arts Company had several marketing companies which sold these dolls using similar boxes, but colored differently. The dolls had several different names including *Kim®*. They had fashionable but inexpensive clothes. The thin jointed legs are an identification feature (see Identification Guide, page 242).

MARKS: None (doll); boxes marked with the name of the marketing company of the doll.

Hi-Heel 'Teen: HP; 8½in (22cm); sleep eyes with painted eyelashes above eyes; platinum hair; excellent flesh color; jointed at neck, arms, legs and above knees; high-heeled feet; 2nd and 3rd fingers molded together and curved toward hand; sharp mold lines on arms and legs; unusually thin legs (see Identification Guide, page 242); standard arm hooks (see Identification Guide, *Hard Plastic Dolls, I,* page 265); head-turning walker; flannel dress with black top trimmed with lace and print skirt; black pillbox-type hat with large red rose; all original; circa 1956-1957. It competed with the Alexander *Cissette®*. (See also *Kim®* dolls, page 140).

MARKS: None (doll); "Beautiful Virga Dolls//Hi-Heel 'Teen//manufactured by Beehler Arts Ltd.//H-H 3" (box)

368.

SEE: *Illustration 368.*
PRICE: $20-25

Hi Heel 'Teen: HP; 8½in (22cm); same characteristics as the other *Hi Heel 'Teen, Illustration 368;* blue taffeta dress and blue net overskirt with glitter; pink high-heel shoes; all original; circa 1956-1957.

MARKS: None (doll); "Beautiful Virga Dolls//Hi-Heel 'Teen//manufactured by Beehler Arts//H-H 3" (box)

SEE: *Illustration 369. Pat Parton Collection.*
PRICE: $20-25   *369.*

213

Vogue Dolls, Inc.

The registered trademarks, the trademarks and the copyrights appearing in italics within this chapter belong to Vogue Dolls, Inc.

Mrs. Jennie Graves, the founder of the Vogue Doll Company, experimented with different materials and types of dolls from 1922 until 1947-1948. With the advent of hard plastic, she changed the material of her composition *Toddles* dolls to hard plastic and continued their popular size and styles. Her first 1948-1949 dolls in the new material look very much like *Toddles*.

She also experimented with a variety of names. The beloved name *Ginny* did not appear until 1952. Other early post-war dolls were *Crib Crowd*, *Far-Away Lands*, *Story Book Characters*, *Sister-Brother Sets* and many others.

This book features some beautiful examples of these early dolls.

Mother and Daughter: HP; 14in (36cm) and 8in (20cm); unusual advertisement for dolls with matching outfits; *Mother* doll similar to a composition doll made about 1943; the composition doll was unmarked; 1949.
The dolls in the photograph on the right were not advertised as *Ginny*. They were just 8in (20cm) dolls with "Sunday Best" clothes.
SEE: *Illustration 370. Playthings*, August 1949.

Painted-Eye Ginny Twins: HP; 8in (20cm); mohair wigs; girl dressed in pink skirt and sweater set; boy dressed in matching pink pants and sweater set; both have stockinette caps; all original; 1948-1950.
MARKS: "Vogue" (head); "Vogue" (body)
SEE: *Illustration 371* (Color Section, page 221). *Sandra Strater Collection.*
PRICE: $275-350 each (depending on outfit)

Cinderella, Prince and Fairy Godmother: HP; 8in (20cm); painted eye; strung; non-walking; 1949. (upper right in advertisement). **PRICE:** $275-350 each
Crib Crowd: HP; 8in (20cm); painted eyes; strung; non-walking; babies; 1949. (center left in advertisement) These dolls were advertised as "miniature mites with curly foundation wigs." **PRICE:** $500-550 each
Vogue Velva Wetting Baby: All HP fittings; 15in (38cm); filled with 100% foam rubber; made and tested in the laboratories of the Fuller Brush Company; will not pull apart under 65 pounds pressure; 1949 (bottom left in advertisement)
SEE: *Illustration 372. Playthings*, September 1949.

370.

372.

Fluffy: HP; 8in (20cm); marked "Fluffy" on box; sleep eyes with painted lashes above the eyes; straight legs; "Poodle" hair; green "poodle" suit; pink and green ears; non-walking; circa 1950.

    MARKS: "Vogue" (head); "Vogue" (body)

    SEE: *Illustration 373. Pat Timmons Collection.*

PRICE: $500-600+

373.

Ginny Cowboy and Cowgirl: HP; 8in (20cm); strung non-walker; sleep eyes with painted eyelashes; girl's eyes are brown; the boy's eyes are blue; both have brown mohair wigs; both wear red felt hats; green center snap shoes; green belts with tiny metal guns; both have plaid shirts; girl has cream-colored leather-type skirt with multi-colored trim at bottom; matching vest is trimmed in red rickrack; boy has same vest; pants are cream-colored felt in back with the front made to look like chaps made of sheepskin; 1951.

    MARKS: "Vogue Doll" (back)

    SEE: *Illustration 374. Athena Crowley Collection.*

PRICE: $300-350 each

374.

Toddler: HP; 8in (20cm); non-walker; strung; sleep eyes with painted lashes above eyes; straight legs; pink satin print dress; matching panties; pink straw hat with cloth daisies; pink shoes; blue socks; circa 1951-1952.

    MARKS: "Vogue" (head); "Vogue" (body)

    SEE: *Illustration 375. Nancy Roeder Collection.*

PRICE: $275-325

375.

Black Ginny: HP; 8in (20cm); sleep eyes with painted lashes; early non-walker; straight legs; pink dress with blue trim; 1952. A walker was made later.

  MARKS: "Vogue" (head); "Vogue" (body)

  SEE: *Illustration 376. Marge Meisinger Collection.*

  PRICE: $700 up (very few sample prices)

Painted Eyelash Ginny: HP; 8in (20cm); blonde poodle cut wig; sleep eyes with painted eyelashes above eyes; green felt coat with red rickrack trim; green checked dress; red ribbon in hair; all original; circa 1952.

  MARKS: "Vogue" (head); "Vogue" (body)

  SEE: *Illustration 377. Marianne Gardner Collection.*

  PRICE: $250-300

Ginny Roller Skater: HP; 8in (20cm); blonde poodle cut wig; sleep eyes with painted eyelashes above eyes; red and white skating costume; red snap shoes with skates; excellent condition with good color; 1952.

  SEE: *Illustration 378. Marianne Gardner Collection.*

  PRICE: $250-350

376.

377.

378.

Continued on page 225.

Terri Lee *Southern Belle* (see page 206).

Terri Lee *Tiny Jerri* and *Tiny Terri* (see page 206).

Virga *Playmate Lolly-Pop* (see page 211).

Richwood *Sandra Sue* (see page 190).

Vogue painted-eye *Ginny Twins* (see page 214). *Sandra Strater Collection.*

Nancy Ann *Roy Rogers* and *Dale Evans* (see page 157). *Nancy Catlin Collection.*

Vogue *Ginny Cowgirls* and *Cowboy* (see page 227). *Marge Meisinger Collection.*

Vogue *Ginny in Trunk* (see page 225). *Dorothy Hesner Collection.*

Valentine *Mona Lisa* (see page 209). *Pat Parton Collection.*

Lenci (Italy) provincial
dolls (see page 144).

Reliable (Canada) *Plassikins* (see page 188).

Bible Doll Co. of America *David* (see page 68). *Eunice Kier Collection.*

Continued from page 216.

Ginny Skater from Sports Series: HP; 8in (20cm); sleep eyes with painted eyelashes; green felt top; pink felt skirt with felt applique; ice skates; mint condition with excellent color; 1952.

    SEE: *Illustration 379. Marianne Gardner Collection.*

    PRICE: $250-300+

Ginny: HP; 8in (20cm); head-turning walker; sleep eyes; came in double fold cardboard travel case; wardrobe includes party dress, straw hat, nightgown, robe, playsuit, towel, slippers, mirror, comb, garden tools, panties, shoes and shampoo cape; 1954. This is the year *Ginny* became a walker.

    SEE: *Illustration 380.* Marshall Field & Co. Christmas catalog, 1954. *Barbara Andresen Collection.*

    PRICE: $400-500 up (very few sample prices available)

Ginny in Trunk with Clothes: HP; 8in (20cm); non-walker; sleep eyes with painted lashes above eyes; straight legs; panties and cape on doll; right side of box has white kimono with red dots, nightgown curlers, booties and soft plastic shoes; left side of box has yellow organdy dress (tagged), straw hat with blue flowers and an extra pair of shoes with ties in center; doll wears sunglasses; circa 1953. The trunk is cardboard with country and steamship labels. It also has a "Dolly Airlines" label.

    MARKS: "Ginny//My Beautiful Real-Looking Hair Can Be//Wet, Combed, Curled & Set" (tag); "Vogue Dolls" (dress tag)

    SEE: *Illustration 381.* (Color Section, page 222). *Dorothy Hesner Collection.*

    PRICE: $400-500 up (very few prices available)

379.

380.

Ginny, the walk and dress doll, comes in her own double fold cardboard travel case. Her marvelous wardrobe includes party dress, straw hat, nightgown, robe, play suit, towel, slippers, mirror, comb, garden tools. She wears panties, shoes, socks and shampoo cape. 8 inches tall, just right to dress and undress, easy to sew extra clothes for. Plastic body, saran hair, wake-and-sleep eyes. Will delight little girls age 6 to 12. **151 T2-77** **$5.95**

Ginny: HP; 8in (20cm); dressed in Easter coat and straw hat; purse with "Ginny" printed on it; Ginny's pup made by Steiff; 1955.

> SEE: *Illustration 382. Playthings,* April 1955.

Ginny: HP; 8in (20cm); straight leg walker; advertisement from 1955 Christmas toy catalog of The May Company in Cleveland, Ohio.
Clothes top row from left to right: 1. gray organdy dress with pink trim 2. checked overalls with yellow jersey and brown cap 3. blue dress with black straw hat 4. cowgirl outfit 5. blue and white Dutch girl outfit. Clothes bottom row from left to right: 1. red dress 2. roller skater 3. bride 4. velvet coat, fur muff and beret.
Ginny's baby sister, *Ginette:* soft vinyl; 8in (20cm)

> SEE: *Illustration 383.*

why has *Ginny* led the Easter Parade and every parade!

QUALITY and STYLE!

above all are the reasons why Ginny is the Fashion Leader in Doll Society

vogue dolls inc. announces that

the established price of Ginny at $1.98 will hold throughout 1955, enabling our customers to enjoy a full margin of profit instead of taking a shorter mark-up and trading down.

VOGUE DOLLS INC.
33 SHIP AVE., MEDFORD 55, MASS.
NEW YORK OFFICE • 200 FIFTH AVE., ROOM 656

Fashion Leader in Doll Society

APRIL, 1955—PLAYTHINGS

382.

Ginny—our miniature walking doll of fashion.

(A) GINNY is the best dressed little lady in all of doll society. Her available wardrobe of more than fifty different outfits—complete with tiny accessories—contains something 'specially smart for every occasion. Only a few of her many costumes are mentioned here. A petite 8" tall, Ginny is just about the cutest thing Santa ever tucked into his bag. She's made of unbreakable plastic, has real eyelashes and life-like Dynel hair that can be combed, dampened and reset. She sleeps, sits, stands, and even walks. Choose Ginny with pigtails or with bangs, blonde or brunette. Wt. 1 lb. Ginny with blonde bangs in her pretty lace trimmed red dress, panties, slippers, and bow.
2A — $2.98

With panties, shoes, socks only. Select from Ginny's wardrobe.
(B) Gray organdy dress, pink trim. 2B — $1.50
(C) Checked overalls, jersey, cap. 2C — $1.50
(D) Blue dress, black straw hat. 2D — $1.98
(E) Complete Cow Girl Outfit. 2E — $1.98
(F) Dutch Girl Costume. 2F — $2.50
(G) Roller Skater. 2G — $3.50
(H) Bride. 2H — $2.98
(K) Velvet Coat, fur muff, beret. 2K — $3.50
Bridesmaid 2NS — $2.98
2A2 — $1.98

Baby sister Ginette.

(L) GINNETTE. Ginny's brand new little sister is so baby-like she actually drinks, wets, and coos. Made of soft vinyl, she has movable arms and legs, and flexible toes and fingers. And she's just 8" tall. Weight 1 lb. Ginnette with diapers and bottle.
2L — $2.98

COSTUME ONLY
Her ruffled nylon playsuit and matching bonnet.
2L2 — $1.98

(M) BABY TOTER. Made especially for Ginnette so that she can be carried wherever her little mother goes. Has zipper and carrying handles.
2M3 — $2.30

by VOGUE DOLL

383.

Ginny Cowgirls and Cowboy: HP; 8in (20cm); different cowboy and cowgirl outfits made by Vogue.

Left to right:

1. Purple felt skirt with gold trim; chartreuse top with rickrack trim; fuchsia vest with gold trim; purple felt cowboy hat; fuchsia boots; carrying a gold gun; Vogue label on dress. *Marge Meisinger Collection.*
2. Green felt skirt with print of horse; red blouse; chartreuse vest with print of steer; carrying a gold gun; Vogue label on dress.
3. Cowboy doll with short blonde hair; green felt cowboy pants with print of horses; red top; chartreuse cowboy hat; carrying a gold gun; Vogue label on suit. *Marge Meisinger Collection.*
4. Blue cowgirl dress with silver black cotton trim at neck and sleeves; silver fringe braid; black leather belt; white holster with silver gun which is molded like the gold guns; Vogue label on dress. *Marge Meisinger Collection.*

SEE: *Illustration 384* (Color Section, page 222).

Ginny: HP; 8in (20cm); bent-knee walker; plastic molded eyelashes; red bathing suit with "Ginny" knit into material; circa 1957-1962.

MARKS: "Vogue" (head); "Ginny Vogue Dolls, Inc. Pat #2687594 Made in U.S.A." (body)

SEE: *Illustration 385.*

385.

PRICE: $125-150

Ginny from Far-Away Lands: HP; 8in (20cm); bent-knee late *Ginny*; series included: 1. *Highlander* 2. *Scandinavian* 3. *Hollander* 4. *Hawaiian* 5. *Oriental* 6. *Israelian* 7. *Alaskan;* 1959.

SEE: *Illustration 386. Playthings,* March 1959.

386.

Girl in Pink: painted HP; 14½in (37cm); lovely wig with hair braided and roller at sides; sleep eyes; painted eyelashes under eyes; closed mouth; early standard arm hook (see Identification Guide, *Hard Plastic Dolls, I,* page 262A); unusually slender body with long legs; all original clothes; pink organdy dress and teddy; pink cotton slip attached to skirt; pink leather buckle shoes; 1st, 2nd and 3rd fingers molded together with the little finger only molded part way; Vogue clothing characteristics; lace trim △▽ on dress; circa 1949.

MARKS: "14" (head); "Made in U.S.A." (body). There is no circle around mark. "Vogue Dolls" (tag sewn into dress)

SEE: *Illustration 387. Shirley Niziolek Collection.*

PRICE: (rare doll — very few sample prices)

387.

Littlest Angel: HP body with vinyl head; 11in (28cm); sleep eyes; straight rooted hair; walker; jointed at neck, shoulders, hips and knees; 1962.

This is from a 1962 Vogue brochure. The *Littlest Angel* is no longer advertised under the Arranbee name. She has now become *Ginny's* cousin and part of the *Ginny* family. She likes to visit the *Ginny* family and bring her complete wardrobe with her.

Top row from left to right:

1. Basic *Little Angel* with panties, shoes and socks.
2. *Picnic Fun:* matching *Ginny* outfit with white cotton deck pants and red print over-blouse.
3. *Patriotic Dress:* white piqué dress with red, white and blue trim.

Bottom row from left to right:

1. Two-piece pajamas.
2. Pink batiste dress with lace trim; satiny bow; rosebuds.
3. Blue dot cotton school dress; crisp white pinafore.
4. Red party dress with full skirt trimmed with lace.

SEE: *Illustration 388. Brochure from the Kathryn Davis Collection.* (See illustrations in Arranbee section of this book. See also the illustrations in *Glamour Dolls of the 1950s and 1960s* under Arranbee.)

388.

Jill: HP; 10in (25cm); sleep eyes with molded lashes; pierced ears; jointed knees; high-heeled feet; painted fingernails; adult figure; arm hook similar to *Ginny.*

Jill was introduced at the Toy Fair in New York in February 1957. The March issue of *Playthings* featured a beautiful pop-up section of the Vogue dolls. This lovely version of *Jill* with the beautiful background folded out of the magazine.

MARKS: "Vogue" (head); "Jill/Vogue, Made in USA, 1957" (body)

SEE: *Illustration 389. Playthings,* March 1957. (See inside title page for photograph.)

PRICE: $75-100 (depending on outfit)

Jill: HP; 10in (25cm); sleep eyes with molded lashes; pierced ears; jointed knees; high-heeled feet; painted fingernails; adult figure; armhole hook similar to *Ginny*; (for *Jill* clothes brochure, see *Hard Plastic Dolls, I,* pages 251-255).

MARKS: "Vogue" (head); "Jill//Vogue, Made in USA, 1957" (body)

SEE: *Illustration 390. Lois Janner Collection.*

PRICE: $85-110 (depending on outfit)

390.

Walkalon Mfg. Company

The registered trademarks, the trademarks and the copyrights appearing in italics within this chapter belong to Walkalon Mfg. Company.

Betsy Walker: HP head; tenite body; 21in (53cm); early key-winding walking doll which walks alone and swings her arms, legs and head; pink organdy dress with Koroseal panties; brown sleep eyes; 1950.

MARKS: None (doll); "Warren// Three Oaks (picture of 3 trees) Michigan" (tag on panties)

SEE: *Illustration 391. Playthings,* August 1950.

Betsy Walker: HP; 20in (51cm); key-winding walking doll; brown sleep eyes; still in working condition; (not shown dressed in original pink organdy dress and bonnet); (see *Illustration 391*).

MARKS: None (doll); "Warren// Three Oaks (picture of 3 trees) Michigan" (tag on panties)

SEE: *Illustration 392. Arline Last Collection.*

PRICE: $75-90 (in working condition) $100+ (mint-in-box)

391.

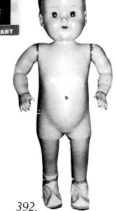

392.

World Wide Doll Club
(Overseas Dolls)

The registered trademarks, the trademarks and the copyrights appearing in italics within this chapter belong to World Wide Doll Club.

Brochure: The Nabisco Wheat Honeys and Rice Honeys offered these dolls as a premium about 1959. The brochure said, "Fabulous dolls...made patiently in little shops and peasant cottages where dollmaking is an art and a loving tradition. Dolls are dressed by artisans with the same deft touches that make their grandmothers' dolls museum pieces. Rich fabrics or home-spun types — whatever material is used is characteristic of the doll-making tradition in the country of origin.

"DOLLS ARE HISTORY IN MINIATURE

"Dolls tell you so much about the land they come from — the customs, station in life, occupation, religion or even the region of the country. And there is always some extra surprise — a coin or perhaps an extra stamp, or some other curiosity. No wonder these dolls inspire interest in history, geography and language!"

Originally these dolls cost $1.00 or $1.25 and two boxtops from Wheat Honeys or Rice Honeys. The coupon was sent to Locust Valley, L.I., N.Y. However, the dolls were mailed to the customer from the country of origin. The dolls' material and construction varied widely as did the costuming. The advertising concept is unusual.

The following dolls were offered:

1. Italy — *Zita* from Palermo and *Valentino* from Tormina.
2. Japan — *Higasa* in kimono and *Ichiro* with samaurai sword.
3. Israel — *Jessica* with pottery jar and *Aaron*, a carpet seller.
4. Korea — *Tai-Mu*, a dancer and *Bock-Dong* who beats a drum.
5. Scotland — *Meg* and *Gregory*, both in a tartan.
6. Greece — *Althea* in native costume and *Tassos* wearing uniform of the Royal Guard.
7. Malta — *Elena* wears the black faldetta and *Nardo* is a fisherman.
8. Holland — *Juliana* in Dutch dress and *Pieter* in Dutch pantaloons.
9. Portugal — *Petita* has an embroidered apron and *Fernando* is a fisherman.
10. Switzerland — *Herta* has a festival costume and *Ludwig* is an Alpine climber.
11. South Africa — *Nomsa* carries a baby on her back and *Fanou* has a spear and shield.
12. Arabia — *Mabruka* is a dancer and *Omar* is a desert sheik.

393.

Your Overseas Doll Gregory from Scotland: HP; 6½in (17cm); sleep eyes with no lashes; sculptured, molded eyebrows; jointed at neck and shoulders only; mold mark runs through sculptured ear; dressed in traditional Stuart plaid Scottish kilt; black wool jacket; white shirt with jabot; Scottish hat; molded slipper shoes which have been painted black; painted-on socks; individual fingers; plastic purse holds Scottish flag and English 1956 farthing with a picture of Queen Elizabeth; circa 1958-59. This doll was probably made by the Sarold Mfg. Co. (see page 202).

MARKS: None (doll); "Nabisco Wheat Honeys or Rice Honeys Collector Dolls from around the world.!"
SEE: *Illustration 393.*
PRICE: $15-20

Heidi: HP; glass eyes; HP eyelashes; mohair wig; painted-on white socks and blue shoes; royal blue skirt; light blue apron; black vest; white blouse; straw hat with ribbons and flowers; all original in box; mailed from Zurich, Switzerland, March 20, 1958. This doll came with a letter explaining the customs and geography of Switzerland. She did not seem to be connected with the Nabisco premium set of foreign dolls but her dress was the same as *Herta* in the Nabisco set.
SEE: *Illustration 394. Carmen P. Smotherman Collection.*
PRICE: $20-30 (without box)

394.

Writing Toys Corporation

The registered trademarks, the trademarks and the copyrights appearing in italics within this chapter belong to Writing Toys Corporation.

Manuel von Rabenau was the inventor-creator of *Rita, the Writing Doll.* He was granted a patent in July 1959 and the doll was marketed in 1962.

Within a few weeks of the patent approval Inez Robb, feature writer of United Features Syndicate, wrote a story which was printed in many newspapers including the *New York Times.* She called *Rita* a "mentally-oriented doll."

Rita's debut was at the 1962 New York Toy Fair. Soon letters of inquiry came not only from dealers in the United States but from France, Argentina, Italy, Mexico, Germany and Japan.

Rita not only could write, but she was attractive and realistic. The original *Rita* was sculptured by Agop Agapoff, well-known New York artist.

Included with the purchase of *Rita* were three word discs, each of which wrote two words — one on each side. Additional discs could be ordered from Writing Toys Corporation.

Rita the Writing Doll: HP with vinyl head; 26in (66cm); battery operated; came with three cams which allowed her to write six words; blue eyes; all original; purchase price in 1962 was $29.95.

    MARKS: "First Run" (back in circle); "Writing Toys, St. Paul USA 1962" (head)

    SEE: *Illustration 395* (doll holding magic slate and stylus). *Mary Elizabeth Poole Collection.*

       Illustration 396 (operating instructions). *Mary Elizabeth Poole Collection.*

    PRICE: $150-200 in operating condition (very few sample prices available)

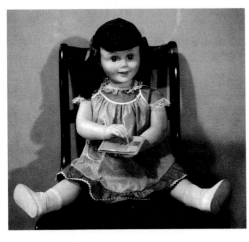

395.

IMPORTANT - for Writing position
Gently push arm holding slate downward until it reaches its *Rita* "STOP" position.

RITA IS A STURDY DOLL DESIGNED FOR YEARS OF ENJOYMENT. HOWEVER, LIKE ANY FINE INSTRUMENT WITH MOVING PARTS, RITA SHOULD NOT BE ABUSED. THE BEST WAY TO HOLD RITA IS BY CRADLING YOUR HANDS UNDER HER LEGS.
(See illustration)

in place. Disc writes two words, one on each side. Whichever side is up, will be the word Rita writes.

ON/OFF SWITCH

To make Rita write, switch on battery-powered motor. The up position is on; down is off.

INSERTING BATTERIES

Insert long-life batteries into openings at Rita's sides. On Rita's LEFT, place battery facing FORWARD. On Rita's RIGHT, place battery facing BACKWARDS.

CHANGING WORD DISKS

When you want to change discs, pull lever down to locking position B. Remove disc.

INSERTING WORD DISKS

To insert word disc, pull lever down and to the right, so lever locks into position B. In order for Rita to start writing promptly, hold disc where two vertical lines are grooved on edge. Place disc on center post (similar to placing a record on a phonograph turntable). Release lever by moving to left and up, gently, until lever is returned to position A, and disc is locked

MAGIC SLATE AND STYLUS

Both the stylus and magic slate are removable, so that when Rita isn't writing, you can give her a nap, hold her in your arms and play with her just as you would any other doll. But remember, Rita is a very special doll and therefore deserves special attention. See next page for instructions on removing stylus and magic slate.

396.

Doll Marks

All of the names in *italics* appearing in the following section are protected names. The legal protections were left off for the readability of the charts and price guide.

By far the majority of the marks for hard plastic dolls were published in *Hard Plastic Dolls I*. Because this means of identification is so important, the marks are repeated and updated in this section. The other sections of the Identification Guide show new information.

NUMBERS

1.	2S	Uneeda
2.	3	Uneeda, Richwood Toys
3.	7/3	Starr
4.	9	Ideal *Lolly*
5.	11VW	Valentine
6.	12	Valentine
7.	14	Roberta, Valentine, Star, De-Sota, Arrow, Ideal Baby Possible Vogue
8.	14R	Belle, Deluxe Reading, Eegee, Natural, Rite Lee, Royal, Sayco
9.	16	Arranbee
10.	16VW	Valentine
11.	P 16	Belle
12.	17VW	Valentine, Arranbee
13.	18V	Nancy Ann
14.	18VW	Valentine
15.	20	Uneeda
16.	20HH	Belle
17.	VP23 or UP17	Ideal
18.	23ARV	Arranbee
19.	25	Uneeda
20.	31AE	Horsman
21.	32	Ideal
22.	49 R & B	Arranbee
23.	65 R & B	Arranbee
24.	74	Arrow
25.	88	Horsman
26.	V91	Ideal
27.	P90-91-92-93-94	Ideal (*Toni* Family)
28.	P90 W	Ideal
29.	128	Valentine
30.	160-170-180	Horsman
31.	170	Baby Barry Toys
32.	180	Roberta
33.	R185	Valentine
34.	190	Wilson
35.	AE 200	Belle
36.	P 200	Ideal
37.	210	Mollye, Arranbee, Uneeda, Roberta
38.	250 R & B	Arranbee
39.	450	Mollye
40.	750	Sayco
41.	AE593	Belle
42.	2252077	Ideal
43.	2675644	American Character
44.	2687594	Vogue

PAT. PENDING — Companies using this mark
1. A & H (Pats. Pending and Pat's Pend)
2. Arranbee
3. Ideal *Posie* (back of knees on roll joint)
4. Ideal
5. Plastic Molded Arts (*Miss Joan*) (Pats. Pending)
6. Pressman (Pat. Pend.)
7. Togs & Dolls
8. Terri Lee
9. Valentine (This company sometimes has both "Made in USA" and Pat. Pending" on back)
10. Virga (Pat's Pend.)

MADE IN U.S.A.

1. American Character *Alice*	6. Hardy Different Toys	11. Roberta
2. Baby Barry Toys	7. Horsman	12. Star
3. Bal	8. Ideal	13. Sayco
4. Cast	9. Imperial	14. Uneeda
5. DeSota	10. Richwood *Cindy Lou*	15. Vogue

SYMBOLS

1. ⬦➔ Arrow
2. ⊗ Mollye
3. △ *Saucy Walker*-type — Ideal Characteristics

LETTERS

1. A	Uneeda	8. E.G.	Eegee
2. A.C.	American Character	9. MK	Ideal
3. AE	American Character, Belle, Deluxe Reading, Eegee, Mary Hoyer, Nasco, New Dolly Toy Company, P. & M. Sales, Sayco, Valentine, Unique	10. P	Ideal
		11. PMA	Plastic Molded Arts
		12. R & B	Arranbee
		13. S	Eegee
		14. s	Sayco
4. Amer. Char.	American Character	15. U	Uneeda
		16. V	Ideal
5. B	Uneeda	17. V4	Effanbee
6. ©	Terri Lee	18. VP	Ideal
7. CDC	Cosmopolitan	19. W	Ideal Walker

Identification Guide
Table of Contents

Arm Hooks

Of all the methods of identifying hard plastic dolls, the characteristics of the arm hooks can be the most helpful. This is especially true of the small walking dolls. Many of the companies seem to have their own special hook even though they purchased bodies from the few doll body companies.

It is recommended that the reader refer to *Hard Plastic Dolls, I* for most of the arm hooks of the better known hard plastic dolls. The following arm hooks are in addition to those in the first book.

WARNING: The collector must be aware of the so-called "marriages" in repaired dolls. Arms seemed to be especially vulnerable in dolls that were strung, and they were often replaced with any small arm available.

A.
1. *Sarold (England) Ginny-type Doll* (bottom arm); metal ring hook.
2. *Rosebud (England) Ginny-type* (top arm: all-plastic hook.
   SEE: *Illustration 397. Marge Meisinger Collection.*

397.

B.
Ontario Plastics Paula Sue: arm hook with squared off plastic piece holding a metal ring.
   SEE: *Illustration 398. Marge Meisinger Collection.*

C.
Nancy Ann Debbie arm hook: each arm has a different hook. The Richwood *Cindy Lou* has the same arm hooks.
   SEE: *Illustration 399. Marge Meisinger Collection.*

398.

399.

D.
Block Baby Walker Arm Hook: This hook is similar to, but not the same as the Nancy Ann *Debbie* hook (see Identification Guide, *Hard Plastic Dolls, I*, page 268U) and the Arranbee *Littlest Angel* and Vogue *Li'l Imp* (see Identification Guide, *Hard Plastic Dolls, I*, page 269Y). This hook is on both the hard plastic head and the vinyl head models.
  SEE: *Illustration 400.*

E.
(from left to right)
Arm Hooks:
1. Plastic Molded Arts *Miss Joan.*
2. Cosmopolitan jointed-arm *Ginger.*
3. Midwestern *Mary Jean.*
  SEE: *Illustration 401.*

F.
Richwood Cindy Lou Arm Hook: similar to Plastic Molded Arts arm hook in *Hard Plastic Dolls, I,* page 265M.
  SEE: *Illustration 402. Marge Meisinger Collection.*

G.
Plastic Molded Arts (PMA) Chubby-Type Doll: unusual arm hook.
  SEE: *Illustration 403. Helen M. Keefe Collection.*

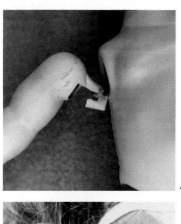

400.

401.

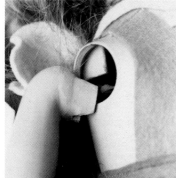

402.

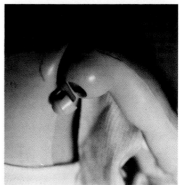

403.

Bodies of 6in (15cm) to 8in (20cm) Ginny-Type Dolls

There was a gradual change in the bodies of the popular small *Ginny*-type dolls. They generally were introduced as non-walker dolls. Then the walking mechanism was added. About 1955 many of the companies added jointed knees.

About the same time, most of the companies started to make both the all-hard plastic doll and the vinyl-headed doll with rooted hair. In general, the vinyl-headed doll cost a little more money but was so popular that the all-hard plastic doll was dropped from the line. Today's collectors prefer the all-hard plastic doll, and it is interesting to note that many more of these dolls seem to have survived. The dedicated collector often finds that it is difficult to locate specific dolls with vinyl heads.

A. (left to right)
1. *A & H. Gigi:* HP; early hip-pin straight-leg walker with original box.
   SEE: *Illustration 404. Kim R. Lusk Collection.*
2. *A & H. Gigi:* HP; bent-knee walker
   SEE: *Illustration 405.*
3. *A & H. Gigi:* HP with vinyl head (not pictured); see *Illustration 14.*

B.
Allison Bonita (left) and American Character Betsy McCall (right): slim walking dolls; *Bonita* has soft vinyl head; *Betsy* has HP head.
   SEE: *Illustration 406. Marge Meisinger Collection.*

404.

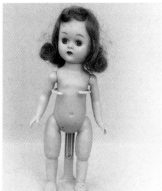

405.

406.

C.

Ginger and Ginger-Type All-HP Bodies: Left to right: 1. Midwestern *Mary Jean*, 8in (20cm) 2. Cosmopolitan *Ginger*, 7½in (19cm) with medium eyes 3. Cosmopolitan *Ginger*, 7½in (19cm) with small eyes.

Mary Jean has the same body characteristics as *Ginger* except for painted feet, an extra 1/2in (1.3cm) in height and a similar but slightly different arm hook (see Identification Guide, page 236). The other two dolls have the standard *Ginger* arm hook (see Identification Guide, *Hard Plastic Dolls, I*, page 266N).

407.

Other *Ginger* characteristics include a mold seam through the middle ear making the center part of the ear higher than the top and the lobe; closed mouth; very faint navel; dimple under the lip that is distinctive; toes all the same length; dots above the toes; some have jointed knees with a crease in front of the ankle; a few have jointed arms (see *Illustration 150*); individual fingers; mold flaw at wrist on palm side; fingernails and joint details are excellent; all are head-turning walkers; glued-on wig; distinctive heel (see *Illustration 251*).

MARKS: None
SEE: *Illustration 407.*

Five of the six *Ginger*-type dolls are shown in *Illustration 408*. The sixth *Ginger* doll is the first doll on the left in *Illustration 409*.

D.

Ginger Bodies: from left to right:

1. Early straight leg with painted eyelashes.
2. Most popular straight-leg *Ginger*; see *Illustration 421* for three variations in eyes.
3. Late bent-knee doll with bent elbows.
4. Vinyl head on hard plastic body.
5. Vinyl head on hard plastic body: Cha-Cha heel.

SEE *Illustration 408. Pat Parton Collection* (first doll on left).

408.

(Left to right) all-HP:

Cosmopolitan Ginger #6: bent knees with straight arms; head-turning walker. *Pat Parton Collection.*

E.

Richwood Sandra Sue: high heels and toe detail; walking mechanism but head does not turn (2nd doll from left).

Richwood Sandra Sue: flat feet and no toe detail; walking mechanism but head does not turn (3rd doll from left).

Roberta Walker, Doll Bodies Mary Lou, Grant Plastics Suzie: painted, molded shoes; non-walker (4th doll from left).

For general characteristics, see the company listings in this book and in *Hard Plastics Dolls, I.*

MARKS: None (dolls)

SEE: *Illustration 409.*

F.

Elite Vicki: Pam facial characteristics and arm hook; dimples above toes which have excellent detail; (this is very different from the *Pam* and *Lucy* doll which have molded slippers); jointed at neck, shoulders hips and knees; two creases at ankles.

MARKS: None (doll); "Elite Creations" (brochure)

SEE: *Illustration 410. Ester Borgis Collection.*

409.

410.

411.

G.
Nancy Ann Muffie (from left to right) #1: HP; straight-leg non-walker; jointed at shoulders, neck and hips; flip Dynel wig with side part; painted eyelashes above eyes; no eyebrows above eyes; molded eyelashes; straight line on seat; 1953.
   MARKS: "STORY BOOK//DOLLS//CALIFORNIA" (back)
   SEE: *Illustration 411.*

Muffie (from left to right) #2: HP; rare straight-leg non-walker; slightly different body and legs; Y on seat; a line below and above front knees; two dimples between knee lines; Dynel flip wig with side part; shorter neck than other dolls; molded eyelashes on sleep eyes; painted eyelashes and eyebrows above eyes; date unknown.
   MARKS: None (doll)
   SEE: *Illustration 411. Mary Ann Watkins Collection.*

Muffie (from left to right) #3: HP; straight-leg walker; Dynel wig in flip style with side part; wig also came in pigtails; molded eyelashes on sleep eyes; painted eyelashes above eyes; no eyebrows; head-turning walker; one straight line on seat; 1954.
   MARKS: "STORY BOOK//DOLLS//CALIFORNIA" (back)
   SEE: *Illustration 411. Mary Ann Watkins Collection.*

Muffie (from left to right) #4: HP; rare unplayed-with doll in box marked "Lori-Ann" (see *Hard Plastic Dolls, I,* page 192); came with a flocked hair twin brother in a second marked "Lori-Ann" box; girl has unusual wig with bangs and two rows of rolled curls held with hairpins; straight-leg head-turning walker; eyelashes and eyebrows above eyes; one straight line on seat; date unknown.
   MARKS: None (doll); "Lori-Ann" (box)
   SEE: *Illustration 411.*

Muffie (from left to right) #5: HP; straight-leg head-turning walker; molded lashes on sleep eyes; eyelashes and eyebrows painted above eyes; one line on seat; circa 1954-56.
   MARKS: "STORY BOOK//DOLLS//CALIFORNIA//MUFFIE" (back)
   SEE: *Illustration 411. Mary Ann Watkins Collection.*

Muffie (from left to right) #6: HP; same as #5 except that it is a bent-knee head-turning walker; painted eyebrows and eyelashes above eyes; one straight line on seat; circa 1954-1956.

> **MARKS:** "STORY BOOK//DOLLS//
> CALIFORNIA//MUFFIE"
> (back)
> **SEE:** *Illustration 412. Mary Ann Watkins Collection.*

Muffie (from left to right) #7: HP with vinyl head; bent-knee head-turning walker; painted eyelashes and eyebrows above eyes; molded eyelashes on sleep eyes; one line on seat; 1956 +.

> **MARKS:** "STORY BOOK//DOLLS//
> CALIFORNIA//MUFFIE"
> (back); large "NANCY
> ANN" (head)
> **SEE:** *Illustration 412.*

Muffie (from left to right) #8: HP with vinyl head; head-turning walker; same doll as #7 except for straight legs; rooted ponytail; 1956 +.

> **MARKS:** "STORY BOOK//DOLLS//
> CALIFORNIA//MUFFIE"
> (back); "Nancy Ann" (in
> small letters on back of head)
> **SEE:** *Illustration 412.*

412.

413.

Muffie (from left to right) #9: HP; plastic walking mechanism; head-turning walker; beautiful, but slightly different skin tone; heavier wide-set legs; eyelashes painted below eyes; plastic eyelashes over sleep eyes; 1967.

> **SEE:** *Illustration 413.*

H.
Ontario Plastics Paula Sue: early non-walking *Ginny*-type.
> **SEE:** *Illustration 414. Marge Meisinger Collection.*

414.

415.

416.

417.

I. (from left to right)
1. *Uneeda:* HP body and vinyl head.
2. *Hollywood:* all-HP.
3. *Allison:* HP body and vinyl head.
4. *Plastic Molded Arts:* HP body and vinyl head.
    SEE: *Illustration 415. Marge Meisinger Collection.*

J.
High-Heel 'Teen: HP; slender figure; jointed at neck, shoulders, hips and knees.
    MARKS: None
    SEE: *Illustration 416.*

K.
Virga, Fortune, Kim, Doll Bodies, Grant Plastics, Niresk, Plastic Molded Arts, Norma, Ginny-Type Walking Dolls: all HP.
    It is difficult to identify these dolls as belonging to a specific company without a box. However, there are differences in the quality of the dolls. For the most part Virga, Fortune, Kim and Norma made dolls of better quality.
    SEE: *Illustration 417.*

K.
Virga, Fortune, Kim, Doll Bodies, Grant Plastics, Niresk, Plastic Molded Arts, Roberta Ginny-Type Walking Dolls: HP with vinyl head.
    MARKS: None
    SEE: *Illustration 418. Patricia Arches Collection.*

418.

L.

1. *Vogue Painted-Eye Early HP Doll:* 8in (20cm); painted eyelashes top and to side of eye; non-walker; jointed at neck, shoulders and hips; 3rd and 4th fingers molded together; two lines at ankle; arm hook (see *Hard Plastic Dolls, I,* Identification Guide, page 267R); circa 1948-1950. Most of these dolls were not yet named *Ginny.*

> MARKS: "Vogue" (head); "Vogue" (body)
>
> SEE: *Illustration 419* (doll on left). *Pat Parton Collection.*

2. *Ginny:* HP; 8in (20cm); sleep eyes with painted eyelashes; heavy hard plastic; (see *Hard Plastic Dolls, I* for further general characteristics and *Illustration 556* for dressed doll); circa 1950-1953. A walking mechanism was added in 1954.

419.

The "poodle cut" wig was used only in 1952. This particular doll was the first one called *Ginny.* She is dressed in a black velvet skirt and organdy top and a straw hat. From this point on all of these small dolls made by Vogue were called *Ginny.*

> MARKS: "Vogue" (head); "Vogue" (body)
>
> SEE: *Illustration 419* (doll on right).

L.

Ginny: HP: 8in (20cm)

420.

3. All HP; pin-jointed straight-leg walker; sleep eyes with molded eyelashes; one line on ankle; other characteristics including arm hooks are the same; 1955-1956.

4. *All HP;* pin-jointed bent-knee walker; sleep eyes with molded eyelashes; other characteristics including arm hooks are the same; 1957-1962.

5. *HP body with vinyl head;* pin-jointed bent-knee walker; other characteristics including arm hooks are the same; the flesh tone of the plastic is very pink; quality of the vinyl in the head is excellent; 1963-1965.

> MARKS: (Left to right) Dolls #1 and #2 "Ginny//Vogue Dolls//Inc.//(Pat. No 2687594)//Made in U.S.A." (body); "Vogue" (head); doll #3 the same except "Ginny" (head)
>
> SEE: *Illustration 420.* Doll #3 *Phyllis Appel Collection;* Doll #5 *Barbara Comienski Collection.*

243

Comparison Chart of "Chubby-type" Dolls

The so-called "chubby" dolls, 10in (25cm) to 12in (31cm), have been favorites of children and collectors since the 1950s. They were really a large *Ginny*®-type doll that children could handle more easily. They had a large wardrobe that could be purchased where the dolls were sold. Each year new clothes were added to the line.

It is often very difficult to identify these dolls. Since they were usually sold in just panties, shoes and socks, very few of these dolls have original clothes. The clothing was purchased in boxes, and it is still possible to find some mint-in-box clothes for these dolls.

The chart below is an attempt to help collectors identify their dolls. It is not perfect, and there are many variations of each brand. In the end, these dolls may have come out of the same factory. There are differences in the quality of both the dolls and the clothes. There are even differences in the quality of the dolls within one company in any given year.

I. MARKS
A. Arranbee *Littlest Angel* (see page 55-62)
1. "65" or "15" (vinyl head) often hard to read; "R & B" (waist)
2. Inverted T (⊥) on *Surprise Doll* (vinyl head)
3. "19" (vinyl head of doll with short, straight rooted hair)
4. "R & B" 11 (vinyl head of doll with short, straight rooted hair)
5. "R & B" (head of all-HP doll)
6. "R & B" (head and back of all-HP doll)
7. "R & B" (back only of all-HP doll)
B. Vogue *Li'l Imp* (see Hard Plastic Dolls I, page 257)
1. "R & B//15" or "16" (vinyl head). It is often hard to read.
2. "R & B//76" (vinyl head). It is often hard to read.
3. "19" (vinyl-headed doll)
C. Block (see pages 69-70)
1. No marks on all-HP *Baby Walker*
2. "Block Doll Products" (vinyl-headed doll)
D. Nancy Ann *Debbie* all-HP "Nancy Ann" in raised letters (head)
   Nancy Ann *Debbie* vinyl head "Nancy Ann" (head)
E. Sayco *Miss America Pageant* doll
1. "s" (vinyl head)
2. "Sayco" (head)
3. None
F. Togs and Dolls *Penny Walker*
   "Pat. Pending" (all HP body)

II. ARM HOOKS
A. Arranbee *Littlest Angel*
1. All-HP dolls
2. Hard plastic dolls with vinyl head
3. *Japanese Surprise* doll with vinyl head.
B. Vogue *Li'l Imp* vinyl head
C. Block all-HP *Baby Walker* or vinyl-headed doll
D. Nancy Ann *Debbie* all-HP
E. Nancy Ann *Debbie* vinyl head
F. Sayco Miss America Pageant doll (vinyl head)

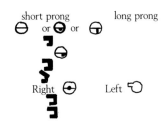

short prong   long prong

⊖ or ⊖ or ⊖

⊖

Right ⊕   Left ↰

III. ELBOW DIMPLES
A. Arranbee *Littlest Angel* all-HP and vinyl head   none
B. Vogue *Li'l Imp* (vinyl head)   none
C. Block with *Baby Walker* all-HP   yes
   Block (vinyl head)   unknown
D. Nancy Ann *Debbie* all-HP and vinyl head   yes
E. Sayco *Miss America Pageant* doll (vinyl head)   yes (close together)

IV. WALKING MECHANISM AND LEGS
A. Arranbee *Littlest Angel*   hip-pin walker with jointed legs

B. Vogue *Li'l Imp*   hip-pin walker with jointed legs
C. Block all-HP *Penny Walker*   regular walking mechanism with
                                                                          straight legs

  Block with vinyl head   regular walking mechanism with jointed knees
D. Nancy Ann *Debbie* all-HP   regular walking mechanism with
                                                                          straight legs

  Nancy Ann *Debbie* with vinyl head   regular walker with jointed knees
E. Sayco *Miss America Pageant* doll with vinyl head   regular walker with jointed knees
F. Togs and Dolls *Penny Walker* all-HP   regular walker

V. MOUTH
A. Arrabnee *Littlest Angel* both all-HP and vinyl   Molded tongue in mouth
B. Vogue *Li'l Imp* vinyl head   Molded tongue in mouth
C. Block both all-HP and vinyl head   Closed mouth — no tongue
D. Nancy Ann *Debbie* all-HP and vinyl head   Closed mouth — no tongue
E. Sayco *Miss America Pageant* doll vinyl head   Closed mouth — no tongue
F. Togs and Dolls *Penny Walker* all-HP   Closed mouth — no tongue

VI. MOLDED HAIR UNDER WIG
A. Arranbee *Littlest Angel* all-HP   Sometimes
  Arranbee *Littlest Angel* vinyl head   Usually no
  Arranbee *Japanese Surprise* doll vinyl head   Molded hair under rooted hair
B. Vogue *Li'l Imp* vinyl head   No
C. Block *Baby Walker* all-HP   Yes
  Block doll vinyl head   No
D. Nancy Ann *Debbie* all-HP   Yes
  Nancy Ann *Debbie* vinyl head   No
E. Sayco *Miss America Pageant* doll vinyl head   No
F. Togs and Dolls *Penny Walker* all-HP   Yes

VII. PAINTED EYELASHES UNDER EYES
A. Arranbee *Littlest Angel* all-HP   wide spaced, short
  Arranbee *Littlest Angel* vinyl head   wide spaced, short
B. Vogue *Li'l Imp* vinyl head   none
C. Block *Baby Walker* all-HP   dark paint
  Block doll vinyl head   medium paint
D. Nancy Ann *Debbie* all-HP   long, dark paint
  Nancy Ann *Debbie* vinyl head   wide spaced, medium paint
E. Sayco *Miss America Pageant* doll vinyl head   none
F. Togs and Dolls *Penny Walker* all-HP   unknown

VIII. POINTED NIPPLES ON BREASTS
A. Arranbee *Littlest Angel* all-HP   no
  Arranbee *Littlest Angel* vinyl head   no
B. Vogue *Li'l Imp* vinyl head   no
C. Block *Baby Walker* all-HP   yes
D. Nancy Ann *Debbie* all-HP   unknown
  Nancy Ann *Debbie* vinyl head   no
E. Sayco *Miss America Pageant* doll vinyl head   no
F. Togs and Dolls *Penny Walker* all-HP   yes

IX. STITCHING AROUND WIG NEAR NECKLINE
A. Arranbee *Littlest Angel* all-HP   no
  Arranbee *Littlest Angel* vinyl head   no
B. Vogue *Li'l Imp* vinyl head   no
C. Block *Penny Walker* all-HP   yes
  Block vinyl head   unknown
D. Nancy Ann *Debbie* all-HP   yes
  Nancy Ann *Debbie* vinyl head   no
E. Sayco *Miss America Pageant* doll vinyl head   no
F. Togs and Dolls *Penny Walker* all-HP   no

Dress-Me Dolls

The following companies sold the "Dress-Me" type of doll. These were usually sold on a wholesale basis to companies which dressed dolls, doll supply shops, doll hospitals, craft shops and doll mail order companies.

1. Block Doll Creations
2. Central Toy Manufacturing Corporation
3. Commonwealth Plastics Corp.
4. Doll Bodies, Inc.
5. Grant Plastics
6. Reliable (Canada)
7. Rosebud (England)

Eyes

A.
Cosmopolitan Ginger Eyes (left to right):
  1. Midwestern *Mary Jean* (large eyes)
  2. Cosmopolitan *Ginger* (medium eyes)
  3. Cosmopolitan *Ginger* (small eyes)
Many of the LARGE EYE dolls with *Ginger* characteristics seem to have been marketed by companies other than Cosmopolitan.
  SEE: *Illustration 421.*

B.
Painted-Eye Ginger: HP; 8in (20cm); first *Ginger.*
  MARKS: None
  SEE: *Illustration 422. Pat Parton Collection.*

C.
Sarold (England) Ginny-type:* unusual unpainted molded eyebrows; (see *Illustration 342*, page 202). The Sarold Company made many small and inexpensive dolls. Most of them had this type of eyebrows. It is an excellent identification feature.

421.

422.

Fasteners
(Gripper Snaps)

Today the value of hard plastic dolls depends on the clothes that they are wearing. Collectors who have dolls without original clothes search for authentic costumes to increase the dolls' historical significance and value. For many years one of the methods of identification has been to look at the gripper snap fasteners.

In this section the doll collector can find a few examples of the fasteners used in the 1950s. This is just a start on this research, but perhaps the reader can use this section as a starting point for a study which will help locate original clothes.

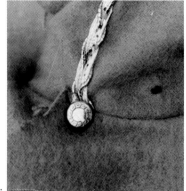

423.

A.

Cosmopolitan Ginger, Fortune Pam, Sayco Miss America Pageant Dolls fastener: the Cosmopolitan *Ginger* clothing is labeled; the Fortune *Pam* and Sayco *Miss America Pageant* clothing is not marked.

    SEE: *Illustration 423. Pat Parton Collection.*

B.

Nancy Ann Muffie and Debbie Snap Closings: two different types of gripper snap closings were used for both dolls. The first was a small snap with a solid top (right). The second was used later and was a snap with a double circle (left).

    SEE: *Illustration 424.*

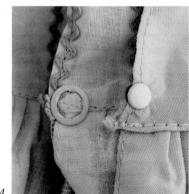

424.

C.

Nancy Ann Style Show Doll with Vinyl Head: the few dolls documented had the same small snap with the solid top (right). In these cases the snaps matched the color of the costume.

    MARKS: "Grippers S M C O" (second larger snap)
    SEE: *Illustration 424.*

D.

Ontario Plastics Paula Sue: unusual white gripper snap closing with several protrusions on top surface.

    SEE: *Illustration 425. Marge Meisinger Collection.*

425.

E.
Vogue Fastener: type of gripper snap fastener usually found on clothes made by the Vogue Dolls, Inc.
Little Imp: "Starlet" on inside of snap.
Early Ginny: hook and eye closing.
SEE: *Illustration 426.*

426.

Foreign Dolls

Foreign dolls pictured in *Hard Plastic Dolls I*

Foreign Dolls Pictured in this Book

Hair Care Dolls

1. Arranbee: *Nanette, the Beauty Shop Doll* came with a beauty kit, curlers and easy instructions for doing hair; 1957; (see page 54).
2. Artisan: *Raving Beauty* advertised that she had Ravon hair that could be shampooed, combed and waved; 1950; (see page 63).
3. Baby Barry Toys: *Baby Barry* came with a "Wave-A-Doll Hair Kit;" (see page 67).
4. Effanbee: *Tintair Honey* came with hair dye, applicator and curlers; 1951; (see page 105).
5. Eugenia: *Perm-O-Wave Pam* came with plastic curlers, a make-up cape, barrette and carrying case; 1949 (see page 108).
6. Fleischaker Novelty Co.: *Little Girl of Today* came with human hair rooted in scalp. She had detailed hair styling instructions; 1951; (see page 111).
7. Fortune Toys, Incorporated: *Starlet the Lustercreme Shampoo* was an advertising doll; circa 1957; (see page 139).
8. Horsman: girl doll came with curlers, brush and comb set; early 1950s; (see page 124).
9. Ideal Toy Company: *Toni* came with a "Play Wave" kit; circa 1950-1955; (see *Hard Plastic Dolls, I*, page 144 and this book, page 135).
10. Pedigree (England): their *Toni*-type doll was almost identical with the Ideal *Toni* and came with a similar wave kit; circa 1953-55; (see page 185).

Rooted Hair in Hard Plastic Head

1. American Character: some *Sweet Sue* dolls have a skull cap with rooted hair glued onto the head; early 1950s; (see *Hard Plastic Dolls, I*, page 43).
2. Fleischaker: *Little Girl of Today* came with human hair rooted in the head; 1951; (see page 111).
3. Monica: *Marion* had hair rooted in hard plastic; circa 1953-55; (see *Hard Plastic Dolls, I*, page 181).
4. Unica (Belgium): HP girl doll has a rubber cap which is holding rooted hair; mid 1950s; (see page 209).

Colored Wigs on Dolls

During the 1950s women and children were experimenting with hair styles and color. It was becoming acceptable, and even fashionable, to have dyed hair. Dolls, especially the small walking dolls and larger ballerina dolls, often had pink, orange, blue, green and other colored hair. Children loved it. This is a partial list of dolls which could be purchased with brightly colored hair.

1. Admiration: *Ginny*-type girl.
2. Cosmopolitan: *Ginger* with the large eyes.
3. Fortune: *Pam*.
4. Grant Plastics: *Suzie* and other small dolls
5. Virga: *Schapiarelli GoGo*, *Lollipop* and *Playmates*
6. Vogue: *Little Imp*.

Saucy Walker-type Dolls

Ideal's *Saucy Walker* and *Saucy Toddler* were very popular, well-made dolls in both boy and girl models. They were also expensive. Other companies, and Ideal itself, made cheaper versions which sold well. Some were marked with the competing company name but many were unmarked or with symbols like △ or AE. They were made of all-hard plastic or a combination of a hard plastic body and vinyl head.

The following companies competed with Ideal and made a *Saucy Walker*-type.

1. Aster Co.
2. Baby Barry: *Baby Barry*
3. Belle: *Playmate Walker* and *Heddi Stroller*
4. Doll-Land Division of Western Stationary Co.: *Angel Locks*
5. Eegee: *Susan Stroller* and *Merry Stroller*
6. P.J. Hill: *Cindy Walker*
7. Horsman: *Ruthie Walker*
8. Imperial: walking girl
9. Midwestern: *Suzy Stroller*
10. Natural: *Bride*
11. P & M: *Paula Mae*
12. Pedigree: walking boy and girl
13. Reliable: *Plassikin*
14. Roddy: boys and girls
15. Uneeda: *Country Girl*

Shoes and Feet

The hard plastic dolls can often be identified by their shoes and feet. The following pictures are in addition to those pictured in *Hard Plastic Dolls, I*.

The following is a reference list for those dolls pictured in *Hard Plastic Dolls, I*. The pages listed are all in *Hard Plastic Dolls, I*.

1. Molded feet from Plastic Molded Arts, A & H, Midwestern and Corrine Dolls (see page 283A).
2. Another type of feet used by Plastic Molded Arts, Peggy Huffman, Playhouse and others (see page 283B).
3. Mold-on PMA Indian (see page 283C).
4. Molded and painted shoe with bow used by A & H, Duchess, Lingerie Lou (Doll Bodies) and Grant Plastics (see page 284D).
5. Shoes used by Virga (Beehler Arts) and Fairyland Dolls (see page 284E).
6. Another molded shoe used by Virga (Beehler Arts) (see page 284F).
7. Fortune shoe with butterfly bow (see page 285G).
8. Another Fortune shoe with a thinner, upper roll (see page 285H).
9. Virga-Fortune and Duchess shoe (see page 285I).
10. Shoe used on dolls sold inexpensively such as Lovely (see page 286J).
11. Molded, painted Roberta shoe with bow (see page 286K).
12. Knickerbocker, S & E and Reliable of Canada (see page 286L).
13. Ideal plastic shoes (see page 286M).
14. A. & H. shoe with bow (see page 287N).
15. Ideal *Princess Mary* shoes (see page 287O).
16. Capezio ballerina shoes (see page 287P).

A.

American Character Sweet Sue Shoes: see *Illustrations 64* through *69* for a picture of an early *Sweet Sue* shoe from the 1952 catalog.

B.

Cosmopolitan Ginger Heel: unusual heel found on *Ginger* and *Ginger*-type dolls. An exception is the bent-knee doll (not pictured). This bent-knee doll has two different characteristics that will help identify it:

1. Two lines above the ankle.
2. Unusual leg and ankle mold seam on the side of the leg.

SEE: *Illustration 427.*

C.

Effanbee Shoes: see *Hard Plastic Dolls, I, Illustration 200* for a picture of the early *Honey Walker* simulated black patent leather slipper.

D.

Ideal Little Girl Shoes: There were two types of shoes made for Ideal little girl dolls during the hard plastic era. 1. Simulated leather with a snap in front. 2. Vinyl shoes with "Ideal" on the sole.

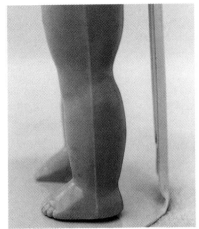

427.

The simulated leather shoes were shown in company catalogs through 1952. (See *Hard Plastic Dolls, I,* page 146. In this book see page 134.) Although some Ideal company advertisements showed these leather-like shoes in 1953, most of the dolls had vinyl shoes from then on through the hard plastic period.

The vinyl Ideal shoes are shown in *Hard Plastic Dolls, I,* page 286, *Illustration 625.* The flower design was only on a few of these vinyl shoes.

Baby and Toddler Shoes: The Ideal babies wore simple high-tie shoes of simulated leather. These can be seen in *Illustration 226.* A few of these high shoes have been seen on all-original *Toni* dolls. *Toni* dolls.

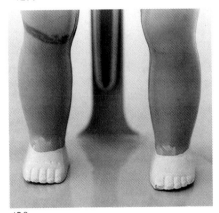

428.

E.

Midwestern Mary Jean: painted shoes showing toes; all other foot characteristics of the Cosmopolitan *Ginger* are the same.

SEE: *Illustration 428.*

F.

Nancy Ann Muffie Shoes: There were two types of shoes; left is the earliest leather-like shoe with a small gripper snap closing; right is an all-plastic buckle shoe which was used on later dolls.

SEE: *Illustration 429.*

429.

G.

Pedigree Small Walking Doll (Ginny-type): two different types of foot construction (see *Illustration 309*); doll on left has painted shoes and socks; doll on right has a regular foot with good toe detail.

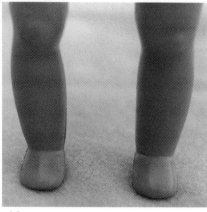

430.

H.

Uneeda Feet (Ginny-type) Doll: the feet on the 8in (20cm) walking doll shows no toe detail.
SEE: *Illustration 430.*

I.

Beehler Arts, Fortune, Virga Molded-on Slippers (Ginny-Type Dolls):
1. Doll on left is a Fortune *Pam.*
2. Doll on right is a Plastic Molded Arts *Joannie.*

Other dolls with the same molded slipper include Doll Bodies *Mary Lu:* Fortune *Ninette, Starlet;* Grant Plastics *Suzie;* Niresk *Joannie;* Norma *Norma;* Roberta *Jeannie;* Virga *Lucy, Playmates* and *Lolly-Pop.*
SEE: *Illustration 431.*

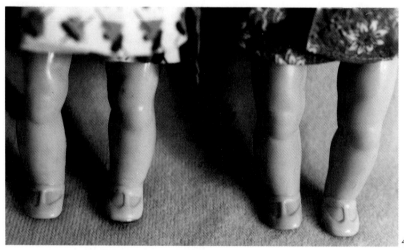

431.

Talking Dolls

1. Art-Doll Creations (English)
2. Joy Toys, Inc. (dolls talk in English, Spanish, French and Portuguese)
3. Pedigree (English)

UPDATED PRICE GUIDE

The following is an updated list of values for the dolls described in this book. Prices in this updated guide - as throughout the book - reflect a range of prices from various parts of the United States. These prices are only given for the specific dolls photographed. These dolls would be in good to *mint* condition box, tag and/or "tissue" mint conditions. Local prices will vary.

If a doll is scarce or very rare, it will be costly. Where dolls are still "coming out of attics" or "readily availabe at garage sales," prices will be lower. Personality dolls are usually more expensive.

Because clothes were important to society in the 1950s, these dolls often had elegant and lovely clothes. Even everyday clothes were fancy and surprisingly well made. As with all dolls, unusual, clothes will add to the quoted prices. Undressed dolls are usually worth 1/4 to 1/3 the value of a dressed doll.

Hard plastic dolls were still available in quantity eight to ten years ago. Today the collector sees fewer and fewer in mint condition and prices have risen. It is not at all uncommon to see unheralded, rare dolls go for remarkable prices at auction, especially when in mint condition. A comparison of the prices in this updated list to the prices in the original 1985 text of this book provides dramatic evidence of the increasing value of these wonderful dolls.

A & H DOLL MFG. CORP.

Mary Todd Lincoln:	$	75-150
Marie Antoinette:	$	75-150
Elizabeth Woodville Grey:	$	75-150
Martha Washington:	$	75-150
Queen Isabella:	$	75-150
Betsy Ross:	$	75-150
Queen Elizabeth I:	$	75-150
Empress Josephine:	$	75-150
Empress Eugenie:	$	75-150
Molly Pitcher:	$	75-150
Priscilla Alden:	$	75-150
Queen Victoria:	$	75-150
Molly Pitcher: 12in (31cm)	$	75-150
Priscilla: 12in (31cm)	$	75-150
Betsy Ross: 12in (31cm)	$	75-150
George Washington:		
8in (20cm)	$	35-40
Gigi: 8in (20cm)	$	35-50
Gigi: 7¹/₂in (19cm)	$	35-45
Gigi & Revolving Carousel		
Wardrobe: 8in (20cm)	$	50-60
Prize Packages:	$	20-25
Dutch Girl in Bell:		
8in (20cm)	$	20-25
Birthstone Dolls:		
9in (22cm)	$	10-12
Costume Styled for *Julie*		
Walking Doll:	$	10-15

ACTIVE DOLL CORPORATION

Scotch Lassie: 7in (18cm)	$	12-15

ADMIRATION DOLL COMPANY

Girl: 7¹/₂in (19cm)	$	10-12

A.H. DELFAUSSE COMPANY

Madmoiselle:	$	45-55

A & H DOLL MFG. CORP.

Donna Dolls Queen		
Elizabeth: 12in (31cm)	$	60-75

ALDEN'S

Lil Megotoo: 8in (20cm)	$	15-20

ALEXANDER DOLL COMPANY, INC.

Beaux Arts Creations Queen		
Elizabeth: 18in (46cm)		$2000-2400+
Beaux Arts Creations		
Princess Margaret Rose:		
18in (46cm)		$2000-2400+
Beaux Arts Creations Lady:		
18in (46cm) (pink)	$	200-2200+
Beaux Arts Creations Lady:		
18in (46cm) (chartreuse)		$2200-2400+
Beaux Arts Creations Lady:		
18in (46cm) (white)		$2200-2400+
Bride: 14in (36cm)	$	450-500+
Ringbearer: 12in (31cm)	$	500-600

Knuckle-head Nellie:
14in (36cm) .... $ 600-1000+
Cinderella: 15in (38cm) .. $ 500-700
Pink Bride: 14in (36cm) .. $ 500-700
Lady with the Rhinestone
Beauty Mark:
21in (53cm) $3000-5000
Champs Elysees:
21in (53cm) $2000-5000
Pink Champagne:
21in (53cm) $2000-5000
Deborah Ballerina:
21in (53cm) $2000-5000
Kathryn Grayson:
21in (53cm) $6000-8500
Kathy: 15in (38cm) ...... $ 400-500+
Maggie: 14in (36cm) ..... $ 450-550
Wendy Bride: 15in (38cm) $ 500-600+
Rosamund: 15in (41cm) .. $ 500-600
Rosamund: 18in (46cm) .. $ 600-800
Annabelle: 15in (38cm)... $ 450-550
Tommy Bangs: 15in (38cm) $ 750-800+
Stuffy: 14in (33cm) ...... $ 700-850
Glamour Girls:
18in (46cm) .... $ 800-900+
Elaine of the Me and
My Shadow Series:
18in (46cm) .... $ 600-800
Victoria of Me and
My Shadow Series:
18in (46cm) .... $ 750-900+
Binnie Walker: 15in (38cm) $ 500-600+
Winsome Binnie Walker:
5in (38cm) .... $ 225-275
18in (46cm) .... $ 250-300
25in (64cm) .... $ 325-400
Mary Ellen: 31in (79cm).. $ 425-500
(1955) costume ..... $ 80-100
Lissy: 12in (31cm) .... $ 325-350
Kelly: 12in (31cm) .... $ 400-500
Cissy: 20in (51cm)-
21in (53cm) .... $ 800-+
Cissy #2283: .... $ 700-800+
Renoir Cissy: 20in (51cm) $ 650-800+
Elise Renoir: 16¹/₂in (42cm) $ 500-550
Cissette: 10¹/₂in (27cm) ... $ 200-225
Cissette Portrette: 10¹/₂in (27cm)
(Gold Rush) .... $ 850
(Gibson Girl) ...... $ 850
(Renoir)........... $ 400-600

(Scarlett) .... $ 400-550
(Agatha) .... $ 550-575
(Godey)........... $ 500
(Southern Belle) ..... $ 450-500
(Melinda) .... $ 375-450
Jenny Lind: 11in (28cm).. $ 650-750
Davy Crockett Boy and Girl:
8in (20cm) .... $ 600-750
Infant of Prague: 8in (20cm)
Angel: 8in (20cm)
(Maggie Mixup face) ... $1000-1050
Bride and Groom:
8in (20cm) .... $ 700-800
Little Women: 8in (20cm). $ 650-725
Little Genius: 19in (46cm) $ 170-190
Quiz-kin: 7¹/₂in (19cm) ... $ 550-650

AMERICAN CHARACTER
DOLL CO. _____

Sweet Sue: 14in (36cm)... $ 240-280
18in (46cm)-20in (51cm) $ 325-350
24in (61cm) .... $ 400-450
30in (76cm) .... $ 525-575
Sweet Sue School Girl:
14¹/₂in (37cm) .... $ 135-150
Sweet Alice: 16¹/₂in (38cm) $ 325-350
Mardi Gras: 15in (38cm) . $ 140-280
18in (46cm) .... $ 325-350
23in (58cm) .... $ 400-450
Sweet Sue Cotillion:
(Costume) .... $ 250-325
Tiny Tears: 11in (28cm) .. $ 75-100
12in (31cm) .... $ 75-100
15in (38cm) .... $ 75-100
18¹/₂in (47cm)...... $ 125-225
Life Size Sweet Sue: ..... $ 525-575+
Sweet Sue wardrobe from
1955 catalog:
Tiny Tears: 13in (33cm) .. $ 300+
Toodles "Potty Baby": 13in
(33cm) & 16in (41cm) .. $ 70-100
Annie Oakley: 18in (46cm) $ 275-325+
Betsy McCall: 8in (20cm)
depending on costume .. $ 165-200
Nanette: 15in (36cm)
depending on costume .. $ 75-200
18in (46cm) depending
on costume .... $ 250-300
23in (58cm) depending
on costume .... $ 400-450

Nanette Cowgirl:
14in (36cm) .... $ 175-200
Nanette with Tiara:
18in (46cm) .... $ 250-280
Nancy Lee: 14in (36cm) .. $ 175-200
Nancy Lee Skater:
20in (51cm) .... $ 300-350
Nancy: 14in (36cm) ...... $ 175-200
Life Size Nanette:
30in (76cm) .... $ 275-350
Nanette Ballerina:
18in (46cm) .... $ 125-150
Littlest Angel: 11in (28cm)
depending on costume .. $ 75-175
Littlest Angel Skier:
11in (28cm).......... $ 125-175
Littlest Angel Skater:
11in (28cm).......... $ 100-125
Littlest Angel in Jodhpurs:
11in (28cm).......... $ 125-175
Littlest Angel: 11in (28cm) $ 75-100
Littlest Angel: 10in (25cm)
walking doll .... $ 175-225
Littlest Angel: 10in (25cm)
head turning walker .... $ 175-225
Littlest Angel Cowgirl:
10½in (27cm) .... $ 125-150
Littlest Angel Ballerina:
11in (28cm).......... $ 100-150
Littlest Angel Bride:
11in (28cm).......... $ 125-150
Littlest Angel in Chinese
Costume: 11in (28cm) .. $ 130-160

ARTISAN DOLL (ARTISAN NOVELTY CO.)

1950 Walking Doll: ...... $ 80-110
Raving Beauty: 20in (51cm)
depending on costume .. $ 200
Raving Beauty:
depending on costume .. $ 325-375
Raving Beauty Walking Doll:
20in (51cm) .... $ 325-375
Raving Beauty: 20in (51cm)
depending on costume .. $ 225-275

AVA MILANO ART DOLL

Pamela: 18in (46cm) ..... $ 200-250+

AWIN TRADING CO. (ENGLAND)

Coronation Walking Guardsman: 24in (61cm)

BABY BARRY TOYS

Baby Barry: 16in (41cm)
with accessories $200-250

BEDDY-BYE AND BYE-BYE DOLL

Travel Doll: 7¼in (19cm)
with costumes & acc. .... $ 50-60

BELLE DOLL & TOY CORP.

Heddi Stroller: 20in (51cm) $ 100-175

BIBLE DOLL CO. OF AMERICA

David: 10in (25cm) ...... $ 50-75

BLOCK DOLL CORP.

Answer Doll: 12in (33cm) . $ 50-75
Baby Walker:
10½in (27cm) .... $ 50-75
Answer Doll: 12in (31cm) . $ 45-55
Chubby-Type:
10½in (27cm) .... $ 50-75
3 Block Doll Creations: .. $ 5-6

BONOMI COMPANY (ITALY)

Annie: .... $ 100-150

CHIQUITA TRINKETS

Chiquita Dolls: .... $ 20-25
Rumbero Doll:
11in (28cm).......... $ 10-15

COMMONWEALTH PLASTICS CORP.

Dress-Me Dolls: 6in (15cm)

D & D MFG. CO.

Nun: 12in (31cm) .... $ 30-50

DIAMONT (GERMANY)

Boy in Lederhosen:
14in (36cm) .... $ 85-110

DE SOTO MANUFACTURING COMPANY

Randy Goes to the Circus: $ 40-55

DOLL BODIES (DOLLS OF FAR-A-WAY-LANDS, INC.)

Cornation Doll: 7½in (19cm)
& 12in (31cm) .... $ 40-50

DOLL BODIES, INC. (ORIGINALLY LINGERIE LOU)

Mary-Lu Walker:
18in (46cm) .... $ 40-45
Mary-Lu: 7¹/₂in (19cm)... $ 12-15
Mary-Lu Walker:
16in (41cm) .... $ 60-85
Dress-Me Dolls: 7¹/₂in (19cm)-
11¹/₂in (29cm) .... $ 5-15
Dress-Me Dolls:
7¹/₂in (19cm) .... $ 12-15
Dolls of Faraway Lands: . $ 10-20

DUCHESS DOLL CORP.

Coronation Doll: 7¹/₂in (19cm)
& 12¹/₂in (32cm) ...... $ 75-100
Dale Evans: 8in (29cm)
depending on costume .. $ 30-50
Miss Valentine of 1951:
7¹/₂in (19cm) .... $ 35-50
Peter Pan and Tinker Bell:
7in (18cm) .... $ 35-55
packaged in box ..... $ 125-135
Alice in Wonderland:
7¹/₂in (19cm) &
12¹/₂in (32cm) .... $ 35-50
Italian Dream Girl:
13in (33cm) (in box).... $ 35-50
Duchess:.............. $ 40-55

EEGEE (GOLDBERGER DOLL MFG. CO., INC.)

Gigi Perreau: 20in (51cm) $ 75-125
Susan Stroller: 23in (58cm) $ 65-75

EFFANBEE DOLL CORP.

Howdy Doody: 19in (48cm) $ 150-200
23in (58cm) .... $ 200-250
Electronic Doll: 28in (71cm)
in working condition.... $ 200-250+
Schiaparelli Doll:
18in (46cm) .... $ 300-400
Tintair Honey: 16in (41cm) $ 350-375
Honey Bride: 14in (36cm) $ 170-200
16in (41cm) depending
on costume .... $ 180-225
18in (46cm) depending
on costume .... $ 195-240
24in (61cm) depending
on costume .... $ 275-325

Honey Walker Ice Skater:
18in (46cm) .... $ 250-350

ELITE CREATIONS

Vicki: 8in (20cm) .... $ 30-40
Vicki Brochure:......... $ 5-10

EUGENIA DOLL COMPANY, INC.

Pam, the Perm-O-Wave Doll:
14in (36cm)
Doll in Child's Dress:
18in (46cm) .... $ 150-175
Doll in Pink Dress in Box:
18in (46cm) .... $ 225-250
Juliette Bridal Doll:
21in (53cm) .... $ 175-200

FLEISCHAKER NOVELTY COMPANY

Little Girl of Today:

FORTUNE TOYS INCORPORATED

Ninette: 8in (20cm) ...... $ 50-60
Pam: (in box) .... $ 50-60
(doll) .... $ 40-50

FURGA (ITALY)

Girl in Blue Dress: 14in (36cm)
depending on costume .. $ 150-175

G.A. DOHERTY CO.

Susan's Crochet Doll Kit:
7in (18cm) .... $ 15-25

G.H. & E. FREYDBERG, INC.

Mary Jane: 17in (43cm) .. $ 250+

GINGER DOLLS

Painted Eye Ginger Nurse:
8in (20cm) .... $ 75-100
Ginger in Mexican Outfit: $ 55-75+
Mouseketeers: .... $ 125-150+
**Ginger in Mouseketeer
Mousekarade Costume:** $ 125-150+
**Ginger in Mouseketeer
Official Talent Roundup
Costume:** .... $ 125-150+
Ginger Ballerina:
7¹/₂in (19cm) .... $ 55-75
Cha Cha Heel Ginger:
8in (20cm) .... $ 55-75+
Ginger:................ $ 50-75

Miss Ginger: 10in (25cm) . $ 80-120
Ginger Doll-Mate:

GRANT PLASTICS, INC.

Donna: 7¹/₂in (19cm) ..... $ 5-10
Eileen: 20in (51cm) ...... $ 15-25
Gretchen: 7¹/₂in (19cm)... $ 5-10
Linda: 12in (31cm) ...... $ 5-10
Karen: 7¹/₂in (19cm) ..... $ 5-10
Kathleen: 11in (28cm).... $ 5-10
Marcia: 7¹/₂in (19cm) .... $ 5-10
Pamela: 8in (20cm) ...... $ 5-10
Priscilla: 12in (31cm) .... $ 5-10
Suzie: 8in (20cm)........ $ 5-10
Sylvia: 18in (47cm) ...... $ 5-10

J.K. FARNELL & CO. LTD. (ENGLAND)

Plastic Dolls:

HARDY DIFFERENT TOYS

Girl in White Dress:
14in (36cm) .... $ 125-145

HOLLYWOOD DOLL MANUFACTURING CO.

Queen for a Day:
6in (15cm) .... $ 30-35
Western Series Cowboy:
5in (13cm) .... $ 20-30
Non-walking doll:
8in (20cm) .... $ 35-45
Rock-a-Bye Baby:
5in (13cm) .... $ 16-20

HORSMAN DOLLS, INC.

Bright Star: 15in (38cm).. $ 100-175+
Little Girl: 16in (41cm)... $ 100-150
Mary Had a Little Lamb:
18in (46cm) .... $ 100-150
Pitter Patty: 19in (48cm) . $ 70-80

IDEAL TOY CORPORATION

Betsy McCall: 14in (36cm) $ 250-300
Betsy Wetsy: 12in (31cm);
16in (41cm) .... $ 80-100
Harriet Hubbard Ayer:
14in (36cm) .... $ 175-195
16in (41cm) .... $ 250-300
Lolly: 9in (23cm) .... $ 25-30
Mary Hartline (Toni P94):
22¹/₂in (57cm) .... $ 750+
Miss Curity: 14in (36cm) . $ 250-325

Plassie: 16in (41cm);
19in (48cm); 22in (60cm) $ 50-100
Plassie Toddler: 14in (36cm)
undressed .... $ 75-100
14in (36cm) dressed in
original clothes .... $ 110-145
Plassie Toddler: 14in (36cm)
sleep eyes .... $ 110-145
Saucy Walker: 22in (56cm) $ 125-150
16in (41cm) .... $ 70-100
Toni: P90 .... $ 250-300
P91 .... $ 350-375
P92 .... $ 400-500
P93 .... $ 525-550
P94 .... $ 600-650+
Toni in Pleated Dress:
21in (53cm) .... $ 550-600
Toni: 16in (41cm) ...... $ 350-375

INEZ HOLLAND HOUSE

Starlet: 7¹/₂in (19cm) ..... $ 30-35

J. HALPERN COMPANY (HALCO)

Baby Flufee: 24in (61cm) . $ 75-100
Bridesmaid: 29in (74cm) . $ 95-120

JOLLY TOYS

Girl in Pink Dress:
16in (41cm) .... $ 70-80

KÄTHE KRUSE

Model Hanne Kruse:
9³/₄in (25cm) .... $ 350-400+
Badebaby: 12in (31cm)... $ 350-375+
Gretchen and Hansel:
16in (41cm) .... $ 450-475
Susi and Jane: 16in (41cm) $ 450-475+
Mimerle: 12in (31cm) .... $ 300-400

KIM DOLLS

Fairy: 8¹/₂in (22cm) ...... $ 35-40
Kim in Jodhpur Outfit:
7¹/₂in (19cm) .... $ 35-40

L. REESE & CO.

Peress Coronation Doll:
15in (38cm) .... $ 300-400+

LENCI (ITALY)

Girl from Sardinia:
6in (15cm) .... $ 40-50
Girl from Valsarentino:
6in (15cm) .... $ 75-100

LOVELY DOLL

U.S. Marine, U.S. Army,
U.S. Air Corps:
  7in (18cm) . . . . $ 20-25

MARY HOYER DOLL MFG. CO.

Doll in 3-piece knitted bathing outfit:
  14in (36cm) . . . . $ 300-400+
Gigi: 18in (46cm) . . . . $ 400-500+
Mary Hoyer Dollies: . . . . . $ 375-400+

MIDWESTERN MFG. CO.

Mary Jean: 8in (20cm) . . . $ 25-35
Suzy Stroller: 16in (41cm);
  19in (48cm) . . . . $ 75-100

MRS. LAVALLE

Cuddlee Bride Walking Doll:
  8in (20cm) . . . . $ 25-30

NANCY ANN STORYBOOK DOLLS, INC.

Muffie: 8in (20cm) . . . . . . $ 150-175+
Muffie: (for doll and
  mint outfit) . . . . $ 150-175+
    (for unopened boxed
    outfit) . . . . $ 40-50
Spanish Muffie: 8in (20cm) $ 80-100
Around the World Muffie:
  8in (20cm) . . . . $ 80-100
Debbie: 10¹/₂in (27cm)
  depending on costume . . $ 125-165
Debbie clothes:
  (boxed outfit) . . . . $ 60-70
Roy Rogers and Dale Evans:
  8in (29cm) . . . . $ 120-145
Nancy Ann Style Show
  Series: . . . . $ 400-475
Nancy Ann Style Show Doll:
  18in (46cm) . . . . $ 300-450+
Sisters Go to Sunday School:
  3¹/₂in (9cm); 5in (13cm) . $ 35-55
Little Sisters Go to School:
  3¹/₂in (9cm); 5in (13cm) . $ 35-55
Easter Dolls: 5in (13cm) . . $ 35-55
Maytime: 6in (15cm) . . . . . $ 35-55
Beauty: 5in (13cm) . . . . . . $ 35-55
See Saw Marjory Daw:
  5in (13cm) . . . . $ 35-55

NIRESK INDUSTRIES, INC.

Nina Ballerina:
  20in (51cm) . . . . $ 50-75

258

Hollywood Bride with
  7-outfit trousseau:
  18in (46cm) . . . . $ 75-95
Janie Pigtails: 8in (20cm) . $ 25-35

NORMA ORIGINALS, INC.

Majorette: 7¹/₂in (19cm) . . $ 15-20
Norma Bride: 8in (20cm) . $ 40-50
Martha Washington:
  7¹/₂in (19cm) . . . . $ 20-25
Groom: 7¹/₂in (19cm) . . . . $ 20-25

OLD COTTAGE TOYS

Scotland Boy: 9in (23cm) . $ 125-175
  12in (31cm)-13in (33cm)
    depending on doll(s) $ 300-1100
Winter Girl in Kate Greenaway Style:
  9in (23cm) . . . . $ 70-95
Amy: 10in (25cm) . . . . . . $ 125-175
Baby: 4³/₄in (12cm) . . . . . . $ 40-45
Goose Girl: (small doll) . . . $ 115-125
  (larger size) . . . . $ 300-325+
Tweedledum and Tweedledee:
  10in (25cm) $1100-1200

ONTARIO PLASTIC INC.

Paula Sue: 8in (20cm) . . . . $ 20-25

P.J. HILL CO.

Cindy Walker: 14in (36cm);
  20in (51cm); 23in (58cm) $ 50-75

P & M DOLL COMPANY

Paula Mae Magic Knee Action Doll:
  (white doll) . . . . $ 50-60
  (black doll) . . . . $ 65-80

P.M.A. DOLLS, INC. (PLASTIC MOLDED ARTS)

Joanie Pigtails: 8in (20cm)
  depending on outfit . . . . . $ 20-40
Joanie Pigtails Wardrobe &
  Travel Case: 8in (20cm) $ 35-40+
Joanie Walker: 8in (20cm) $ 25-25
Joanie-the Wedding Belle:
  8in (20cm) . . . . $ 35-40
Stepping Steppers:
  11in (28cm) . . . . $ 20-25
Chubby Type Girl:
  10¹/₂in (27cm) . . . . $ 20-30
Miss Joan: 12in (31cm)
  depending on costume . . $ 25-40
Little Miss Joan: 9in (23cm)
  depending on costume . . $ 25-40

PARIS DOLL COMPANY

Rita Majorette:
  29in (74cm) . . . . $ 150-200+
Rita: 29in (74cm) . . . . $ 150-200+
Rita: 31in (79cm) . . . . $ 150-200+

PEDIGREE COMPANY SOFT TOYS, LTD. (PETER DARLING LTD.)

Coronation Doll: 27in (69cm)
Little Princess: . . . . $ 125-150
Doll in Knit Outfit:
  22in (56cm) . . . . $ 100-125
Pin-up Doll: 14in (36cm)
  in original clothes . . . . . . $ 100-125
Costume Dolls:
  6¹/₂in (15cm) . . . . $ 40-50
Delite Doll: 7in (18cm) . . . $ 10-12

PRESSMAN TOY CORP.

Fever Doll with Hospital Bed:
  7in (18cm) . . . . $ 50

REINA DOLL CORP.

Best Dressed Doll in America:
  13in (33cm) . . . . $ 15-25

RELIABLE TOY CO. LTD/LTEE.

Cornation Dolls:
Plassikins: 15in (38cm) . . . $ 75-100
Dress-Me Doll: 12in (31cm) $ 10-15
Indian: 11in (28cm) . . . . . . $ 25-30

RICHWOOD TOYS, INC.

Sandra Sue Skater:
  8in (20cm) . . . . $ 125+
Louisa May Alcott Dolls, Beth, Amy, Marmee, Meg and Jo:
  (without box) . . . . $ 125+
  (with box) . . . . $ 200+
Sandra Sue Outfits: (outfits mint-in-zippered plastic bag) . . . . $ 45-65+
Sandra Sue Accessories:
  white hat, shoes and
  jewelry . . . . $ 35-40
  formal dress . . . . $ 50-60
  playsuit . . . . $ 45+
Cindy Lou: 14in (36cm)
  in dress . . . . $ 125-150
  in long dress . . . . $ 145-175

Cindy Lou "Round the Clock Fashions":
  (boxed outfits) . . . . $ 50-60

ROSEBUD (ENGLAND)

Baby: 5¹/₂in (14cm) . . . . . . $ 35-50
Fairy Dolls: 6¹/₂in (16cm) . $ 50-75
Baby Rosebud Toddler:
  6¹/₂in (17cm) . . . . $ 30-45
Miss Rosebud:
  7¹/₂in (19cm) . . . . $ 55-85
Miss Rosebud: 7in (18cm) $ 55-85
Sarold Girl: 7in (18cm) . . . $ 45-85
Miss Rosebud:
  7¹/₂in (19cm) . . . . $ 45-85

SAROLD (ENGLAND)

Girl: 8in (20cm) . . . . $ 30-40

SAYCO DOLL CORPORATION

Miss America Pageant Doll-Wave:
  10³/₄in (27cm) . . . . $ 55-75
  (outfits) . . . . $ 25-50
Dream Girl Costume:
  8in (20cm) . . . . $ 15-20

SOCIÉTÉ FRANÇAIS FABRICATION BÉBÉ ET JOUETS

Girl: 15in (38cm) . . . . $ 85-125+

STANDARD DOLL CO.

Miniature Character Doll:
  15in (38cm) . . . . $ 20-25
  8in (20cm) . . . . $ 10-12

STEPHANIE PLAYTHINGS, INC.

Stephanie and Stephan:
  30in (76cm) . . . . $ 80-90

TANZPUPPE-SWEETHEART (WESTERN GERMANY)

Vatican Guard: 7in (18cm) $ 25-35

TERRI LEE, INC.

Terri Lee and Jerri Welcome a New Baby Sister: 16in (41cm) . . . . $ 250-325
Gene Autry:
  16in (41cm) (nude) . . . . . $ 750
  (all original) $1450
Benjie: 16in (41cm) . . . . . . $ 750+
Southern Belle:
  16in (41cm) . . . . $ 450-550

Tiny Terri Lee: 10in (25cm) $ 160-170
Tiny Jerri: 10in (25cm) . . . $ 180-190

TOGS AND DOLLS CORP. ____

Mary Jane: . . . . $ 225-300

UNEEDA DOLL
COMPANY, INC. ____

Needa Toddles:
22in (56cm) . . . . $ 65-85
Magic Fairy Princess Doll:
18in (46cm) . . . . $ 100-125

UNICA (BELGIUM)____

Blonde Rooted Hair Doll:
14in (36cm) . . . . $ 45-55

VALENTINE DOLLS, INC. ____

Mona Lisa: 12in (31cm) . . $ 100-125
Ballerina Doll: . . . . $ 45-65
Dressmaker Doll: . . . . $ 45-65

VIRGA DOLL COMPANY____

Lolly-Pop Walking Doll:
8in (20cm) . . . . $ 100-125+
Playmate in Jodhpurs:
8in (20cm) . . . . $ 100-125+
Schiaparelli GoGo Skater:
8in (20cm) . . . . $ 100-135+
Lucy: 9in (23cm) . . . . $ 50-80
Play-Pals Walking Doll:
9in (23cm) . . . . $ 50-80
Hi Heel 'Teen:
8½in (22cm) . . . . $ 35-40+
Hi Heel 'Teen: 8½in (22cm)
(blue dress) . . . . $ 35-40+

VOGUE DOLLS, INC. ____

Coronation Doll:
8in (20cm) . . . . $1500-1800+
Painted-Eye Ginny Twins:
8in (20cm) . . . . $ 350-375+

Cinderella, Prince &
Fairy Godmother:
8in (20cm) . . . . $ 350-375
Crib Crowd: 8in (20cm) . . $ 550-600
Fluffy: 8in (20cm) . . . . . . $ 700+
Ginny Cowboy and Cowgirl:
8in (20cm) . . . . $ 300-350
Toddler: 8in (20cm) . . . . . . $ 350-375
Black Ginny: 8in(20cm) . . $ 700+
Painted Eyelash Ginny:
8in (20cm) . . . . $ 375-400+
Ginny Roller Skater:
8in (20cm) . . . . $ 375-400+
Ginny Skater from Sports
Series: 8in (20cm) . . . . . $ 350-375
Ginny: 8in (20cm) . . . . . . $ 400-500+
Ginny: 8in (20cm) bent-knee
walker . . . . $ 165-175+
Littlest Angel: 11in (28cm)
depending on costume . . $ 75-175
Jill: 10in (25cm) depending
on outfit . . . . $ 75-100
Jill: 10in (25cm) . . . . $ 100-160

WALKALON MFG. COMPANY__

Betsy Walker: 20in (51cm)
(in working condition) . . $ 90-110
(mint-in-box) . . . . $ 110-135

WORLD WIDE DOLL CLUB
(OVERSEAS DOLLS)____

Heidi: . . . . $ 35-45+

WRITING TOYS
CORPORATION ____

Rita the Writing Doll:
26in (66cm) . . . . $ 175-225

INDEX

OTHER BOOKS BY THE AUTHORS

Cloth Dolls Identification & Price Guide 1920s and 1930s
Expansive photo guide to cloth dolls made by Lenci, Nora Welling, Chad Valley and many others. Lavishly illustrated with a bevy of beautiful photos plus packed with detailed descriptions to make identification simple. Loaded with 1990 values by the best selling author of the **Hard Plastic Doll** series. Features 47 color and 271 b/w photographs. 256 pages. 5¹/₂" x 8". PB. Item #H3979. $12.95

Compo Dolls 1928-1955 Identification and Price Guide
A long-awaited, much needed guide to composition dolls aids collectors with those favorite postwar friends. 428 photographs with 130 in color, display difficult-to-identify dolls augmented by a bevy of 208 pages of detailed text contain the most-up-to-date accurate values. An indispensable book for modern doll collectors! 208 pages. 8¹/₂" x 11". HB. Item #H4389. $25.00

Compo Dolls, Vol. II 1909-1928
Compo Dolls II is a companion volume to **Volume I**, featuring the early prewar character dolls of 1909-1928. 302 photographs with 135 appearing in color, display difficult-to-identify dolls. Information is dedicated to the marks, characteristics and company stories of both the small and large manufacturers. Included is an identification section and up-to-date values. 176 pages. 8¹/₂" x 11". HB. Item #H4691. $25.00

Hard Plastic Dolls, Vol. I, 3rd Revised Edition
An indispensable identification and price guide for every collector wanting to know more about hard plastic dolls of the 40s and 50s and their collectors values. 304 pages. 5¹/₂" x 8". PB. #H4638. $14.95

Hard Plastic Dolls, Vol. II.
Second revised volume of a multitude of additional hard plastic dolls with identification and values. More than 43 color and 394 b/w photos to aid the collector in studying and valuing their dolls. Organized both by type of doll and their manufacturer, this is a deluxe easy-to-use reference book. Includes most current prices. 256 pages. 5¹/₂" x 8". PB. Item #H3823.

Santa Dolls & Figurines Price Guide Antique to Contemporary
Discover valuable information about your favorite Santa collectibles from the information and price guide as well as the legends of Gift-Givers from other countries. Enjoy the different styles of Santa dolls, figurines, paper dolls and postcards and their costumes in 121 gorgeous color photographs and 146 b/w photographs. 160 pages. 5¹/₂" x 8". PB. Item #H4412. $14.95

European Costumed Dolls: Value and Identification Guide
The first book in a series dedicated to preserving the historical and cultural perspectives of different countries. **European Costumed Dolls** contains a multitude of dolls with identification and values in an easy-to-use reference style. Admire the costumes and beauty of the 125 color and b/w photos of these unique **European Costumed Dolls**. 160 pages. 6" x 9". PB. Item #H4741, $14.95

Your HF Digital Companion

By Steve Ford, WB8IMY

Published by: **The American Radio Relay League**
225 Main Street, Newington, CT 06111

Foreword

Picture how text is sent via radio. On the VHF, UHF and microwave bands, it's relatively easy. On the HF bands, however, it's another matter entirely! Not only are the digital signals squeezed into smaller chunks of spectrum, they have to contend with fickle propagation and a much higher level of interference.

Immediately after World War II, amateurs began using surplus radio teletype, or RTTY gear. For decades thereafter, the musical warblings of RTTY stations could be heard as they conversed over hundreds and thousands of miles. Fading and interference caused errors in reception, and the equipment was big and noisy but, most of the time, RTTY worked. In the early 1980's, the era of the personal computer brought RTTY to the desktop and added a new word to the Amateur Radio lexicon: AMTOR. The synchronized, chirping rhythms of AMTOR signaled the beginning of virtually error-free digital communications on the HF bands.

RTTY and AMTOR remain with us in the '90s—and they are as enjoyable and fascinating as ever. New modes such as CLOVER, PacTOR and G-TOR have joined their ranks, providing spectacular improvements in the quality of digital transmission and reception.

Steve Ford, WB8IMY, is about to take you on a tour of these intriguing modes. Along the way you'll learn how to build and operate your own digital station. If you're new to Amateur Radio, I encourage you to explore HF digital communications. You're in for a lot of excitement! If you're a veteran in need of fresh opportunities, this book points the way.

The HF digital modes have a great deal to offer: relaxed, conversational communications; challenging contests; rare DX contacts; public service operations and much more. As you'll discover in *Your HF Digital Companion*, you don't need to be a digital expert to get started. All that's required is the capacity for awe and wonder!

David Sumner, K1ZZ
Executive Vice President
February 1995

A note from the publisher: This book is based on the ARRL's *Your RTTY/AMTOR Companion*, published in 1993. New chapters have been added on PacTOR, CLOVER, HF packet and G-TOR, reflecting the increased interest in these modes. In addition, we've updated other parts of the book, including the Resource Guide, and added two appendices—HF Digital Bulletin Boards, and Technical Descriptions of CLOVER, G-TOR and PacTOR.

Contents

CHAPTER 1

What's That Racket In My Radio?

I f you've spent time exploring the Amateur Radio HF bands, I'll bet you've heard some pretty strange stuff. I'm not talking about the occasional operator who appears to be a few sandwiches short of a picnic, so to speak. No, I'm referring to the odd sounds that you'll find just above the CW portions of the bands.

Let's take a trip through this strange landscape. Do you hear warbling, musical signals? They've been around for decades and veteran amateurs recognize them immediately as *radioteletype*. Although there are many radioteletype codes, the ham custom is to refer to *Baudot* or *Murray* radioteletype as *RTTY* (pronounced "ritty"). Twist the dial a bit further and you're likely to hear a chorus of electronic crickets. These are the chirping dialogs of *AMTOR* (*AM*ateur *T*eleprinting *O*ver *R*adio) stations. Keep hunting and you may also hear the unusual sounds of *PacTOR*, *CLOVER* and *G-TOR*. And what about those raspy, high-pitched bursts? Those are the unmistakable signatures of *packet*.

These are the primary HF *digital* modes. They're called digital modes because the communication involves an exchange of digital data between one station and another. In the case of *AFSK* RTTY, for example, letters typed on a keyboard are translated into data by a computer or data terminal. Another device, usually a *multimode communications processor* (*MCP*), accepts the data and converts it to whatever encoded audio tones are required. The tones are sent to the transmitter and away they go! At the receiving end the same process occurs in reverse: The tones are translated back into data and displayed as text on a computer or terminal screen.

Who Cares?

Why should you care about HF digital modes? If you have something to say, isn't it easier to pick up a microphone or grab a CW key? The answer depends on how effectively you want to communicate.

With the exception of RTTY, all digital communications modes include some form of error detection. This means the text from your station will arrive at its destination *without errors*. It will be received exactly as you sent it—complete with typographical, spelling and grammar glitches. (You can't expect your communications system to correct those problems, too!)

Can you say the same thing for a phone or CW conversation? Well…yes, as long as conditions are decent. Even when noise and interference are severe, the human brain has a remarkable ability to recover meaningful information. However, your mind also has a tendency to use imagination to fill some of the gaps. You may *think* you understood everything correctly, but did you?

A microprocessor-based system isn't burdened with imagination. It receives the data correctly, or it doesn't—

So What Can I do with the HF Digital Modes?

I thought you'd never ask! Here's a partial list...

❏ Enjoy conversations with amateurs throughout the world. The somewhat slower pace of the digital modes allows you to compose your thoughts and express yourself clearly. As a result, you'll find that conversations are friendly and relaxing.

❏ Work rare DX. Many DXpeditions operate RTTY and other digital modes in addition to SSB and CW. By using your digital capability, you'll have an extra edge on the competition!

❏ Access mailbox systems. By connecting to a mailbox, you can read bulletins, drop off messages for other operators or read messages that have been left for you.

❏ Use AMTOR *APLink* systems. An APLink system is your gateway to the packet radio network. You can post messages on an APLink and they'll be forwarded to the VHF/UHF packet network for delivery to hams at their local packet bulletin boards. Packet-active hams can also send messages to you via the APLink system.

❏ Perform public-service work. In emergency situations, the digital modes are often in the spotlight. If disaster strikes in a distant part of the world, digital operators become communications lifelines. For example, injury lists and detailed requests for aid are easily handled by RTTY and AMTOR stations. The National Traffic System also depends on digital modes to move vital messages throughout the world.

❏ Participate in contests that *really* test your skills as a digital operator!

there's no room for random speculation. Its attention span never wanders, no matter how long it has been operating. It proceeds with its instructions diligently and patiently until you tell it otherwise. As a result, the digital modes are highly effective and reliable. With recent developments in digital signal processing (DSP) and innovations such as G-TOR and CLOVER, hams are swapping digital data even under very poor signal conditions!

Although there are obvious practical benefits to using HF digital modes, you can't forget the greatest benefit of all: they're *fun*! Operating the HF digital modes is a unique experience. It's always thrilling to send a RTTY CQ and watch your screen as a stranger—across the continent or half a world away—responds to your call. As the text

The more the better when it comes to contesting! Jon, KB9ATR (third from the left) did a multioperator effort in the ARRL RTTY Roundup to get more people interested in digital communications.

appears, you read it eagerly, the same way you'd read the opening pages of a good novel. A few years ago I enjoyed a fascinating RTTY conversation with a commercial airline pilot. I kept sending one question after another (How much thrust does an engine on a Boeing 767 develop?) and he patiently answered each one. I printed the text of the conversation and I still have it today.

Other digital modes are just as enjoyable. Even though I've made hundreds of AMTOR contacts, I still get a tingle whenever I establish a *link* to another station. My transceiver begins switching rapidly back and forth from transmit to receive. The room is filled with a rhythmic chirp-chirp melody as the data exchange begins. The letters creep across the screen in fits and starts. A conversation has begun!

Since RTTY, PacTOR and AMTOR are the most popular HF digital modes in use today, they are the primary focus of this book. I'll also introduce you to HF Packet, CLOVER and G-TOR.

A Short History Lesson

In the sense that we interpret the word "digital" today, RTTY has the distinction of being the granddaddy of HF digital communications. RTTY dates back to World War II when the military began connecting mechanical teletype machines to HF radios.

At first they tried simple on/off keying to send text, but that didn't work very well. The receiving equipment couldn't always tell the difference between a signal and a burst of noise. After some further experimentation, the designers switched to *frequency shift keying* (*FSK*). This approach used two specific tones to indicate the on/off (*MARK/SPACE*) signals. FSK was a success and RTTY as we know it today was born!

Hams adopted RTTY after the war ended and by the

early '50s it was a well-established mode. Initially it found a home on VHF, but later became more popular on the HF bands. (RTTY is seldom heard on the VHF bands today.)

For several decades, hams relied on surplus teletype machines for their RTTY stations. These mechanical monsters were slow, noisy and often dirty (they had a nasty tendency to drip oil on the floor!). Operators had to read the text on paper as it was printed. The keyboard was a bit unusual, mainly due to the nature of the Baudot code.

With Baudot, all letters are capitalized (upper case). All numbers from 0 through 9 are available along with some limited punctuation. To send numbers or punctuation, a special *FIGS* character must be sent *first*. To return to alphabetical letters, a *LTRS* character must be sent. On the original teleprinters you had to press the FIGS key whenever you wanted to send numbers or punctuation. To return to alphabetical letters, you had to press the LTRS key (see Fig 1-1). You can imagine how difficult it must have been to master the keyboards of those old machines!

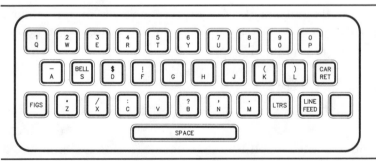

Fig 1-1—The old teleprinters featured a keyboard layout similar to the one shown here. Notice the FIGS key in the lower left corner. You had to press this key before sending punctuation or numbers. Pressing the LTRS key returned you to the "letters" mode. Although these vintage units have all but disappeared, the need to shift from FIGS to LTRS and back again remains. This is now handled automatically by software.

Al, RC2AZ, is an active RTTY operator in Russia. He built virtually all the equipment shown in this photograph!

Some ancient teletype machines remain, but most RTTY enthusiasts rely on computerized systems. The Baudot code is still the same, however, and the FIGS/LTRS shift is still required. No need to worry about your typing skills, though. The FIGS/LTRS shift is handled automatically. All you have to do is type and your software and hardware will take care of everything else. Rather than reading the text on flowing sheets of paper, you'll see it on your monitor screen.

RTTY has fulfilled its promise of transmitting the written word throughout the world. When band conditions are good and signals are optimal, RTTY is efficient and accurate. But what happens when conditions are less than ideal? That's when RTTY shows its weak side. Interference from other transmitters, fading and electrical noise cause errors in RTTY communications. Mild interference will cause a few letters to be deleted here and there. Severe interference can turn the entire text to gibberish!

Commercial maritime communication systems relied on RTTY for decades, but the inability to detect errors was a persistent problem. It could even have life-threatening consequences. What if a maritime weather service tried to alert ships of an approaching storm? The RTTY-transmitted warning had to be repeated over and over to give the ships a decent chance of copying the entire message.

The pressure to create a more reliable teletype system lead to the development of *TOR* (Teleprinting Over Radio), commonly known today as *SITOR* (Simplex Teleprinting Over Radio). Instead of sending the text in one long transmission, the TOR method sends only a few characters at a time. The receiving station checks for errors using a bit-ratio-checking scheme. If all characters are received error-free, the receiving station sends an *acknowledgment* or *ACK* signal and the next few characters are transmitted. If an error is detected, a *nonacknowledgment* or *NAK* signal is sent. This tells the transmitting station to repeat the characters. The result is digital communication *without* errors—a major improvement over previous RTTY systems. The rapid error-checking dialog—known as *Mode A* or *ARQ*—creates the distinctive chirping sounds associated with SITOR communications.

In the early 1980s, the Federal Communications Commission approved SITOR techniques for Amateur Radio use. Peter Martinez, G3PLX, adapted SITOR coding and developed AMTOR. AMTOR was tailor-made for the personal-computer era and it quickly became popular. (The advent of PCs also made *ASCII* RTTY possible using a *complete* character set including upper- and lower-case letters. However, its use remains somewhat limited today because of its lack of error detection.)

AMTOR uses the same limited character set as RTTY, but the coding is different. AMTOR sends 7 data bits per character instead of 5 used by RTTY. Like RTTY, AMTOR can send only upper-case letters. (This is changing, however. See the sidebar, "Upper/Lower Case AMTOR.") AMTOR shares another aspect with RTTY: it sends data by using frequency-shift keying.

You Take the High Tone and I'll Take the Low Tone

Understanding the nature of frequency-shift keying, or FSK, is important if you're going to be an informed digital operator.

Let's start with data. I'm sure you've heard that the fundamental language of all computers is binary *machine code*. In a binary-number system, you're only dealing with 0s and 1s. This is a natural situation for a computer since

---

Upper/Lower-Case AMTOR

AMTOR evolved from commercial TOR and SITOR, which in turn evolved from Baudot radioteletype. One of the handicaps of this evolution was that AMTOR could send only upper-case letters and limited punctuation. Peter Martinez, G3PLX, and Victor Poor, W5SMM, have created an extension of AMTOR, using the *null* code as an upper/lower-case shift signal for receiving stations.

By using upper/lower-case AMTOR, additional punctuation symbols are transmitted as well. In fact, the W5SMM version of APLink includes all of the standard punctuation symbols. For this reason, some operators refer to mixed-case AMTOR as *ASCII AMTOR*. It really isn't the full ASCII character set, but it's close.

At the time this book went to press, only the HAL PCI-3000 and AMT series controllers supported upper/lower-case AMTOR. No doubt other manufacturers will incorporate this feature as it becomes more popular. Stations using upper/lower-case AMTOR—including APLink BBSs—are fully compatible with upper-case-only users.

---

it's comprised of a multitude of solid-state *logic* switches that can only be *on* or *off* ("high" or "low"). So, an "on" condition represents a binary 1 while an "off" condition represents a binary 0.

If you use wires to connect two computers, the on/off voltage states are communicated from one machine to another easily. But let's make the situation more complicated and move the computers several hundred miles apart. Now what are you going to do? Radio seems like a natural choice, but you can't send high/low voltage states over the air...or can you?

What if you translated the changing voltages to changing *tones*? A device known as a *multimode communications processor*, or *MCP*, will do this nicely. You could use 2,125 Hz to represent a binary 1 and 2,295 Hz to represent a binary 0. Feed those tones to the audio input of an SSB transceiver operating on lower sideband, for example, and they'll be transmitted as signals at specific points below the *suppressed carrier frequency*. The 2,125-Hz tone will create a signal 2,125 Hz below the suppressed carrier. The 2,295-Hz tone will create a signal 2,295 Hz below the suppressed carrier. Subtract the frequency of the high tone from the low tone and you get 170 Hz. In other words, the signal *shifts* 170 Hz to represent a 1 or 0. Shifting voltages have become shifting RF signal frequencies! As we discussed previously, the tone that represents a binary 1 is called the MARK. The signal that represents a binary 0 is called the SPACE (see Fig 1-2).

At the receiving end of the path, you'll need to convert the signals back into binary high/low voltage states. MCPs are designed with audio filters to detect the MARK and SPACE signals and produce corresponding data pulses. Feed those data pulses to a computer running *terminal* software and—trumpet fanfare please!—text appears on the screen.

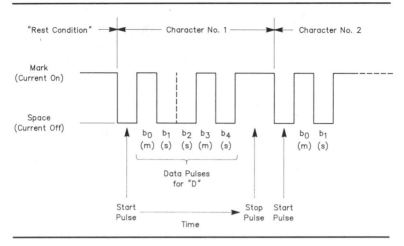

Fig 1-2—This is a diagram of RTTY MARK and SPACE signals as the letter "D" is sent. A start pulse begins the character, followed by the 5 bits that define it (b_0 through b_4). By looking at the bits, you can see that "D" is MARK-SPACE-SPACE-MARK-SPACE. A stop pulse signals the end of the character and another start pulse begins a new character. These MARK and SPACE signals appear as shifting audio tones at the receiver. They are fed to a multimode communications processor (MCP) to be decoded back into data and displayed as text.

Most digital modes use frequency-shift keying to pass information from one station to another. A 170-Hz shift between the MARK and SPACE is the Amateur Radio standard. A few hams use an 850-Hz shift, an artifact from the early VHF RTTY days. Commercial SITOR stations often use a 425-Hz shift. Most MCPs available today offer all three shifts. However, many MCPs fudge the 170-Hz shift to accommodate HF packet as well as RTTY and AMTOR (see the sidebar "Shifty MCPs").

FSK or AFSK?

In our previous example, the shifting tones were

Shifty MCPs

Most multimode communications processors (MCPs) use a 200-Hz shift for RTTY and AMTOR operation (mark = 2110 Hz, space = 2310 Hz). These tones are used for HF packet radio as well. They are compatible with standard 170-Hz shift tones (2125/2295 Hz) since the center frequency (2210 Hz) is the same. In weak-signal conditions, using a 200-Hz shift places you at a disadvantage. Both you and the other station (possibly using 170-Hz shift) must resort to *straddle tuning* to achieve true transceive operation.

It's possible to obtain optimum performance by retuning the MCP receive filters and transmitter tones to match the 2125/2295-Hz standard. While this technique offers a noticeable improvement, you should *not* attempt the adjustment unless you are thoroughly familiar with your MCP and possess all the necessary test equipment. (Most MCP manuals *do not* describe this procedure.) A botched realignment will probably void your MCP warranty!

supplied to the transmitter via an audio input jack. Technically speaking, this is *audio* FSK or AFSK. There is another method known as *direct* FSK. What's the difference? If you're using *direct* FSK, the data pulses from your MCP are *not* converted to MARK and SPACE tones. Instead, they're applied to the FSK input of an SSB transmitter where they shift the frequency of the master oscillator up and down (see Fig 1-3).

So which is better—direct FSK or AFSK? Some hams believe that FSK is a "purer" method of transmitting digital information because it minimizes distortion and harmonics. Other hams argue that if the transmitter isn't over-modulated, AFSK transmissions are just as pure. You'll find large numbers of amateurs using one method or the other, although the majority seem to favor the AFSK

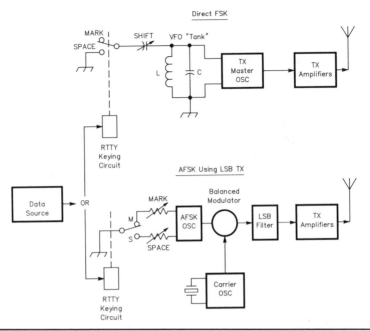

Fig 1-3—Many digital modes rely on direct frequency shift keying (FSK) or *audio* frequency shift keying (AFSK). The upper portion of the diagram illustrates direct FSK. The MARK and SPACE data is applied to a keying circuit that "pulls" the master oscillator in the SSB transmitter, causing it to shift its frequency. In this example, the SHIFT capacitor is added in parallel to the VFO whenever a SPACE pulse is applied.

In the lower portion of the diagram, the MARK and SPACE data is applied instead to an AFSK oscillator (usually this oscillator is inside the MCP. The oscillator generates tones that are fed to audio amplifiers within the SSB transceiver and, ultimately, to its balanced modulator. Regardless of whether you use AFSK or FSK, the result at the receiving station is the same.

approach because some transceivers do not feature an FSK input. The important thing to remember is that whether you use AFSK or direct FSK, the result at the receiving station is the *same*.

If you already own an HF SSB transceiver, you're well on the way to creating your digital station. The next item you'll need is a terminal program, an MCP and a computer or data terminal. As you'll see in the following chapter, there are many ways you can keep costs to a minimum. And if you don't own an HF transceiver, shop around for an inexpensive used radio.

Turn the page…and let's start building your HF digital communications station!

CHAPTER 2

Building Your HF Digital Station

I'll bet you thought this was going to be one of the most difficult chapters in the book. Well, don't let the idea of building an HF digital station intimidate you. Depending on how complex you want to get, it can be as simple as attaching a few cables and making a couple of adjustments.

Take a look at Fig 2-1. This is a diagram of a basic

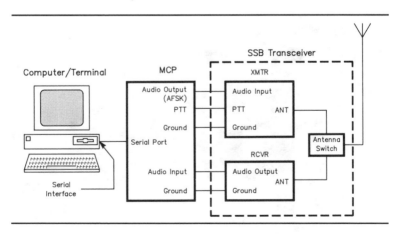

Fig 2-1—All you need is a computer or data terminal, a multimode communications processor and an SSB transceiver. As you'll read in this chapter, used equipment is often adequate. In some cases, you don't even need a computer!

digital station. As you can see, there are three critical areas: the computer, the radio and the MCP. We'll start from the left side of the diagram and work our way across... beginning with the computer.

Does it Compute?

If you're like many hams, you probably have a computer of some kind at your station. (If you don't, bear with me. I have some suggestions for you, too.) Computers are ideal for any digital mode. When running the proper software, they become the perfect interface between you and your equipment.

Does it matter what type of computer you're using? Not really. As long as it can communicate with the MCP, you're in business. To make this possible, it must be equipped with an EIA-232-E *serial* port (more commonly called an RS-232 port), or a TTL (transistor-transistor logic) interface. Most MCPs connect to serial ports with little difficulty. Many also

G0ARF just completed a successful ARRL RTTY Roundup contest despite gale-force winds and two power outages.

work with TTL interfaces. Check the MCP specifications *before* you make your purchase. Make sure it will communicate with your computer!

Software is another area of concern. To talk to your MCP you need a *terminal* program. Why is it called a terminal program? Well, when your computer is communicating with the MCP, it's functioning as a data terminal. It displays information received from the microprocessor and allows you to respond via the keyboard.

Large business-system computers often work in the same manner. The main processor is tucked away in a room by itself while the employees communicate with it using data terminals scattered throughout the building. There's a microprocessor inside your MCP and it also needs a terminal to communicate with the outside world. Your computer can't provide that function by itself—unless it receives the proper instructions. In other words, you can make it *behave like a data terminal* by running terminal software.

Terminal software doesn't have to be complex or expensive. If you're presently using a program to access telephone bulletin board systems or on-line services (such as CompuServe or Prodigy), you may be able to use the same software to talk to your MCP. There are also specific programs that provide many useful features—including "help" messages, split-screen displays for incoming and outgoing text and so on. A number of software sources are listed in the Resource Guide. I encourage you to write for their catalogs and see what's available for your computer. I think you'll be pleasantly surprised to discover how clever— and inexpensive—many of the programs are.

But I Don't Own a Computer!

Don't despair if you're "computationally impaired."

The market is glutted with new and used computers in every price range. Who knows? Maybe you can get by *without owning a computer at all.* (Say *what*? Read on and you'll see!)

So what kind of computer do you need? The answer is up to you. IBM PCs and compatibles are the standard of the Amateur Radio community, but if you choose an Apple, Commodore, Atari or other machine, you won't be left out. The greatest incentive for owning a PC is the huge amount of Amateur Radio software that's available.

If you have the funds to buy new equipment, buy the best computer you can afford. Believe me, you won't regret it. Try to look beyond Amateur Radio applications. Would you like to do your household finances on the computer? Maybe you'd like to play some games, too. Buy a machine that will suit your needs for years to come. Here's a quick shopper's checklist for new computers:

❏ How much software is available for the computer? It may be the greatest machine ever built, but it won't be able to do much without software! Keep ham applications in mind. Can it run the programs that appeal to you the most?

❏ What kind of monitor is available? CGA used to be the popular choice, but it's been superseded by high-resolution VGA and Super VGA monitors. When it comes to digital hamming, the distinctions aren't very important. In fact, CGA is fine. However, if you're thinking of running games and other graphics-oriented software, buy the VGA or Super VGA option.

❏ Check out the disk drives. Does it have at least two floppy drives? Good. How about a hard disk? Any new computer worth owning should have a hard drive—and the bigger the better.

❑ How about memory? 640 kbytes of RAM (Random Access Memory) is the practical minimum, although more is always better!

❑ How fast is the computer? The speed of a computer is expressed by the speed of its clock, in MHz. The faster the clock, the more efficient the computer. For most digital applications, speed isn't all that important. (I use an old 7-MHz IBM-XT for my HF digital operating. It's fast enough for me.) Once again, however, you have to consider the future. Complex software runs best at higher speeds. Many types of software now *require* high-speed machines to perform properly.

The guidelines we've just discussed concern *new* computers, but there are an awful lot of older machines waiting to be purchased. Visit a hamfest or computer flea market and you'll find many used computers for sale. Refer to the new-computer guidelines while you're bargain hunting. If you're willing to compromise on features (128 K of memory instead of 640 K, one disk drive, etc), you can pick up a used Tandy Color Computer, Commodore, Atari and others for well under $100. Raise your sights a bit higher and you'll discover Apples and IBMs for less than $300, depending on the machine. Remember the standard warning when shopping at flea markets: let the buyer beware! Plug it in and make sure it works *before* you part with your cash.

HF Digital Without a Computer

Yes, it *is* possible to operate most HF digital modes (except CLOVER) without the services of a computer. When you use a computer with terminal software, you're telling the computer to behave like a data terminal. Well, why not use the real thing?

At hamfest and computer flea markets you'll often find used data terminals for sale. Many amateurs take this approach to digital operating because it's very inexpensive. At one hamfest, I saw a fellow selling a truckload of used terminals for $10 each!

As you've probably guessed, there are some potential pitfalls in the used-data-terminal game. Consider the following factors carefully before you reach for your wallet:

❏ Check the condition of the terminal. Look at the screen closely. Do you see shadowy lines where the phosphor coating has deteriorated after years of constant use? (On some overused terminal screens you'll actually be able to see horizontal lines where the text was displayed!) This is a sure indicator of a terminal that's seen better days.

❏ If you want to save the text from your conversations, a data terminal may not be the best choice. Most terminals do not contain disk drives. Some terminals *do* support printers. You may have to pay a little more, but at least you'll have the means to save text.

❏ When you purchase a data terminal, you get the terminal software that's stored in its permanent ROM (Read-Only Memory). If you want to try other programs, you're out of luck. Remember: a data terminal is *not* a computer.

Used data terminals are excellent if you want to get started while keeping your costs to a minimum. If you don't think you'll ever have a need to save data for later use, a terminal is a fine alternative to a full-fledged computer. This is especially true if you have no other use for a computer. On the other hand, you'll be missing out on much of the fun and versatility of the HF digital modes by not having a computer in the shack.

You *Can* Get There from Here: MCPs

Computers (or data terminals) and SSB transceivers are about as incompatible as you can imagine. Send digital data directly to a transceiver and you'll get the radio equivalent of "Huh?" ("Arrgh" may be more like it!) Send receive audio from a transceiver directly to a computer and you'll get a similar response. The transceiver is analog and the computer is digital. How shall the twain meet?

Some computers incorporate analog to digital converters—and vice versa—and they can be used to send and receive RTTY on a limited basis. (The Tandy Color Computer is a typical example.) However, most computers need an external device to function as the bridge between the analog and digital worlds. That's the function of the MCP.

Multimode communications processors (MCPs) are byproducts of the packet radio revolution. As packet terminal node controllers (TNCs) became popular, the market was ripe for a device that included packet, RTTY, CW, AMTOR and other modes in a single box. The manufacturers responded and before long the first MCPs made their appearance.

Since the mid '80s, multimode communications processors have gained a strong foothold in the amateur community. Their main advantage is convenience. By sending commands from a computer or data terminal, the operator can jump from one mode to another in a split second. Several MCPs feature special companion software that heightens the convenience factor even further. For example, when using Kantronics' *Hostmaster* software with the Kantronics *KAM*, it's possible to operate packet while *simultaneously* operating other digital modes.

The digital signal processing revolution has had an impact on multimode communications processors as well.

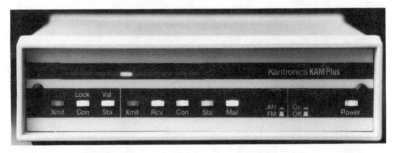

Multimode communications processors (MCPs) such as these offer RTTY, AMTOR, PacTOR, packet, CW, NAVTEX and other modes in a single device.

DSP-based MCPs are truly multimode devices! Rather than using specific internal hardware (various integrated circuits) to process signals, DSP units use *software* to accomplish the same thing. Theoretically, a DSP multimode communications processor will never be obsolete—regardless of new modes that may appear in the future. To operate in a new or different mode, all the DSP device needs is new software!

Radios and Amplifiers

When it comes to RTTY, just about any SSB

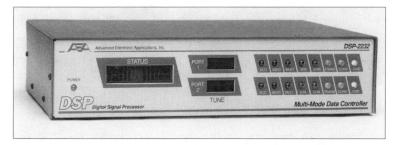

AEA's DSP-2232 is typical of the new series of multimode communications processors that incorporate digital signal processing (DSP). All of the data processing is accomplished with *software*, not hardware. As a result, adding a new mode is as simple as adding new software!

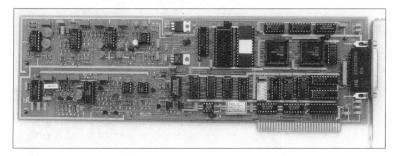

The HAL Communications PCI-3000 is a RTTY/AMTOR controller that fits *inside* an IBM PC or compatible.

transceiver will do the trick, regardless of age. Other digital modes are less flexible because of their rapid transmit/receive switching cycles.

As a rule of thumb, HF transceivers manufactured after 1984 should be able to accommodate the rapid-switching modes. This is not to say that you can't use older radios. I once used a vintage 1977 Kenwood TS-820S transceiver with excellent results. Even my ancient Drake TR-4 transceiver can clatter its relays fast enough to make an AMTOR contact!

Some hams worry about relay failure when running the digital modes with older equipment. There is some cause for concern, but I wouldn't lose sleep over it. Relays are pretty hardy devices. When you're operating, they may sound as though they're about to undergo what the military calls "energetic disassembly." Try to ignore it and watch your screen instead!

FSK vs AFSK

You can operate in the AFSK mode by feeding the audio output from your MCP directly to the microphone jack, or auxiliary audio input, of your SSB transceiver. Just be careful not to overdrive your rig. If your radio has a MIC GAIN control and an ALC meter, adjust the control to keep the tones from exceeding your maximum ALC level. *Do not* use speech processing or compression.

What if your radio includes an FSK mode? Is it "true" FSK as we discussed in Chapter 1? In most cases, the digital pulses from your MCP are used to key an audio oscillator/modulator inside the transceiver. What is labeled as "FSK" is often AFSK in disguise! Even so, the oscillator/modulator in the transceiver may be superior to the one in your MCP. By using the FSK input, you'll gain a superior signal. The transceiver will also add sharper receive filters in the FSK mode, which is a big plus when operating on a crowded band (more about filters later).

Receive Audio

Receive audio is easy to obtain if the rig has an external speaker jack. You'll really be in HF digital heaven if you own a radio that features an auxiliary fixed-level output such as a phone-patch jack! It puts you in the enviable position of being able to supply a constant audio level to your MCP regardless of your front panel VOLUME control setting. Once you've established contact, you can turn down the volume and continue without disturbing anyone else in the house. If your radio lacks an auxiliary audio output or external speaker jack, you'll need to tap the audio at the speaker. A simple Y connector will do the job nicely.

Are you Stable?

Operator stability is a matter for mental health professionals and will not be discussed here. When it comes to radios, though, *frequency* stability is a prime concern. RTTY is a very forgiving mode. Your radio can drift off frequency and you'll still be able to copy clean text—to a point. When you've drifted too far, a gentle nudge of the VFO control will put you back on target.

Don't expect the same flexibility with the other digital modes. If your radio drifts too far off the frequency, the link will cease altogether! Quick action will place you back on the proper frequency, but it may be too late.

Modern rigs employ digital synthesis and/or phase-locked loops to provide rock-solid stability. Older radios—particularly tube-type rigs—are not as stable and can drift quite a bit as they heat up. If you're using a vintage transceiver, allow about 15 minutes of warm-up prior to operating RTTY; 30 minutes for other modes.

As long as we're on the subject of frequency, I highly recommend transceivers with digital frequency displays. Why? If you're trying to communicate with a station on a particular frequency, it helps to have a display that's accurate and easy to read. For example, when I want to access the WA1URA/9 APLink system on the 20-meter band, I just dial up 14.071.30 MHz. There is very little guesswork. Of course, digital frequency displays don't always tell the truth (see the sidebar, "Frequency Displays Never Lie—Do They?").

Something's Burning

Output power is a major consideration. RTTY and Mode B (FEC) AMTOR are *100% duty cycle* modes—meaning that the transmitter is keyed *continuously* during each transmission. (By contrast, CW typically has a 50% duty cycle and SSB even less.) Making a long RTTY or Mode B AMTOR transmission is the equivalent of keying your transceiver at full output and holding it there for several minutes!

Some transceivers are designed to cope with this kind of punishment. They feature heavy-duty power supplies, cooling fans and so on. Make *very* sure your rig is rated for full output at 100% continuous duty—don't just assume it is! If it isn't, plan on operating with your output power reduced at least 50%. On the receiving end, the difference between full output and 50% output is insignificant. The penalty for pushing your radio beyond its limits is severe. We're talking expensive tube or transistor replacements!

Turning up the Power

Most hams enjoy a lifetime of digital operating using only the output power their transceivers provide. In fact,

Frequency Displays Never Lie—Do They?

The amateur standard for specifying a digital frequency is to specify the frequency of the MARK signal. While this is a logical approach, the MARK frequency can be *different* from what your rig's fancy multidigit display tells you it is!

If you're using your transceiver in the LSB mode, your digital display indicates the *suppressed carrier frequency*. In most cases you can subtract 2125 kHz to determine your MARK frequency. On the other hand, if you're in the FSK mode, you'll discover that calculating the exact frequency is *not* a matter of simple subtraction! It all depends on what rig you're using.

Some radios (ICOM and Ten-Tec units, for example) show the MARK frequency. Others indicate the SPACE frequency (TS-930 and TS-940 in particular). Others show the *suppressed carrier frequency* (just like LSB operation). And still others show F_0—the imaginary center frequency between MARK and SPACE. (MARS stations specify F_0.) If in doubt, read your manuals.

It's also important to note that digital frequency displays are *not* frequency meters! Usually, three or four oscillator stages, in addition to the VFO, determine the rig's output frequency. If a frequency error occurs anywhere other than the VFO, it may *not* be evident in the display. Your display reading can easily be several hundred or even a few thousand hertz off! Buying the "high stability option" (if available) will improve the frequency stability of your transceiver, but it usually won't correct your display calibration. If you really want to know your exact frequency, buy a frequency counter, attach a short wire antenna and measure your MARK signal frequency while sending continuous MARK pulses. This technique works on *all* radios.

when propagation conditions are good and interference is minimal, most digital modes are exceptional performers at low power levels. (I once made an AMTOR contact with just a couple of watts to a dipole antenna!) But what if you're gripped with the urge to burn the airwaves with raw, unadulterated power? You need an *amplifier*!

Choosing an amplifier is not a matter to be taken lightly. Remember the 100% duty cycle problem? Well, your amplifier must also be rated for 100% duty cycle operation if you intend to run it at full output on RTTY or Mode B AMTOR. If you think repairing a transceiver is expensive, wait until you cook a couple of amplifier tubes or fry a high-voltage power supply.

Don't forget about switching speeds. The amplifier must be able to switch from transmit to idle very rapidly (in a few *milliseconds*) if you expect to use it with AMTOR ARQ and the other fast-switching modes. Not all amplifiers

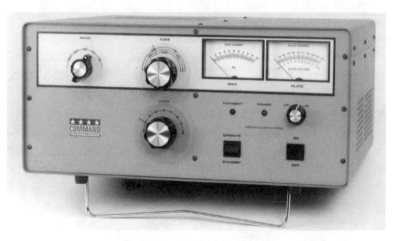

If you want to run high-power, you'd better buy an amplifier that can withstand 100% duty cycle transmissions. High transmit/receive switching speeds are also required. This Command Technologies HF-2500 amplifier is typical of units rated for heavy duty service.

are able to accomplish this, so do your research carefully. When shopping for an amp, look for "full QSK" capability. That usually—but not always—means that the unit can switch fast enough for digital use.

I won't deny that there are advantages to running high power. In contests and DX competitions, it sometimes takes that extra push to cut through the interference. High power can also make the difference when propagation conditions are poor. Still, your amplifier may be more of a headache than a help. Producing more RF can cause interference to your home electronics equipment (TVs, telephones, stereos, VCRs) *and* your neighbor's. That extra RF may also find its way into your computer or MCP. If you're operating AFSK and overdriving your transceiver, the amplifier will make the problem even worse—and may attract the attention of the FCC!

So am I steadfastly against high-power? Not at all. Just make sure you consider every aspect before you spend your money, or reach for the ON switch.

Filters

Take a moment to glance at the frequency guide in Chapter 3 (Table 3-1). You'll see right away that the HF digital modes are squeezed into fairly tight subbands. If you add increasing PacTOR, G-TOR and CLOVER activity, the playing field can get crowded in a hurry! This is particularly true on 20 meters, the most popular digital band.

So how do you separate the signals you want from the signals you don't? You need a device that rejects as much interference as possible without mangling the signal you want to receive. If you're lucky, your HF transceiver will be equipped with a 500-Hz *IF filter* that you can select from either the LSB or FSK mode.

Many transceivers also offer selectable *audio filters*. If an audio filter is well designed, it will pass digital tones while reducing or rejecting signals from other stations operating near your frequency.

Some transceivers are not as flexible as others when it comes to filter selection. When operating AFSK RTTY, for example, most hams place their radios in the lower-sideband (LSB) mode. Many transceivers restrict you to a 2.4-kHz SSB filter in this mode. This is fine if the band isn't too crowded. Under congested conditions, however, a 2.4-kHz filter just doesn't do the job! This is another reason why many digital operators use the FSK mode, if it's available. In the FSK mode, the transceiver may provide a narrower IF filter.

If the IF filters in your rig are either too narrow or too wide, don't lose hope! You may be able to buy an IF filter from the manufacturer and install it in your radio. If that option isn't available, you'll have to consider an *outboard* audio filter.

An outboard filter is easy to install and use. You simply feed the receive audio to its input jack; the filtered audio is available for your MCP at its output jack. Until recently, all active audio filters were based on resistor/capacitor networks. By changing the value of one component or the other, you change the filter's bandwidth. As far as the audio signal is concerned, it's a bit like opening or closing a window depending on how much air you want in the room. These filters work very well for everything from SSB to HF digital to CW.

Digital Signal Processing, or *DSP*, has caused a revolution in audio filter design. DSP filters do not use resistor/capacitor networks. Instead, the incoming audio is converted into digital data for processing by specialized DSP software. The software searches

Tunable outboard filters such as this Autek unit will greatly improve your ability to copy digital signals in crowded band conditions.

through the signal data, rejecting noise and interference according to the desired bandwidth. The result is translated back into audio for use by your MCP. DSP filters are exceptional when it comes to rejecting noise and certain types of interference. Ignition noise from a nearby car, for example, is removed completely. Some DSP filters "seek and destroy" interfering carriers— such as when someone decides to tune their radio on or near your operating frequency!

You can make your own audio filters or buy them. There are a wide variety of designs to choose from. The most important thing to keep in mind, however, is that audio filters are not miracle devices. They'll make it much easier for you to operate on crowded bands, but they can't reject *all* interference. Even a DSP filter can't block a signal that's sitting right on your frequency!

Narrow filters (audio or IF) are *not* required to operate HF digital. I've managed to operate in contest conditions with wide SSB filters, although my score wasn't very

Digital signal processing (DSP) has revolutionized audio filters.
Here is a unit designed by Dave Hershberger, W9GR. It was
featured in September 1992 *QST*. You can build it yourself for
less than $150! All it takes is a flick of the switch to select
optimal digital filtering.

impressive. The best advice is to get some on-the-air
experience before you purchase an extra filter. Depending
on where you operate and under what conditions, you may
decide you don't need it after all.

Putting it all Together

As you begin installing your components, remember to
establish good RF ground connections between each piece
of equipment. RFI can be a major headache with solid-state
devices. Computer birdies, for example, can make reception
miserable. Your transmitter can also wreak havoc with your
computer. I've used ¹/₂-inch copper braid for my ground
connections with good results. Many RFI experts now
advocate using ¹/₂-inch wide copper *straps*. Regardless of

the material you choose, make the ground connection your *first* priority.

Keep all cables as short as possible. A 20-foot audio cable makes a marvelous antenna for RFI. Try to locate all equipment close together and limit cables to no more than six feet in length. Inexpensive audio cables will work just fine. However, a piece of RG-58 coax with phono connectors has superior shielding. (Don't waste your money on expensive, gold-plated audio cables.) If you have an RFI problem, try improving the grounds and cable shielding first. Contrary to audio grounding techniques, ground the cable shields at *both ends*.

As you hook up your equipment, read your MCP, computer and transceiver manuals thoroughly. You'd be surprised at how much grief you'll avoid with an hour or so of light reading!

Pay special attention to the following...

❏ If you need to make custom cables, make sure you have the correct wires connected to the correct pins. Faulty wiring is a major cause of start-up problems (see Fig 2-3).

❏ Your MCP and your computer/terminal must communicate with each other at the same data rate.. If you're using a computer with terminal software, you can change the software settings to match whatever your MCP requires. Data terminals, however, often have a *fixed* data rate. In this case, you'll have to change the rate within the MCP. Some MCPs use an *autobaud* routine that repeats a message several times at various data rates. When you see the message in plain text, you know the data rate is correct for your terminal or computer.

❏ Depending on the age of your radio, the keying circuitry

Keying Older Rigs

MCPs use solid-state switching for transmitter control. Solid-state switching is fast and efficient. It's perfect for modern transceivers, but it can cause problems when used with older gear—especially tube-type radios.

Marrying today's technology to yesterday's equipment can be a challenge, but it's not impossible. One easy solution is to buy a small 12-volt relay and wire it as shown in Fig 2-2. The relay acts as an isolator between the MCP and the rig. The MCP keys the relay which, in turn, keys the transmitter. More elegant solutions are possible using solid-state devices. See "Cheap and Easy Control-Signal Level Converters" by James Galm, WB8WTS, in February 1990 *QST*, pages 24-27.

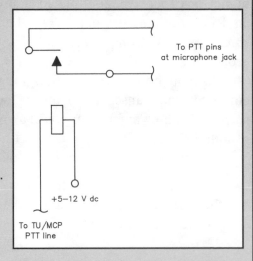

Fig 2-2—If you can't get your MCP to key an older radio, an inexpensive relay will solve the problem.

inside your MCP may not be compatible. You may wire everything properly, only to find that your transceiver will not switch to the transmit mode! Older radios often have problems with solid-state switching used by modern MCPs. See the sidebar, "Keying Older Rigs."

If you have your station up and running, there's

nothing else to do but get on the air and start enjoying the HF digital modes. The operating techniques for some modes differ considerably. Let's start with the easiest: RTTY.

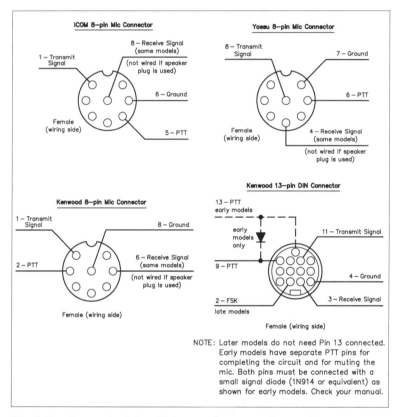

Fig 2-3—General wiring diagrams for several popular microphone connectors. Note that PTT is the *push-to-talk* lead used to key the radio on and off. Because manufacturers can change wiring configurations at any time, always check your manual before connecting your MCP to your transceiver. If you intend to run FSK instead of AFSK, see your transceiver manual for the appropriate connections (usually on the rear panel).

CHAPTER 3

Your First RTTY Conversation

I t's natural to feel tense during your first RTTY conversation. Communicating by keyboard may seem a bit strange unless you already have experience with packet radio or computer-aided CW. Even so, I think you'll be pleasantly surprised to discover just how easy RTTY can be!

Before attempting your first contact, spend some time copying RTTY signals. Take a look at the common HF digital subbands shown in Table 3-1. Depending on propagation conditions, you're likely to find plenty of

Table 3-1

HF Digital Subbands (including HF packet)

(MHz)

1.800 - 1.840
3.590 - 3.635
7.080 - 7.105
10.130 - 10.150
14.070 - 14.099, 14.101 - 14.112
18.100 - 18.110
21.070 - 21.100
24.920 - 24.930
28.070 - 28.189

RTTY activity in the middle portions of these subbands. The 20-meter segment is especially popular. On weekends you'll encounter wall-to-wall signals here! Use your MCP to eavesdrop on some of these conversations. In the process you'll learn your first digital skill: how to use your tuning indicator.

Am I Tuned In?

The answer to this question is easy. If you see meaningless gibberish—or nothing at all—you're not tuned in!

Every MCP features some sort of tuning indicator, depending on the type of equipment you're using. In days gone by, RTTY operators would attach oscilloscopes to their terminal units and tune the signals until they saw the classic "crossed bananas" display (see Fig 3-1). As technology advanced, many terminal units included tiny built-in oscilloscopes that performed the same function.

MCPs often use LED indicators. The Kantronics KAM, for example, features an indicator comprised of several LEDs arranged in a horizontal bar. When the LEDs at opposite ends of the bar flash in sync with the RTTY signal, you know you have it tuned properly. Before you

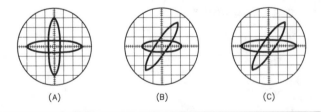

(A)   (B)   (C)

Fig 3-1—Oscilloscope-type tuning indicators produce patterns like these. Pattern A is the classic "crossed bananas," showing that the RTTY signal is tuned properly. At B the receiver is slightly off frequency, while C indicates that the transmitting station is using a shift that differs from the MCP setting.

attempt your first contact, read the MCP manual carefully to familiarize yourself with the operation of your indicator.

What Is That Signal?

As we discussed in Chapter 1, most RTTY operators use lower sideband transmissions with a 170-Hz frequency shift between the MARK and SPACE signals. The commonly used data rate is 60 words per minute, often expressed as 45 baud. But what if you stumble upon two operators who aren't conforming to "conventional" practices? Your indicator says you're tuned in properly, but nothing coherent prints on your screen!

It looks like you'll need to do a little detective work. Check the following:

❑ Is the signal "upside down"? The RF frequency of the MARK signal is usually higher than the RF frequency of the SPACE signal, but there is no law that dictates this standard. With most MCPs, all it takes is a push of a button or keyboard key to invert the normal MARK/SPACE frequency relationship.

❑ Are the operators really using 170-Hz shift at 45 baud? For example, many RTTY operators prefer to run at 75 baud (100 WPM) when exchanging lengthy files. To complicate matters, an operator may also decide to use an 850-Hz shift.

It may be of some comfort to know that these situations are uncommon. You may encounter RTTY at 75 baud or higher, but most operators stick to 45 baud. The use of inverted MARK/SPACE signals and odd frequency shifts is relatively rare.

Listen to the Action

Let's say you've successfully tuned in a RTTY signal. Unless you happen to be monitoring during a contest—

which we'll discuss later in this book—a typical RTTY conversation may look like this:

I FINALLY TOOK DOWN MY OLD VERTICAL AND REPLACED IT WITH A DIPOLE CUT FOR 40 METERS. YOU KNOW WHAT I FOUND OUT? I CAN FORCE FEED THAT DIPOLE WITH MY ANTENNA TUNER AND USE IT ON 20, 15 AND 10 METERS. N9GOR DE WA1MBK K

WA1MBK DE N9GOR . . . . REALLY? THAT SOUNDS PRETTY INCREDIBLE. I HAD NO IDEA YOU COULD DO THAT. I BET THE SWR IS VERY HIGH ON THE OTHER BANDS SINCE THE DIPOLE WOULD NOT BE RESONANT ON THOSE FREQUENCIES. WHAT ABOUT THE RF YOU LOSE IN YOUR FEED LINE? WA1MBK DE N9GOR K

N9GOR DE WA1MBK . . . FEED LINE LOSS IS NOT A PROBLEM EVEN WITH A HIGH SWR. AS LONG AS YOU USE OPEN WIRE FEED LINE, THE LOSS IS SO SMALL IT DOES NOT MATTER. A GOOD ANTENNA TUNER IS THE KEY . . . N9GOR DE WA1MBK K

And so it goes, back and forth at a leisurely pace. When an operator is not sending data, you'll hear a continuous tone or a rhythmic *bee-bee-bee-bee* signal. The rhythmic signal is known as the *diddle*. The MCP is simply switching back and forth between MARK and SPACE signals while awaiting more data from the operator.

The call signs at the beginning and end of each transmission are optional, as long as you identify at least once every 10 minutes. Still, some habits are hard to break and you'll find that RTTY operators often open and close their transmissions with an exchange of call signs. This is made easier by the fact that many modern MCPs feature automatic call sign exchange capability. You simply enter

The impressive RTTY station of KC1YZ. Note the AEA model PK-232 MCP immediately in front of his keyboard (just to the left of his transceiver).

the call sign of the other station *once*. After that, you can generate the entire <his call sign>-DE-<your call sign> sequence by pressing a single key.

Did you notice the **K** used to signify the end of each transmission? It's a RTTY custom to use CW prosigns in conversations. Depending on the operator, he or she may send a **K** (over to you), **AR K** (end of message, over to you) or **KN** (over to you *only*). When the conversation is over, it's common to use **SK** to signal the end of the contact. RTTY operators also adopt the CW custom of abbreviating words. In the sample conversation shown above, "frequencies" may be sent as "freqs."

Time to Pounce!

Enough monitoring! Now it's time for action. What if

you're eavesdropping on a QSO and you see that it's about to end?

N9GOR DE WB8IMY . . . I HAVE TO RUN, WAYNE. DINNER WILL BE READY IN AN HOUR AND I STILL HAVE NOT FINISHED MOWING THE LAWN. HAVE A GOOD WEEKEND AND I HOPE TO CHAT WITH YOU AGAIN . . . . N9GOR DE WB8IMY SK

WB8IMY DE N9GOR . . . NO PROBLEM. GLAD I HAD THE CHANCE TO DISCUSS ANTENNAS WITH YOU. I LEARN SOMETHING EVERY DAY. SEE YOU LATER . . . WB8IMY DE N9GOR SK

Looks like N9GOR is still available. Why not give him a call? Since you were able to copy the transmissions, chances are good that your MCP is already set for the proper data rate, shift and MARK/SPACE frequency relationship. (A quick check never hurts, though!) Switch your MCP to the transmit mode and start typing...

N9GOR N9GOR DE N6ATQ N6ATQ N6ATQ

N9GOR N9GOR DE N6ATQ N6ATQ N6ATQ K K

[switch back to receive]

Make sure to repeat your call sign several times. After all, N9GOR knows his own call, but he doesn't know *yours*! Send your transmission in several short lines rather than one long line.

If the other operator is able to copy your signal, you may see a response like this:

N6ATQ N6ATQ DE N9GOR N9GOR . . . THANKS FOR THE CALL. NAME HERE IS WAYNE WAYNE AND I AM LOCATED IN MILWAUKEE MILWAUKEE WISCONSIN WISCONSIN. YOUR RST RST IS 579 579 . . . BACK TO YOU . . . N6ATQ DE N9GOR K K

Split-Screen Software Makes it Easier

There is one feature that I consider to be almost indispensable to digital operators: split screen capability with a type-ahead buffer. As fancy as it sounds, this simply means that you'll have the ability to start entering your response while the other station is still transmitting.

In most cases, the incoming text from the other station is displayed in a separate area of the screen. Your responses can be typed into another area as you read the operator's comments. This may be confusing at first, but with a little practice you'll master the split-screen technique.

By using your type-ahead buffer, you'll be able to make comments or ask questions right away. If the other operator makes an interesting remark about his or her job, for example, will you remember to ask about it when it's your turn to respond? With type-ahead capability, you can ask your question the moment it occurs to you. When it's time for you to transmit, you can be sure it will be sent along with your other text.

The ability to type ahead also makes the conversation flow smoothly. When the other station has finished sending, all you have to do is switch to the transmit mode and continue typing. Your MCP will start transmitting everything you've entered so far. If you're a good typist, you'll finish before your system "catches up" to you. As far as the receiving station is concerned, he or she sees nothing but smooth-flowing text—just like reading a commercial teletype!

I'm a terrible typist and type-ahead capability allows me to hide this fact from other hams. I keep my transmissions short so that I always finish my comments before the type-ahead buffer is empty. The other operators think I'm a great typist, of course! When I get too long-winded, however, my MCP sends all my pre-typed text before I can finish. The smooth-flowing transmission comes to a grinding halt and I'm exposed as the hunt-and-peck operator I really am!

Notice how N9GOR sends the important information *twice*. He doesn't know how well you are receiving his signal, so he wants to make sure that you won't miss his name, city, state and so on. This is always a good technique to use when you aren't sure of the signal path between your station and another.

Wayne has sent your signal report (RST) and it's 579. The first digit from the left is your readability (R), the second is relative strength (S) and the third is tonal quality (T). In this case, a 579 RST means that he is receiving you very well, your signal strength is moderate and your RTTY tones are good. A perfect RST would be a 599, but a 579 is fine. You can be reasonably certain that he is receiving everything you're sending. Go ahead and tell him who you are and where you are. Don't forget to give him a signal report, too!

[switch to transmit]

N9GOR DE N6ATQ . . . . HELLO WAYNE. NAME HERE IS CRAIG CRAIG AND I AM IN ESCONDIDO ESCONDIDO CALIFORNIA CALIFORNIA. YOUR RST RST IS 599 599. THIS IS MY FIRST RTTY CONTACT. I AM USING A MODEL PK232 MCP AND A KENWOOD TS-820S TRANSCEIVER. ANTENNA IS A DIPOLE UP 30 FEET. SO HOW COPY? N9GOR DE N6ATQ K

[switch to receive]

These are the preliminaries of most digital contacts. Some hams are very proud of their station equipment and will give you a brief rundown of their entire setup. In the earlier days of RTTY, messages such as these were created in advance and stored on reels of paper tape. When fed to a teleprinter, the holes punched in the paper tape were translated into MARK and SPACE signals for transmission.

If you own a computer, you can create and store "canned" messages of your own and save them on diskette or magnetic tape. Depending on the type of software you're using, a single keystroke will send the entire message automatically! Many RTTY operators store and send their station descriptions in this manner, although the process is still known by its old namesake: the *brag tape*! Consult your software manual to learn how to create your own brag tapes and other stored messages.

Once you're past the introductions, the real conversation begins. If you're nervous and can't think of anything to say, start asking questions. What does the operator do for a living? What does he think about his equipment? How many DX contacts has he made? People enjoy talking about their interests and one question usually leads to another. Your conversation doesn't have to be technical; talk about anything that enters your mind!

Is There Anybody Out There?

If you can't find someone to talk to, consider calling CQ. You never know what you'll turn up!

[switch transmitter on]

CQ CQ CQ CQ CQ CQ CQ DE WB8IMY WB8IMY WB8IMY

CQ CQ CQ CQ CQ CQ CQ DE WB8IMY WB8IMY WB8IMY

CQ CQ CQ CQ CQ CQ CQ DE WB8IMY WB8IMY WB8IMY K K

[switch to receive]

A CQ should be long enough to attract attention, but short enough to avoid boring the other station. Repeat your call sign often so the operator on the other end has a decent

Bad Habits

As you scan the RTTY subbands, you'll find some operators sending long streams of RYs at the beginning of their transmissions.

RYRYRYRYRYRYRYRYRYRYRYRYRYRYRYRY CQ CQ CQ CQ CQ CQ CQ CQ DE WB8QVC WB8QVC WB8QVC K K

This is another artifact from the early days of RTTY when it was necessary to make sure that mechanical teleprinters were ready to copy a transmission. In the modern era of computers and data terminals, this is unnecessary. Many operators find these long RY streams highly irritating since they do nothing but waste time and band space. Try to avoid the RY habit. If you have something to say, such as calling CQ, go ahead and say it. You don't need to send a meaningless string of letters in advance.

You may also find operators who make frequent use of the date/time function included in their MCPs. Many units have this feature but, thankfully, most operators don't use it except in contest or public service situations. What does it do? It inserts the time and date (local or UTC) as part of the transmitted text. Usually it appears at the end of a transmission, but may pop up at the beginning. You may also see it at the end of stored messages.

Unless you're in desperate need of a clock, do you really want to know what time it is? Probably not. Now turn the tables. Do you think the other station cares to be informed of the date and time? I think you get the idea! Time and date "stamping" is a waste of RF in most cases. Veteran RTTY operators consider it a nuisance, although most will be too polite to tell you!

chance of getting it right. You may have to send your CQ more than once before you're noticed. Storing your CQ on disk makes it easy to send it again without retyping.

If you don't receive an answer, don't lose hope. Just move to another frequency or band. Before calling CQ, it's good practice to ask if the frequency is in use. Perhaps you've just tuned onto a frequency and it *seems* to be unoccupied. Don't let appearances fool you! You often hear only one side of a conversation—and that side may be listening at the moment!

Checking the frequency is easy. For example, I'd send:

QRL? QRL? DE WB8IMY WB8IMY K K

If the frequency is occupied, someone will let me know right away. On the other hand, if no one replies, I can assume it's safe for me to go ahead and call CQ.

It's a DX Pileup!

Sooner or later you're bound to encounter the fascinating phenomenon known as the *DX pileup*. You'll know when you've found a pileup because it will sound like pure pandemonium!

Pileups are the result of a desirable DX station coming on the air. What makes a DX station worthy of a pileup? If the operator is in a country that is not heard on the air often, that country is considered "rare DX." Any transmission from that part of the globe is a major event and it quickly attracts hordes of hams eager to make a contact.

The first CQs from a rare DX station snag the few hams who are lucky enough to be near the frequency at the time. More join the fray as they discover what's going on. DX *PacketClusters* also sound the alarm on the VHF frequencies and bring operators by the dozens. Within minutes you have a huge number of stations chasing the same goal: the hapless DX operator! As soon as he finishes a contact, everyone starts calling at once! You can imagine how this would sound in your receiver.

When you hear a pileup in progress, the first thing to

do is monitor the exchanges. Determine the DX station's call sign and see if you can copy his signal. When the FR5ZU/G group began calling for contacts from Reunion Island, here is how it looked at my station.

DE XE1/JA1QXY ... XE1/JA1QXY ... XE1/JA1QXY ... BK BK

XE1/JA1QXY DE FR5ZU/G ... UR 599 599 BK TO U ... KN

QSL UR 559-559 TKS QSO DE XE1/JA1QXY

XE1/JA1QXY sends his call sign several times and is heard by FR5ZU. Signal reports are exchanged quickly and the contact is over in a matter of seconds! Notice the heavy use of Q signals and abbreviated words to speed the process. The DX station is fair game once again and two operators slug it out for the prize . . .

DE W2JGR DE W2JGR DE W2JGR DE W2JGR K

FR5ZU/G DE NJØM NJØM NJØM PSE K

NJØM uses the traditional approach while W2JGR tries repeating his call sign preceded by **DE** ("from"). His tactic pays off and he wins.

W2JGR DE FR5ZU/G ... GOOD MORNING ... UR 569 569 ... BK

FR5ZU/G DE W2JGR ... TNX ... UR 579 579 NAME JULES ... QSL??? BK

FR5ZU passes along a signal report and shoots it right back to W2JGR. W2JGR gives his report and sends his name (Jules) as well. At the end of his transmission, he asks if the DX station copied everything ("QSL?").

QSL ES 73 ... FR5ZU/G QRZ KK

FR5ZU sends a quick "QSL" to mean, "Yes, I got it all" along with his best wishes. He immediately sends QRZ to signal that he is ready for another contact. That's NJØM's cue to try again!

DE NJØM NJØM NJØM PSE KK

What you've seen here is less than five minutes of a DX pileup that lasted over an hour! Pity the DX operator at the other end of this melee. He has to do his best to sort out readable call signs among the rampaging signals. Sometimes the interference is so severe, he sees nothing but a wild jumble of letters on his screen.

The best you can do is be patient and keep calling. The rules of DX courtesy say that you shouldn't transmit if a contact has already been established. If you keep transmitting, you may get the attention of the DX station in a way you'd never expect—he'll refuse to answer you for the remainder of the operation! Also, if the DX operator tries to control the mayhem through techniques such as working stations by call sign areas (1s, 2s, 3s and so on), don't buck the system. All you'll manage to do is anger the person you're trying to contact!

It's a "Split Decision"

What if you discover a rare DX station, but you don't hear a pileup? No matter how long you listen, you only seem to copy one side of the conversation—his! This is the telltale sign of a DX station that is *working split*. In other words, he is listening on one frequency and transmitting on another.

For some DX stations, working split is the only way to manage a pileup. This is especially true when a pileup gets too large and begins to disintegrate into chaos. Without the ability to work split frequencies, the DX station may be buried under a torrent of competing signals. Even if he manages to sort out a call sign, making contact is difficult because of interference from other stations who are continuing to call.

A good DX operator will always make it clear that he is working split and will indicate where he's listening for replies. You may see something like this:

CQ CQ DE 5U7M 5U7M UP 10

or...

QRZ DE 5U7M LISTENING 21.085 TO 21.090

The DX operator, 5U7M, is telling everyone that he is listening for calls 10 kHz above this frequency ("UP 10"), or that he is listening between 21.085 and 21.090 MHz specifically.

KB2BBW takes RTTY on the road! With his Toshiba laptop computer, AEA MCP and Uniden 10-meter transceiver, he has a fully equipped, 10-meter mobile RTTY station.

To contact a DX station using a split-frequency scheme, you'll need a transceiver that can transmit on a frequency other than the receive frequency. Many modern transceivers feature *dual VFOs* for this purpose. Other rigs have the capability to use a *remote VFO* (a second VFO in a separate enclosure).

If you have remote or dual-VFO capability, leave your receiver tuned to the DX station and move your transmit frequency to the desired spot. Check your equipment carefully and make sure you know exactly where you are transmitting and receiving. Whatever you do, *don't transmit on the DX station's frequency.*

CHAPTER 4

Time to Start Chirping with AMTOR

AMTOR is a one of the most fascinating HF digital modes. Its signals sound peculiar; even its name has a mysterious quality! (Doesn't the word "AMTOR" seem like something out of a science-fiction movie?)

In reality, AMTOR is a close cousin to RTTY. What sets it apart is its ability to detect errors. Unlike RTTY, AMTOR provides HF digital communications with a consistent level of accuracy.

Two types of AMTOR are used most often in Amateur Radio: *FEC* (or *Mode B*) and *ARQ* (or *Mode A*). When you hear those odd *chirp-chirp* signals, you're listening to ARQ AMTOR. FEC, on the other hand, sounds like very fast RTTY. Before you make your first AMTOR contact, let's take a moment to talk about both modes.

It Looks so Nice, I Sent it Twice

FEC stands for *Forward Error Correction*. This is a synchronized mode where every character is sent twice. The receiving station takes full responsibility for sorting out the errors. This means that an FEC transmission is strictly a one-way affair. The receiving station cannot ask for a repeat if it detects an error.

As the FEC transmission begins, the receiving station synchronizes itself to the transmitter. This synchronizing process may take as long as 10 seconds. When the first character is received, it's tested for the correct 4:3 bit ratio. (Remember our discussion of the bit-ratio test in Chapter 1?) If it passes the test, the character is assumed to be okay and is printed on the screen. If not, the system waits for the repeat and checks it, too. With any luck, the character will pass the test on the second try. Another failure, however, will cause the system to print a blank space or underline character.

Most AMTOR operators use FEC to send CQ in the hope of establishing an ARQ connection. Although it's not a common practice, you can also use FEC to carry on complete conversations. Like RTTY, *any* SSB transceiver is capable of operating in the FEC mode. Just be sure to watch your output power! FEC is a 100% duty-cycle mode. You may need to decrease your output by as much as 50% to avoid damaging your equipment.

Shaking Hands with ARQ

ARQ is a generic data term that means *A*utomatic *R*epeat re*Q*uest. In the ARQ mode, the *information sending station* (*ISS*) sends its text in bits and pieces. It transmits a group of three characters in a single burst and then switches to the receive mode. The *information-receiving station* (*IRS*) checks the characters for the 4:3 bit ratio and then transmits a control character. The control character means "Acknowledged. Send the next three" (*ACK*) or, "Not acknowledged. Repeat the last three" (*NAK*). If the ISS doesn't receive a reply (due to fading signals or interference), it repeats the characters anyway. Each station gets its turn to be the IRS or ISS.

It's fair to say that when you're using AMTOR ARQ

Ed Joy, AA4TH, is justifiably proud of his high-performance RTTY/AMTOR equipment. Whenever Ed needs to run *power*, he gets the full legal limit from his modified Gates HFL-2500 amplifier (background)!

there are really *two* conversations taking place. First, there is the conversation between you and the other amateur. Secondly, there is the conversation—often referred to as *handshaking*—going on between your hardware and the hardware at the other station. For as long as you and the other ham converse, your stations are locked into an intricate dance of signals. Of course, as in all dances, timing is everything!

ARQ Timing

AMTOR ARQ is precisely timed so that both stations know exactly when the other station is transmitting and

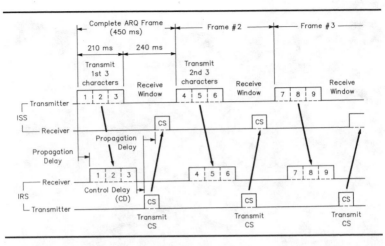

Fig 4-1—A typical AMTOR ARQ timing cycle. The dark arrows indicate the signal path from the information sending station (ISS) to the information receiving station (IRS) and vice versa. Notice how transmitted data does not reach the receiving stations instantaneously. This is caused by propagation delays. Propagation and equipment delays determine the maximum— and minimum—distance over which you can communicate.

listening. This is why high-speed transmit/receive switching is important when it comes to AMTOR equipment. A slow transceiver may still be in the act of switching when it should be listening or transmitting.

A typical ARQ transmission/acknowledgment sequence is illustrated in Fig 4-1. It may look complicated, but the concept is far simpler than the diagram!

A 450-ms ARQ cycle starts when the ARQ *link* is established. (Two stations enjoying an AMTOR ARQ conversation are said to be "linked.") The sending station (ISS) sends three AMTOR characters, which takes 210 ms. After receiving and checking the characters, the receiving station sends its ACK/NAK control signal (CS). The ISS has a 240-ms receive *window*. The CS character must arrive at the ISS before the window "closes," or the ARQ link will eventually fail.

The IRS requires 70 ms to send the CS character. That leaves 170 ms to spare (240 ms – 70 ms = 170 ms). Sounds like we've beaten the clock so far, doesn't it? The catch, however, is that we haven't considered all the possible delays that can take place. After all, even radio waves aren't instantaneous. They travel at the speed of light. The delay they induce is called the *propagation delay*. The propagation delay depends on the distance between the two stations.

Keep in mind that our goal is to communicate over varying distances. The distance may vary from "zero" (two stations a short distance apart) to halfway around the world. Taking the speed of radio waves into account, it takes about .067 seconds (67 ms) for a signal to travel halfway around the world. Since the ARQ signals must pass *both ways* within each cycle (ISS to IRS and IRS to ISS), we need *twice* that time for the total propagation delay (134 ms). If you subtract 134 ms from 170 ms, we still have 36 ms remaining. That's plenty of time—or is it?

Don't forget that equipment delays take a significant bite out of our spare time. The MCPs at each station add a *1 bit period* delay. That's 10 ms for each MCP, or 20 ms total. If slow-switching (60 ms) transceivers are used at both stations, an additional 120 ms is added to the delay (60 ms × 2 = 120 ms). Add the 20-ms MCP delays and our total equipment delay has now reached 140 ms! We've used all of our spare time with an extra 104 ms for good measure. (36 ms – 140 ms = –104 ms) This long-distance AMTOR link is doomed!

If both stations have very ultra-fast transceivers (8 ms), the total equipment delay can be reduced to 36 ms (16 ms for the rigs and 20 ms for the MCPs). The signals will reach each station in time to maintain the link.

Now let's look at the opposite extreme. Consider two AMTOR stations side by side. The propagation delay is effectively zero. Let's also assume that the IRS sends its ACK/NAK control character immediately after receiving

Flexible Timing

One possible solution to the AMTOR ARQ timing problem is the control delay (CD). This is the delay between the time the IRS receives a data pulse and the time it sends its ACK/NAK character. Here are some guidelines for adjusting your control delay:

❑ If you're working a nearby station (2500 miles or less), set your control delay in the range of 30 to 50 ms.

❑ If you're working a distant station (more than 2500 miles), set your delay to a lower value (10 to 20 ms).

❑ If you call a station and the station can't seem to maintain the link, try adjusting *your* control delay.

❑ If another station calls you and *you* can't maintain the link, the calling station must adjust his or her delay.

Not all MCPs will allow you to adjust the control delay. If this is the case with your equipment, don't let it stop you from trying AMTOR. There are some stations you won't be able to contact, but there are many other stations you *will* be able to contact—depending on propagation and equipment delays.

There is another programmable delay in most AMTOR controllers and MCPs: the *transmit delay* (TD). Transmitters don't reach full output instantly. Since this is the case, the transmit delay tells the MCP to hesitate before sending the data. I find that practically all HF transmitters work correctly if you set TD to 10 ms. This parameter can remain fixed since it will be valid for all AMTOR contacts. Of course, remember that your transmit delay—and the transmit delay used by the other station—will increase the total time delay in the ARQ link.

the ISS data. If the transmit/receive switching delays at the ISS are too long, ISS equipment will still be switching when it should be receiving. Thus, it will never hear the control-character transmissions.

As I'm sure you've guessed, your AMTOR communications range is limited by distance, and the speed at which your equipment operates. You'll find, for example, that you can't seem to work stations that are located beyond a certain distance (measured in *thousands* of miles). You'll also discover that you have a *minimum* range as well. The point to remember is that there are a *lot* of AMTOR operators within range of your station—more than enough to keep you busy for a very long time! Besides, you may be able to make a few adjustments that will extend your maximum range, or reduce your minimum range. See the sidebar, "Flexible Timing."

Eavesdropping on AMTOR

Most MCPs include some sort of *listen* mode. The listen mode allows you to tune to an ARQ contact in progress and print the text *without* being part of the link. You need a bit of patience when using the listen mode since it doesn't include the error-correcting feature. You'll see plenty of errors and repeated characters, but at least you can follow the discussion.

Listen mode also works differently, depending on the MCP you're using. The listen mode in some controllers automatically senses and switches to ARQ or FEC. Other units monitor only ARQ transmissions in the listen mode and must be manually switched to the standby mode to monitor FEC signals.

Switch your transceiver to LSB and your MCP to the listen mode. Now hunt for a chirping ARQ signal. I suggest that you look for a strong signal between 14.070 and 14.080 MHz. (Twenty meters isn't the only band with AMTOR activity, but it's one of the most popular.) When you've tuned the signal correctly—remember to watch your indicator—you should see characters within 15 to 20 seconds. If not, try another signal. On some controllers, you may have to reset the listen mode to restart the synchronizing process. With practice, you should be able to copy an ARQ signal with ease. The listen mode may drop out of sync at times, especially when one station ends its transmission and switches from ISS to IRS. This is normal since the listen mode can only synchronize to one station at a time.

Now, find an FEC signal. At first, FEC may be hard to differentiate from RTTY. An FEC transmission includes special synchronizing characters, but they're often sent only once per line of text. It can take 10 seconds or more to receive these synchronizing characters—longer if you miss them or get a noise burst when they're sent. Some MCPs send extra FEC synchronizing signals and these signals will be easier to receive. Practice tuning FEC before you attempt your first AMTOR contact.

Let's Call CQ!

Switch your MCP to the FEC mode. (Some MCPs omit this step. They permit you to send FEC while in the ARQ mode.) An AMTOR CQ should include both your call sign *and* your SELCAL code (see the sidebar, "What's Your SELCAL?").

[switch your MCP to transmit]

[send a blank line]

CQ CQ CQ DE WB8IMY WB8IMY WB8IMY (WIMY WIMY WIMY)

CQ CQ CQ DE WB8IMY WB8IMY WB8IMY (WIMY WIMY WIMY)

CQ CQ CQ DE WB8IMY WB8IMY WB8IMY (WIMY WIMY WIMY) K

[switch back to receive]

What's Your SELCAL?

Before you can operate AMTOR ARQ, you have to choose your *selective call identifier*, or *SELCAL*. When AMTOR stations wish to communicate in ARQ, this is the code that must be used to establish the link. The SELCAL code uses *only* letters, and we choose letters that match at least part of our call signs. Some examples are:

Call Sign	CCIR-476 SELCAL	CCIR-625 SELCAL
KS9I	KKSI	KSIIXXX
WA9YLB	WYLB	WAIYLBX
W1AW	WWAW	WAAWXXX
WB8IMY	WIMY	WBHIMYX

(CCIR-476 is the name of the recommended technical specifications for the version of TOR that's most popular on the amateur bands today.)

Most amateurs use only the CCIR-476 SELCAL configuration. The letter combinations shown for CCIR-625 are strictly my own choice—you can use others.

Most MCPs feature a special command that will allow you to store your SELCAL in memory. (In the Kantronics KAM, for example, the command is "MYSEL." In the PK-232, it's "MYSELCAL.") This is an important step! Without a SELCAL, other AMTOR stations will not be able to call and link to you in the ARQ mode.

But Wait a Minute! What is CCIR-625?

CCIR-625 is a revised AMTOR/SITOR international standard. It was devised to address two problems: (1) the four-character CCIR-476 code was too limited to provide different SELCALs to all stations, and (2) under some circumstances, a CCIR-476 station could re-link with an incorrect station if the original link failed. CCIR-625 allows *seven* characters in its SELCAL, automatically identifies both stations at link-up, and also tightens the specifications for FEC synchronization.

Newer AMTOR controllers include both modes, but CCIR-476 is compatible with both new and old equipment. In a few years, however, CCIR-625 may become the dominant Amateur Radio AMTOR format.

The last step is *very* important! Your AMTOR controller must return to *standby* to be ready to receive an ARQ call. Most AMTOR controllers have two different ways to end an FEC transmission: one command returns the controller to the standby mode and another returns to the FEC mode. Be sure to check your manual!

Also remember to send your FEC CQ with lots of short lines terminated with carriage returns. Why? It allows receiving MCPs to quickly synchronize with your signal. The faster they synchronize, the sooner they'll copy your message.

If someone wants to chat with you, they'll call you in ARQ using the SELCAL code you sent (WIMY in our example). If you don't get an answer, try again. Keep your calls short—don't get fancy or long-winded!

Let's assume that someone is answering your call. You hear the familiar chirp-chirp-chirp as they send your SELCAL over and over. In the meantime, your MCP is decoding the signals. Does the received SELCAL match yours? Yes! At this point you may hear a tone or chime followed by a message telling you that you're linked to the other station.

The AMTOR dance has begun, but who calls the tune? Well, a station that answers (in ARQ) the FEC call of another station is the *master*. It sets the timing parameters and the other station—the *slave*—must synchronize to its signals. In this case, the station that called you is the master and you're the slave. Throughout the conversation, the master and slave roles remain fixed.

Anatomy of an ARQ Conversation

Once an ARQ link begins, the exchange of ACKs and NAKs goes on *continuously*—even if no one is sending information. If you and the other operator decided to leave your keyboards and grab a snack, your stations would chirp mindlessly back and forth to each other. I wouldn't recommend this as a standard operating practice, though!

When a station calls you and establishes a link, you're the IRS. Just wait patiently for the other operator to send his greeting...

WB8IMY DE KU7G ...
HELLO! MY NAME IS BOB AND I LIVE IN
WASHINGTON STATE IN THE SHADOW OF
MOUNT ST HELENS. YOUR RST IS 589.
BACK TO YOU ... +?

Notice how Bob leads off with his call sign and yours. This is important since all you've exchanged so far are you SELCALs. He sends a brief greeting and ends it with **+?**. This strange-looking character is the *over* command. It allows the stations to trade places from ISS to IRS. Bob is turning the link over to you so you can reply.

Over to You

There is a very important point to remember about AMTOR ARQ: *each station must turn the link over to the other station at the end of every exchange.* (This has nothing to do with the master/slave timing relationship.) The normal procedure is to type **+?** to switch the link. With many MCPs, the **+?** is sent by tapping a single key. In effect, this control code says, "Let's turn the link around. You're the ISS now." When the link switches, you'll hear a distinct change in the chirping rhythm.

Recognizing that there are times when the IRS operator (receiving station) would like to immediately break in and make a comment, most MCPs include a *forced over* command. A forced over causes an immediate link reversal, even if the ISS operator is still typing or has text in his transmit buffer. The exact command used to cause a forced over varies between units. Use the forced over sparingly; it's rarely needed, but very handy at times.

When I made my first AMTOR ARQ contact, I didn't understand the idea of turning over the link. I sent my name, location and signal report, and then sat back and waited for a response. It wasn't long before I began to wonder why the other station wasn't answering. Our transceivers were chirping happily to each other, so everything *seemed* to be okay. I saw the letters "ISS" flashing in the corner of my screen, but I really didn't know what they meant. (Like many hams, I often dive right into a new mode without reading my manuals.) Finally, the other station realized that he had a greenhorn on his hands. He sent a forced over and began to patiently explain the meaning of ISS, IRS and why I had to turn the link over to him!

The Conversation Continues

So Bob has turned the link over to you. Now you're the ISS and he's the IRS. Why not send a short greeting and a signal report, too?

HELLO, BOB. YOU ARE SOUNDING FINE HERE IN CONNECTICUT. I LIVE IN A TOWN CALLED WALLINGFORD AND MY NAME IS STEVE. YOUR RST IS 599.

There is no need to repeat the information as you might do during a RTTY exchange. With the ARQ ACK/NAK system, the other station either receives your text or doesn't! With rare exception, the text is never garbled on the receiving end. If there is trouble on the frequency (due to fading or interference), the flow of incoming or outgoing text will slow down or stop altogether.

It sounds like Bob lives in an interesting place. Maybe you should ask him about it.

WERE YOU LIVING NEAR MOUNT ST HELENS WHEN IT ERUPTED BACK IN 1979? KU7G DE WB8IMY +?

Good! You remembered to turn the link over. Now Bob can respond.

YES, I WAS JUST MOVING INTO MY NEW HOME WHEN THE MOUNTAIN BLEW ITS TOP. THERE WERE ASHES EVERYWHERE! I COULDNT DRIVE TO MY NEW JOB BECAUSE OF ALL THE ASH IN THE ENGINE. I STILL HAVE SOME OF IT IN JARS IN MY BASEMENT! +?

Now you have the start of a fascinating conversation! As with RTTY, you can type your comments while you're receiving his. When the link turns over, your system will begin sending the pretyped text automatically. All good things must come to an end, however...

WELL, STEVE, I HAVE TO GET UP VERY EARLY TOMORROW AND DRIVE ALL THE WAY TO BOISE, IDAHO. I THINK I SHOULD GET TO BED SOON OR I WILL NEVER HEAR THE ALARM CLOCK. THANKS FOR THE GREAT CONVERSATION. I REALLY ENJOYED IT. GO AHEAD AND MAKE YOUR FINAL COMMENTS AND THEN YOU CAN DOWN THE LINK. 73 . . . WB8IMY DE KU7G SK +?

Bob says you can "down the link"? What does that mean? It simply means that he is asking you to send the *end* command that will terminate the ARQ link between your stations.

GOODNIGHT, BOB. HAVE A GOOD TRIP. HOPE TO LINK UP WITH YOU AGAIN ONE OF THESE DAYS. 73 . . . KU7G DE WB8IMY SK

Most MCPs feature a single keystroke that sends the end command (some label it "disconnect"). If you're in doubt, you can do it manually by sending **ZZZZ.**

That's it! The link is broken and the conversation is over. If another station has been eavesdropping, he or she may call now. Only two stations at a time can be linked via

AMTOR ARQ. If anyone else wishes to talk to you, they must wait until the conversation ends.

Answering an AMTOR CQ

What if you're prowling through the digital subbands and you see someone calling CQ? The first order of business is to load the *other station's* SELCAL code. Be careful not to change your own in the process! Obviously, there are two SELCAL codes involved: your SELCAL and the SELCAL of the other station. To help keep this straight, MCPs label your SELCAL as *MYCALL*, *MYA*, *MYSEL* or *LOCAL CALL* (LC).

Most MCPs will prompt you to enter the SELCAL of the other station:

SELCAL? ____

Some units (such as the Hal PCI-3000) include a call directory that lists several calls in a menu format. Still other controllers label the SELCAL to be sent as the *remote call* (RC), or sometimes *HISCALL*. Consult your manual to determine the correct label and the proper procedure to enter the other station's SELCAL.

Once you've entered the SELCAL, your station will begin chirping it over and over. If the link isn't established within a certain period of time, the transmissions stop. With luck, the other station will hear your signals and start the link. You're the calling station, so you're the master now. All the timing parameters for this conversation will be dictated by *your* station. Since you started the conversation, you're also the ISS at the moment. Send your opening remarks and start having fun!

APLink: Your Window on the VHF Packet World

APLink is a bulletin board system (BBS) program designed by Vic Poor, W5SMM, to provide message store-

You don't need three computers to operate AMTOR, but KG5EG puts them all to good use. His neat station layout makes it easy for him to operate any mode he desires.

and-forward capability for AMTOR users. APLink allows stored messages to be shared between two computer ports— one port for an HF AMTOR controller and another for a VHF packet TNC. Messages can be read or stored by an AMTOR station on HF, or by a packet station on VHF. As a result, APLink provides a connection (no pun intended!) between AMTOR operators and the VHF packet network.

The APLink Scanning BBS

Frequency-scanning APLink stations first appeared in Europe as the brainchild of G3PLX. They're now common in the United States and they're spreading worldwide.

A scanning APLink BBS uses the programmable memories and scanning options of newer HF transceivers. When the BBS is not in use, its receiver continuously scans the programmed frequencies. A BBS station often scans four or five bands and two or three different frequencies within each band. A complete scan can take 15 to 30 seconds.

The scan pauses for 2 to 5 seconds on each frequency. If the BBS station hears its own SELCAL being sent by a potential user, scanning ceases and an ARQ link is established. If the frequency is busy, or the BBS SELCAL is not heard, the BBS resumes scanning.

This frequency-scanning technique allows one BBS to serve stations at varying distances—regardless of propagation conditions. If you can't connect to an APLink BBS on 20 meters, for example, try again on another band. Eventually you'll find a band that offers a good path between you and the APLink BBS. It's a very clever way to make the best use of our available HF spectrum and propagation!

If you want to connect to a scanning APLink BBS, you must: (1) know the exact frequencies the BBS is scanning, and (2) be able to accurately set your transmitter to those frequencies. Scanning BBS stations have files that list the exact frequencies they monitor. When you first connect to an APLink BBS, download its frequency list so you'll know where to find it the next time. In Appendix A you'll find a list of APLinks and other automated digital stations.

Before attempting to use an APLink station, listen to several of the listed frequencies and see if you can hear the BBS communicating with other stations. This will tell you whether the BBS is busy (calling it will do no good if it is), and the quality of the BBS station's signal at your QTH. When you finally call the BBS, choose a frequency where its signal is strong and stable.

Most APLink operating commands will be familiar to packet users. As is the case with many packet BBS systems these days, APLink stations have disabled their command list response. This means that you may only see **GA +?** when you initially establish the link ("GA" means "Go Ahead").

Sending a private message via APLink is very similar to packet, but **AT** is used in place of @. For example, on an

APLink BBS you'd enter: **SP WAØQKL AT WØAMN**
rather than **SP WAØQKL @ WØAMN**. (Even this is
changing with the advent of upper/lower-case AMTOR.
These APLink stations *do* use @ in their message format—
just like packet.)

I use APLink to send mail to a packet-active friend in
Dayton, Ohio—about 1200 miles from where I live in
Connecticut. Sure, I could send the message via the regular
packet network, but it might take several days to reach him.
APLink offers a time-saving shortcut! I link with the
WA1URA/9 APLink in Fort Wayne, Indiana—not far from
Dayton in terms of packet networking. After I enter my
message, the APLink uses VHF to transfer it to my friend's
local packet bulletin board, usually within one hour! He can
send his reply on VHF back to the WA1URA/9 APLink.
The next time I establish a link to the system, it will tell me
that I have mail waiting.

Let's Give it a Try!

What you're about to see is text from an actual link
with the WA1URA/9 APLink system. I select 14.071.4
MHz (suppressed carrier frequency) and begin calling by
sending the SELCAL **WURA** in the ARQ mode. Within
seconds, we're linked!

My transmissions are shown in italics. Note that I
don't need to use the **+?** command to turn the link over.
APLink expects each command to be followed by a carriage
return and a line feed. When it senses this, it sends a forced
over to switch the link automatically.

DE WA1URA/9 APLINK 6.MT STANDBY

NEED HELP? TYPE 'HELP' (CR)

. . . PLEASE LOGIN+?

LOGIN WB8IMY

WB8IMY DE WA1URA/9 QRU GA+?

("QRU" means there's no mail waiting for me. If I *did* have mail waiting, I'd see "QTC" followed by the message number. Before I proceed, I ask for a list of recent users.)

LR

USERS IN THE LAST 24 HOURS:
9K2DZ   GB7SCA   KAØJRQ   KB1PJ   KB8NH
KD4B   KE5HE   KK4CQ   NØIA   N2JAW
NRØS   UA9QRA   TG9VT   VE6PD   W7DCR
W7IJ   WA4DDX   WB3EPC   WB8IMY WG1I
ZS5S

GA+?

(I think I'll perform a test by sending mail to myself! I'll be curious to see how long it takes for the message to arrive at my local packet BBS in Connecticut.)

SP WB8IMY AT W1NRG.CT.USA.NA

CONFIRM . . . SP WB8IMY AT W1NRG.CT.USA.NA (YES/NO) +?

YES

MSG NR 61497 GA SUBJ/MSG+?

(This is the tricky part for new users. The APLink wants me to enter the subject of the message *on a line by itself.* After that, I'm free to go ahead and enter the rest of the message.)

TEST MESSAGE
This is an APLINK test message being sent back to my home packet PBBS.
NNNN

(Notice how I ended the message with NNNN, also on a line by itself.)

WB8IMY DE WA1URA/9 NR 61497 FILED GA+?

(My message has been filed in the system as message number 61497. While I'm linked, I'll check for any NTS traffic to be delivered.)

LT

MSG	TS	SIZE	TO	AT	FROM	FILED(Z)	SUBJECT
61490	TY	474	NTSMN	NTSMN	W7DK	0913/1340	GILBERT MN (218)749
61489	TY	468	NTSIL	NTSIL	W7DK	0913/1338	MIDLOTHIAN IL (708)687
61474	TN	502	38346	NTSMS	N1JBR	0913/1005	GREETING
61472	TY	517	93550	NTSCA	WA1GDJ	0913/0957	PALMDALE 805-947
61444	TY	331	96703	NTSHI	N2JAW	0912/2352	WELFARE - KAUAI HI (808)826
61418	TN	599	63108	NTSMO	N4UAV	0912/1724	ST LOUIS MO 314-534
61410	TY	582	55313	NTSMN	N1MQR	0912/1027	QTC BUFFALO (612-477)

WB8IMY DE WA1URA/9 GA+?

(It doesn't look like there's anything waiting for delivery to my area of the country. I'll leave the APLink for now and check back in a few days.)

LOGOFF

WB8IMY DE WA1URA/9 SK

In case you're wondering, my test message arrived at the W1NRG packet bulletin board 6 hours later!

In addition to sending messages, you can read informative bulletins and access other information. Once you feel confident with AMTOR, try working an APLink

WRU Answer-Back

Most AMTOR controllers and all commercial SITOR controllers include an automatic station identification feature called "Who Are You" (WRU). This feature dates back to mechanical Teletype machines. The concept involves sending a special character code that triggers an automatic response from another station—usually its call sign.

AMTOR WRU works like this:

1. My WRU feature is active and I have text in my *ANSWERBACK* storage (my call sign).
2. Your station is the ISS and you send the WRU code.
3. My AMTOR controller responds with a *forced over* and becomes the ISS.
4. My station sends its ANSWERBACK text followed by *over* (+?).

Note that it should be the station called (mine in this example) that forces the first *over*. If your MCP doesn't handle the exchange in this manner, using your WRU feature can create some *very* confusing situations! For this reason, you may not care to use the WRU function unless you are also using APLink.

system! See Table 4-1 for a list of common APLink commands. A list of APLinks and other automated digital stations can be found in Appendix A.

Table 4-1

Common APLink Commands

❏ Commands to APLink on its AMTOR port should always be on a new line and end with CR.

❏ The user should avoid transmitting the "+?" sequence. APLink knows when it is its turn to send. APLink will change the link direction, as needed.

❏ Arguments shown in square brackets [like this] are optional. Arguments shown in point brackets <like this> are not optional and must be included.

A—Abort the current output; return to GA+? prompt
CANCEL <num>—Cancels message <num> if originated by you
F—Abort the current msg
LOGIN <call>—Logs you into the system
LOGOFF—Same as LOGOUT
LOGON <call>—Same as LOGIN
LOGOUT—Logs you off
H—Send the help file
L—List all non-bulletin, non-private messages
L [number]—List all non-bulletin, non-private messages equal to or greater than (number)
LTO or **LM**—List all messages to you
LTO [call]—List all messages to <call>
LFM—List all messages from you
LFM [call]—List all messages from <call>
LB—List new general interest bulletins
LB [number]—List general interest bulletins from [number] and higher
LT—List all NTS messages
NTS—List all unforwarded NTS messages (may be restricted)
LU—List all registered users
LR—List all stations that have logged on during last 24 hours
RN or **RM**—Read all new messages addressed to you
R [number]—Read message [number]
RH [number]—Read message [number] including routing headers
RI—Read the Intercept File (for forwarding to home BBS)
RF— Read the Auto-Fwd File (to see how AMTOR routing is done)
SP <call>—Send a private message to <call>, end with NNNN
SP <call1> AT <call2>—Send a private message to <call1> to be forwarded by packet to BBS with call sign of <call2>
ST <zip>AT NTS<st>—Enter (Send) an NTS message
SB [name]—Enter (Send) a bulletin to "name"; End with NNNN
SB [name1] [AT name2]—Enter a bulletin to be forwarded; End with NNNN
T—Talk to the SYSOP
V—Read version number
III Anywhere on a command line cancels the command

CHAPTER 5

Exploring PacTOR

O nce upon a time, AMTOR was the undisputed king of the HF digital modes. Yes, there was RTTY, but it lacked the ability to detect and correct errors. When the going was rough, AMTOR was always the winner. HF packet came along in the mid-80s, but it proved to be too slow for many applications. AMTOR retained its crown.

Then, in 1990, a new challenger appeared. This mode combined the best of packet and AMTOR while adding a few innovations of its own. It ran circles around both AMTOR and packet, doing things neither mode could accomplish individually. The advantages were self evident and hams quickly embraced the challenger. As this book goes to press, *PacTOR*—the AMTOR/packet fusion—is about to win the title of the most popular HF digital mode. In just a few short years it overthrew king AMTOR and won the top spot in the hearts of most digitally active hams. To understand PacTOR's success, you have to understand how it works.

Bonnie King, KD4BNV, does her hamming from the keyboard with PacTOR. *(photo by Conard Murray)*

The Gory Details

PacTOR was developed in Germany by Hans-Peter Helfert, DL6MAA, and Ulrich Strate, DF4KV. Like packet, PacTOR supports the complete ASCII character set. This means that you can send upper- and lower-case letters as well as binary files (computer software and other information).

Like AMTOR and packet, PacTOR sends error-free information by using a *handshaking* system. When the data is received intact, the receiving station sends an ACK signal (for *acknowledgment*). If the data contains errors, a NAK is sent (for *nonacknowledgment*). In simple terms, ACK means, "I've received the last group of characters okay. Send the next group." NAK means, "There are errors in the last group of characters, send them again." This back-and-forth data conversation sounds like crickets chirping. In the case of PacTOR, the long chirp is the data and the short chirp is the ACK or NAK. AMTOR and PacTOR sound similar when you hear them, but PacTOR is the mode with the extended chirps.

Memory ARQ

With AMTOR and packet, a group of characters must be repeated over and over if that's what it takes to deliver the information error-free. This results in slow communications, especially when conditions are poor.

PacTOR handles the challenge of sending error-free data in a different and interesting way. As with AMTOR, each character block is sent and acknowledged if it's received intact. If signal fading or interference destroys some of the data, a NAK is sent and the block is repeated—just like AMTOR. The big difference, however, involves *memory*.

When a PacTOR-equipped MCP receives a mangled character block, it analyzes the parts and temporarily memorizes whatever information appears to be error-free. If the block is shot full of holes on the next transmission as well, the MCP quickly compares the new data fragments with what it has memorized. It fills the gaps as much as possible and then, if necessary, asks for another repeat. Eventually, the MCP gathers enough fragments to construct the entire block (see Fig 5-1)! This is a tremendous improvement over AMTOR and packet where the character block is often repeated many times before it finally makes it through unscathed. PacTOR's *memory ARQ* feature dramatically reduces the need to make repeat transmissions of damaged data. This translates into much higher throughput.

The Need for Speed

When it comes to transmit/receive switching speeds, PacTOR is somewhat more liberal than AMTOR. An AMTOR station sends a block of characters and waits up to 240 ms for a reply (an ACK or a NAK). PacTOR, on the

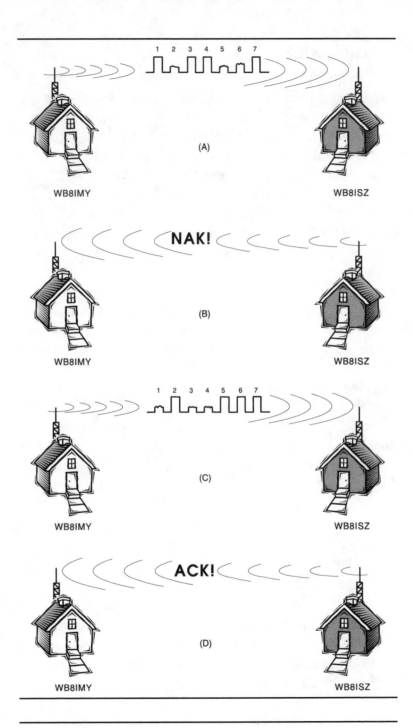

other hand, waits 290 ms. This extra 60 ms is critical for communication over long distances. Any SSB transceiver capable of switching from transmit to receive within 90 ms can be used for PacTOR. This encompasses virtually all rigs made since 1980.

PacTOR has the capability to communicate at varying speeds according to band conditions. Under good conditions, PacTOR will accelerate to 200 baud. It can go even faster (up to 400 baud) by compressing text data through the use of *Huffman* coding. If conditions deteriorate, however, PacTOR will automatically slow back down to 100 baud—which is still considerably faster than AMTOR. You can switch speeds manually or, as most PacTOR operators prefer, allow the system to switch by itself.

The "Everyman" Mode

With memory ARQ, and the ability to change data rates automatically, PacTOR allows you to enjoy conversations under conditions that would easily disrupt AMTOR or packet. Any ham, even those with very modest stations, can use PacTOR to communicate effectively on the HF bands.

Fig 5-1—Memory ARQ at work. WB8IMY sends data to WB8ISZ (A), but bits 2, 5 and 6 are corrupted. The MCP at WB8ISZ's station memorizes the good data as well as the positions of the corrupted bits. It sends a NAK (B) to demand a repeat of all the data. On the next transmission (C), bits 1, 3 and 4 are corrupted, but that's not a problem. WB8ISZ's MCP has these bits stored in memory from the first transmission. What's important is the fact that bits 2, 5 and 6 made it through intact. They're the *missing bits* from the first transmission. These bits are combined with the ones in memory and the entire data segment is complete! WB8ISZ now sends an ACK (D) for the next batch. (A PacTOR data segment is actually 192 bits long when operating at 200 bit/s; 80 bits long at 100 bit/s.)

Amplifiers, beams and other expensive toys are definitely *not* required to enter the world of PacTOR. (I've had several PacTOR contacts while running as little as 5 W to a dipole antenna!)

What Do I Need to Run PacTOR?

Assembling a PacTOR station is very simple. All you need are the following:

❏ An SSB transceiver (PacTOR data can be sent via AFSK or FSK)

❏ A data terminal or a computer running terminal software

❏ A multimode communications processor (MCP) with PacTOR capability

Most popular MCPs have PacTOR built-in. They include: the PacComm PTC, MFJ-1278, Kantronics KAM Plus, AEA PK-232MBX, AEA PK-900 and the AEA DSP-2232. See the Resource Guide for addresses and telephone numbers. If you own an older version of these MCPs *without* PacTOR, upgrades are available. Contact the

The PacComm PTC was one of the first PacTOR MCPs available in the US. Within a couple of years, other manufacturers followed with their own PacTOR-capable MCPs.

manufacturer. PacTOR is also available on the HAL Communications PCI-4000/M CLOVER card for IBM-PCs and compatibles.

When assembling your PacTOR station, use the same guidelines discussed in Chapter 2. If you're already set up with an MCP for the other digital modes, you don't need any extra equipment to operate PacTOR.

Calling CQ on PacTOR

If you read the AMTOR chapter, you'll recall that you send CQ on AMTOR using the *FEC* mode. The same is true for PacTOR, although PacTOR FEC is unique to this mode. An MCP in the AMTOR mode cannot read a PacTOR FEC transmission.

Tune through the digital subbands until you hear what sounds like a fast RTTY signal. As you lock-in the signal, your MCP will indicate that it is trying to synchronize with the FEC transmission. Within a short time you should begin to see text on your screen.

You can always identify an AMTOR CQ because the operator must list his or her SELCAL in the text.

CQ CQ CQ CQ CQ DE WB8IMY WB8IMY (WIMY) (WIMY) K K

That's easy enough, but what about this?

CQ CQ CQ CQ CQ DE WB8IMY WB8IMY WB8IMY K K

Is this a PacTOR or G-TOR CQ? There's no way to tell! Both modes use complete call signs rather than SELCALs. To alleviate the confusion, many HF digital operators are adding their *mode* to their CQ message. This is a good practice to follow. Put your MCP in the *PacTOR standby* mode and let's call CQ.

[Switch your MCP to PacTOR FEC transmit]

[Send a blank line]

CQ PacTOR CQ PacTOR CQ PacTOR DE WB8IMY WB8IMY WB8IMY

CQ PacTOR CQ PacTOR CQ PacTOR DE WB8IMY WB8IMY WB8IMY

CQ PacTOR CQ PacTOR CQ PacTOR DE WB8IMY WB8IMY WB8IMY K K

[Switch your MCP back to receive]

Any station that's monitoring your signal will know exactly which mode you're using—and will reply accordingly. When you send CQ, use several short lines of text rather than a few long lines. This helps stations synchronize to your signal more easily.

Once you make contact, the conversation flows along just like AMTOR (see Chapter 4). The station that answered your call is the *ISS* (information sending station) and you're the *IRS* (information receiving station). When he sends his "hello," he'll probably use the *over* command to flip the link. (Consult your MCP manual and/or software documentation concerning the over command.) Now you're the ISS and he is the IRS. Introduce yourself and ask a question about where he lives, or what he does for a living. Use the over command to flip the link again. A conversation is underway!

Answering a CQ

Answering a CQ in PacTOR is straightforward. Depending on the software you're using, it may be as simple as entering:

CALL N1BKE

or, **CONNECT N1BKE**

at the **cmd:** prompt. Some types of software streamline the process even further. There may be pop-up boxes where you simply enter a call sign.

PacTOR has a clever feature that comes in handy when you're trying to connect to a distant station. If the station is more than about 5000 miles away, use the exclamation mark (!) in your connect request. This forces the MCP to lengthen the time it waits to receive an ACK signal from the station, allowing more time for your signal to reach him and his ACK to return. For example:

CONNECT !HS1CHG

Working a PacTOR BBS

Although live conversations are the rule with PacTOR, there are lots of BBSs as well. You'll find that they're almost identical to packet systems. When you connect to a PacTOR BBS, you'll see something like this:

**Welcome to WB8SVN's PacTOR BBS in Placentia, CA.
Enter command:
A,B,C,D,G,H,I,J,K,L,M,N,P,R,S,T,U,V,W,X,?,* >**

After you enter a command you *do not* need to send the over code. The BBS will flip the link automatically after it receives the command from you.

You can use PacTOR BBSs to exchange messages with other PacTOR operators. And with PacTOR's ability to handle binary data, you can even download small programs from the BBS and run them on your computer!

Many AMTOR APLinks and BBSs now respond to PacTOR calls as well. If you spot an AMTOR operator using an APLink, give it a try after he's finished. There's a good chance that it will answer your PacTOR call. You'll find a list of digital BBSs in Appendix A.

Finally, most PacTOR-capable MCPs have mailbox

functions. You can use your PacTOR mailbox as a convenient way to pick up messages from friends when you're not at the keyboard. Remember the FCC rules about unattended operation, though. Don't leave your mailbox on the air when you're not able to monitor and control your station.

PacTOR-2

The state of the art never remains fixed. This is as true of PacTOR as it is of any communication mode. At the 1993 Dayton HamVention the inventors of PacTOR unveiled their newest creation: *PacTOR-2*.

PacTOR-2 pushes the HF performance envelope much farther than PacTOR, providing higher throughput while generating a signal that only occupies about 500 Hz of spectrum. To achieve this remarkable performance, the creators rely on digital signal processing (DSP) and extremely fast microprocessors.

The complex *pi/4-DQPSK* modulation system used by PacTOR-2 requires DSP technology. With DSP you let the *software* decide the composition of the signal, not the hardware. DSP is much more flexible, allowing you to create the signal you want without having to worry about hardware filters and so on. The trade-off is that you must use high-speed microprocessors to handle all the incoming and outgoing information at a decent rate.

As you might guess, PacTOR-2 is so complex it cannot be adapted for use in a conventional MCP. The DSP requirements alone are way beyond virtually all MCPs in the Amateur Radio market today. With this in mind, the developers decided to build and market their own PacTOR-2 multimode controllers. These devices are capable of operating in CW, RTTY, packet and AMTOR in addition to PacTOR-2. A PacTOR-2 controller was shown at the 1994 Dayton HamVention.

PacTOR-2 is also *backward compatible* with PacTOR (should we call it PacTOR-1?). That is, a PacTOR-2 operator can communicate with a PacTOR operator and vice versa. It's difficult to predict the future of PacTOR-2. For this mode to become popular in the United States, a substantial number of amateurs must be willing to abandon their present equipment and buy PacTOR-2 controllers. Ultimately, the marketplace will decide the fate of PacTOR-2.

CHAPTER 6

Connecting with HF Packet

When you think "packet," VHF and UHF probably spring to mind. Although it's true that most packet activity takes place on the VHF and UHF bands (especially 2 meters), you'll find it lurking on HF as well. If you tune through the upper ends of the HF digital subbands, you'll hear the high-pitched, buzzing choruses of dozens of packet stations. Twenty meters is the most popular band for HF packet, but you'll encounter this mode on other bands, too.

Every MCP on the market today has HF packet capability. So do a number of packet-only TNCs. The widespread availability of equipment is the engine that's driven much of the packet activity on the HF bands. Before we dive into the nuts and bolts of packet operating, however, let's take a brief look at how this mode works.

Getting the Information Through

Let's say that I wanted to transmit the contents of this book from my computer to your computer. I could establish a radio link to your station and use it to send everything to

Dave Patterson, WB8ISZ, enjoys operating HF packet while his cat Sam looks on.

your computer in one transmission. It sounds easy so far, doesn't it?

Why don't we make our example a little more challenging? We'll add two more hams on the same frequency. These guys don't want to send books to each other, but they do want to swap lengthy opinions on the latest music. I'm quick on the trigger, however, so my station transmits first. The entire text of this book is suddenly flying across the airwaves in a long, continuous stream of data. My signal is occupying the frequency, so the other hams have to stand by until I'm finished.

At long last my transmission ends. Now the other hams can send their information. But wait! During my transmission there were bursts of noise and interference that destroyed some of the data. You can't have a book with errors, so there is only one thing I can do: send the entire book again! Without hesitation, my computer switches on the transmitter and repeats the outrageously long transmission.

By this time everyone is staring at their computer screens and muttering, "This is ridiculous. There must be a better way." Of course, they're right!

Making a Big Job Smaller

Let's use the same example, but this time we'll use packet techniques to get the job done. The first step is to establish a connection between our stations. We say our stations are *connected* when the packet transmission and reception protocols are active and we're ready to transfer data. (A protocol is a formal, standardized way of doing something. Clubs often use Robert's Rules of Order to keep meetings civilized. Robert's Rules of Order are a set of protocols.) In the case of packet, the protocol is known as *AX.25*.

My station begins by digesting the text of the book and constructing a number of "byte-sized" packets for transmission. The packets are lined up in proper order like airplanes sitting on a taxiway waiting to take off. Within a fraction of a second, the first packet is on its way.

Your station receives the packet and checks it for errors. In the meantime, a timer has started back at my station. If I don't hear from you before the timer reaches zero, the packet is sent again. For the moment we'll assume that my first packet arrived error-free. Your station communicates this fact by sending a special signal known as an ACK, or acknowledgment. When I receive your ACK, my next packet is transmitted.

"Hold on!" you say. "What happens if your station doesn't hear my ACK for some reason?" If your ACK arrives distorted and unreadable—or not at all—my timer simply continues to count down to zero. Eventually, my station will resend the first packet. When you receive the first packet again, your station will, in effect, say, "What's going on here? I already have this packet. Send the next one!" It indicates its displeasure by transmitting what is known as a reject frame. When I receive the reject, my station will automatically send the next packet.

Through this process of timers, ACKs and rejects, all of my packets will arrive at your station in one piece—and vice versa. When signals are strong and clear at both stations, the packets are transmitted and acknowledged in rapid-fire sequence.

During the silent periods between our transmissions, the other hams can send their packets, too. Packet is extremely patient. If a station has a packet to send and another station is transmitting on the frequency, it will wait until the transmission stops before trying to send its data. Packet is also very persistent. A packet will be transmitted and retransmitted many times before the system finally gives up and breaks the connection.

The Special Problems of HF Packet

Noise and interference are deadly to packet, and the HF bands have both in abundance. All it takes is the corruption of *one* bit of data and an entire packet data frame is ruined. The receiving station won't accept it, which means the transmitting station must try again. When you listen to packet signals, the first thing you notice is that some of the bursts are relatively long—up to 3 seconds or more. That's an eternity when you're sending data. It's also more than enough time for a pop of static or a blip of interference to wreck everything.

The HF bands are also prone to fading. Even a slight fade is enough to cause data loss. By combining the effects of noise, interference and fading, you set the stage for frustration. When conditions deteriorate, throughput suffers. The act of sending a simple greeting can take several minutes. (Oops! Lost a couple of bits! We'll have to send that frame again. And again. And again...)

This is why so many hams ultimately turn to other digital modes such as AMTOR, G-TOR, PacTOR and CLOVER when they need to pass information on HF efficiently. This is not to say that packet doesn't have its place on the HF bands. When signal conditions are good, it performs quite well. There are still many VHF and UHF bulletin boards throughout the world that depend on HF packet to move mail over great distances. And there are great opportunities to enjoy fascinating conversations on HF packet. The key to success is patience!

Equipment Requirements

The standard digital station setup we discussed in Chapter 2 is all you need for HF packet. You can use almost any SSB transceiver, operating in either LSB or USB. Packet isn't a rapid-fire handshaking mode like AMTOR or PacTOR, so you *don't* need a transceiver that can switch from transmit to receive quickly. This opens the door to using older, less expensive radios. Even so, you may need to lengthen the delay your TNC or MCP imposes between the time it keys the transmitter and the time the data tones are actually sent. Older transceivers need a little extra time to close their relays and come up to full output power. Check your TNC or MCP manual for a command called **TXDelay**. Adjust the TXDelay value *upward* if you have difficulty operating packet with an older radio.

Most HF packet operators use AFSK. They feed the audio from the TNC or MCP directly to the transceiver's microphone jack or auxiliary audio input. Be careful to observe your ALC meter and adjust your **mic gain** control to prevent overdriving your rig. If your radio has selectable receive filters and/or noise blankers, use them cautiously. HF packet signals are quite wide and it doesn't take much to distort them!

Depending on the type of MCP or TNC you're using, you may have to send a command to place it in the HF packet mode. On some units it's simply a matter of sending a command such as **HF ON**. On others you may need to adjust the data rate through the **HBAUD** command. Below 28 MHz only 300-baud packet is legal. So, you may have to send a command such as **HBAUD 300** to place your TNC or MCP in the HF packet mode.

An HF Packet Tour

Before you enjoy your first HF packet conversation, spend some time prowling through the bands. HF packet can be a little confusing at first glance

Set up your TNC or MCP so that you can monitor all packet data—even packets not intended for you. In some units the **MCOM** command is used (**MCOM ON**). In others it is part of the **MONITOR** command. Check your TNC or MCP manual.

When you find a packet signal, tune *very carefully*. If your TNC or MCP has a bargraph type tuning indicator, you're ahead of the game. You can use it to get your radio on the correct frequency with little trouble. Packet signals can be tuned without an indicator, but it is quite difficult. With practice, however, you'll learn to do it by ear. That is, you'll know you're close when you hear the packet signal at a certain pitch.

Don't expect to see information on your screen right away. You may have to wait for the next transmission (after you've stopped tuning) before data is displayed. And if conditions are so-so, you may have to wait even longer.

Mail Forwarding

Of all the activity you'll see on HF packet, *mail forwarding* is the most common. The global packet system is made up of VHF and UHF networks that serve local areas. The bulletin boards in these networks pass mail between each other on VHF and UHF frequencies when they can, but sometimes the routes require leaps of hundreds or thousands of miles. Unless the bulletin board operator has the ability to relay mail via amateur satellite, the next best choice may be HF packet.

The act of relaying packet mail from one point to another is known as *forwarding*. Messages and bulletins travel on VHF or UHF until they reach stations with HF packet forwarding capability. A station must have more than an HF transceiver and a TNC to be a forwarder. An HF mail forwarder keeps appointments with other stations on specific frequencies. Elaborate software checks each incoming message from the local network and "decides" which HF station should receive it. The messages are stored until they can be relayed via HF packet to the appropriate station.

Let's say that you've stumbled upon some forwarding in progress. It may look like this:

WØXK>N4HOG:
ö_îywl*°_ÛòÊ\$£¶ØæHÅ'G^›2%T´JÜ·_y7™o,ÖÓ Tnx for QSL   0´á_îîq,_

WØXK>N4HOG:
ç‰   »_áY∂|ÚÎf'_x"¯°xö®;=»8À‡¿Í¥c_CaueJó &__ÓÛúÿ_OQçy@}/YÔÀÂ_J›3—sé ¿ –Ÿ‹mïV=

WØXK>N4HOG:
Ïø,pßÁ%-%ŸAÜ¥k6M—ß2ŒF¯‰•_A'Rq+>3åQ ±9M_òa&1¿£:ûµ_...ûÔø ·k#@ ,Ù~RM\$8ËÌ-†Xµ

No, there's nothing wrong with your computer! These stations are using a type of data compression to make it easier to send large amounts of data. The result on your screen, however, looks like this. If you see stations passing traffic without compression, this is more typical of what you'll see:

XF3R>XE1M-15:
Another ham (80 years old!) told me about a mode called PACTOR.

XF3R>XE1M-15:
Another ham (80 years old!) told me about a mode called PACTOR.

XF3R>XE1M-15:
Another ham (80 years old!) told me about a mode called PACTOR.

XF3R>XE1M-15:
I never heard of this before!

XF3R>XE1M-15:
Has anybody further info?

XF3R>XE1M-15:
Thanx in advance.

XF3R>XE1M-15:
73....Joss.

Notice that parts of this message were repeated several times. I bet you can guess why! Noise, interference or fading must have caused errors on the receiving end. A few repeats were required to get the message through.

Bulletin Boards and Mailboxes

HF packet gives you the opportunity to connect with bulletin board systems (PBBSs) throughout the world. By connecting with a bulletin board, you can view messages and bulletins concerning every topic imaginable! Of course, you can do the same thing on VHF packet, but DX bulletin boards offer a perspective you won't find elsewhere. What are the big issues among hams in Argentina, for example? Connect to an Argentinean PBBS and find out!

PBBS activity is easy to spot. Most hams request a list of the latest bulletins when they connect, so look for any station that seems to be sending such a list. Here is an actual example copied on 20 meters:

VE4GQ>WB4TDB:
8965   BF   1967 ALL @MAN VE4SYG 07-Jun MRS BYLAWS

8964   B$ 1587 SALE @ALLCAN VO2APL 04-Jun LOTS OF THINGS FOR SALE

8961   B$ 1012 SALE @ALLCAN VO2APL

8960   B$ 414 WANTED @CANADA VE4YE 07-Jun

8956   B$ 2986 RSGB @CANADA VE6EQ 05-Jun RSGB MAIN News 5th June

8955   B$ 2603 RAC @CANADA VE3LVO 05-Jun $$$ STONEWALLING? $$$

Some PBBSs are able to serve more than one station at a time, so you may see several messages going to one station, then another. We'll discuss how to connect to a PBBS a little later.

As you comb through the packet signals you may also run into data that *looks* like it's coming from a PBBS, but it isn't. For example:

[KPC2-5.00-HM$]
16000 BYTES AVAILABLE
Thanks for checking in. Please leave a message and I'll get back to you. 73, Bill/W1KKF.
ENTER COMMAND: B,J,K,L,R,S, or Help >

This is the typical sign-on message you'll receive from a packet *mailbox*. These mailbox functions are common features on TNCs and MCPs. Depending on the model you've purchased, you may have one at your fingertips right now!

Although they look similar, there are major differences between PBBSs and mailboxes. Notice, for example, that this packet mailbox has only 16,000 bytes of data storage available. Packet mailboxes store all of their incoming and outgoing messages in solid-state RAM (random access memory). The typical RAM capacity of a packet mailbox is only about 32 kbytes. True PBBSs, on the other hand,

Unattended Operation

When you discover the convenience of having your own HF packet mailbox, it's tempting to simply leave it on the air around the clock. If you do, you'd better be able to prove that you're in control of your station at all times. Unless you have a special temporary authority (STA) issued by the Federal Communications Commission, it is *illegal* to operate an HF station unattended! (When this book went to press, the rules concerning unattended HF operating were under review by the FCC.)

STAs are difficult to obtain and the FCC isn't likely to grant one just so that you can operate a mailbox 24 hours a day. The STAs that apply to HF packet were issued to a small group of stations involved in mail forwarding. This is not to say that you cannot forward mail or perform any other legal function with your packet station. Just make sure you're present at your station location when you're doing it!

The easy solution to the mailbox dilemma is to put it on the air at specific times when you know you'll be available. Tell your friends that your mailbox will be running from, say, 7 PM to 11 PM, Monday through Friday.

usually store data on *hard disks* with several *megabytes* of capacity.

You'll also notice that the *command line* (**ENTER COMMAND: B,J,K,L,R,S, or Help >**) is much shorter than those you'll see on most packet bulletin boards. That's because packet mailboxes have very limited capabilities. This one will allow you only to send mail (S), read mail (R), list messages (L), kill messages (K), see a list of stations heard recently (J) and disconnect (B).

With their meager memories and limited features, packet mailboxes are not intended to perform like real PBBSs. Instead, packet mailboxes are convenience devices. They allow stations to connect and exchange mail. This makes it easy for friends to drop off messages (and read replies). If you decide to set up your own HF packet mailbox, be careful to observe FCC rules concerning unattended operation.

Live Conversations

Live conversations are common on HF packet, perhaps more common than on VHF and UHF packet. You'll recognize them right away because they're just lines of text flying back and forth from one station to another. For example:

WB8IMY>N6ATQ:
So did you get your new vertical up last weekend? >>>

N6ATQ>WB8IMY:
No, it rained like crazy. There's no way I was going to lay radial wires in the mud! >>>

Note the use of >>> at the end of each line. Many packeteers use this symbol to let the other stations know that it's their turn to comment. You'll also see **BTU** (back to you) and **K** used in the same manner.

Calling CQ

Before you attempt an HF packet connection, check your receive audio level. Adjust the level control until the RCV or DCD indicator on your TNC or MCP glows when a packet is received (tune in some packet signals to test this). If the indicator blinks in response to noise on the frequency, you have the audio level set too high.

The next step is to send a *CQ* (general call) to flush other hams out of the woodwork. You can send your CQ as a single, *unconnected* packet, but you must be in the converse mode to do so. (If you're in the command mode, enter **CONV** at the **cmd:** prompt.) When you're not connected to another station, everything you enter while in the converse mode is sent as an unconnected packet. Any station that receives the packet without errors will be able to read it. Since it's sent without an established connection, an ACK from another station isn't required or expected.

Sending a CQ this way is easy. Just type a brief message and hit your **ENTER** or **RETURN** key. For example:

CQ, CQ from NØMZR in Palmyra, Missouri. K

The problem with this approach is that the CQ is sent only once. What if a burst of interference prevents someone from receiving it? What if you sent your CQ just seconds before a lonely packeteer arrived on the frequency? To send CQ more than once, you'd have to type the entire line over and over.

Fortunately, there's an easier way to send multiple CQs. Your TNC or MCP is equipped with a **BEACON** function. When the beacon is activated, your TNC will transmit unconnected packets repeatedly until you turn it off.

The content of your beacon packet is determined by

your **BTEXT** parameter. BTEXT stands for "beacon text" and it contains the actual text of your CQ message. Simply switch to the command mode and enter something like this:

BTEXT CQ CQ from N6ATQ in Escondido, California

When you're ready to start, enter the **BEACON** command along with the beacon *rate*.

BEACON EVERY *N*

N usually equals a certain interval of time. In some TNCs and MCPs, for example, 1 is equal to 10 seconds. So, **BEACON EVERY 1** will cause the TNC to transmit an unconnected packet containing your BTEXT message every 10 seconds. **BEACON EVERY 3**, on the other hand, would cause the packet to be transmitted every 30 seconds (10 × 3). Timing can differ from one unit to another, so check your manual carefully.

What beacon rate should you select? If the frequency is busy, keep your beacon rate low (once per minute or longer). If the frequency is unoccupied, you can beacon at a much faster rate. The key is knowing when to stop. Sending beacons on a quiet frequency should net a response within a few minutes. If it doesn't, turn off the beacon (**BEACON EVERY 0**) and try another frequency. If someone answers your call, you may need to switch to the command mode and turn off the beacon.

Using a PBBS

Connecting to a PBBS is the same as connecting to any other packet station. Monitor the packet frequencies and watch for bulletin board activity. When you find one, make your connect request and have fun! Let's pretend we've discovered the W1NRG-4 PBBS.

CONNECT W1NRG-4

If the other station hears you, you'll be rewarded with:

*** CONNECTED TO W1NRG-4

Very good! You've made the connection. Now the PBBS will send its sign-on information to you.

Welcome to W1NRG's MSYS PBBS in Wallingford, CT Enter command: A,B,C,D,G,H,I,J,K,L,M,N,P,R,S,T,U, V,W,X,?,* >

That's a big list of commands and we don't have the space in this book to discuss each one. A list of common PBBS commands is shown in Table 6-1. Would you like to see what bulletins are available on the PBBS? The *LB* (List Bulletins) command will do the trick. You can read a message by sending the letter *R* followed by the message number.

Table 6-1

Common PBBS Commands

General Commands:

B	Log off PBBS.
Jx	Display call signs of stations recently heard or connected on TNC port x.
N x	Enter your name (x) in system (12 characters maximum).
NE	Toggle between short and extended command menu.
NH x	Enter the call sign (x) of the PBBS where you normally send and receive mail.
NQ x	Enter your location (x).
NZ n	Enter your ZIP Code (n).
P x	Display information concerning station whose call sign is x.

S	Display PBBS status.
T	Ring bell at the Sysop's station for one minute.

Information commands:

? *	Display description of all PBBS commands.
?	Display summary of all PBBS commands.
? x	Display summary of command x.
H*	Display description of all PBBS commands.
H	Display summary of all PBBS commands.
H x	Display description of command x.
I	Display information about PBBS.
I x	Display information about station whose call sign is x.
IL	Display list of local users of the PBBS.
IZn	List users at ZIP Code n.
V	Display PBBS software version.

Message commands:

K n	Kill message numbered n.
KM	Kill all messages addressed to you that you have read.
KT n	Kill NTS traffic numbered n.
L	List all messages entered since you last logged on.
L n	List message numbered n and messages numbered higher than n.
L< x	List messages *from* station whose call sign is x.
L> x	List messages addressed *to* station whose call sign is x.
L@ x	List messages addressed for forwarding to PBBS whose call sign is x.
L n1 n2	List messages numbered n1 through n2.
LA n	List the first n messages stored on PBBS.
LB	List all bulletin messages.
LF	List all messages that have been forwarded.
LL n	List the last n messages stored on PBBS.
LM	List all messages addressed to you.
LT	List all NTS traffic.
R n	Read message numbered n.
RH n	Read message numbered n with full message header displayed.
RM	Read all messages addressed to you that you have not read.

Table 6-1 Continued

S x @ y   Send a message to station whose call sign is x at PBBS whose call sign is y.

S x   Send message to station whose call sign is x at this PBBS.

SB x   Send a bulletin message to x at this PBBS.

SB x @ y   Send a bulletin message to x at PBBS whose call sign is y.

SP x @ y   Send a private message to station whose call sign is x at PBBS whose call sign is y.

SP x   Send a private message to station whose call sign is x at this PBBS.

SR   Send a message in response to a message you have just read.

ST x @ y   Send an NTS message to station whose call sign is x at PBBS whose call sign is y.

ST x   Send an NTS message to station whose call sign is x at this PBBS.

File transfer commands:

Dx y   From directory named x, download file named y.

U x   Upload file named x.

W   List what directories are available.

Wx   List what files are available in directory named x.

Wx y   List files in directory named x whose file name matches y.

Trouble on the Frequency

If there's a problem with your connection to another station, the STA (status) indicator on the front panel of your TNC or MCP may provide the first clue. When the path is very good, all packets will be received and acknowledged right away. You'll see the STA indicator flashing on and off as this takes place. If the STA remains on—even after you've sent a very brief message—it means that your TNC or MCP is still waiting for ACK signals from the other station. An STA that's still glowing long after you've entered the last line of your message is a sure sign of trouble. The culprit could be weak signals at either end of the path. Another likely suspect is interference.

If interference is severe, or propagation is poor, how long will your TNC/MCP keep trying before it finally gives up? It all depends on the **RETRY** parameter. Your unit was probably shipped with its **RETRY** parameter set at 10. In other words, it will transmit a packet 10 times without acknowledgment before terminating the connection. You *can* set your **RETRY** parameter to zero, forcing your TNC/MCP to repeat its packets endlessly, but this is poor operating practice. If the signal path between you and another station is so poor that it takes 20 or 30 "retries" to get a packet through, why bother? Unless it's an emergency situation, you'll only cause frustration for yourself and additional congestion for everyone else.

In the end it doesn't matter if it's interference or poor propagation that eventually pushes your TNC or MCP to its limit. When the **RETRY** count is exceeded, you'll see:

Retry count exceeded

***DISCONNECTED

A ccording to legend, Ray Petit, W7GHM, was working on a revolutionary new HF digital communication system in his home lab. His wife stopped by just in time to see a display of the received signal pattern on Ray's oscilloscope. "That looks just like a clover," she remarked. The new mode didn't have a name and his wife's description seemed appropriate enough. Why not simply call it *CLOVER*?

What is CLOVER?

CLOVER is an advanced HF digital communication system that Ray Petit developed in a joint venture with HAL Communications of Urbana, Illinois. CLOVER uses a four-tone modulation scheme. Depending on signal conditions, any of *ten* modulation formats can be selected manually or automatically. Six of the modulation systems employ phase-shift modulation (PSM); two use amplitude-shift modulation (ASM); and two use frequency-shift modulation (FSM). Each tone is phase- and/or amplitude-modulated as a separate, narrow-bandwidth data channel.

As you might guess, the resulting CLOVER signal is very complex!

For example, when the tone pulses are modulated using quadrature phase-shift modulation (QPSM), the differential phase of each tone shifts in 90° increments. Two bits of data are carried by each tone for a total of eight bits in each 32-

CLOVER Bandwidth

As we've already discussed, space is a premium in the HF digital subbands. That's why it's important for any HF digital mode to be as *narrow* as possible.

With a 2-kHz bandwidth, an HF packet signal is nearly as wide as a voice transmission. You can't squeeze too many packet signals onto the band before serious interference begins (just listen to the HF packet activity on 20 meters!).

AMTOR improves the situation with a 1 kHz bandwidth, but that's still awfully wide for the available space. PacTOR transmissions have about the same bandwidth. If we expect to use the HF bands for efficient digital communications, we need to provide room for many more signals.

And then along comes CLOVER! As remarkable as it may seem, CLOVER manages to conduct extremely efficient communications while using only 500 Hz of spectrum! Two CLOVER signals could occupy the space of one AMTOR signal. *Four* CLOVER signals could fit in the same amount of spectrum required for one HF packet signal.

This narrow bandwidth is yet another prominent feature of CLOVER. Of course, a narrow-bandwidth signal requires more careful tuning. That's why the HAL PC CLOVER software includes an on-screen tuning indicator. You can also understand why your transceiver must be very stable to operate CLOVER. With a 500-Hz wide signal, all it takes is a little bit of drift and you're way out of the ballpark!

ms frame. The resulting block data rate is about 250 bits per second. CLOVER is capable of even higher data rates when using 16-phase, four-amplitude modulation (16P4A). In this format, CLOVER perks along at 750 bit/s.

The complex, higher-speed modulation systems are used when conditions are favorable. When the going gets rough, CLOVER automatically brings several slower (but more robust) modes into play.

Even with these ingenious adaptive modulation systems, errors are bound to occur. That's where CLOVER's Reed-Solomon coding fills the gaps. Reed-Solomon coding is used in all CLOVER modes. Errors are detected at the receiving station by comparing check bytes that are inserted in each block of transmitted text. When operating in the ARQ mode, CLOVER's damaged data can often be reconstructed without the need to request repeat transmissions! This is a major departure from the techniques used by packet, AMTOR and PacTOR. Of course, CLOVER can't always repair data; repeat transmissions—which CLOVER handles automatically— are sometimes required to get everything right.

With the combination of adaptive modulation systems and Reed-Solomon coding, CLOVER boasts remarkable performance—even under the worst HF conditions. The only Amateur Radio digital mode with the potential to approach CLOVER's performance is PacTOR-2, and possibly G-TOR (under certain conditions).

CLOVER Handshaking

As you may recall, PacTOR and AMTOR both use an *over* command to switch the link so that one station can send while the other receives. CLOVER links must be switched as well, but the switching takes place *without* using *over* commands.

When two CLOVER stations make contact, they can send limited amounts of data to each other (up to 30 characters in each block) in what is known as the *chat mode*. If the amount of data waiting for transmission at one station exceeds 30 characters, CLOVER automatically switches to the *block data mode*. The transmitted blocks immediately become larger and are sent much faster. The other station, however, remains in the chat mode. Because of precise frame timing, all of this takes place without the need for either operator to change settings, or send *over* commands. The CLOVER controllers at both stations "know" when to switch from transmit to receive and vice versa. And what if both stations have large amounts of data to send at the same time? Then they *both* switch to the data block mode. This high degree of efficiency is transparent to you, the operator. All you have to do is type your comments or select the file you want to send—CLOVER takes care of everything else!

CLOVER features an FEC mode similar to that used by AMTOR, PacTOR and G-TOR. You use the CLOVER FEC to call CQ, or to send transmissions that can be received by several stations at once. (In the CLOVER ARQ mode, only two stations can communicate at a time.) CLOVER shares another characteristic with AMTOR: the use of SELCALs. When attempting to contact another CLOVER station, you must send its SELCAL first.

What Do I Need to Run CLOVER?

The requirements for a CLOVER station differ substantially from those of other HF digital modes. They are:

❏ An SSB transceiver. The transceiver must be very stable (less than 30-Hz drift per hour). It should also include a frequency display with 10-Hz resolution. The audio output from the CLOVER controller is fed to the audio

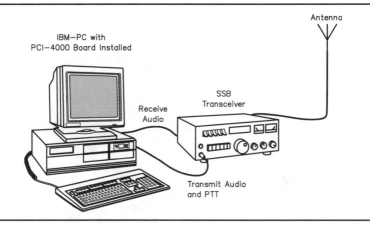

Fig 7-1—A diagram of a typical CLOVER station. The HAL Communications PCI-4000 CLOVER card plugs into an IBM-PC or compatible computer. The transmit audio and PTT (push-to-talk) cable connects from the PCI-4000 to the audio input of the transceiver. The receive audio is routed from the transceiver to the PCI-4000.

input of the transceiver (CLOVER uses AFSK, not FSK). Receive audio is supplied to the controller from the external speaker jack or other source (see Fig 7-1).

❏ An IBM-PC computer or compatible. The computer must be at least a 286-level machine.

❏ A PCI-4000 CLOVER controller board. All CLOVER controllers are available exclusively from HAL Communications (see the Resource Guide for details). The HAL PCI-4000 CLOVER controller is installed *inside* the computer using any available expansion slot (see Fig 7-2). The board uses a dual-microprocessor design and digital signal processing to achieve signal modulation and demodulation.

❏ HAL PC-CLOVER software. This is supplied by HAL Communications and is included with every PCI-4000

Fig 7-2—Installing a PCI-4000 CLOVER controller is as easy as opening our computer cabinet and sliding the card into an empty expansion slot. The cables connect to the outside edge of the card.

controller. It is *not* a terminal program. The PC-CLOVER software is the instruction set of the PCI-4000 itself! It's loaded into the PCI-4000's memory each time you decide to operate. This approach makes it easy to update the PCI-4000 in the future. You simply buy a new diskette or download the software from a BBS.

The original PCI-4000 CLOVER controller offered CLOVER *only* and the cost was approximately $1000. In early 1994, HAL Communications introduced the PCI-4000/M—a multimode CLOVER controller. In addition to CLOVER, the PCI-4000/M includes AMTOR, PacTOR and RTTY. The cost had dropped to about $800 at the time this book went to press.

CLOVER on the Air

When this chapter was written, CLOVER signals were

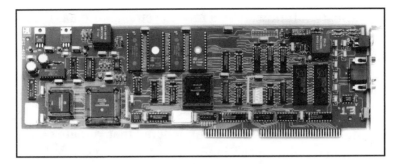

The HAL Communications PCI-4000 CLOVER controller. It plugs into the expansion slot of an IBM-PC or compatible computer (286 or higher).

not common on the bands. Most of the CLOVER activity was confined to 30 and 20 meters. Part of the reason was the cost of the PCI-4000 and the fact that the original version could only operate CLOVER.

Most CLOVER-equipped stations are dedicated to relaying high-volume message traffic. This makes casual CLOVER operating the exception rather than the rule (although you will find a few CLOVER BBSs on the air). With the advent of the less expensive, multimode PCI-4000/M, this scenario is almost certain to change. You may see more CLOVER operators getting on the air just to chat.

CLOVER signals are relatively easy to recognize. The data bursts vary in length. Some are short, while others can last several seconds. The signals make a staccato *brrrrr* sound rather than the chirping rhythms of AMTOR, PacTOR and G-TOR.

CLOVER Conversations

When it comes to on-the-air operating, CLOVER is different from any of the modes we've discussed so far. To call CQ, for example, you switch to the **MODE** menu, highlight **CQ** and press **ENTER**. The PCI-4000 sends a CW identification followed by a raucous stream of data. Unlike other digital modes, you do not see "CQ CQ CQ" flowing across your screen. In fact, you see nothing at all.

The PCI-4000 sends CQ in the form of data signals that appear as CQ "flags" to other CLOVER stations. When another CLOVER operator tunes in your signal, all he sees is a statement on his screen announcing that you are calling CQ. At that point he can ignore you or press a single key to establish a CLOVER connection.

Once the conversation has started, it is similar to HF packet. Because there are no *over* commands, you need to let the other station know when you've completed a statement. For example:

**Hello! My name is Steve
and I live in Wallingford, Connecticut. I am new to
CLOVER. What do you think of it? >>>**

Without >>>, BTU, K or a similar symbol at the end of my statement, the other operator might inadvertently jump in after the end of the first line. This can be very confusing for everyone!

While you're watching the conversation, it's easy to get distracted by the receive/transmit status table in the upper right corner of the screen. The table displays the modulation format in use at the moment, the signal-to-noise ratio, tuning error, phase dispersion, error-correction capacity and transmitter output power (as a percentage of full output). The table is split into horizontal rows labeled "MY" and "HIS." Not only do you see your own parameters changing, you see the changes taking place *at the other station!* (CLOVER accomplishes this feat by periodically swapping station data.) Who is enjoying the best receive conditions? Which station is doing the greatest amount of error correcting at the moment? Just look at the table!

Adaptive Operating

The PCI-4000's adaptive behavior is fascinating. As signal conditions fluctuate during a conversation, the PCI-4000 raises and lowers the audio level to the input of your transceiver. This causes a corresponding change in output power.

For example, when my CLOVER station learns that you are receiving me extremely well (based on the signal-to-noise and error-correction data supplied by your station) it may automatically drop my power to a mere 6% of full output. If conditions deteriorate, my output may jump to 50% or even 100%. In other words, CLOVER uses only as much power as it needs to maintain the link at any given time. Imagine how our bands would sound if every mode had this capability!

CHAPTER 8

G-TOR

O n New Year's Day 1994, WØXI and WK5M of the Kantronics Corporation transmitted a 9718-byte file from their station in Kansas to WA4EGT in California on 20 meters. Despite mediocre band conditions, the file was transferred in just 5 minutes and 20 seconds. They used a digital mode never heard before on the HF bands: *G-TOR*. Immediately thereafter, the file was transmitted again, this time using PacTOR. It took 20 minutes and 15 seconds—nearly four times slower. Throughout the month of January these tests were repeated with over 1,000,000 bytes transferred error-free. The average character/second rate for G-TOR was 23.7; for PacTOR 8.64. More testing and tweaking followed until March 1, 1994, when G-TOR made its official debut.

Equipment Requirements

As this book went to press, G-TOR was available in only one multimode controller: the Kantronics *KAM Plus,* specifically those units sold after March 1, 1994. Owners of earlier KAM Plus MCPs can upgrade to G-TOR by simply purchasing and installing a version 7.0P EPROM chip. Hams who own older KAMs can also add G-TOR, but they must purchase the version 7.0E enhancement board. If you already own a KAM with an enhancement board, all you need is a 7.0E EPROM. The address and telephone number of the Kantronics Corporation are listed in the Resource Guide. Kantronics has also offered to license G-TOR to other MCP manufacturers and several have shown interest. (MFJ plans to add G-TOR to their 1278 MCP in 1995.)

If you have an SSB transceiver that will switch from transmit to receive in less than 100 ms (most will), you should be able to use it for G-TOR with little difficulty. You can operate G-TOR in direct FSK or AFSK. Most G-TOR operators are using AFSK, however.

No special software is required other than a terminal program to interface with the MCP. The exception is the G-TOR *monitoring* software, which we'll discuss in a moment.

Who Put the "G" in G-TOR?

G-TOR is an acronym for *G*olay-coded *T*eleprinting *O*ver *R*adio. Golay coding is the error-correction system created by M. J. E. Golay and used by the *Voyager* space-craft. Sending billions of bytes of data across the Solar System required a scheme to ensure that the information could be recovered despite errors caused by interference, noise, and so on. If Golay coding could meet that challenge, the engineers at Kantronics wondered if it could be applied to digital communication on the HF bands as well.

To create G-TOR, Kantronics combined the Golay coding system with full-frame data interleaving, on-demand Huffman compression, run-length encoding, a variable data rate capability (100 to 300 bit/s) and 16-bit CRC error

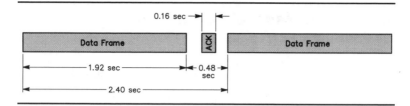

Fig 8-1—G-TOR timing. A complete G-TOR cycle is 2.40 seconds long. The data frame requires 1.92 seconds to transmit. After that, there is a 0.48-second "window" of silence while the sending station waits for the receiving station to acknowledge. The 0.16-second ACK must arrive before the window closes or the data frame will be transmitted again.

detection. G-TOR system timing is liberal enough to permit long-distance communication (see Fig 8-1).

The G-TOR waveform consists of two phase-continuous tones (BFSK) spaced 200 Hz apart (MARK = 1600 Hz, SPACE = 1800 Hz). However, the system can still operate at the familiar 170-Hz shift (MARK = 2125 Hz, SPACE = 2295 Hz). The optimum spacing for 300-bit/s G-TOR transmissions would normally be 300 Hz. In the interest of keeping the bandwidth as close to 500 Hz as practical, some small amount of performance is traded off to save bandwidth.

One of the primary causes of reduced throughput on synchronous ARQ signals (such as those used by AMTOR and PacTOR) is errors in the acknowledgment signal (ACK). To reduce unnecessary retransmissions due to faulty ACKs, G-TOR uses *fuzzy* ACKs. This system allows receiving stations to tolerate a small number of errors in an ACK signal, rather than ignoring it completely and automatically resending the data. If you want the details of this complex protocol, I suggest you read "G-TOR: A Hybrid ARQ Protocol for Narrow Bandwidth HF Data Communication" by Phil Anderson, WØXI, in the May 1994 *QEX* (the ARRL experimenter's magazine).

G-TOR vs PacTOR vs AMTOR: A Nonscientific Test

As a KAM Plus owner, I was intrigued to say the least when I first heard about G-TOR. The announcement made substantial claims about G-TOR's ability to surpass PacTOR and even rival CLOVER in terms of overall throughput. Not that I disbelieved Kantronics' claims, but this was something that I had to witness in my own shack. I contacted Kantronics and purchased a replacement EPROM for my KAM Plus. It arrived within days and soon I was on the air.

My first test was with Karl Medcalf, WK5M, of Kantronics. We met on 14.085 MHz. I was running an ICOM IC-745 transceiver connected to a dipole approximately 30 feet off the ground. My average RF output was 100 W. WK5M was using a similar setup, although his antenna was a triband beam on a 50-foot tower. When we established communication, Karl gave me a 579 signal report. He was booming into my station with a 599+. There was moderate interference. Neither of us were using signal filtering beyond that provided by our 2.3-kHz IF filters.

The first test was with PacTOR. Karl sent a 9,718-byte ASCII file which I received within 8 minutes and 15 seconds for an average data rate of 157 bit/s. We switched to G-TOR and Karl resent the file. This time I received the complete text in only 3 minutes and 35 seconds, an average data rate of 362 bit/s. To illustrate the robust nature of G-TOR, Karl sent the file a third time, but with his RF output reduced to only 5 W. Throughput suffered as you'd expect, but the entire file still made it across at an impressive rate of 290 bit/s (see Fig 8-2).

G-TOR was clearly superior to PacTOR under average conditions, but how would we fare under truly abominable conditions? (Karl and I didn't have time for an AMTOR test and I was curious to see how it would compare, too.)Larry Wolfgang, WR1B, ARRL Senior Assistant Technical Editor, upgraded his KAM with G-TOR firmware and we met on the air at 14.070 MHz.

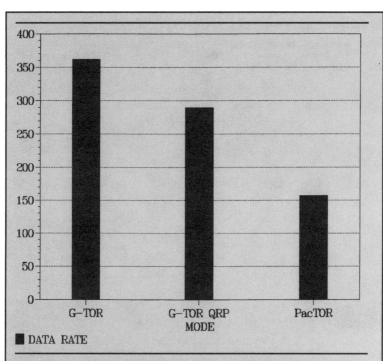

DATA RATE

Fig 8-2—A comparison of PacTOR vs G-TOR in tests
between WB8IMY and WK5M using a 9718-byte file. The
test took place on 20 meters with good band conditions and
moderate interference.

His transceiver is a Kenwood TS-820 working into a
triband beam pointed *away* from my location. Once
again, neither of us were using filtering beyond that
provided by our fixed IF filters (2.3 kHz).

The band had effectively shut down for the
evening. Even though we enjoyed interference-free
conditions, noise levels were very high. Since Larry
lives only 40 miles away, I received his 100 W signal
via groundwave. It was extremely weak. I could *just*
hear his FEC test transmissions above the noise
(actual copy was spotty). Larry said that I was
somewhat louder on his end, but barely. These were
the awful conditions I was hoping for!

Continued from page 5

We began with AMTOR. I sent a 3934-byte ASCII text file, which Larry received within 20 minutes for an average data rate of 26 bit/s. The link was maintained continuously throughout the test, although Larry noted several errors in the received text.

PacTOR fared somewhat better. The same file was sent in 16 minutes and 6 seconds for an average data rate of 33 bit/s. Larry received the file error-free.

Finally, we tried G-TOR. Larry received the file in 6 minutes and 7 seconds for an average data rate of 86 bit/s—$2^{1}/_{2}$ times faster than our PacTOR test! At one point during the transfer I was astonished to see my KAM indicate that it had momentarily surged to a data rate of 300 bit/s. The results of all three tests are illustrated graphically in Fig 8-3.

Signal conditions remained fairly constant throughout the tests. We attempted to transfer the file using HF packet, but it was impossible to establish and maintain a connection. It would have been interesting to attempt a CLOVER test over the same path, but neither of us were equipped for that mode.

With all these innovations, G-TOR performs quite well despite noise, fading and interference. It runs circles around AMTOR and is capable of passing information at two to three times the rate of PacTOR. No, G-TOR isn't as supercharged as CLOVER or PacTOR-2, but it offers impressive performance at less than half the cost.

G-TOR in Action

G-TOR is surprisingly easy to operate. If you're familiar with AMTOR or PacTOR operating, G-TOR is essentially the same. When you're in the G-TOR mode, you

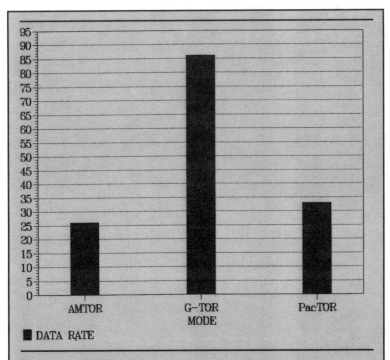

Fig 8-3—Average data rates during tests on 20 meters between WB8IMY and WR1B. The size of the test file was 3934 bytes. Received signals were weak at both stations and noise levels were high. We attempted the file transfer using HF packet, but conditions were too poor to permit a connection.

use AMTOR FEC to call CQ. This allows your transmission to be copied by as many stations as possible. If someone wants to talk to you, they respond in G-TOR using your full call sign.

When you call CQ, let the stations know that you're fishing for G-TOR contacts. Remember that AMTOR stations may be tuning in. Here's an example of a typical G-TOR CQ:

CQ CQ CQ CQ CQ—G-TOR
CQ CQ CQ CQ CQ—G-TOR
CQ CQ CQ CQ CQ—G-TOR
DE WB8IMY WB8IMY WB8IMY
Standing by for G-TOR calls. K K

Once the G-TOR link is established, the station that called you is the ISS, or *information sending station*. It's up to him to speak first. While he is transmitting, you're the *information receiving station*, or IRS. You flip these IRS/ISS roles back and forth by sending an "over" code. Like PacTOR, G-TOR can transfer ASCII or binary information.

If you copy someone calling CQ G-TOR, you simply switch to the G-TOR standby mode. Establishing a connection is as easy as entering the word G-TOR followed by the call sign of the station you wish to contact. For example:

GTOR WB8IMY

You can monitor the G-TOR data rate by glancing at the MCP front panel. When the **STA** LED is off, the rate is 100 bit/s. A flashing **STA** indicates 200 bit/s and a steady **STA** means that you're perking along at 300 bit/s. The data rates change automatically based on the quality of the link. Links always begin at 100 bit/s. If the number of correctly received frames exceeds a preset value, the receiving station will request a speed increase to 200 or 300 bit/s. If the link deteriorates, the data rate will automatically ratchet downward. You can also set the data rate manually.

The G-TOR mode supports the KAM Plus mailbox. If you set the **ARQBBS** command *ON*, any connecting station will receive the mailbox prompt. You'll also find a number of BBSs that accept G-TOR connects. See the list in Appendix A.

Monitoring G-TOR

The KAM Plus (and all other MCPs) include a *listen* mode for monitoring AMTOR and PacTOR conversations. You simply tune in a signal, switch to the listen mode and follow the chat.

The Kantronics KAM Plus does *not* feature a G-TOR listen mode. The task of decoding a G-TOR transmission while performing other functions (such as receiving packet on the KAM's VHF port) is too much for the microprocessor.

Kantronics provides a solution with their *G-MON* software. By using *G-MON*, you can eavesdrop on G-TOR links with *any* KAM that has WEFAX capability. You can also use *G-MON* with the WEFAX function of other Kantronics TNCs such as the KPC-2 and KPC-3 to monitor G-TOR activity. *G-MON* is provided with new KAM Plus units as well as their upgraded *HostMaster II+* software. You can also purchase *G-MON* separately from Kantronics for a nominal fee. (As this book went to press, MFJ had not released details of how the G-TOR listen mode will be implemented in the 1278 MCP.)

G-MON is essentially a terminal program. By placing the KAM Plus in the *GSCAN* mode, you can monitor data frames being exchanged between two linked G-TOR stations. Your computer is doing quite a bit of processing under *G-MON*, so you must run the software on a reasonably fast machine—preferably a 286 or faster PC. Using *G-MON*, you can eavesdrop on G-TOR conversations. There is no error correction under *G-MON*, so you'll receive a number of mutilated frames. Even so, you'll be able to follow the conversations and identify the stations most of the time.

G-TOR signals sound similar to PacTOR when you hear them on the air. The difference is the G-TOR data bursts are somewhat longer—nearly two seconds in length. With a little practice you'll be able to sort out the signals with ease.

G-TOR's Future?

If enough hams and manufacturers jump aboard the G-TOR bandwagon, the future of this mode is bright. G-TOR offers a substantial improvement in HF digital communications at a price that many amateurs can afford. Will it succeed in head-to-head competition with CLOVER, PacTOR and PacTOR-2? Time will tell.

CHAPTER 9

Digital Contesting

When was the last time you enjoyed a good, clean fight? No, not the bare-knuckle variety! I mean a good-natured battle between you and your fellow digital enthusiasts on the HF bands. The goal of the conflict is simple: contact as many stations as possible during the time allotted.

Contesting is fun regardless of the mode, but it is especially exciting on the digital modes. A good contest will sharpen your skills as an operator—and prove how long you can stare at a monitor before your body *demands* sleep! Contests are also excellent tests of your station equipment. It's fascinating to review your post-contest data and discover patterns. (Did most of your contacts seem to come from a particular area of the globe? Where was your most distant contact?)

If you're gunning for new states or countries to clinch an award, a contest is one of the best times to grab them. You can send a QSL card for a contest contact just as you would for a normal conversation. And if you're lucky enough—or skilled enough—to win in a contest category, you'll receive a handsome award.

David, WBØQIR, beat his local antenna restrictions by running coax out to the antenna on his car! He bagged a total of 153 contacts during the ARRL RTTY Roundup.

Don't fall into the trap of thinking that your station isn't up to the challenge of a contest. Brute force and racks of rigs don't necessarily create winners. The real key is *skill*. It's knowing, for example, when to hunt-and-pounce, or when to sit at one frequency and call "CQ Contest." It's watching the shifting propagation and checking various bands for new activity. In so many contests, it isn't the wealthy operator who wins, it's the *smart* operator!

Most HF digital contests involve the use of RTTY, AMTOR, ASCII or packet. At the time of this writing, PacTOR, G-TOR and CLOVER were not popular contest modes, but you can expect that to change very soon.

There are ten major digital contests each year. Let's discuss each one in capsule form. For more detailed information on these contests and others, check *QST* magazine or the *Digital Journal Contester's Guide* (see the Resource Guide).

**Okay, so I only made 53 contacts during the ARRL RTTY
Roundup. I still managed to earn this attractive certificate!**

ARRL RTTY Roundup

The ARRL RTTY Roundup is one of the most popular
digital contests of the year. It takes place on the first full
weekend of January, beginning at 1800 UTC Saturday and
ending at 2400 UTC Sunday. The eligible modes include
RTTY, AMTOR, ASCII and Packet. (Packet contacts must
be *direct*; no repeating devices allowed.) All bands from 80
through 10 meters can be used except 30, 17 and 12 meters.

US stations must exchange signal reports and the states
where they are located; Canadian stations provide signal
reports and provinces. DX stations must send signal reports
and a serial number beginning with 001.

EA RTTY Contest

This contest is sponsored by the Seccion Territorial

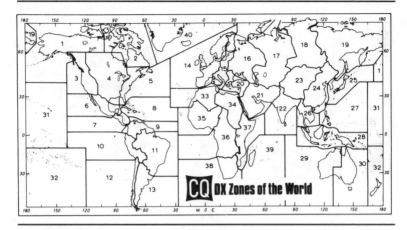

Fig 9-1—The CQ world zone map. Many contests require that you exchange your CQ zone along with other information.

Comarcal De Ure De Aranda De Duero in Spain. (Now you understand why everyone just calls it the EA RTTY Contest!) The contest gets underway on the first full weekend of February starting at 1600 UTC Saturday and ending at 1600 UTC Sunday. All bands except 30, 17 and 12 meters may be used.

Spanish stations must send signal reports, province prefix and CQ zone (see Fig 9-1). All others send signal reports and CQ zones.

ADRS World-Wide RTTY WPX Contest

The American Digital Radio Society sponsors this contest on the first full weekend of February. The contest starts at 0000 UTC Saturday and ends at 0000 UTC Sunday.

All HF digital modes are valid for contacts. Only the 80, 40, 20, 15 and 10 meter bands can be used. Competition categories include Single Operator (high power, low power, or single band) and Multi Operator (single transmitter or multiple transmitters).

Catch a Glimpse of a RTTY Contest

What's it really like in the heat of a RTTY competition? See for yourself! The following is actual text copied during the 1992 CQ/Digital Journal contest.

CQ CQ CQ CONTEST DE HB9CAL HB9CAL HB9CAL PSE K

HB9CAL HB9CAL DE W9IT W9IT W9IT W9IT K

(W9IT tries to answer, but HB9CAL responds to another station instead)

GMØILB DE HB9CAL RR TNX . . . RST 599 ZONE 14 QSL? GMØILB DE HB9CAL PSE K

(W9IT tries again and succeeds)

HB9CAL HB9CAL DE W9IT W9IT W9IT K

W9IT W9IT DE HB9CAL UR RST 599 599 ZONE 14 QSL? K

THANK YOU . . . 599-ZONE 04-ILLINOIS . . . GOOD LUCK . . . HB9CAL DE W9IT SK

(Shifting to another frequency, we find N9ITX calling CQ)

CQ CQ CQ CONTEST DE N9ITX N9ITX K

N9ITX DE W9JJX W9JJX UR 579 ZONE 04 INDIANA K

(N9ITX misses W9JJX's state and desperately asks for a repeat)

STATE STATE STATE AGAIN PSE DE N9ITX K

N9ITX DE W9JJX STATE IS INDIANA INDIANA INDIANA OK? K

W9JJX DE N9ITX . . . 599 . . . ZONE 04 IL QSL? K

ROGER ROGER. TNX AND 73 DE W9JJX SK

Stations exchange an RST signal report and a three-digit contact number beginning with 001 as the first contact. Point multipliers are based on the prefix of the call signs of the stations you contact. Examples include: N8, W8, HG1, WB2, KC2 and so on.

Certificates will be awarded to the highest-scoring stations. Plaques are also available.

BARTG RTTY Contest

BARTG stands for British Amateur Radio Teleprinter Group. Their contest begins at 0200 UTC Saturday on the third full weekend of March. It ends at 0200 UTC Monday. All bands except 30, 17 and 12 meters may be used.

Stations must exchange signal reports, the time in UTC (here's a good use for your automatic date/time function!) and a QSO number. Your first QSO is number 001. Your second is 002 and so on.

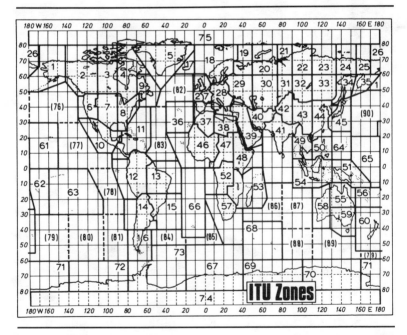

Fig 9-2—ITU zones of the world. In some competitions, your *ITU* zone is required rather than your CQ zone.

SARTG AMTOR Contest

The SARTG AMTOR Contest—sponsored by the Scandinavian Amateur Teleprinter Group—is probably the most popular AMTOR-only contest. You'll encounter it on the third full weekend of April from 0000 to 0800 UTC Saturday, 1600-2400 UTC Saturday and 0800 to 1600 UTC Sunday. (Nice of them to provide 8-hour rest breaks!) All bands are fair game except 30, 17 and 12 meters.

Stations contact each other initially using FEC (mode B), but *must* switch to ARQ (mode A) to exchange the contest information. The exchange consists of a signal report, name and QSO number starting with 001.

VOLTA RTTY DX Contest

The Como SSB/RTTY club and the Associazoione

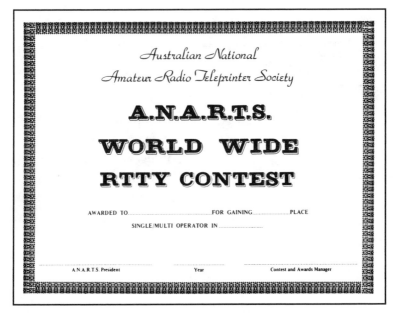

Depending on your final score, you might earn this award for participating in the ANARTS RTTY contest.

Radioamatori Italiani sponsor the VOLTA RTTY DX Contest to honor the Italian discoverer of electricity, Alessandro Volta. It takes place during the second full weekend of May from 1200 UTC Saturday to 1200 UTC Sunday. All bands except 30, 17 and 12 meters may be used.

To score, the exchanges must include a signal report, QSO number (beginning with 001) and ITU zone number (see Fig 9-2).

ANARTS RTTY Contest

The Australian National Amateur Radio Teleprinter Society (ANARTS) sponsors a late spring contest that really brings out the DX activity. The contest starts at 0000 UTC Saturday on the second full weekend of June. It ends at 0000 UTC the following Monday. All amateur bands except 30, 17 and 12 meters are eligible and all digital modes including packet may be used (packet contacts must not use repeating devices).

The official exchange is a signal report, time (in UTC) and ITU zone number.

SARTG RTTY Contest

The Scandinavian Amateur Teleprinter Group sponsors their second contest of the year—this one a RTTY contest—in late summer. The contest takes place on the third full weekend of August from 0000 to 0800 UTC Saturday, 1600 to 2400 UTC Saturday and 0800 to 1600 UTC Sunday. All bands except 30, 17 and 12 meters are eligible.

The exchange for this contest is very simple: a signal report and QSO number starting with 001.

CQ/Digital Journal Contest

Cosponsored by *CQ Magazine* and the *Digital*

Journal, the CQ/Digital Journal competition ranks with the ARRL RTTY Roundup as one of the most popular digital contests. Look for it in the last full weekend of September, beginning at 0000 UTC Saturday. The contest ends at 2400 UTC Sunday. All digital modes including packet may be used (no unattended operation or contacts through gateways or digipeaters). Every amateur band is eligible except 30, 17 and 12 meters.

Stations within the continental US and Canada exchange signal reports, state or province and CQ zone number (see Fig 9-1). All other stations send signal reports and CQ zones.

JARTS RTTY Contest

The Japanese Amateur Radio Teletype Society inaugurated the JARTS RTTY contest in 1992. The contest is held on the third weekend of October from 0000 UTC Saturday to 2400 UTC Sunday. This is a RTTY-only contest on all amateur bands except 30, 17 and 12 meters.

The contest exchange is a bit unusual: signal report and *operator age*. JARTS rules specify that an age of "zero" is acceptable from female operators. (No kidding.)

WAE RTTY Contest

The final contest of the calendar year is the German WAE RTTY competition on the second week of November. It begins at 1200 UTC Saturday and ends at 2400 UTC Sunday. All bands except 30, 17 and 12 meters may be used.

The exchange is a straightforward signal report and QSO number beginning with 001.

Digital Contest Software

You can streamline your contest operating—and

increase your scores—by using specialized contest software. Many of these programs harness the power of your computer to provide handy features such as automatic contact logging. All you have to do is make the contacts and the computer will maintain your log!

The software packages listed below are primarily for IBM PCs and compatibles. Even so, contact the manufacturers to see if they market other versions for your computer.

ARIES
PO Box 830
Dandridge, TN 37725
tel 615-397-0742
Works with the KAM, PK-232 and HK-232 MCPs

COMPRTTY II
David Rice, KC2HO
144 N Putt Corners Rd
New Paltz, NY 12561
tel 914-255-3273
Works with the KAM, PK-232, MFJ-1278 MCPs as well as the PCI-3000

SCOTCHLG
Hal Blegen, WA7EGA
2021 E Smythe Rd
Spangel, WA 99031
Works with the PK-232 MCP only

Wyvern Technology
Ray Ortgiesen, WF1B
35 Colvintown Rd
Coventry, RI 02816
tel 401-823-RTTY
Works with the KAM, PK-232 and MFJ-1278 MCPs

An HF Digital Glossary

Terms in italics appear elsewhere in this Glossary.

ACK: An abbreviation for "acknowledgment." AMTOR stations exchange ACKs to verify that data has been received without errors.

AFSK: An abbreviation for "audio-frequency-shift keying." A method of digital transmission that is accomplished by varying the frequency of an audio tone applied to the microphone or auxiliary audio input of a transmitter.

AMTOR: An acronym for Amateur Teleprinting Over Radio. A popular method of digital communication on the HF bands.

ANSWERBACK: (AMTOR only) The programmable message that is sent when a receiving station receives a *WRU* (Who Are You?) command.

APLink: A bulletin board system (BBS) program created by Vic Poor, W5SMM. Messages and files may be accessed by either HF AMTOR or VHF packet-radio stations.

ARQ: Automatic repeat request. This is the error detection mode of AMTOR, PacTOR and CLOVER. ARQ signals are easily recognized by their chirp-chirp sound. An ARQ link can be established only between two stations.

ASCII: An acronym for American Standard Code for Information Interchange (usually pronounced *as-key*). A standard method of encoding data so it can be understood by many different computers.

autobaud: A routine used by some *MCPs* to automatically adapt to the serial data rate of a computer or *terminal*.

Baudot: A term commonly used among Amateur Radio RTTY operators to specify a 5-bit teletype code.

bit: The shortest data pulse used to make a RTTY character. The *Baudot* code uses 5 data bits. *ASCII* code uses 8 bits (7 data plus one parity bit).

bit/s: An abbreviation for "bits per second," a measurement of the rate at which data is transferred from one device to another.

capture: To save incoming data to a disk file for later use.

CD: Control delay (AMTOR/PacTOR). A time delay inserted by the *slave IRS* between the end of its reception of the *ISS* data "chirp" and the transmission of its *Control Signal*.

CLOVER: A modulation and data protocol created by Ray Petit, W7GHM. CLOVER uses PSK and ASK modulation on a pulsed tone sequence. CLOVER modulation levels are adaptive and data may be sent at rates 10 to 100 times that of AMTOR or HF packet radio. The CLOVER signal bandwidth (500 Hz at −50 dB) requires half the spectrum of AMTOR and a quarter that of HF packet radio.

Control Signal: The single character sent by the *IRS* to acknowledge (*ACK*) or not-acknowledge (*NAK*) the data sent by the *ISS*. The ISS repeats characters when a NAK (or no response) is received from the IRS.

data rate: The rate at which data is sent from one station to another. 45 baud is the standard RTTY data rate (speed = 60 WPM). 50 baud (66 WPM), 57 baud (75 WPM), and 75 baud (100 WPM) may also be used. 110 baud is the common data rate for HF ASCII RTTY.

data terminal: A device that allows a human operator to communicate with a *TU* or *MCP*.

digital signal processing: Using software rather than hardware to encode or decode digital signals for various modes.

download: The act of requesting and receiving specific data from another station.

DSP: An abbreviation for digital signal processing.

dumb terminal: A basic *data terminal* that provides only input and output functions. It cannot store or process data.

EIA-232-E: A data voltage and load protocol used by most computer devices for data pulses. An EIA-232-E *MARK* pulse has a negative voltage between –3 and –25 volts. A *SPACE* pulse is positive between +3 and +25 volts. Commonly referred to as *RS-232-C*.

End: The control command sent by an AMTOR station to end an *ARQ* link.

FEC: Forward error correction. A digital mode that may be used to send a message to more than one receiving station. Each character is sent twice to provide error correction. FEC is also called "Collective Broadcast" mode in commercial usage.

FIGS: A RTTY/AMTOR control character that signals the printer to shift to the FIGureS case.

firmware: Software stored in an integrated circuit memory chip.

floppy disk: Removable magnetic disks used to store digital data.

Forced Over: A command that can be initiated by the *IRS* to force a change in the channel direction (*IRS* to *ISS* and vice versa). The command used to cause a forced over varies with the controller or *MCP*.

FSK: Frequency-shift keying. Modulating a transmitter by using the data signal to shift the carrier frequency.

G-TOR: An acronym for Golay-coded Teleprinting Over Radio. A method of digital communication developed by Kantronics and introduced in 1994.

hard disk: Nonremovable magnetic disks used to store large amounts of data.

ISS: Information-sending station. The station that is sending information on the *ARQ* link. The ISS may be either the *master* or *slave* station.

IRS: Information-receiving station. The station that is receiving information on the *ARQ* link. The IRS may be either the *master* or *slave* station.

Listen: The mode of an MCP that allows it to monitor ongoing *ARQ* (and *FEC* and *SELCAL*) transmissions. Listen mode does not include error correction. Listen mode is generally not included in commercial *SITOR* controllers.

LTRS: A RTTY/AMTOR control character that signals a shift to the letters case.

MARK: The ON pulse state of a data signal. Also the "1" digital logic state.

Master: The station that establishes the *ARQ* link. The master station designation remains fixed for the duration of the ARQ QSO, regardless of which station is sending information. The master station sets the timing for both stations in an ARQ link.

MCP: An abbreviation for Multimode Communications Processor. A digital device designed to provide packet, CW, RTTY, fax, PacTOR and AMTOR communications as well as other modes. Also known as a multimode data controller.

Modem: A *MO*dulator-*DEM*odulator device that translates digital data pulses into audio tone frequencies or vice versa.

NAK: Not-acknowledge. The *IRS* response that tells the *ISS* station, "The last three characters were not received correctly. Please repeat last three characters."

NTS: National Traffic System. An ARRL-sponsored system for relaying messages throughout the nation and the world. NTS is supported by packet networks as well as CW, phone, RTTY and AMTOR.

Over: The control command that switches the roles of the two *ARQ* stations—*IRS* becomes *ISS* and ISS becomes IRS.

PacTOR: A modification of AMTOR and packet radio developed by DL6MAA and DF4KV. PacTOR uses the ASCII character code and adaptive data rate control to provide two to four times faster data throughput than AMTOR or HF packet radio.

PBBS: An abbreviation for Packet Bulletin Board System. A repository for packet mail, bulletins and other information within a local packet network.

port: A circuit that allows a one device (such as a computer) to communicate with another device (such as an *MCP*).

PTT: An abbreviation for Push To Talk. On a transceiver microphone, the button that's used to key the transmitter.

RAM: An acronym for Random Access Memory. A data storage device that can be written to and read from. Commonly used to refer to memory chips within a computer or other microprocessor-controlled device.

RS-232-C: The former standard for interfacing computers and/or *terminals* to other devices such as *TUs* and *MCPs*. It was replaced by *EIA-232-E*, although many still use the term RS-232 when referring to a "standard" interface.

RTTY: An acronym for Radioteletype (usually pronounced *ritty*). One of the oldest methods of digital communications. RTTY is still popular on the HF bands.

SELCAL: Selective call. The special letter (or number) sequence sent at the beginning of an AMTOR or CLOVER call in *ARQ* mode. An ARQ link will be established only when the transmitted SELCAL letters match those programmed at the desired station. Amateurs make up SELCAL codes as contractions of their amateur call signs; commercial ARQ stations are assigned numerical codes.

serial port: A circuit that permits one device to communicate with another by sending information bit-by-bit. Computers and *data terminals* often communicate with *TUs* and *MCPs* through their serial ports.

shift: The frequency difference between the *MARK* and *SPACE* pulses. The standard RTTY/AMTOR shift is 170 Hz.

SITOR: Simplex Teleprinting Over Radio. A commercial name for *ARQ* ship-to-shore communications.

Slave: The *ARQ* station that is called in an ARQ link. The slave designation remains fixed for the duration of the ARQ QSO. The slave always synchronizes its timing to that of the *Master* station.

SPACE: The OFF pulse state of a data signal. Also known as the "0" digital logic state.

split-frequency: Using a different frequency for transmitting and receiving.

Standby: The resting state of an AMTOR, PacTOR or CLOVER controller. When the programmed *SELCAL* or call sign is received, the controller automatically switches to *ARQ* mode and establishes the link. When called in *FEC* mode, the controller automatically switches to FEC mode and prints the message.

start bit: The first bit sent in an asynchronous data transmission. The START bit is always a SPACE with a time duration equal to one data bit. For example, Baudot RTTY uses one start bit.

stop bit: The last data bit sent in an asynchronous data transmission. The stop bit is always a MARK pulse. With Baudot coding, the stop bit may be 1.41, 1.5, or 2 times the length of a data bit. In HF ASCII, the stop bit is two times the length of a data bit. At ASCII data rates greater than 110 baud, the stop bit is generally the same length as the data bit.

store and forward: The act of receiving data (messages or bulletins) and then storing them temporarily until they can be passed along to the next station.

switching delays: The delays associated with changing a transceiver or transmitter/receiver system from transmit to receive and back again.

TD: Transmit delay. A programmable time delay that blocks data transmission until the transmitter has reached full power.

terminal: A device that allows a human operator to communicate with an *MCP* or *TU*. Also known as a *data terminal*.

terminal software: Software that allows a personal computer to imitate (emulate) the functions of a *data terminal*.

terminal unit: A modem-type device dedicated to RTTY operating. It transforms digital data into *AFSK* tones or *FSK* pulses for transmission. A terminal unit also converts received audio to digital data. Also known as a *TU*.

throughput: A measure of the effectiveness of a data system. The throughput rate is the number of data elements per unit time (characters, bytes, or bits) that can be passed from one station to another without error. The throughput of AMTOR under ideal conditions is 6.67 characters per second (cps).

TTL: A type of digital interface based on transistor-transistor logic. For example, some personal computers offer a TTL interface rather than an EIA-232-E interface.

TU: See *terminal unit*.

upload: To send a data file or message to another Amateur Radio station.

WRU: Who Are You? A signaling system that lets one AMTOR controller automatically obtain identification from the other station. When enabled, reception of the FIGS-D ($) AMTOR code reverses the channel direction (over), sends text stored in the *ANSWERBACK* message, and restores channel direction (second over). WRU is often used by *APLink*.

Resource Guide

Books

The ARRL Operating Manual. American Radio Relay League, 225 Main St, Newington, CT 06111, tel 203-666-1541.

Digital Contester's Guide, Digital Journal, PO Box 2550, Goldenrod, FL 32733-2550. $13

G-TOR: The New Mode, Kantronics Corp, 1202 E 23rd St, Lawrence, KS 66046-5006, tel 913-842-7745.

Newsletters

The Digital Journal, PO Box 2550, Goldenrod, FL 32733-2550. 15 issues/year. $20 US, Canada and Mexico; $35 elsewhere.

Equipment Manufacturers

Advanced Electronic Applications (AEA), PO Box C2160, Lynnwood, WA 98036-0918, tel 206-774-5554. (MCPs and TNCs)

HAL Communications Corp, PO Box 365, Urbana, IL 61801, tel 217-367-7373. (RTTY terminal units and CLOVER equipment)

Kantronics, 1202 E 23rd St, Lawrence, KS 66046, tel 913-842-7745. (MCPs and TNCs)

MFJ Enterprises, Box 494, Mississippi State, MS 39762, tel 800-647-1800. (MCPs and TNCs)

PacComm, 4413 N Hesperides St, Tampa, FL 33614-7618, tel 813-874-2980. (PacTOR equipment and TNCs)

Digital Software Sources

Please note that the products and addresses shown below are subject to change. Unless otherwise noted, send a self-addressed envelope with 2 units of First-Class postage when requesting information.

Apple (see also Macintosh)

Cotec, 13462 Hammons Ave, Saratoga, CA 95070.

Ham-Soft, PO Box 443, Galena Park, TX 77547-0443. Send $1 for catalog.

W1EO, 39 Longridge Rd, Carlisle, MA 01741.

Atari

ElectroSoft, 3413 N Duffield Ave, Loveland, CO 80538.

Langner, John, 115 Stedman St, #H, Chelmsford, MA 01824-1823, tel 508-256-6907.

Color Computer (Tandy)

Dynamic Electronics, PO Box 896, Hartselle, AL 35640, tel 205-773-2758.

Commodore

AMSOFT, PO Box 666, New Cumberland, PA 17070-0666, tel 717-938-8249. Catalog $1.

Colorburst, PO Box 3091, Nashua, NH 03061, tel 603-891-1588.

G & G Electronics, 8524 Dakota Dr, Gaithersburg, MD 20877, tel 301-258-7373.

Ham-Soft, PO Box 443, Galena Park, TX 77547-0443. Send $1 for catalog.

WB1FOL, 77 Wentworth St, Malden, MA 02148.

IBM PCs and compatibles

AMSOFT, PO Box 666, New Cumberland, PA 17070-0666, tel 717-938-8249. Catalog $1.

American Digital Radio Society, PO Box 2550, Goldenrod, FL 32733-2550. (*Express 2.0* software for CLOVER)

American Software, PO Box 509, Suite M16, Roseville, MI 48066-0509.

Colorburst, PO Box 3091, Nashua, NH 03061, tel 603-891-1588.

Comtech Research, 5220 Milton Rd, Custar, OH 43511.

Dynamic Electronics, PO Box 896, Hartselle, AL 35640, tel 205-773-2758.

Ham-Soft, PO Box 443, Galena Park, TX 77547-0443. Send $1 for catalog.

InterFlex Systems Design Corp, PO Box 6418, Laguna Niguel, CA 92607-6418.

Kasser, Joe, G3ZCZ, PO Box 3419, Silver Spring, MD 20918.

K-Quest, PO Box 92877, Southlake, TX 76092.

Renaissance Software & Development, Killen Plaza, Box 640, Killen, AL 35645, tel 205-757-5928.

Rice, David, 144 N Putt Corners Rd, New Paltz, NY 12561.

Schnedler Systems, 25 Eastwood Rd, PO Box 5964, Asheville, NC 28813, tel 704-274-4646.

Wyvern Technology, 35 Colvintown Rd, Coventry, RI 02816, tel 401-823-RTTY. (RTTY contest software)

Macintosh

Ham-Soft, PO Box 443, Galena Park, TX 77547-0443. (Send $1 for catalog.)

Krueger, Kevin, 1780 Ruth St, Maplewood, MN 55109, tel 612-770-0370. (contest software)

ZCo Corporation, PO Box 3720, Nashua, NH 03061, tel 603-888-7200.

Zihua Software, PO Box 51601, Pacific Grove, CA 93950, tel 408-372-0155.

HF Digital Bulletin Boards and Mail-boxes Worldwide

T his information was complied by Craig McCartney, WA8DRZ, and is accurate as of March 1, 1995. Please note that operating schedules and frequencies change without notice.

The three-letter code *following* the first line of each station listing indicates the software command set:

APL - AmTOR/Packet Link (W5SMM)
KCQ - W8KCQ mailbox software
PAM - Personal AmTOR Mailbox (W5SMM)
PLX - G3PLX AmTOR mailbox
RLI - WØRLI Packet/CLOVER mailbox
Win - WinLink - APLInk for Windows (W5SMM)
Oth - Other

The letter(s) that *precedes* each frequency line designates the digital mode(s) used on the indicated channels:

A - AMTOR, CCIR-476 (100 baud, 170 Hz shift)
C - CLOVER (500 Hz occupied bandwidth)

P - PacTOR (100/200 baud, 200 Hz shift)
R - RTTY
X - HF Packet, AX.25 (300 baud, 200 Hz shift)

Some BBS and mailbox systems also accept G-TOR connects.

United States—West

These digital stations located west of the Mississippi River in the continental United States operate 24 hours a day (unless noted) on the mark carrier frequencies (LSB for CLOVER) listed.

All frequencies shown in kHz

AA5BJ Dusty in Ruidoso (.NM.USA.NA)
A 7075 10132 10134 14065.

AA7HS Steve in Yakima (#APL.WA.USA.NA) APL
A 28128 21074 21077 14069 14070.5 14071.5 14073 14077 Days
A 7069 7070 7071 7073 7075.5 3605.37 3627 Nights

K5VMX Bob in Spring (Houston) (.#SETX.TX.USA) Win
A 7068 7069 7070 7071 10129 14071.5 18105 21074 25915 28125
C 7065 7067 7068 10135 10136 14065
C 14066 14067 14068 18105 21066 24911 28128

K7BUC Del in Phoenix (.AZ.USA.NA) APL
A 7071 10140 14071.5 14073.5 14074 21073.5 (Day)
A 3627 7071 10140 14071.5 14073.5 14074 (Night)

K7SLI Jim in Marysville (.#NWWA.WA.USA.NA) APL
A 3625 3627 3629 7069 7071 7073 10127 10128 10129
A 14069 14071 14073 21074 21076 21078

KAØJRQ Larry in Glenwood (Omaha) (.IA.USA.NA) Win
A 3623 3624 3622 7071 7075.5 7073 10125 10127 10128
A 14073 14077 18105 21075 24915
C 3630 7065 7067 10134 10135 14065 14067 18105 21075 24911

KB6BT Walter in Saratoga (San Francisco)
(@N6LDL.#NOCAL.CA.USA.NA) Oth
P 10138 14079 21079

KC7J Ron in Tacoma (.WA.USA.NA) APL
P 18107

KD7UM Dave in Salt Lake City (.#SLC.UT.USA.NA) APL
A 3621 3623 3627 7073 7075 7077 10127 10129
A 14069 14073 14077 21071 21075 28127

KE5HE Jim in Hearne (.#STX.TX.USA.NA) Oth
P 10138 14078

KS5V Ed in Canyon Lake (San Antonio/Austin) (.#STX.TX.USA.NA) APL
A 7071 (Day), 3620 (Night)

NØIA/7 Bud in Las Vegas (.#SONEV.NV.USA.NA) Win
AP 7069 7073 7075 10131 10133 14071
AP 3625 3627 3629 (0200-1300z)
AP 14075 18105 21073 24913 28127 (1300-0200z)
C 7067 7069 10134 10135 14067
C 3630 7066 7068 (0200-1300z)
C 14069 18105 21067 21069 (1300-0200z)

N5DST Scott in Houston (.#SETX.TX.USA.NA) Win
A 3622 3623 3624 7068 7069 7071 10125 10126 10127 10128 10140.5
A 14069 14070.5 14071.5 14072.5 14073.5 18102.5 21072.5 21074 21076

N5TC Tom in College Station (.#STEX.TEX.USA.NA) Win
A 3622 7069 7071 7073 10126 14068.5
C 3628 7066 7067 10135 10136 14078 18106

N6EQZ/7 NEQZ Ted in Renton (Seattle) (#APL.WA.USA.NA) Win
AP 3625 3627 7069 7071 7072 7074 7077 10128 10130 14069
AP 14072 14073 14077 18099 21073 21075 28073 28125

N6IYA John in Felton (.#NOCAL.CA.USA.NA) RLI
C 7064 7065 7066 7067 7068 7069
C 14064 14065 14066 14067 14068 14069 (Days)

N7CR Rory in Spokane (.#SPOKN.WA.USA.NA) APL/RLI
A 3622 3627 3629 7069 7071 7073 10126 10128
A 14069 14072 18102 21075 24915
C 3624 3630 3634 7064 7066 7068 10135 10136
C 14066 14067 18105 21066 24911

NA7P Greg in Edmonds (Seattle) (.WA.USA.NA) APL
A 14069

NZ2T/5 Bob in Southlake (Dallas/Ft Worth) (.#DFW.TX.USA.NA) Win
A 7069 7071 7073 7075 10123 10125 10127 10135 14069 14071 14073
A 18101 18107 21073 21077 24915

WØLVJ/7 Mike in Spanaway/Graham (.WA.USA.NA) APL
A 3605.37 (Primary), 7069 (Secondary)

WØRLI/7 Hank in West Linn (.OR.USA.NA) RLI
C 7065 7067 7068 (Night), 14065 14067 21065 21067 21068 (Day)

W2USA/7 Ft. Lewis ARA, Fort Lewis (.WA.USA.NA) APL
A 28147.9

W5VBO/7 Brian in Peoria (Phoenix) (.AZ.USA.NA) APL
A 3622 3625 7069 7071 7073 10125 10126 10127 10128
A 14070.5 14071.5 14072.5 18102 18105.5 28125

W5XO Dennis in Gause (.#CENTX.TX.USA.NA) RLI
C 3625 3630 7066 7067 7068 7069 10135 10136 14066 14067 14068 14069
C 18084 21066 21067 21069 24924 28084

W7DCR Gary in La Pine (.OR.USA.NA) APL
A 3622 7069 7075.5 10126 10127 10128 14069 14070.5
A 14072.5 18105.5 21072.5 21076 21079 24915 24925

WA8DRZ/6 Craig in Redwood City (San Francisco)
(.#NOCAL.CA.USA.NA) APL
AP 10128 10129
AP 14068.5 14069.5 14070.5 14071.5 14072.5 14073.5 14074.5 14075.5

WB5UJO Hoppy in Marlin, Texas (.TX.USA.NA) Win
A 7075

WI7D Jeff in Las Vegas (.#SONEV.NV.USA.NA) Win
AP 3621 3623 3627 7069 7075 7077 10127 10129 10139.5
AP 14069 14072 14073 14077 18099 21073 21075 24925 28073 28125

United States—East

These mailbox stations located east of the Mississippi River in the continental United States operate 24 hours a day (unless noted) on the mark carrier frequencies (LSB for CLOVER) listed.

All frequencies shown in kHz

AA5AU Don in New Orleans (.LA.USA.NA) APL
A 14066

K1HB Fred in Boston (.MA.USA.NA) Oth
P 7042 10147 14079 14085 21079 28079

K1UOL Bob in Bethel (.CT.USA.NA) APL
A 14071.5

K2PPH Glenn in Buffalo (#WNY.NY.USA.NA) APL
A 14069 14072 14074 14078 21074 28074

K4CJX Steve in Nashville (.#MIDTN.TN.USA.NA) Win
A 3622 7070.5 7072.5 10126 10128 14070 14072 21074
C 3630 7066 7067 7068 10135 10136 14066 14067 14068 21066

K4YZU Bill in Magnolia (#SKY.KY.USA.NA) APL
A 7069 7070 7070.5 7071 7072.5

KC9PX Joe in Janesville (WI.USA.NA) APL
A 3620 3622 3627 7068 7069.9 7070.5 7072.5 7075.5 1817 1819
A 14069 14070.5 14072.5 14073.5 14075 21072.5 21076 21079 28075
28128

KD4OM Jim in Hickory (.#HKY.NC.USA.NA) APL
A 7070.5

KK4CQ Harvey in Pensacola (.#PNSFL.FL.USA.NA) APL/RLI
A 3622 7070 7070.5 7071 7076 10126 10128 21074 21076
A 14070 14071.5 14072.5 28070 28128
C 3630 7066 7068 10135 10136 14066 14067 14068 28128

N2HOS Jim in New York (.NY.USA.NA)
C 3630 7066 14066 18106 21066
N2JAW Ron in Trenton (.NY.USA.NA) APL
A 3622 7071 7072.5 7075.5 10128 10140.5 14068 14071.5 14073.5 21072.5

N3EXW Louis in Rockville (.MD.USA.NA) APL
A 14068

N8PGR Hans in Cleveland (.#NEOH.OH.USA.NA) Win
AP 3622 3623 7068 7072 10127.50 10138.00 18101.50 14068 14073
AP 14075 14076 14078 14080 21073 21075 21080 28075 28080

W1FYR Alan in Gilsum (.NH.USA.NA) APL NTS ONLY
A 3620 3622 7068 7071 7072.5 10126 10128 10130 14068 14070
A 14071.5 14072.5 14073.5 18102.5 18105.5 21072.5 21074 21079

W2NRE Warren in Scarsdale (.NY.USA.NA) Win
A 3620 3622 7070 7072 10126 10128 14066 14068 14070 14076
A 18105 24915 28074
C 3630 7066 7068 10135 10136 14066 14068 18106 21066

W2TKU/4 Al in Sarasota (.#SRQFL.FL.USA.NA) Win
A 7070 7076 14072 14076 14078 21074 21080
C 7066 7068 10136 14066 14067 14068 21064 21066

W4KAU Dick in Cohutta (.#APL.GA.USA.NA) APL
A 7070.5 7072 7075.5 7076 10126 10128
A 14069 14070.5 17072.5 14076 21072.5 21074

W4NPX Bob in Charlottesville (.#CVA.VA.USA.NA) Win
A 3620 3627.87 7063.87 7065.87 7068 7070 7072
A 10126 10128 10132.87 10133.87
A 14063.87 14065.87 14070 21063.87 21074 28128
C 3630 7066 7068 10135 10136 14066 14068 21066 28130.13

W5KSI Angelo in New Orleans (.#NOLA.LA.USA.NA) APL
A 3620 3622 7069 7071 7075.5 14068 14070 14073.5 14074 14079
A 21074 21075 21079 28074 28075

W8KCQ Bill in Worthington (.OH.USA.NA) KCQ
AP 3645 7071 7073.5 10128 14079 14080 18107.5 21079 28079

W9MR Ken in Keensburg (.#SEIL.IL.USA.NA) Win
A 3620 3622 3624 7070 7072 7074 7076 10128 10140
A 14068 14070 18104 21072 24925

W9UWE Julius in Chicago (.IL.USA.NA) Oth
P 14079 14085 21079 21081 28075

WA1URA/9 Frank in Grabill (Fort Wayne) (.IN.USA.NA) Win
A 3620 3622 7071 7075.5 10128 10139.5
A 14069 14070.5 14071.5 14073.5 14075 21074 21076 21079
C 3624 3625 3630 7066 7067 7068 10135 10136
C 14066 14067 14068 21066 21068
P 3622 7072 7077 10122 10127 1072
P 14077 18107 21072 21077 24907

WA2MFY Peter in Gladstone (.NJ.USA.NA) KCQ
AP 3622.5 3642 3645 7071 7073.5 7075.5 7076.5 7077 7081.5 10128
10129.5
AP 14068 14068.5 14069 14069.5 14070.2 14070.5 14073.5 14074 14079
14080
AP 18107.5 21070.5 21073.5 24915 28074 21075 21076 21079 28071
C 3610 7065 7069 10135 10136 10141.5 14065 14066 14067 14072 14078
C 18100 21065 21070 24925 28084

WA7SJN/9 Bill in Indiana (.IN.USA.NA) RLI
C 7064

WA9FCH/4 John in Reston (.VA.USA.NA) APL
A 7070.5 7071 7072.5 7075.5 10128 10139.5 10140.5 10140
A 14068 14070.5 14071.5 14072.5

WA9WCN Bob in Lapel (Indianapolis) (.IN.USA.NA) Win
C 7065, 7066 7067 7068 10135 10136 14066 14067 14068 21066
C 3625 3630 7065 7066 7067 7068 (Nite Only)
P 7070 7072 10126 10128 18102 14074
P 3624, 7070, 7072 (Nite Only)
(Nite: 2300-1200z)

WB8APD Dave in Willoughby (Cleveland) (.OH.USA.NA) APL
A 14071.5

WD8NIK Frank in Warren (Detroit) (.#SEMI.MI.USA.NA) Win
A 7068, 7070, 7071, 7072.5 or 7076

WX4J Earl in Switzerland (.#SWITZ.FL.USA.NA) APL
A 3618 3620 3624 7069 7071.5 7073.5 7075.5
A 14071.5 14072.5 14073.5 21072.5 21074.5

North/South America

These digital stations in North and South America
(outside of the continental US) operate 24 hours a day
(unless noted) on the mark carrier frequencies listed.

All frequencies shown in kHz

AH6IH Bill in Honolulu, Hawaii (#APL.HI.USA.OC) APL
A 14068

AL7LS Bruce in Delta Junction, Alaska (.AK.USA.NA) APL
A 14072.5

HC5K Ted in Cuenca, Ecuador (.ECU.SA) Oth
AP 21073 21074 21075

KB8JLV Stan in Adak, Alaska (.#ADAK.AK.USA.NA) APL
A 14070.5 (1700-0600z)

KP4GE Ramon in Caguas, Puerto Rico (.PR.USA.CAR.NA) Win
A 14068 18105 21072
C 14065 14066 18102 21065 21066

LU3EX in Argentina (.ARG.SA)
P 14072 21072

TG9SO Roberto in Guatemala City, Guatemala (GTM.NA) APL
A 21074 (Day). 7068 (Night)

TIØRC Radio Club of Costa Rica in San Jose (.#SJO.CRI.NA) APL
A 14068

VE2FK Claude in Montreal, Quebec, Canada (.CAN.NA) KCQ
AP 7071 7072 7073.5 7076 7077 14066 14068.5 14074 14079 14080

VE2IMQ Claude VE2DLC, in Rimouski, Quebec
A 7073.5 7077 14064.88 14065.88 14066.88 14.067.88–
A 18069.88 18107.5 21070.5 21073.5

VE3AWC Dave in Richmond Hill, Ontario, Canada (.ON.CAN.NA) KCQ
AP 7071 7073.5 7077 14078 14079 14080

VE3EG Roy in Aurora, Ontario, Canada (.ON.CAN.NA) KCQ
AP 7071 7073.5 7076.5 7077 (0700-0900 & 1000-2300 EDT)
AP 14080 (0900-1000 EDT)

VE3PAO Peter in Coldwater (Orillia), Ontario, Canada
(#CON.ON.CAN.NA) APL
A 14068.5

VE7CIZ George in British Columbia, Canada (.#VANC.BC.CAN.NA) Oth
AP 14071
AP 10119 (2300-0400z)

VO1BBS Hugh in Seal Cove, Newfoundland (.NF.CAN.NA) Win
A 14068.5

VP8BFH Bob in Port Stanley, Falkland Islands (.STLY.FALK.SA) APL
A 14066 (1030-2330z)

W6HTH William in Honolulu, Hawaii (.HI.USA.OC) APL
A 14070.2

WP2B/XE2 Reg in Punta Banda, Mexico (.BCN.MEX.NA) APL
A 10127 10128 10129 14068.5 10469.5 14070.5 14071.5 2170 21074 21076

ZF1GC Frank in Bodden Town, Grand Cayman Island
(#GC.CYM.CAR.NA) Win
A 14070.5 14071.5 14072.5 14073.5 14074.5 14075.5 14076 21080
(1100-0300z Weekdays, 1100-2200 Fri, 0000-0300z Sat)

Europe

These digital stations in Europe operate 24 hours a day
(unless noted) on the mark carrier (LSB for CLOVER)
frequencies listed.

All frequencies shown in kHz
5B4AEJ in Cyprus (.CYP.AS) Oth
P 14068

9AØAPL Croatian Amateur Radio Assoc. in Zagreb, Croatia (.HRV.EU)
APL
A 14072

CT1BT Teles in Evora, Portugal (.CTEV.PRT.EU) APL
A 7037 7039 14075.5 14078 21076.5 28077.5

DJØOW in Germany (.DEU.EU) Oth
AP 14079

DKØBLN in Germany (.DEU.EU) Oth
AP 3581 7040 14078 14081 21081 28075

DJØMCS in Germany (.DEU.EU) Oth
AP 14068

DJ2HZ in Germany (.DEU.EU) Oth
AP 3584.9 7040

DKØMHZ in Germany (.DEU.EU) Oth
AP 3587 7040 14073 21073 28073

DKØMTV Guenter (DJ8CY) in Mainz, Germany (.DEU.EU) PLX
A 3581 7038 14075 14078 14081 21081 28075

DLØBN in Berlin, Germany (.DEU.EU) Oth
AP 3581 14079 21081 28075

DL1WX in Germany (.DEU.EU) Oth
AP 7034

DL2FAK in Germany (.DEU.EU) Oth
AP 14079

DL6FZ in Germany (.DEU.EU) Oth
AP 3582 3586 7036 7038 7041 14078 14080 21082 21084 28082

DL7AMW in Germany (.DEU.EU) Oth
AP 14079 14080 21081 28075

EA8CAP in Canary Islands (.ESP.EU) Oth
AP 3581 7038 10141 14072 14073 14071.4 14082 14083
AP 18107 21082 21083 24928

GB7EMX Kit in Aberdeen, Scotland (.#75.GBR.EU) APL
A 3587.5 3588 3588.5 3589 7038 7039 7040 10145 10146
A 14075 14076 14077 14078 21080 21081 28075 28076

GB7SCA John in Plymouth, England (.#44.GBR.EU) PLX
AP 3587.5 3588.8 3589 7038 7040 7041 10145 10146
AP 14071 14075 14076 14077 14078 14098 21071 21080 28075

GB7SIG Blandford in Dorset, England (.#45.GBR.EU) APL
A 3587.5 3588.5 3589 7038 7039 7040 10145 10146
A 14076 14077 14078 18105.5 21080 21081 28075

HB9AK Paul in Meilen (Zurich), Switzerland (.CHE.EU) PLX
P 7041 14071 14098 21071
A 3581 3583 3588 3589 7038 7040 10141 10146
A 14071.5 14072 14075 14078 21080 21085 28075 28080
C 14098

HB9BJJ in Switzerland (.CHE.EU) Oth
AP 7042 10141 10143 10147 14076 14085

HB9CJC in Switzerland (.CHE.EU) Oth
AP 7041

I5FLN Luciano in Florence, Italy (.ITA.EU) APL
A 14069 (2100-0500z), 21070 (0800-1700z)

IKØNNT Sergio in Rome, Italy (.ITA.EU) APL
A 14078

LAØFA in Norway (.NOR.EU) Oth
AP 7034

LA5JEA Platform 16/11-S in the North Sea (.#NORTHSEA.NOR.EU) APL
A 3581.5 3587.5 7038 7039 14068 14071 14075 21072.5 21075 21077

LZ2BE Bob in Razgrad, Bulgaria (.BGR.EU) APL
A 3582 7036 7038 10146 14074 14078 21074

OE4XBU Rudi in Eisenstadt, Austria (.AUT.EU) Win
AP 14067.5 14073 14075 14078 21067.5 21073 21075.5

OH2BAW Staffan in Esbo (Helsinki), Finland (.FIN.EU) APL
A 3581.5 3587 7038 10146 14071 14076 21077.5 28077.5

ON6RO Rene in Louveigne, Belgium (.BEL.EU) Win
AP 14068.5 14070.5 14073 14074 14075 21073 21075.5 21.077

PAØQRS Piet in Krimpen (Rotterdam), Netherlands (.#NH2.NLD.EU) APL
A 7034 7037 14067 14070 14072 21082 28082

PAØRVR Richard in Papendrecht, Netherlands (.#ZH2.NLD.EU) Win
A 14070 14075 14080 18105 (1200 - 2200 UTC)
P 14070 14075 14080 18105 (2200 - 1200 UTC)

SL5BO Claes in Enkoping (Stockholm), Sweden (.SWE.EU) APL
A 14077 (or 14078)

SM4CMG Bo in Sweden (.SWE.EU) APL
A 21077

SM6FMB Sven near Gotenburg, Sweden (.SWE.EU) APL
A 7037 7038 7039 10109 10128 10145 10146 14069 14070 14075 14076 14078
A 18102.5 18105.5 21072 21074 21075 21076 28074

U5WF Vladimir in Lvov, Ukraine (.LVV.UKR.EU) APL
A 14075 (except contests)

UA4LCQ Yuri in Ulyanovsk, Russia (.#ULY.RUS.EU) APL
A 14075 21075

Africa/Middle East

These digital stations in Africa and the Middle East operate 24 hours a day (unless noted) on the mark carrier (LSB for CLOVER) frequencies listed.

All frequencies shown in kHz

4X6SL Kuti in Petach-Tikva (Tel-Aviv), Israel (.ISR.AS) APL
A 14071 (1800-0600z), 21071 (0600-1800z)

5NØFDR in Nigeria (.NGA.AF) Oth
P 14078

9K2DZ Abdul in Kuwait City (.KWT.AS) APL
A 7071 10128 14066 14070 14074 14076.5 14079
A 21076 21076.5 21079 18105.5 24925

9K2EC Mohsin in Kuwait (.KWT.AS) Win
A (KKEC) 14066 14071 14072 14079 18105.5 21071 21081 28079
C 14066 14082.12 21066 21082.12
P 14080 21080

9X5LJ Jacques in Kigali, Rwanda (.#KGL.RWA.AF) APL
A 14073 (1700-0500 NA), 21073 (0500-1700 EU)

SU1ER Ezzat in Heliopolis, Cairo, Egypt (.CAI.EGY.AF) Win/PCC
A 14068 or 14070
C 14070.12 or 14072.12
(Daily 1500-2000z, Fri/Sat 0600-0900z)

TU2BB Felix in Abidjan, Ivory Coast (.CIV.AF) APL
A 14076 (Night), 21076 (Day)
(weekends closed)

TY1PS Peter in Cotonou, Benin (.BEN.AF) Win
A 14072 14078 21072 21078 28072 28078
C 14064 14066 21066
(0630-1400z Beam 120, 1400-1900z Beam 010, 1900-0630z Beam 310)

V51NH Nico in Windhoek, Namibia (.NAM.AF) APL
A 14070

ZS5S Joe and Mary in Howick, South Africa (.NTL.ZAF.AF) APL/RLI
A 7037 14069 14073 21069 21073
C 7039.1 14066 21066
P 7036 7037 14069 14073 21069 21073
X 7043 10143 14109

ZS6KM Mario in Pretoria, South Africa (.TVL.ZAF.AF) APL
A 14075 (0430-0700z) NA
A 21075.5 (0700-1800z), 14075 (1800-2000z) EU

Asia and Oceania

These digital stations in Asia and Oceania operate 24 hours a day (unless noted) on the mark carrier (LSB for CLOVER) frequencies listed.

All frequencies shown in kHz
9M2CR Colin in Port Dixon, Maylaysia (.MYS.AS) PLX
P 14072 14074 14076 14078

BV5AF Bolon in Taiwan (.TWN.CHN.AS) APL/RLI
A 14069 14072 14075 14077 14079 21070 21072 21076
C 10135 14084 21084

BV5AG Katy in Taiwan (.TWN.CHN.AS) APL
A 21072

DU1AUJ Lynn in Quezon City, Philippines (.SCAN.PHL.OC) APL
A 14070 (1300-2300z), 21070 (2300-1300z)

DU3HF Francis in Manila, Philippines (.MNL.PHL.OC) APL
A 7020

DU9BC Fred in Davao City, Philippines (.DVO.PHL.OC) APL
A 7012.8 (2300-1000z), 14072 (1000-2300z)

DU9WX Dodong in Iligan City, Philippines (.PHL.OC) APL
A 7012.8

FK8BK Louis in Noumea, New Caledonia (.NCL.OC) APL
A 14066 (0700-1300z)

HSØAC Ray in Thailand (.#APL.THA.AS) APL
A 14069.5

JA1JTA Mike in Sagamihara, Japan (.JPN.AS) APL
A 14070 (Sat/Sun only)

JA3FJ Goro in Chiba, Japan (.JPN.AS) PLX
AP 14071 14072 14074 14076 14078

JA5TX Mitsuo in Kochi, Japan (.JPN.AS) PLX
AP 14071 14072 14074 14076 14078

JR3TMW
P 14072

VK2AGE Gordon in Goonellabah (Lismore), Australia (.NSW.AUS.OC)
Win
A 7045 10109 14075 14077 21076
(NA 0000-0600z, 0700-0800z & 1030-1130z
AF 0600-0700z, EU & AS 0800-1030z, 1130-0000z)

VK2EHQ Peter in Kulnura (Sydney), Australia (.NSW.AUS.OC) APL
A 14070.5

VK2OG Peter in Quaker's Hill (Sydney), Australia (.NSW.AUS.OC) APL
A 14069 (NA 2000-1200z, EU 1200-2000z)

VK2FPV Paul in Sydney, Australia (.NSW.AUS.OC) APL
A 21069 (weekends)

VK3WZ John in Melbourne, Australia (VIC.AUS.OC) APL
A 14075

VK6PK in Australia (#WA.AUS.OC) Oth
A 14075.5

VK6TN Ernie in Glen Forrest (Perth) (.#WA.AUS.OC) PAM
A 14071 (VK/ZL 0100-0500z, NA 1000-1400z EU 1400-0100z)
A 21079 (AF/VU 0500-0800z, Far East 0800-1000z)

VU2DPG Dieter in New Dehli, India (.DEL.IND.AS) APL
A 14079 (1400-0330z), 21079 (0330-1000z), 21079 (1100-1400)
X 21115 (1000-1100z)

ZL1ACO Neill in Pukekohe (Auckland), New Zealand (.PUK.NZL.OC)
APL
A 10128 14070.5 14072.5 14073.5 14075 14075.5 21076 21079

ZL4AK Bill in Oamaru, New Zealand (.OAU.NZL.OC) APL
A 10109 10111 10126 10127 10128 (0530-2000z)
A 14069 14070.5 14071 14072 14074 14075 14077 21074 21076 21079
28074
(2000-0530z)

Appendix B

Technical Descriptions: CLOVER, G-TOR and PacTOR

Foreword

In 1989, the League issued a challenge to amateurs to develop ways of improving the performance of packet radio in the high frequency bands. Instead of responding with improvements to AX.25 packet radio, designers came up with different strategies to provide for efficient HF data communication technologies, namely PacTOR, CLOVER, and G-TOR. These initiatives by individuals and design teams in the United States and Germany, quickly gained industry sponsorship. Products supporting these technologies are currently available on the market, and in use by radio amateurs worldwide. Because of these improvements in HF communications efficiency, these systems have found applications by other radio services.

The technical descriptions that follow are intended to document the manifest technical characteristics of these systems. They are not intended as complete system definitions, as they should be obtained from the respective manufacturers because they may contain intellectual property rights.

These systems carry no specific endorsement by the League except to applaud the innovative work by their developers. We encourage further study and development of HF digital communications in the amateur services.

David Sumner, K1ZZ
Executive Vice President
February 1995

CLOVER

1. INTRODUCTION

CLOVER is a digital communications mode that conveys 8-bit digital data over narrow-band high-frequency radio. It can also transfer ASCII text and executable computer files without using the additional control characters required in other digital modes, which decrease throughput. It measures signal conditions, and automatically changes modulation format and data throughput to match current link quality. Reed-Solomon data encoding provides forward error correction (FEC) within each data block to repair many errors without the need for retransmission.

2. WAVEFORM

The CLOVER waveform consists of four tone pulses, each of which is 125 Hz wide, spaced at 125 Hz centers. The four tone pulses are sequential, with only one tone being present at any instant and each tone lasting 8 ms. Each frame consists of four tone pulses lasting a total of 32 ms, so the base modulation rate of a CLOVER signal is always 31.25 symbols per second. Data is conveyed by changing the phase and/or amplitude of successive pulses at the same frequency. These changes are made only at the instants midway between the peaks of two successive pulses when their amplitudes are zero. The measured CLOVER modulation spectra is tightly confined within a 500 Hz bandwidth, with outside edges suppressed 50 dB to prevent interference to adjacent frequencies. Unlike other modulation schemes, the CLOVER modulation spectra is the same for all modulation formats. Additional key parameters of CLOVER modulation include a symbol rate of 31.25 symbol/s (regardless of the type of modulation being used), 2:1 voltage (6 dB power) crest factor, and a ITU-R emission designator of 500H J2 DEN or 500H J2 BEN.

3. TRANSMISSION PROTOCOLS

CLOVER normally operates over half-duplex links and uses a Reed-Solomon algorithm to provide FEC. This FEC may be used alone in FEC mode or combined with an Automatic Repeat reQuest (ARQ) protocol in ARQ mode to acknowledge each individual data block. The ARQ mode provides an effective adaptive control system which constantly measures the signal-to-noise ratio, frequency offset, phase dispersion, and errors on each block of received data. CLOVER evaluates these measured parameters and selects the best modulation format for the respective propagation conditions. The receive modem sends commands to the transmitting modem indicating which modulation format should be used for the next transmission. This process ensures selection of an optimum modulation format, allowing CLOVER to operate even with multipath and other HF propagation impairments.

4. REED-SOLOMON ERROR DETECTION AND CORRECTION ALGORITHM

Reed-Solomon FEC is used in all CLOVER modes. This is a powerful byte and block oriented error-correction technique, not available in other common HF data modes, and it can allow the receiving station to correct errors without requiring a repeat transmission. Errors are detected on octets of data rather than on the individual bits themselves. This error correction technique is ideally suited for HF use in which errors due to fades or interferences are often "bursty" (short-lived) but cause total destruction of a number of sequential data bits. Error correction at the receiver is determined by "check" bytes which are inserted in each block by the transmitter. The receiver uses these check bytes to reconstruct data which has been damaged during transmission. The capacity of the error corrector to fix errors is limited and set by how many check bytes are sent per block. Check bytes are also "overhead" on the signal and their addition effectively reduces the efficiency and therefor the "throughput rate" at which user data is passed between transmitter and receiver. Efficiencies of 60%, 75%, or 90% can be invoked by using successively lower levels of Reed-Solomon encoding for error correction, or 100% efficiency by bypassing this algorithm. Better propagation conditions do not require as much error correction, which means the amount of overhead decreases and the efficiency increases.

5. SIGNAL CHARACTERISTICS

CLOVER normally uses six different modulation formats which are automatically selected to best compensate for the propagation conditions. These formats are described in the following chart:

CLOVER MODULATION FORMATS

Modulation	Description	Data Rate(bps)
2DPSM	Dual-diversity Binary Phase Shift Modulation (PSM)	62.5
BPSM	Binary PSM	125
QPSM	Quadrinary PSM	250
8PSM	8-level PSM	375
8PSM/2ASM	8-level PSM, 2-level Amplitude Shift Modulation	500
16PSM/4ASM	16-level PSM, 4-level Amplitude Shift Modulation	750

6. IDENTIFICATION

Call signs are exchanged during linking, and each station identifies every few minutes, all automatically.

7. CLOVER CONTROL BLOCK (CCB)

Each transmission uses a CLOVER Control Block (CCB) to provide synchronization and mode information. Only one CCB is sent per transmitter-ON cycle. The CCB is always sent using a 17-octet block size and a 60% Reed-Solomon encoder efficiency. The CCB uses 2DPSM modulation in the FEC mode and BPSM modulation in the ARQ mode. The CCB is followed by one or more Error Corrector Blocks (ECBs) of data. In FEC mode, the CCB serves as a preamble to the data block which announces the modulation format and the sending station call sign. In ARQ mode, the CCB follows transmission of one or more data blocks and is used to announce the modulation format to be used by the other station during its next transmission.

8. ERROR CORRECTION BLOCK (ECB)

The data field contains one or more ECBs of error-correction encoded data. One of the variable parameters in CLOVER modulation is the length of the ECB which can be 17, 51, 85, or 255 octets long, always sent at a fixed channel rate of 31.25 bit/s. This is analogous to packet length. However, in this case, block length and the number of Reed-Solomon correctable errors are proportional, with longer blocks being able to correct more errors without requiring repeat transmissions. The effective data rate varies with the type of modulation and the encoder efficiency, going up to 750 bit/s under optimum conditions.

9. FEC MODE

This mode allows a sending station to transmit data to one or more receiving stations. FEC mode is a one-way transmission that cannot repeat transmissions for error correction or use adaptive waveform selection. Therefore, the sending station must choose a transmitting modulation format in advance and assume that conditions between the sending station and all other stations are adequate for the chosen mode. The Reed-Solomon algorithm is used to provide receive error correction in FEC mode with a 60% code rate. Both BPSM and QPSM modulations use 85-character blocks, and the default modulation format is 2DPSM in FEC mode.

The first CCB frame begins with 2.048 seconds of carrier. A 32-ms carrier-off gap immediately follows this frame and each of the following frames. This first CCB frame becomes identical to all of the following (recurrent) CCB frames from this point on. The next frame sent is a 64-bit synchronization sequence which also lasts 2.048 seconds. All subsequent blocks are immediately preceded by a 32-ms reference tone pulse sequence. The CCB is next, and it is followed by from 3 to 9 ECBs.

10. ARQ MODE

ARQ is a two-way point-to-point mode which provides fully adaptive and error-corrected communications between two stations that are linked together. As in the case of FEC, a varying number of ECBs are sent in each ARQ time frame. The number of ECBs and other timing parameters are adjusted so that the total time for each ARQ frame is exactly 19.488 seconds, regardless of modulation waveform combination used. The full advantages of adaptive waveform control and error correction via repeat transmission are provided to these two stations. Data is communicated between both ARQ stations by adding a series of ECBs of data following the CCB. Although the CCB's waveform parameters remain fixed, the waveform of the ECBs is adaptively adjusted to match current propagation conditions. The throughput rate during ECB transmissions is generally much higher than that used for the CCB, because the ECB uses longer blocks and high-rate modulation waveforms to expedite data transfer. All ARQ link maintenance operations are performed at the CCB level.

ARQ ECBs are always 255 bytes long. The Reed-Solomon code rate is set for 150, 188, or 226 8-bit data bytes per ECB depending upon the ARQ bias selected (Robust, Normal, or Fast, respectively). The default bias setting is Robust. Both stations send CCB frames, which last 2.720 seconds. A limited amount of data may be exchanged within the CCBs (called Chat Mode), although large quantities of data are transferred through the ECBs. Unlike packet radio, CLOVER selectively repeats only those blocks which fail Reed-Solomon correction, not all blocks following a failed block. ARQ is an adaptive mode that does not use 2DPSM modulation.

11. MONITORING CAPABILITY

LISTEN mode permits additional stations to monitor all traffic between linked ARQ mode stations. Call signs of all CLOVER stations being monitored are also displayed, since CLOVER stations automatically identify every few minutes.

CLOVER REFERENCES

Ford, Steve: "HAL Communications PCI-4000 CLOVER-II Data Controller" (Product Review), *QST*, American Radio Relay League, Newington, CT, May 1993, pp. 71-73.

HAL Communications: "CLOVER Glossary," Engineering Document E2000, Rev. D, HAL Communications Corp., Urbana, IL, November 1992.

HAL Communications: "PCI-4000/CLOVER-II Interface Specifications," Engineering Document E2001, Rev. G, HAL Communications Corp., Urbana, IL, March 1993.

HAL Communications: "PCI-4000 CLOVER-II Data Modem Reference Manual" and "PC-CLOVER Operator's Manual," HAL Communications Corp., Urbana, IL, November 1992.

Henry, George W. and Ray C. Petit: "CLOVER - Fast Data on HF Radio," *CQ*, CQ Communications, Hicksville, NY, May 1992, pp. 40-44.

Henry, George W. and Ray C. Petit: "HF Radio Data Communication: CW to CLOVER," *Communications Quarterly*, CQ Communications, Hicksville, NY, Spring 1992, pp. 11-24.

Horzepa, Stan (ed); George W. Henry and Ray C. Petit: "CLOVER Development Continues," "Gateway," *QEX*, American Radio Relay League, Newington, CT, March 1992, pp. 12-14.

Petit, Ray C.: "CLOVER is Here," *RTTY Journal*, Fountain Valley, CA; January 1991, pp. 16-18; February 1991, pp. 12-13; March 1991, pp. 16-17; April 1991, p. 10.

Petit, Ray C.: "CLOVER Status Report," *RTTY Journal*, Fountain Valley, CA, January 1992, pp. 8-9.

Petit, Ray C.: "The 'CLOVERLEAF' Performance-Oriented HF Data Communication System," *QEX*, American Radio Relay League, Newington, CT, July 1990, pp. 9-12.

Townsend, Jay: "CLOVER - PCI-4000," *RTTY Journal*, Fallbrook, CA, April 1993, pp. 3-4; May/June 1993, p. 20.

G-TOR

1. PROTOCOL

G-TOR (Golay-Teleprinting Over Radio) can be viewed, in part, as a variant of the Automatic Link Establishment (ALE) protocol, outlined in MIL-STD-188-141A. G-TOR combines the error correcting properties of ALE, including Forward Error Correction (FEC) coding and full-frame interleaving, the Automatic Repeat reQuest (ARQ) cycle of Packet and a new application of the invertibility of the Golay code, to produce a faster new mode.

2. DATA FRAME STRUCTURE

G-TOR is a synchronous transmission system with a data frame duration of 1.92 seconds and a 0.48-second window between data frames, for a total cycle time of 2.40 seconds regardless of transmission rate. Data frames are 192, 384, or 576 bits long sent at 100, 200, or 300 symbols/sec, respectively, with the data rate dependent on band conditions. Each data frame consists of a Data field and Status byte, followed by a two-byte Cyclic Redundancy Check (CRC). No start or ending flags are added to any of the frames, thus lowering overhead and resulting in improved frame efficiency relative to AMTOR and PacTOR. The Data field contains 21, 45, or 69 eight-bit bytes sent at 100, 200, or 300 symbols/sec, respectively. The Status byte provides the frame number identification, data format (whether standard 8-bit ASCII or Huffman compressed), and a command (data, turnaround request, disconnect, or connect) for a total of 8 bits.

3. ACKNOWLEDGEMENT (ACK) FRAME STRUCTURE

ACK frames are used to acknowledge correct or

incorrect receipt of data frames, to request changes in transmission speed, and to change the direction of information flow. There are five different ACK frames: Data frame received without error (send next frame), Data frame error detected, Speed-up, Speed-down, and Changeover. Each of the ACK frames consists of two eight-bit bytes sent from the information-receiving station to the information-sending station at 100 symbols/sec, for a duration of 0.16-second during the 0.48-second window between data frames. The Changeover ACK frame initiates a changeover in information flow direction by starting out with a two-byte Changeover ACK (which causes the information-sending station to stop sending) followed by 19 data bytes, a single status byte, and a two-byte CRC, for a duration of 1.92 seconds (the same as a data frame). None of the ACK frames are interleaved; however, each is generated from a set of pseudo-random numbers and up to three bit-errors are allowed per ACK, thus reducing needless retransmissions from faulty ACK signals. Hence the ACKs are called *fuzzy*. Link quality, denoted by a set number of consecutive good or bad frames, determines link speed.

4. ASCII CHARACTERS AND HUFFMAN / RUN-LENGTH COMPRESSION

G-TOR frames are sent in normal ASCII or are Huffman and run-length encoded, depending upon which is more efficient on a frame-by-frame basis. The Huffman table for G-TOR is unique: It differs from the PacTOR table in that it emphasizes English over German character usage and upper and lower case characters are swapped automatically (frame-by-frame) in a third attempt to compress data - hence Huffman forms A and B.

5. GOLAY ERROR-CORRECTION CODING AND INTERLEAVING

G-TOR uses extended Golay coding which is capable of correcting three or fewer errors in a received 24-bit code word. The Golay code used in G-TOR is a half-rate code, so that the encoder generates one error-correction bit (a parity bit) for every data transmitted. Interleaving is also used to correct burst errors which often occur from lightning, other noise, or interference. Interleaving is the last operation performed on the frame before transmission and de-interleaving is the first operation performed upon reception. Interleaving rearranges the bits in the frame so that long error bursts can be randomized when the de-interleaving is performed. When operating at 300 symbols/sec, the interleaver reads 12-bit words into registers by columns and reads 48-bit words out of the registers by rows. The de-interleaver performs the inverse, reading the received data bits into registers by rows and extracting the original data sequence by reading the columns. A long burst of errors, for example 12-bits in duration, will be distributed into 48 separate 12-bit words before the error correction process is applied. This effectively nullifies the errors. Both data frames and parity frames are completely interleaved. In addition, by using the invertibility characteristic of Golay code words, data frames are always alternated with data frames coded in Golay parity bits. In this way, G-TOR can maintain full speed (when band conditions are good) - rather than fall to rate-1/2. Receiving parity bits can be used as data or as parity.

6. LINK INITIALIZATION

To establish a link, the information-sending station transmits the call sign of the intended receiver. Once the information-receiving station has synchronized, it sends an ACK to the information-sending station and data transmission begins.

7. SIGNAL CHARACTERISTICS

G-TOR uses frequency-shift keying like PacTOR and packet radio. At 300 symbols/sec, and with the recommended frequency shift of 170 or 200 Hz, G-TOR's spectral characteristics are almost identical to those of packet radio.

8. ERROR DETECTION AND ARQ CYCLE

G-TOR provides error correction by using a combination of both ARQ retransmission and forward error-correction. The error- detection code transmitted with each frame is a 2-byte CRC code, the same used in the AX.25 packet protocol, and it is used to determine if the frame was received correctly before error correction is initiated and after error correction is completed, to ensure that the error-correction process has successfully removed all errors in the packet. Although the CRC error-detection code is used on every frame to detect errors, the Golay error-correction procedure is skipped unless errors are detected. This ability to skip unnecessary error correction is extremely valuable since forward error correction is very costly in terms of throughput. The Golay code used in G-TOR is a half-rate code, with one error-correction bit required for every information bit; however, by using the invertibility of the extended Golay code, the half-rate transmission result normally encountered with FEC systems is avoided. Frames made up of parity bits can be fully converted to data frames. Received frames are synchronized, de-interleaved, decoded and checked for proper CRC. If the frame is found to be in error, the

---

information-receiving station will request that the matching parity frame be sent. If the parity (or data) frame that follows is found to be correct, that frame is acknowledged. If, however, it too is in error, it is combined with the previous data (or parity) frame in an attempt to recover the original data bits. In this way the system has three chances to recover the original data from the transmission of one data and one parity frame. If unsuccessful, the ARQ cycle begins again. The dispersal of noise-burst errors via interleaving, combined with the power of the Golay code to correct 3 bits in every 24, usually results in the recovery of error-free frames.

G-TOR REFERENCES

Anderson, Phil: "G-TOR's Evolutionary Improvements!" Kantronics Inc., Lawrence, KS, 1994.

Anderson, Phil: "HF ARQ Protocols," *RTTY Digital Journal*, April 1994.

Anderson, Phil, and Glenn Prescott: "Error-Correcting Codes," *RTTY Digital Journal*, March 1994.

Anderson, Phil, Michael Huslig, Glenn Prescott, and Karl Medcalf: "G-TOR: The New, Faster HF Digital Mode for the KAM Plus," *RTTY Digital Journal*, March 1994, pp. 1-2.

Ford, Steve: "G-TOR vs. PacTOR vs. AMTOR: A Nonscientific Throughput Test," *QEX*, American Radio Relay League, Newington, CT, May 1994, p. 18.

Kantronics: "G-TOR: The New HF Digital Mode for the KAM Plus and KAM Enhancement Board," Kantronics Inc., Lawrence, KS, 1994.

Karn, Phil: "Toward New Link-Layer Protocols," *QEX*, American Radio Relay League, Newington, CT, June 1994, pp. 3-10.

Prescott, Glenn, Phil Anderson, Mike Huslig, and Karl Medcalf: "G-TOR: A Hybrid ARQ Protocol for Narrow Bandwidth HF Data Communication," *QEX*, American Radio Relay League, Newington, CT, May 1994, pp. 12-19.

PacTOR

1. PROTOCOL

PacTOR can be viewed as a combination of two earlier digital modes, packet radio and AMateur Teleprinting Over Radio (AMTOR). PacTOR provides improved throughput because its transmission speed adapts to the quality of the link and it uses Huffman compressed characters. PacTOR operates over half-duplex links and uses an Automatic Repeat reQuest (ARQ) protocol, acknowledging each individual data packet with a short Control Signal (CS). Some PacTOR implementations provide a Memory-ARQ feature to determine and store the relative strength of each received bit. Copies of corrupted frames stored this way are correlated with frames received later, to provide a coding gain for improved error correction.

2. PACKET LENGTH AND ACKNOWLEDGMENT

PacTOR is a synchronous transmission system with a packet duration of 0.96 second, a CS duration of 0.12 second, and an idle time of 0.17 second for a total cycle time of 1.25 seconds. The idle time is required for turaround procedures and settling, which allows for a maximum distance of about 20,000 km as in AMTOR. Clock reference is crystal controlled with an internal standard to at least 15×10^{-6} accuracy. The initiating station is the Master, and the other station is the Slave. PacTOR subjects each received packet to a Cyclic Redundancy Check (CRC) which triggers an ARQ for packets failing the CRC. The receiving station provides acknowledgement by sending a CS. Repetition of the same CS indicates a request for a packet to be repeated. The CS has a standard length of 12 bits and is always sent at 100 baud.

3. PACKET COMPOSITION AND BAUD RATE

Packets are either 96 bits long sent at 100 bauds or 192 bits long sent at 200 bauds, with the data rate dependent on conditions. Each packet consists of a Header byte, Data field, and Status byte, followed by the CRC byte given twice. The Header byte consists of the 8-bit pattern for 55 hexadecimal and is used for synchronization, Memory-ARQ, and listen mode. The Data field contains 64 bits if sent at 100 bauds or 160 bits if sent at 200 bauds. Its format is normally Huffman-compressed ASCII, with conventional 8-bit ASCII as the alternative. The Status byte provides the packet count, data format (whether standard 8-bit ASCII or Huffman-compressed ASCII), break-in request, and QRT bit, for a total of 8 bits. The CRC calculation is based on the ITU-T polynomial $xE16+xE12+xE5+1$. The CRC byte is calculated for the whole packet starting with the data field, without Header, and consists of 16 bits. There are four different Control Signals, identified as CS1, CS2, CS3, and CS4, the functions of which are explained below.

4. LINK INITIALIZATION

To initiate a PacTOR connection, the Master station sends a special synchronization packet which contains the standard Header byte followed by the call sign (address) of the Slave station in both a 100-baud and a 200-baud bit pattern. (Each address field allows for up to eight characters, with the character 0F hexadecimal following the call sign in each unused space.) This allows the 200-baud bit pattern to determine the quality of the channel: The Slave responds with CS1 (4D5 hexadecimal) if the 200-baud bit pattern was received without error, or CS4 (D2C hexadecimal) if not, which leads to an instant reduction of data rate to 100 bauds. After receiving the first CS1 or CS4 from the Slave, the Master sends the first data packet with Header=AA hexadecimal and packet count=1. System specific data, including the Master call sign, is sent automatically at the beginning. If the Slave is busy, it can both acknowledge and reject a connection by sending one CS2 (AB2 hexadecimal) each time it receives a correct synchronization pattern. The Master terminates its connect request after receiving CS2 twice in succession.

5. CHANGING SPEED

The decision regarding a speed change is made at the receiving end, by automatically evaluating the data input rate and packet statistics including error rate and number of retries. The receiving station transmits CS1 (acknowledge) following each correctly received packet, or CS4 (speed change request) following receipt of a bad 200-baud packet. The data contained in each unacknowledged 200-baud packet is automatically repeated at 100 bauds. This repetition requires several 100-baud packets because of the smaller Data field. If the receiving station acknowledges a correctly received 100-baud packet with CS4, the transmitting station sends the next packet at 200 bauds. If the following 200-baud packet is not acknowledged after an operator-selectable number of attempts (normally two), the speed is automatically set back to 100 bauds.

6. CHANGING DIRECTION AND ENDING CONNECTION

The receiving station can change to transmit by sending CS3 (34B hexadecimal) as a break-in request at the head of its first data packet. At the end of a connection, special end of contact (QRT) synchronization packets are transmitted which contain the receiver address in the reversed order. This process is repeated until the sending station has received the acknowledgement.

7. ASCII CHARACTERS AND HUFFMAN COMPRESSION

PacTOR normally uses ASCII characters that have been compressed with a Huffman algorithm. This Huffman compression reduces the average character length for improved efficiency. The Annex shows the Huffman compressed equivalent of each ASCII character used in PacTOR, with the least significant bit (LSB) given first. The length of individual characters varies from 2 to 15 bits, with the most frequently used characters being the shortest. This results in an average character length of 4 to 5 bits for English text, instead of the 8 bits required for normal ASCII.

8. SIGNAL CHARACTERISTICS

PacTOR uses frequency-shift keying (FSK). With the recommended frequency shift of 200 Hz, PacTOR can be received through a filter with a bandwidth as narrow as 600 Hz.

PacTOR REFERENCES

Helfert, Hans-Peter, and Ulrich Strate: "PacTOR - Radioteletype with Memory ARQ and Data Compression," *QEX*, American Radio Relay League, Newington, CT, October 1991, pp. 3-6.

Horzepa, Stan: "PacTOR: Better HF Data Communications for the Rest of Us?", *QST*, American Radio Relay League, Newington, CT, February 1993, p. 98.

Rogers, Buck: "PacTOR - The New Frontier," *CQ*, CQ Communications, Hicksville, NY, July 1993, pp. 88-95.

Van Der Westhuizen, Mike: "A Practical Comparison Between Clover and Pactor Data Transfer Rates," *CQ*, CQ Communications, Hicksville, NY, February 1994, pp. 40-42.

PacTOR Huffman Compression

Char	ASCII	Huffman (LSB [sent first] on left)	Char	ASCII	Huffman (LSB [sent first] on left)
space	32	10	I	73	11110010
e	101	011	T	84	11110100
n	10	0101	O	79	000101000
i	105	1101	P	80	000101100
r	114	1110	1	49	001010000
t	116	00000	R	82	110000010
s	115	00100	(	40	110011011
d	100	00111	)	41	110011100
a	97	01000	L	76	110011101
u	117	11111	N	78	111100000
l	108	000010	Z	90	111100110
h	104	000100	M	77	111101010
g	103	000111	9	57	0001010010
m	109	001011	W	87	0001010100
<CR>	13	001100	5	53	0001010101
<LF>	10	001101	y	121	0001010110
o	111	010010	2	50	0001011010
c	99	010011	3	51	0001011011
b	98	0000110	4	52	0001011100
f	102	0000111	6	54	0001011101
w	119	0001100	7	55	0001011110
D	68	0001101	8	56	0001011111
k	107	0010101	H	72	0010100010
z	122	1100010	J	74	1100000110
.	46	1100100	U	85	1100000111
,	44	1100101	V	86	1100011000
S	83	1111011	<FS>	28	1100011001
A	65	00101001	x	120	1100011010
E	69	11000000	K	75	1100110100
P	112	11000010	?	63	1100110101
v	118	11000011	=	61	1111000010
O	48	11000111	q	113	1111010110
F	70	11001100	Q	81	1111010111
B	66	11001111	j	106	00010100110
C	67	11110001	G	71	00010100111

Char	ASCII	Huffman (LSB [sent first] on left)
-	45	00010101111
:	58	00101000111
!	33	11110011101
/	47	11110011110
*	42	001010001100
"	34	110001101100
%	37	110001101101
'	39	110001101110
_	95	111100001100
&	38	111100111001
+	43	111100111110
>	62	111100111111
@	64	0001010111000
$	36	0001010111001
<	60	0001010111010
X	88	0001010111011
#	35	0010100011011
Y	89	00101000110101
;	59	11110000110100
\	92	11110000110101
[	91	001010001101000
]	93	001010001101000
<DEL>	127	110001101111000
~	126	110001101111001
}	125	110001101111010
I	124	110001101111011
{	123	110001101111100
'	96	110001101111101
^	94	110001101111110
<US>	31	110001101111111
<GS>	29	111100001101100
<ESC>	27	111100001101101
<EM>	25	111100001101110
<CAN>	24	111100001101111
<ETB>	23	111100001110000
<SYN>	22	111100001110001
<NAK>	21	111100001110010
<DC4>	20	111100001110011

Char	ASCII	Huffman (LSB [sent first] on left)
<DC3>	19	111100001110100
<DC2>	18	111100001110101
<DC1>	17	111100001110110
<DLE>	16	111100001110111
<RS>	30	111100001111000
<SI>	15	111100001111001
<SO>	14	111100001111010
<FF>	12	111100001111011
<VT>	11	111100001111100
<HT>	9	111100001111101
<BS>	8	111100001111110
<BEL>	7	111100001111111
<ACK>	6	111100111000000
<ENQ>	5	111100111000001
<EOT>	4	111100111000010
<ETX>	3	111100111000011
<STX>	2	111100111000100
<SOH>	1	111100111000101
<NUL>	0	111100111000110
<SUB>	26	111100111000111

About The American Radio Relay League

The seed for Amateur Radio was planted in the 1890s, when Guglielmo Marconi began his experiments in wireless telegraphy. Soon he was joined by dozens, then hundreds, of others who were enthusiastic about sending and receiving messages through the air—some with a commercial interest, but others solely out of a love for this new communications medium. The United States government began licensing Amateur Radio operators in 1912.

By 1914, there were thousands of Amateur Radio operators—hams—in the United States. Hiram Percy Maxim, a leading Hartford, Connecticut, inventor and industrialist saw the need for an organization to band together this fledgling group of radio experimenters. In May 1914 he founded the American Radio Relay League (ARRL) to meet that need.

Today ARRL, with more than 170,000 members, is the largest organization of radio amateurs in the United States. The League is a not-for-profit organization that:

- promotes interest in Amateur Radio communications and experimentation
- represents US radio amateurs in legislative matters, and
- maintains fraternalism and a high standard of conduct among Amateur Radio operators.

At League Headquarters in the Hartford suburb of Newington, the staff helps serve the needs of members. ARRL is also International Secretariat for the International Amateur Radio Union, which is made up of similar societies in more than 100 countries around the world.

ARRL publishes the monthly journal *QST*, as well as newsletters and many publications covering all aspects of

Amateur Radio. Its Headquarters station, W1AW, transmits bulletins of interest to radio amateurs and Morse Code practice sessions. The League also coordinates an extensive field organization, which includes volunteers who provide technical information for radio amateurs and public-service activities. ARRL also represents US amateurs with the Federal Communications Commission and other government agencies in the US and abroad.

Membership in ARRL means much more than receiving *QST* each month. In addition to the services already described, ARRL offers membership services on a personal level, such as the ARRL Volunteer Examiner Coordinator Program and a QSL bureau.

Full ARRL membership (available only to licensed radio amateurs) gives you a voice in how the affairs of the organization are governed. League policy is set by a Board of Directors (one from each of 15 Divisions). Each year, half of the ARRL Board of Directors stands for election by the full members they represent. The day-to-day operation of ARRL HQ is managed by an Executive Vice President and a Chief Financial Officer.

No matter what aspect of Amateur Radio attracts you, ARRL membership is relevant and important. There would be no Amateur Radio as we know it today were it not for the ARRL. We would be happy to welcome you as a member! (An Amateur Radio license is not required for Associate Membership.) For more information about ARRL and answers to any questions you may have about Amateur Radio, write or call:

ARRL Educational Activities Dept
225 Main Street
Newington, CT 06111-1494
(203) 666-1541
Prospective new amateurs call: 800-32-NEW-HAM
(800-326-3942)

Index

Notes

Notes

Notes

Notes

Notes

Notes

HF DIGITAL
COMPANION

PROOF OF
PURCHASE

FEEDBACK

Please use this form to give us your comments on this book and what you'd like to see in future editions.

Where did you purchase this book?

☐ From ARRL directly   ☐ From an ARRL dealer

Is there a dealer who carries ARRL publications within:

☐ 5 miles   ☐ 15 miles   ☐ 30 miles   of your location?   ☐ Not sure.

License class:

☐ Novice   ☐ Technician   ☐ Technician with HF privileges
☐ General   ☐ Advanced   ☐ Extra

Name _____   ARRL member? ☐ Yes ☐ No

_____ Call sign _____

Daytime Phone ( ) _____ Age _____

Address _____

City, State/Province, ZIP/Postal Code_____

If licensed, how long? _____

Other hobbies _____

_____

Occupation _____

For ARRL use only	HF Dig
Edition 1 2 3 4 5 6 7 8 9 10 11 12	
Printing 1 2 3 4 5 6 7 8 9 10 11 12	

From _____

_____

_____

EDITOR, HF DIGITAL COMPANION
AMERICAN RADIO RELAY LEAGUE
225 MAIN ST
NEWINGTON CT 06111-1494